VISUAL DISOBEDIENCE

DISSIDENT ACTS, edited by Macarena Gómez-Barris and Diana Taylor

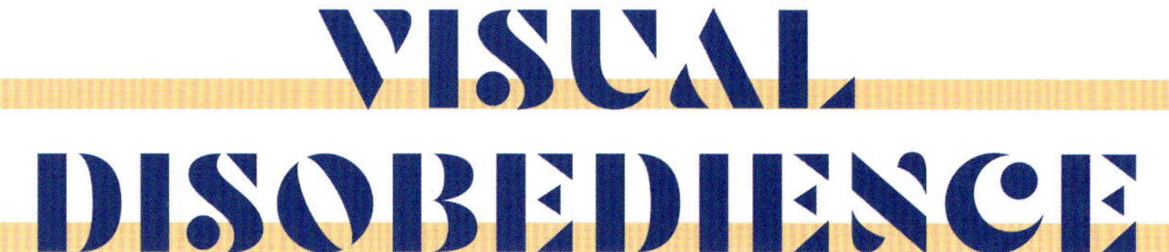

VISUAL DISOBEDIENCE

Art and Decoloniality in Central America

KENCY CORNEJO

Duke University Press *Durham and London* 2024

Printed in South Korea on acid-free paper ∞
Project Editor: Livia Tenzer
Designed by Courtney Leigh Richardson
Typeset in Garamond Premier Pro and Raginy
by Westchester Publishing Services

Library of Congress Cataloging-in-Publication Data
Names: Cornejo, Kency, author.
Title: Visual disobedience : art and decoloniality in Central America / Kency Cornejo.
Other titles: Dissident acts.
Description: Durham : Duke University Press, 2024. | Series: Dissident acts |
Includes bibliographical references and index.
Identifiers: LCCN 2023040715 (print)
LCCN 2023040716 (ebook)
ISBN 9781478030546 (paperback)
ISBN 9781478026334 (hardcover)
ISBN 9781478059608 (ebook)
Subjects: LCSH: Art, Central American—Political aspects. | Art, Central
American—Social aspects. | Art and social action—Central America. |
Art and society—Central America. | Politics and culture—Central America. |
Postcolonialism and the arts—Central America. | Decolonization in art.
Classification: LCC N6560.2 .C67 2024 (print) | LCC N6560.2 (ebook) |
DDC 701/.03—dc23/eng/20240228
LC record available at https://lccn.loc.gov/2023040715
LC ebook record available at https://lccn.loc.gov/2023040716

Cover art: Edgar Calel, *B'atz constelaciones de saberes*, 2015.
Diptych photograph, back view. © Edgar Calel. Courtesy of the artist.

Para mi padre, RENE B. CORNEJO,

y mi madre, BLANCA R. CORNEJO,

modelos de fuerza, amor, resistencia,
y los más importantes maestros de mi vida.

CONTENTS

ILLUSTRATIONS

ACKNOWLEDGMENTS

This project was conceptualized, researched, written, and revised across the years, in multiple spaces, and with the support of many people. The list is too extensive to include in full but I extend my gratitude to everyone for every contribution.

First, this book would not be possible without all the artists and cultural workers in Central America who supported me and this project from its very inception and across ten years of research travel. They spent hours in dialogue with me; some traveled with me across lakes and mountains, some shared rare catalogs and resources, and some facilitated meetings and connections with other artists. Others reminded me to take a break and let the beauty of the lakes, oceans, volcanoes, food, music, and beautiful people of the region serve as inspiration. Some accompanied me to visit family members and others invited me into their own family homes. It is impossible to name everyone in this space, but special recognition goes to Ronald Morán, Adán Vallecillo, Benvenuto Chavajay, Sandra Monterroso, Antonio Mena, Edgar Calel, Fernando and Ángel Poyón, Regina Galindo, Danny Zavaleta, Yasser Musa, Joan Duran, Rosina Cazali, Anabella Acevedo, Bayardo Blandino, José Pablo Ramírez, Juanita Bermúdez, Muriel Hasbun, Jorge de León, Lucy Argueta, Fabricio Estrada, Ruben Silhy, Raúl Quintanilla, Patricia Belli, Ernesto Calvo, Gustavo Larach, Jhafis Quintero, Walterio Iraheta, Guadalupe Maravilla, Beatriz Cortez, Yasmin Hage, Cristina Cuadra, Natalia Domínguez, Ernesto Bautista, Ernesto Salmeron, Mauricio Kabistan, Victor "Crack" Rodriguez, and Miguel A. López.

This book first developed at Duke University, where I benefited from the support of many, including Kristine Stiles, Esther Gabara, Richard Powell, and Walter Mignolo. Their own intellectual interventions and critical thinking were foundational for the development of concepts and ideas in my work.

I am eternally grateful to my community of friends for their support during those years, especially Yuridia Ramirez, Alicia Barrientos, Fredo Rivera, Raúl Moarquech Ferrera-Balanquet, Fari Nzinga, Zach Blas, Jeannette Acevedo Rivera, the folk at El Kilombo Intergaláctico, and Jasmina Tumbas, who was my most trusted friend and political ally from day one. Financial support for initial research travel during those years was made possible with a Latin American and Caribbean Studies Research Grant, a Fulbright-Hays Doctoral Dissertation Research Abroad (DDRA) Fellowship, and a Ford Foundation Dissertation Completion Fellowship.

This book was heavily revised while I was at the University of New Mexico. My colleagues Szu-Han Ho, Kirsten Pai Buick, Ray Hernandez-Duran, Ana Alonzo-Minutti, Marcella Ernest, Aaron Fry, and Myra Washington were a source of support and friendship. I am grateful to them. I also thank Mary Tzongas, Claudia X. Valdes, Bernadine Hernández, Francisco J. Galarte, Rebecca Schreiber, Amy L. Brandzel, and Elizabeth Quay Hutchison, who offered support in many ways. Much of the material in this book was shared with graduate students in my Central American art seminars at UNM. Their engagement was a constant reminder of the urgency of this work, and I'm especially grateful to the Central American students who reminded me this material was personal and political for them as well, including Martin Wannam, Hazel Batrezchavez, Jeannette Martinez, Joselin Castillo, Alexandra Rivas, Manuel Criollo, and Ezekiel Acosta. Additional travel to Central America was made possible with funding from the University of New Mexico, including the College of Fine Arts and the Feminist Research Institute. Image reproduction for this book was supported with a UNM Research Allocations Grant, a WeRi Investing in Faculty Success Program Grant, and a CFA Creative Research grant. In the greater Albuquerque community, I am most thankful to Victor Chacon, Beva Sanchez-Padilla, Gabrielle Marie Uballez, Sue Shuurman, and Farah Nousheen for their friendship and support and Samia Assed for her political solidarity, friendship, and radical inspiration.

The various invitations to present my work in progress at institutions afforded valuable feedback at different parts of the manuscript and at various stages of its development. Many thanks go to Tamara Toledo, Claire Bishop, Cristina Gonzalez, Kaitlin M. Murphy, Anita Huizar-Hernández, Ester E. Hernández, José David Saldívar, Patricia Fernandez-Kelly, Shannon Speed, Macarena Gómez-Barris, Claudia Sandoval, Luis Vargas Santiago, Jennifer Jolly, and Claudia Milian. Each preparation and conversation was a contribution to my thinking and the development of this book.

Writing is both a solitary and a collective endeavor and I'm indebted to many friends and colleagues whose company offered joy and encouragement during the writing of this book, especially when I returned home to Compton, California. My thanks to Maylei Blackwell, Claudia Sandoval, Sylvia Zamora, Ana Paulina Lee, Juan Herrera, Lauren Aguilar, and Milo Alvarez. I am also grateful to all who offered a change of scenery for my writing. I was blessed to be able to do some of the writing for this book from cafés in downtown Puebla, Mexico, thanks to Arquetopia: International Art Residency, or with a beautiful view of Lake Coatepeque in El Salvador thanks to Laberinto Projects. In Beirut, Lebanon, the conversations with Anjali Nath, Manu Vimalassery, Hatim El-Hibri, Anaheed Al-Hardan, Samhita Sunya, and Adam Waterman were invaluable. And in Belo Horizonte, Brazil, Simon Njami, Daniel W. Coburn, Daniella Géo, Bruno Vilela, Guilherme Cunha, and Brígida Campbell offered insights and discussion that were instrumental in earlier phases of my research. Simon Njami offered the best reminder—to always be me. All these encounters fueled both my spirt and my writing at various stages of this book.

I am also indebted to Leticia Alvarado, Laura Perez, Tatiana Reinoza, Robb Hernandez, Adela Licona, Ana Paulina Lee, Arely Zimmerman, Colleen Jankovic, and my sister Xiomara Cornejo, who all read different chapters of the manuscript. Thank you for your time, careful consideration, thoughtful feedback, and unwavering encouragement, especially Colleen Jankovic for reading the manuscript in its entirety. An interdisciplinary community of intellectuals, thinkers, doers, and activists provided a source of inspiration and accountability. I am grateful to Central American studies scholars and writers Claudia Milan, Arturo Arias, Arely Zimmerman, Maritza Cárdenas, Kirsten Silva Gruesz, Ana Particia Rodríguez, Cary Cordova, Leisy Abrego, Suyapa Portillo Villeda, Cecilia Menjívar, Karina Alma, and Roberto Lovato. I am inspired by scholars committed to decolonizing knowledge, the university, and the arts, and I am especially grateful for conversations with Nelson Maldonado Torres, Nitisha Dillon, Shellyne Rodriguez, Tatiana Flores, Saudi Garcia, MónicaRamón Rios, and members of the Curators and Educators for Decolonization group.

At Duke University Press, Ken Wissoker's guidance and kindness, especially amid the unpredictability of a pandemic and multiple family emergencies, has been encouraging and comforting beyond what I can express. I am grateful to the Duke team for answering my many questions and to the anonymous readers for their careful reading and feedback; thank you for making this book better. Any errors in the book are entirely my own. To Diana Taylor and Macarena Gómez-Barris, coeditors of the Dissident Acts series, thank you for believing in this book. I am especially grateful to Macarena Gómez-Barris, who has been a constant source of encouragement, support, and friendship and a true example of what feminist decolonial solidarity can be.

Finally, I am everything I am because of my family. To my parents, Rene and Blanca Rosa Cornejo, thank you for inspiring the love in this book. To my sisters, Xiomara and Edlin Cornejo, and my brother, Rene Cornejo, thank you for your support and encouragement. And of course, to my furry family members, our dogs Xocomil, Boogie, Uma, Koko, and Lulu, your love and loyalty are unrivaled.

I'm also grateful to my family in El Salvador, especially my cousin Katherine Siliézar, who was a companion during many travels in El Salvador. My tías, Morena Cornejo and Deisy Palacios, may you rest in peace, thank you for reminding me how strong Salvadoran women have always been. Manuel Huerta, you have taught me more than you realize; thank you for being by my side during the final phases of this project. To everyone listed and not listed, I extend my gratitude for being part of this journey.

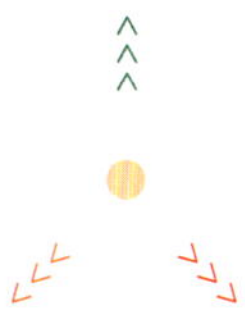

INTRODUCTION

Against Visual Coloniality

Artists, curators, and cultural workers all waited eagerly to view the anticipated exhibition *Ante América*. After inaugurating in Bogotá, Colombia, in 1991 and traveling to the United States in 1993, the exhibition arrived in San José, Costa Rica, where it was hosted by El Museo de Arte y Diseño Contemporáneo in 1994. It was one of several Latin American art exhibitions in the United States and Europe fueled by a growing interest in multiculturalism and an attempt to address the growing Latina/o populations, albeit doing so through the promotion of Latin American art.[1] *Ante América*, curated by Gerardo Mosquera, Rachel Weiss, and Carolina Ponce de León, was of particular interest for Central Americans because its curators presented it as one of the first Latin

American exhibitions curated from the "inside" and proposed an expanded geographical vision of Latin America by including artists from South America, the Caribbean, and of African descent together with Chicana/o and Native American artists. Yet, when *Ante América* arrived in Costa Rica, many in the region were surprised at the blatant omission of Central American artists from this hemispheric approach. During the exhibit's theoretical encounter, audience members questioned the curators on the Central American absence from their vision, to which the curators replied that they were simply unaware of any artistic activity taking place in Central America.[2]

The exclusion of seven countries (Guatemala, Belize, El Salvador, Honduras, Nicaragua, Costa Rica, and Panama) from *Ante América* revealed to attendees the nature of disappearance of an entire region from a hemispheric artistic framework, even when led by desires for diversity. Some understood that under the layer of innocent unfamiliarity lie assumptions shaped by colonial logics on *who* makes art and from what geopolitical locations, for as US curator Dan Cameron noted in a review of the show, the three areas overlooked in the exhibition all shared the most prominent Indigenous populations in Latin America.[3] Moreover, the curators' selection of the Central American country as a destination for the exhibition but not considering it as a site of artistic presence reiterated to others the perception of the region as a consumer rather than a creator. These realizations became the impetus for a series of regional dialogues, artistic initiatives, curatorial visions, art spaces, and a new cultural infrastructure led by Central Americans that propelled the artistic scene of postwar Central America for years to come, producing renowned artists now included in national and international exhibitions, collections, and biennials around the world.[4] And yet, such moments of disappearance for Central American art are still repeated in both research and curatorial projects that collectively form and uphold canons in Latin American art in which Mexico, Brazil, and Argentina are defined and amplified as Latin American art centers by the inferred voids around them.

The deeper implication of cultural erasure, however, is not limited to inclusion on gallery walls but ripples into sociopolitical spheres in which negation of a people's culture is historically tied to the negation of a people's history and humanity. For Central Americans, visibility and invisibility extend beyond aesthetics or exclusion from the canons of art and into the denial and erasure of our very existence. Deletion occurs through blatant exclusion of historical narratives, reduction into objects of gaze, disappearance into homogenized groups and geographies, or existence as targets of empire. Nation-states' investment in ideologies of mestizaje (an anti-Indigenous and anti-Black project) continue to perpetuate the myth of whiteness, relegating Indigenous peoples to a romantic past and disallowing Blackness in the region.[5] These types of erasures are reinforced by an amalgamation of anti-immigrant, anti-refugee, anti-Black, anti-Indigenous, and anti-LGBTQ sentiments in the United States that force migrants into obscurity.[6]

Border zones further amplify Central American imperceptibility. Maritza E. Cárdenas has theorized the nonrecognition of US Central Americans as the "Other Than Mexican" logic, or "OTM"—an acronym first used by US Border Patrol to taxonomize immigrants, and a logic that propels the "unintelligibility" of Central Americans beyond the border.[7] Central Americans' incomprehensibility, and by extension the unrecognizability of their creative productions, is only reversed when they are read/seen by institutions and political entities as subjects of suffering and destitute. Thus, Central America remains hypervisible in US imaginaries as a tropical site of misery and violence in need of intervention, while artistic and cultural production from the region remains little known, or unimaginable. This obscurity further parallels what Sarita Echavez See calls "imperial forgetting" in her own work on the Filipino American context as a process in which US empire forgets it is empire by categorically erasing those it subjugates and denying them the space and language needed for the exploration and articulation of their culture and history.[8]

Nonetheless, artists in Central America continue to defy a multiplicity of erasures, whether it be forceful disappearance, cultural elimination, historical deletion, or the normalization of institutional forgetting. In 2003, Guatemalan artist Regina José Galindo created *¿Quién puede borrar las huellas?*, one of the most iconic performances of Central American contemporary art in reaction to the repression of historical memory. The state had just approved General José Efraín Ríos Montt's candidacy to presidency despite his involvement in genocide during the country's civil war (1960–96). Throughout his 1981–82 tenure, Ríos Montt oversaw the rape, torture, displacement, infanticide, and murder of more than 1,771 Ixil Maya people in Guatemala. Outraged at the state's historical amnesia, Galindo, dressed in black, walked silently and barefoot from the Constitutional Court of Guatemala to the National Palace, two institutions and symbols of power (see figure I.1). She carried with her a basin of human blood, only pausing periodically to place her feet inside before leaving a trail of bloody footprints between the two locations. As she walked, Galindo passed before a line of policing figures, protectors of the nation-state, and after an hour ended the action with two feet pointing toward the National Palace—the last of the blood-spattered footsteps—where she left the basin of blood and walked away.

As inferred by the performance's title, *¿Quien puede borrar las huellas?* (Who can erase the traces?), Galindo confronted the Constitutional Court

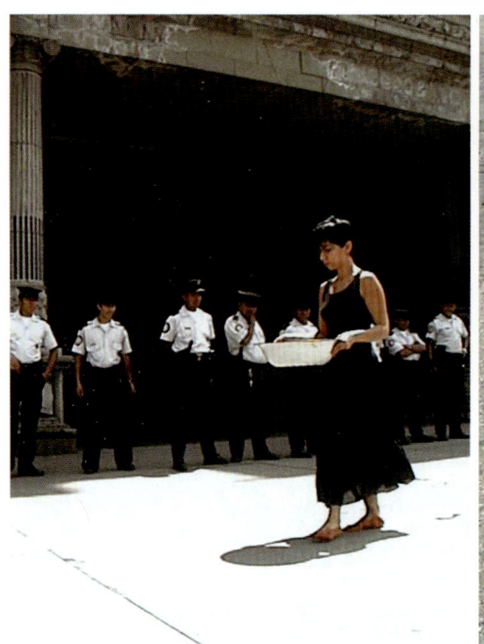

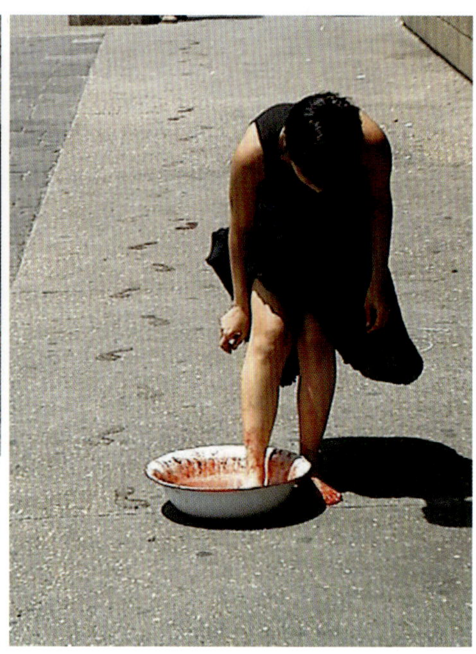

FIGURE I.1.
Regina José Galindo, *¿Quién puede borrar las huellas?*, 2003, performance. Courtesy of the artist.

with its historical amnesia, rejected its narrative of peace and justice, and located nation-state institutions as accessories to crimes against humanity. Though pained and enraged, Galindo did not utter a word or a scream. Instead, with her own body, she materialized a trail of bloodstained footmarks that metaphorically made visible the people most erased by the nation-state; the red stains created a ghostly presence of the thousands of Maya Indigenous people murdered and disappeared under Ríos Montt (see figure I.2). Her corporal gesture evoked the ephemeral and the fragility of life and memory in Guatemala while she refused to let the state expunge its role in Indigenous extermination from the collective and historical memory. Beyond the forgetting of genocide, she condemned Guatemala's use of systematic erasure to facilitate reoccurrences of state-sanctioned oppression.

Visual Disobedience defies imperial forgetting and the erasure of our humanity by offering a panorama of art across three decades in Central America. The forty artists and over eighty artworks analyzed in this book attest to both the experimentation and the abundance of creativity and art making in the region, and to a critical understanding of how colonial legacies and US empire fuel the mass exodus of refugees and asylum seekers arriving at the US-Mexico border. I specifically focus my attention on a postwar context, beginning in the 1990s, when the region transitioned into a period of reconciliation following years of US intervention, revolution, and occupation. Yet, as I show, the afterlives of violence have produced new emergent manifestations with ongoing displacement, racial and gender violence, and criminalization and repression that cause the current exodus and dispossession of Central Americans.

Guatemalan artist Jorge de León gestured at this perpetuity of violence in another iconic performance of the region, *El círculo* (The circle)(2000). During his action, the artist inserted a needle and thread through his lips in a circular motion, sealing his lips shut as a testimony to the continuity and cyclical nature of violence in a so-called postwar region (see figure I.3). Metaphorically, he enacted the repeated sequence of silencing and violence that, despite the signing of peace accords in 1996 that ended a thirty-six-year-long war in Guatemala, remained a common form of repression through fear tactics and unresolved injustices. De León was not only physically drawing and visualizing with the needle and thread but also feeling this painful act. His performance conveyed the continuous muzzling of historical pain and scarring on the collective body in the rotation of state and imperial aggression that the artists in this book address.

The so-called postwar context further marks a transitional moment for the region and its creative expression, both politically and conceptually, which includes a new postwar understanding of historical violence beyond the Cold

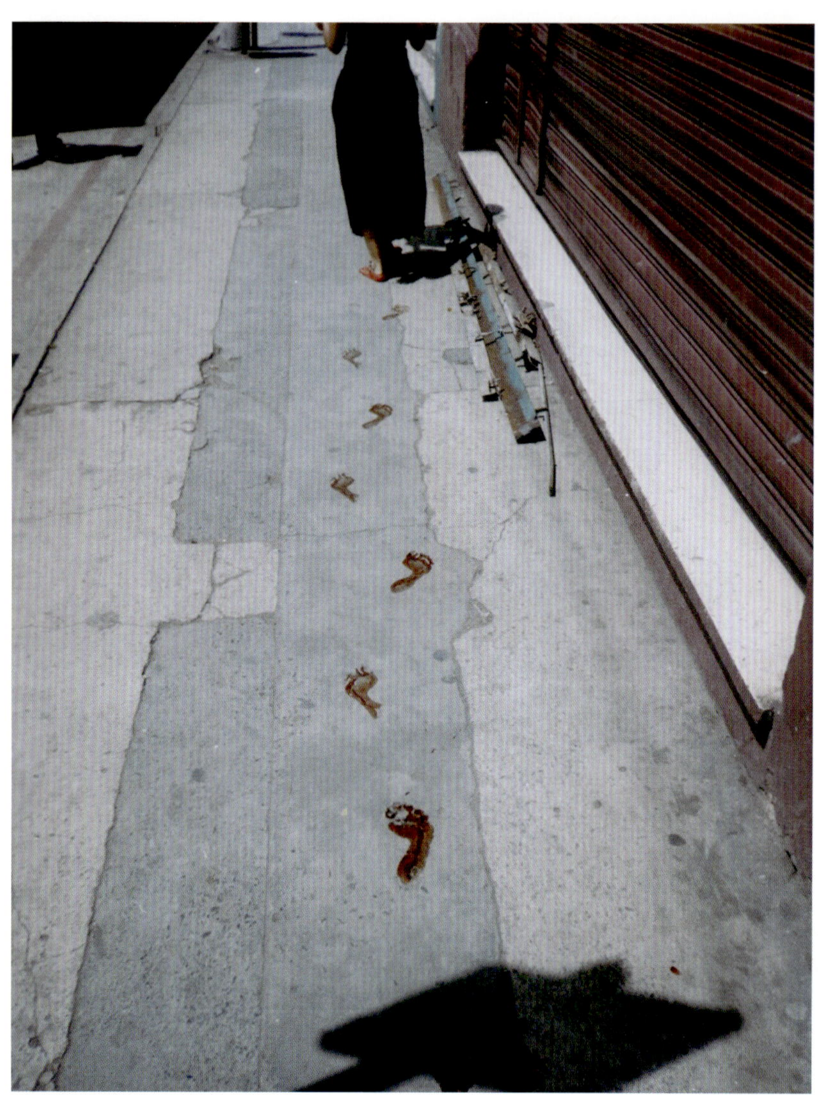

FIGURE I.2.
Regina José Galindo, *¿Quién puede borrar las huellas?*, 2003, performance. Courtesy of the artist.

FIGURE I.3.
Jorge de León, *El círculo: Festival octubre azul*, 2000, performance. Photograph by Regina José Galindo. Courtesy of the artist.

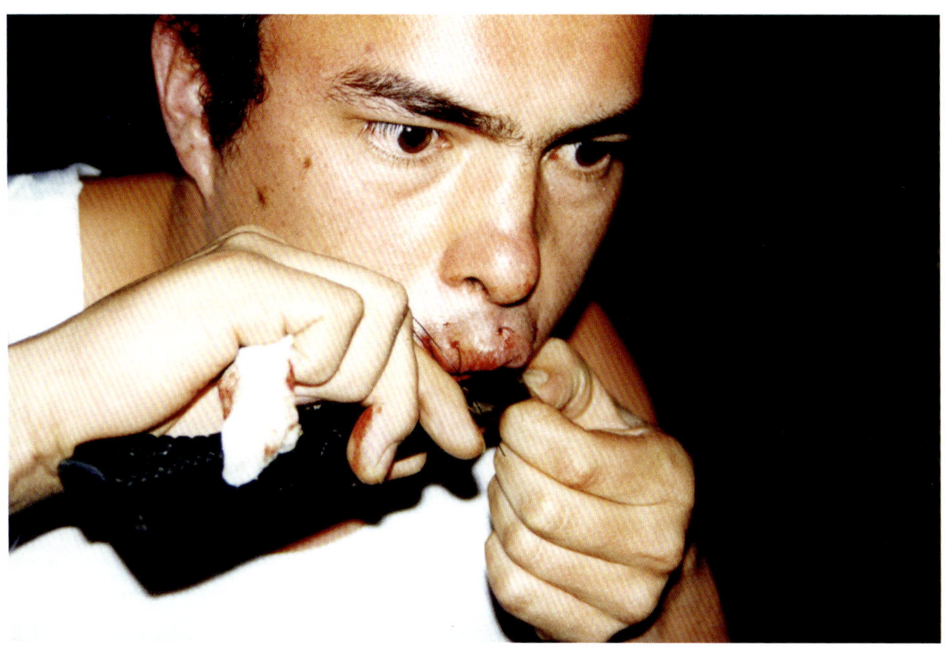

War or left-/right-wing rhetoric of the decades prior, and an innovative critical visual language that includes performance, conceptual, installation, new media, and video art. This shift is evidenced in the works of activists and artists like Nicaraguan-born Elyla (Fredman Barahona), who turns to embodied performance to push against the left- and right-wing binaries that dominate Nicaraguan politics. In *Ni azul blanco ni rojo negro* (Neither blue white, or red black) (2019), the artist walked to the Nicaraguan Embassy from La Carpio, a poor neighborhood in San José, Costa Rica, where thousands of Nicaraguans settled during the conflict in the 1980s to 1990s and remain marginalized by the government (see figure I.4). During the procession, the artist carried a baby doll half-covered in red-black (a reference to the Sandinista Revolution of the 1970s) and the other half in blue-white (a reference to the now Sandinista political party led by Daniel Ortega), thus binding patriarchal revolution with contemporary neoliberal politics. Physically engulfed in a black dress, the artist mourned the failures of both groups in their attempts at liberation and the colonial legacies still entrenched in Nicaragua that sanctioned a shared exclusion of queer, nonbinary, and Afro-descendants from visions of the ideal nation-state. Instead, the artist pushed for anticolonial conversations that center queer, feminist, Afro, and Indigenous perspectives and autonomy.[9] These interconnected creative dialogues as briefly exemplified with Galindo's, de León's, and Elyla's actions offer a new imaginative use of the body and space for critical interventions into issues of racial, gendered, and colonial violence not previously addressed during years of conflict in the 1970s and 1980s.

While important scholarship has analyzed the social and political nuances that form the region's history and current political climate, to date no US academic book has offered a history of Central American art, analyzed the correlation between visuality and the legacies of colonialism as they manifest in the isthmus, or examined the resulting and ongoing decolonial practices in art.[10] However, with this book I seek not to insert Central American art into Western canons from which it has been excluded but rather to expose, disrupt, and dismantle the colonial logic behind systemic violence in the region by theorizing creative acts that counter the politics of seeing and invisibility that have been used against Central Americans across borders in multiple ways. The emergence of Central American art histories thus requires a decolonizing disruption of disciplinary confines and hegemonies in the art world and knowledge production, to dismantle boundaries located not only in geographical spaces and geopolitical borders that displace migrants but also in conceptual, intellectual, and philosophical venues from which Central Americans, and other marginalized groups, have long been negated and excluded—including the artistic realm.

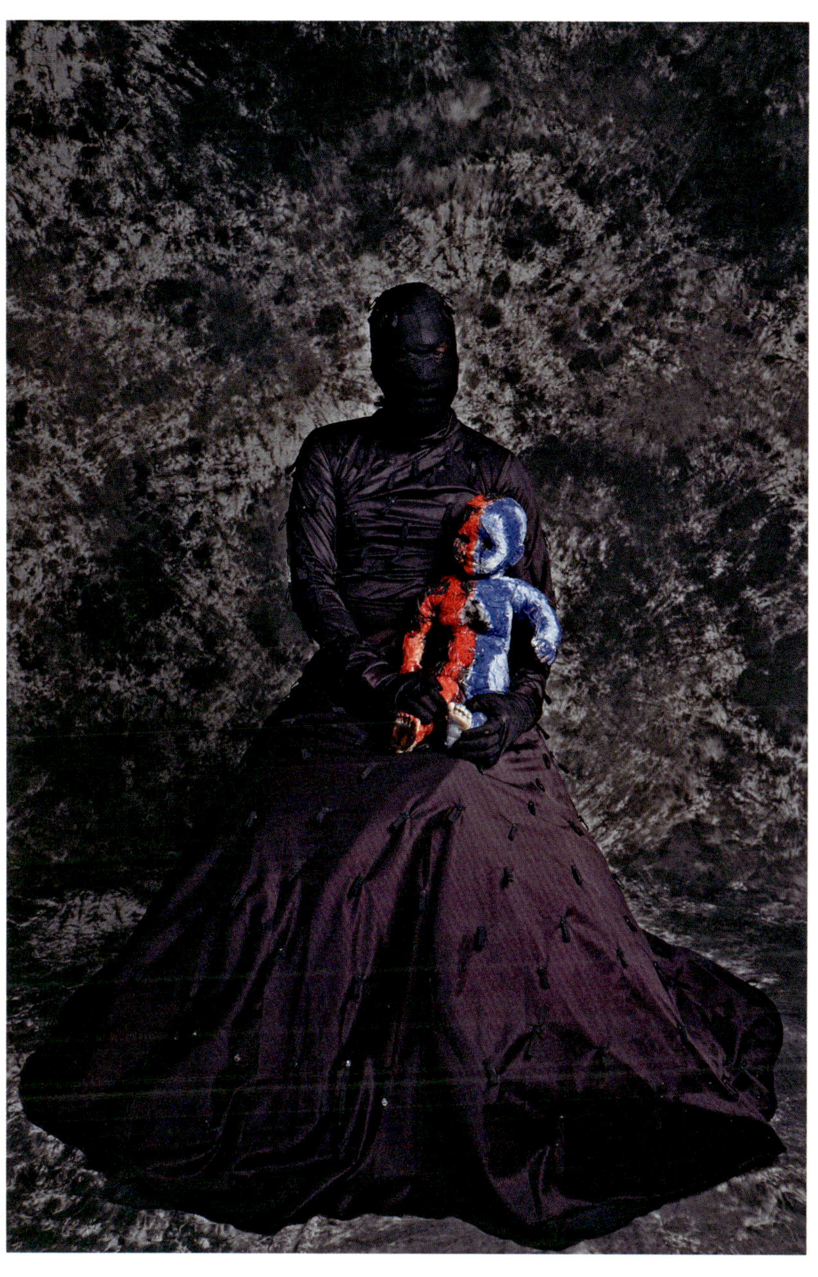

FIGURE I.4.
Elyla (Fredman Barahona), *Ni azul blanco ni rojo negro*, 2019, performance. Courtesy of the artist.

Visual Disobedience thus offers a contemporary art history of postwar Central America through decolonial aesthetics, by which I mean an anticolonial reconfiguration of visuality, art, and its principles from the perspective of those whom colonial logics place outside the realm of Western art histories, theories, and practices. I propose "visual disobedience" as a tactic of resistance within decolonial aesthetics—it is a defiance of both state repression and visual coloniality; it is an act of praxis and protest against colonial logics and toward the decolonization of art and knowledge. Throughout the chapters of this book, I frame the practices of Central American artists as collectively forming a visual disobedience that attests to the most pressing issues for the region and its diaspora, from Indigenous genocide to femicide, anti-LGBTQ violence, mass migration, criminalization, and prison captivity. My analysis of visual disobedience in the context of these themes both introduces an array of established and emerging artists and offers a critical foundation for understanding the recent Central American exodus at the center of US anti-immigrant policies.

DECOLONIALITY AND DECOLONIAL AESTHETICS/AESTHESIS

In *La virtualidad del cuerpo: Aparecer y desaparecer en tiempos de guerra* (The virtuality of the body: Appearing and disappearing in time of war) (2020), a performance critiquing the erasure of Afro-diasporic artists from art spaces, Afro–Costa Rican artist Marton Robinson eliminated the white walls of the gallery altogether and centered the Caribbean jungle as a site of knowledge and creation (see figure I.5). In the video performance, the artist pours a white glue liquid over his head as a reference to the whitening agenda of nation-states in Central America, whose investments in ideologies of mestizaje continue to perpetuate the myth of whiteness.[11] As the glue covers the majority of his head and upper torso, the artist also evokes the white marble sculpture, its connotation of Western high art, of European ideals of beauty, and its placement in white Eurocentric art histories. Robinson, who at one point mimics the European classical white sculpture, begins to wipe the white liquid from his face and head, ultimately exposing a failed whitening process over the artist, and thus his corporal resistance to Black erasure in the art world and in the geopolitical spaces he navigates. The artist connects a racist logic of whitening of Central American peoples with whitening of art spaces and art systems and the masking, disappearance, and reappearance of the politicized Black body. Importantly, Robinson's critiques extend beyond Costa Rica, into a deeper relationship and history between aesthetics and colonialism that perpetuate assumptions already fused into the structures, definitions, and values of the art world.

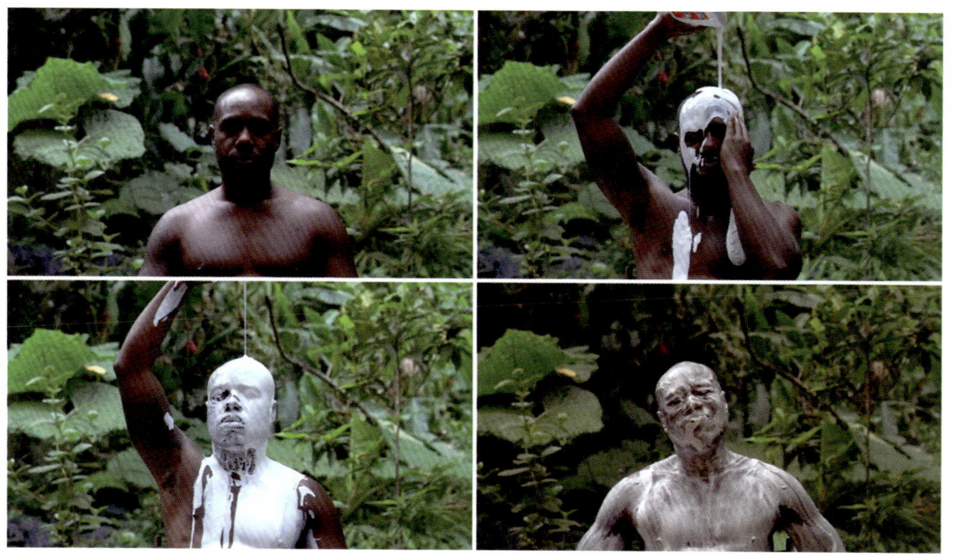

FIGURE I.5.
Marton Robinson, *La virtualidad del cuerpo: Aparecer y desaparecer en tiempos de guerra*, 2020, video performance (stills). Courtesy of the artist.

Because the Western concept of "art" is entrenched in colonialism, which together with US empire is at the core of contemporary Central American struggles, this study engages the theorization of decolonial aesthetics by artists, cultural workers, and scholars from the Global South. The term *aesthetics* is a historically determined Western notion and invented formal category with which to theorize the senses of a human subject. It reflected a set of principles determined by European intellectual men that focused on specific human subjects whose senses and subjectivity they believed were the *only* ones that mattered—themselves. Taste was considered a matter of reflection on the senses that only the evolutionary superior species could engage. According to racist Darwinian ideas of the time, that meant Western upper-class men. Those unable to reflect on the senses, that is, non-Western people, the "underdeveloped" or "backward," could simply only be immersed in their senses.[12] Consequently, in early Western art, aesthetics became a body of knowledge that implicitly centered art and its sensorial reception, especially vision, as the domain of European men. All others (racialized and colonized peoples) were relegated to the subject matter depicted in art, but not the producers or receptors whose sensibilities, creativity, and subjectivity required intellectual consideration. As the philosophy of aesthetics was increasingly intertwined with class and race, aesthetics became a category of judgment and by extension of morality and humanity. That is, aesthetics not only upheld the idea of inferior and superior races but also perpetuated the idea that racial hierarchies determined appreciation for beauty and artistic abilities, thus undermining the creative expression of subjugated peoples as a way to reinforce hierarchies of human civilization.[13] Aesthetics became a colonizing philosophical category, as Robinson reminds us in his video performance.

Attempts to decolonize aesthetics have led some anticolonial thinkers to the conclusion that no term attached to *aesthetics* (i.e., *political*, *radical*, or even *decolonial*) would stop it from being a colonizing category rooted in Western ontologies that reproduce colonial logics and narratives. The Jamaican philosopher Sylvia Wynter proposed a differentiation between aesthetics and its colonial counterpart by referring to them as "Aesthetics 1" and "Aesthetics 2." The former (Aesthetics 1) relates to the perception of the world through the senses, and the latter (Aesthetics 2) is the colonization of the senses through the theorization of beauty and taste as defined by Eurocentric thought.[14] The discourse of Aesthetics 2, she claims, not only projects the class-specific taste of Europeans as the general and "universal" taste of the developed world but is also imbued with codes that coerce behavior from subjugated people that condition them to live in a colonial world.

Indigenous proposals to combat aesthetics as a colonizing system emerge across the hemisphere. To reclaim the senses and orality in Indigenous knowledge making, Bolivian sociologist Silvia Rivera Cusicanqui proposes two epistemological and pedagogical methodologies of praxis. These approaches, which she calls "historia oral" (oral history) and "sociología de la imagen" (sociology of the image), prioritize Indigenous oral and visual forms to decenter the written word as the only valid means of instituting history.[15] Meanwhile, art historian Jolene Rickard, citizen of the Tuscarora Nation (Haudenosaunee), drawing from her own subjectivity and family history, rejects the Eurocentric notion of sovereignty. Instead, she theorizes a Haudenosaunee understanding of "visual sovereignty" as a dominant expression of Indigenous self-determination, renewal, and resistance and as a better method for reading the interrelated space of colonial gaze, deconstruction of colonized image and text, and Indigeneity in relation to the settler state.[16]

Along the lines of Wynter's arguments, members of the modernity/coloniality/decoloniality collective project conclude that aesthetics colonized *aesthesis*, a term that defines the perception of the world by the senses that they use as a replacement for Wynter's Aesthetics 1.[17] The group proposes a revival and recuperation of aesthesis (Aesthetics 1) as a way of sensing-knowing-doing in the world.[18] What differentiates their framing from a "postcolonial" art framework is the concept of "coloniality" and "decoloniality" as coined by Peruvian sociologist Aníbal Quijano. Coloniality describes a system of domination conceived through racial divisions, in which the European/Western colonization of political and economic spheres continues to be intricately linked to the colonization of knowledge systems at the world scale.[19] While colonialism refers to the historical moment of colonization, coloniality refers to its continuity into the present as an ideological and epistemic tool of domination. Interventions by feminist theorists and philosophers further expand coloniality to include overlooked gendered-raced-sexualities, exposing gender, gendered logics, and the category of "woman" to be additional colonial concepts.[20]

The ongoing occupation of land through settler colonialism and the coloniality of knowledge through institutions continue to inform policies and state laws affecting racialized peoples in Central America, whether to justify the forced sterilization of women in Guatemala; the theft of sacred lands under government control in Honduras; the erasure of Indigenous histories and languages in El Salvador; the oppression of Afro-descendants in the region, especially in Belize, Guatemala, Nicaragua, Honduras, and Panama; the abduction and imprisonment of migrant children at the border; or the rationalization of genocide. As I elaborate in the next section, visuality is also entrenched in coloniality. Because we are conditioned to subscribe to Western hegemonies through the coloniality of knowledge, Walter Mignolo proposed a rejection, or "delinking," of coloniality and theorized "epistemic disobedience" as an act of insubordination against the hegemony of Eurocentric knowledge.[21] For me, the term was an invitation to question the role of art and visuality within coloniality—as these are also embedded in colonial projects and upheld through its institutions, such as archives, museums, and universities. How can we locate, historicize, and theorize the defiance of creatives most affected and erased by Western modernity, racial capitalism, and the colonial matrix of power?

While building on these conversations of decolonial aesthetics/aesthesis, my interest in *Visual Disobedience* is less in contesting a philosophical category and more in exposing how coloniality and decoloniality function in Central America through the sensing-knowing-doing of creatives. I do so by centering anticolonial acts of resistance. Placing these creative acts within a decolonial aesthetics framework allows me to move beyond institutional critique of art, and beyond coloniality as subject matter in art (i.e., depictions of colonial suffering), toward honoring the praxis of Central American art and creativity historically denied to us. Thus, the subtle acts, delicate movements, and brief moments of being through which subjugated peoples reassert their existence are as key in my framing of decolonial aesthetics as are the long-term battles and historical engagements with decolonization that receive recognition. Every moment, every gesture, is already a defiance that calls for the death of coloniality when one's own existence is an act of insubordination, as it is often in Central America for poor, racialized, and gendered people, and as Galindo, de León, Elyla, and Robinson show in their actions.

We can view these artists' brief moments of creative embodied resistance as what Macarena Gómez-Barris calls "decolonial gestures," which she defines as the "smaller spaces and moments of decolonization, in relation to racial and settler colonial projects."[22] The term is useful for me in identifying and centering embodied acts of creativity in service of decolonization rather than focusing on the commodified product that is often valued in Western art. Brevity or subtleness should not be mistaken as futile, for decolonial gestures are assertions of existence and a defiance of erasure that moreover decenter colonial structures and frameworks of knowledge, history, and memory. Therefore, valuing both the archive and the repertoire, as theorized by Diana Taylor, for this book I'm less interested in creative things as fetishized relics and more interested in creative decolonial *acts* and *who* enacts them, with all the history and resistance behind them.[23]

An attention to multiple geographies of reason is crucial to a decolonial aesthetics in Central America since the region shares a history with other geopolitical spaces of creative erasure brought on by colonialism. For instance, Nelson Maldonado-Torres notes the unique position of the Caribbean in the creation of its own decolonial aesthetics.[24] Topologically, the Caribbean is an archipelago that under multiple colonial empires also gave way to multiple decolonialities. Maldonado-Torres reminds us that the Caribbean, as the first site of colonial encounter between the Old World and the New World, was ground zero for brutal practices of colonization and dehumanization in the making of the modern/colonial world. Thus, a consortium of pioneering decolonial thinkers who emerged from the Caribbean (i.e., Frantz Fanon, Aimé Césaire, Sylvia Wynter, Édouard Glissant, and Maldonado-Torres himself, among others) pointed to the decolonized body and the decolonized senses as necessary for decolonization. As Maldonado-Torres explains, "Aisthesis is a key zone of struggle as it defines how subjects relate to their own bodies and encounter everything in their temporal spatial horizon."[25]

The topology of Central America, like that of the Caribbean, has also shaped its political history and, as I show in this book, the relation to its spatial and temporal environment. Communities along the Atlantic Coast of Central America, like the Garinagu and other Afro-descendant populations, identify with Black Caribbean culture due to their history as descendants of Afro-Caribbean people and their proximity to the islands. Others perceive the seven Central American countries as islands due to the tropical nature and the isolation perpetuated by decades of war. However, in their exhibition on Caribbean art, scholars and curators Tatiana Flores and Michelle Ann Stephens refute archaic frameworks of fragmentation, instead asserting a continuity of connections among the Caribbean islands, which one could also extend to Central America.[26] Yet, topologically, Central America is an isthmus—a strip of land, a narrow passage, flanked by the Pacific and Atlantic Oceans on either side. It is a bridge that connects North America with South America, that is neither North nor South, nor the Caribbean, yet is at the center of it all. It is the center of the Americas. Poet Pablo Neruda once called it "the waist of America" in reference to corporate colonization: "The United Fruit Company / reserved for itself the juiciest / the central seaboard of my land, / America's sweet waist," which it baptized "Banana Republics."[27] That geographic location made the region a target of US imperialism and the geopolitical embodiment from which its artists sensed the world.

But what comes of such a struggle, in which a body *senses* and thus *makes sense* of its own spatial and temporal context, a context shaped by coloniality?

In her study on South American Indigenous and Afro–Latin American communities, whose territories have been made into "extractive zones," Macarena Gómez-Barris reveals what she describes as "submerged perspectives"—those ways of perceiving otherwise that offer possibilities of decolonization unintelligible to capitalist and colonial powers.[28] Though focusing on sites targeted by extractive capitalism in Ecuador, Peru, Chile, Colombia, and Bolivia, Gómez-Barris offers a framework with which to consider ways of seeing from other zones ravaged by racial capitalism and extractivism, such as Central America. From corporate colonization by the United Fruit Company to land occupation and violence with the Panama Canal, the region faces ongoing and extractive colonial projects such as land theft, privatization of water, and the building of hydroelectric dams that disproportionately affect Indigenous and Afro–Central American communities and make them chiefly vulnerable to governmental repression. Yet from underneath that heavy cloak of such extractive violence, their creative acts both reveal alternative perspectives and expose the incomplete project of modernity.

Naming, loving, and writing from those turbulent spaces that produce submerged perspectives is another form of delinking from the Eurocentrism of the discipline of art and art history and another component of decolonial aesthetics. For me, as a US Central American art historian, daughter of Salvadoran immigrants, it is necessary to dispel what Colombian philosopher Santiago Castro-Gómez describes as hubris *of the zero point*.[29] The zero point refers to that geopolitical grounding from which one thinks and produces knowledge but which in European modernity and imperialism is imagined as an *invisible* location. That invisible location, which in fact truly centers a European positionality as a point of observation, has been passed off as a "universal point of view" and is still enforced in Eurocentric fields as *objectivity*. In contrast, decolonial aesthetics is rooted in seeing, feeling, thinking, and creating from the embodiments of those who are erased, subjugated, colonized, or previously colonized, and acknowledges creations from those specific geopolitical groundings as valid ways of knowing and being in the world.

What these decolonial thinkers point us to in the many possibilities of decolonial aesthetics is that the sensing-knowing body and the geopolitical space from which it senses and enunciates produce alternative ways of seeing that are incomprehensible to colonialism and empire—ways of seeing that defy the heavy cloak of colonization by piercing through it with insubordinate existence and love for oneself and one's communities. It is that love that Maya Kaqchikel artist Edgar Calel summons in his series Kit Kit (2014) (see figure I.6). When Calel learned of his grandmother's passing in 2014, he was consumed with loving memories of her chanting "kit, kit, kit, kit" when she called birds to feed them corn seeds. From his grief and coming to terms with an utterance he would no longer witness, Calel used clay earth, the very substance she had now become, to depict a repetition of the monosyllable "kit" in different scales, positions, and directions all across the walls of his grandmother's humble house in Comalapa, Guatemala. What appeared as an abstract visual distortion is in fact an acoustic intervention with a range of volume mimicked by the different scales of the word and not only honors the memory of his grandmother but transforms the space into an archive and repertoire of her song since passersby who read the words perform her melody. Calel further re-creates Kit Kit in public and in artist spaces during his travels, thus carrying with him the onomatopoeic sound that evokes his grandmother in all dimensions of space and time and that has become a sort of artist signature that further fuses them in life and creation (see figure I.7). Calel's variations of Kit Kit extend beyond the visual and embody a Maya sensing-knowing way of love, memory, and ancestral honoring.

When we understand how the violence of settler colonialism and coloniality repress ways of seeing/sensing/knowing/being in site-specific locations—whether in Palestine, Turtle Island, the Caribbean, the Philippines, the Amazon, or, as I show in this book, Central America—and when we think and write from those spaces, the practice of re-existence becomes all the more radical, and the possibilities of decolonial aesthetics innumerable. Artists are central to this process because decoloniality is lived and embodied and theorized by the people on the ground who are directly affected by multiple systems of oppression. *Visual Disobedience* begins in the recognition that decoloniality does not reside in the academy. Therefore, it centers artists as creative makers, thinkers, and theorists. It is a book from a Central American diasporic perspective in dialogue with artists on the ground who are collaborators and friends, who dismantle Western concepts of aesthetics and their colonial products through a disobedience that is visual, embodied, and activated in real space and time, and multisensorial all at once—a resistance rooted in the very human faculties a *colonizing* aesthetics philosophically denies them.

VISUAL COLONIALITY

When we fail to locate a direct correlation between a colonized aesthetics and visuality to land dispossession, forced poverty, war and genocide, and other realities of subjugated peoples, a decolonial aesthetics becomes a mere slogan in a long list of empty signifiers.[30] In proposing a decolonization of art, or a decolonial aesthetics, it is necessary to also establish how colonized aesthetics have

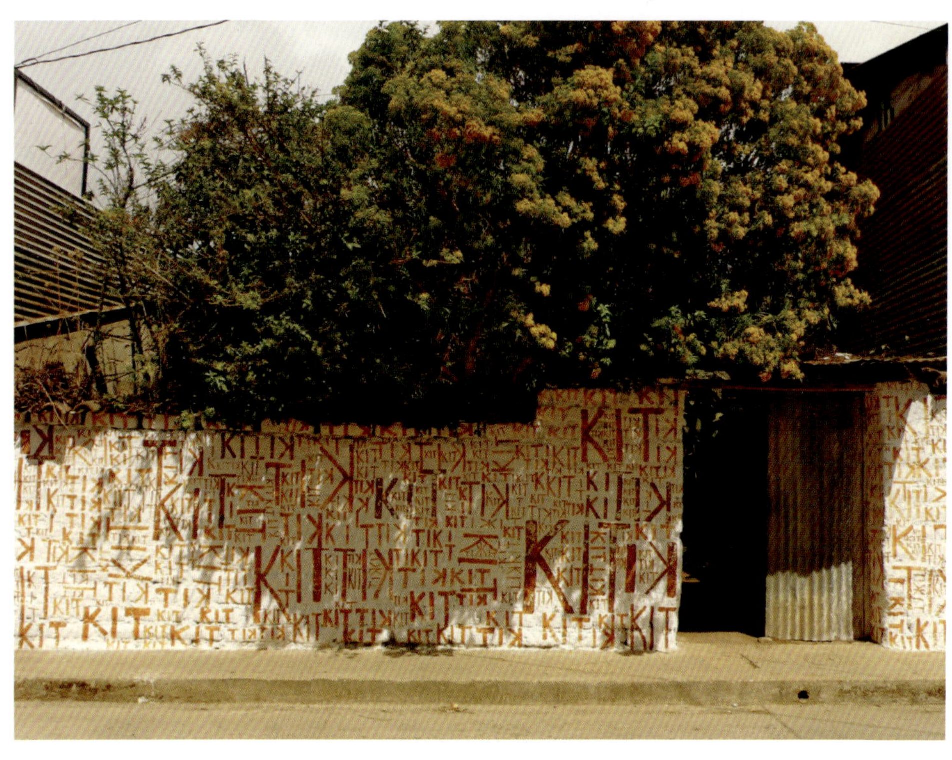

FIGURE I.6.
Edgar Calel, Kit Kit series, 2014, mural. © Edgar Calel. Courtesy of the artist.

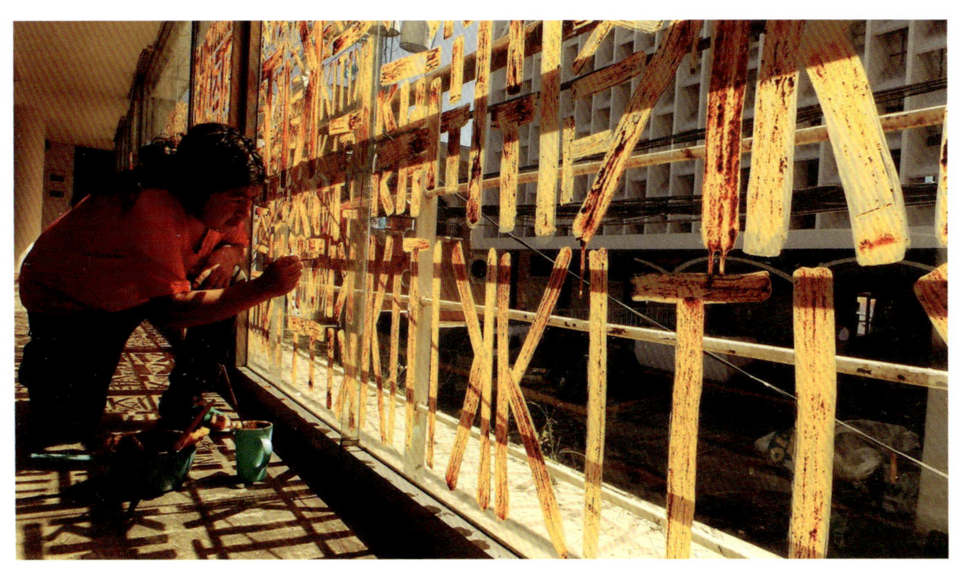

FIGURE I.7.
Edgar Calel, Kit Kit series, 2017, window mural. © Edgar Calel. Courtesy of the artist.

come to violate humanity in tangible ways. To do so, I ask, where do we locate it in actual space and time beyond abstract concepts? This inquiry into specificities of colonial violence leads to a more explicit question regarding this book: in the praxis of what I call visual disobedience, what exactly is being disobeyed? To build on the vocabulary needed to name sites of colonial violence, I propose that there are concrete ways colonization has appropriated visuality into a colonizing tool beyond the philosophical category of aesthetics, what I call *visual coloniality*. With this phrase I build on Quijano's concept to specifically address the colonization of creativity, images, and artistic production of those who've been made into subject matter (the topic of an artwork, the thing seen in an artwork) that is then transformed into a *tool* of domination in the service of colonization. I'll elaborate on just three mechanisms of visual coloniality: visual erasure, visual thingification, and visual extractivism, three different but entangled forms of colonial violence affecting us across space and time.

VISUAL ERASURE

The power of our creative history, and the threat it poses to empire, is often underestimated, in part because we have been fed colonial lies that as a violent region on the peripheries of modernity we have no art, that it only existed once long ago and is now extinct, that we are now incapable of artistic sophistication, or that it can only be "gifted" to us in solidarity by others. Yet I want to remind us that the creative force of the native inhabitants of the region was so powerful that it posed a threat to European domination at the time of conquest. Thus, to visually and epistemically remove that threat, visual erasure was an initial and deliberate project of colonialism that continues into contemporary time. As Ariella Aïsha Azoulay reminds us in the context of art and its constitutive imperialism, colonial plunder is not a concluded event but an ongoing process.[31]

In Mesoamerica—what is now Central America—architecture, murals, calendars, and codices that are often preserved today as popular tourist sites or in museums and collections held an epistemic value for Maya people before conquest. They convey a sophisticated visual and spatial system designed for astronomical calculation, recordkeeping, and the preservation and transmission of histories and cosmologies. Like the performances, ceremonies, and ritual acts that took place at these sites, this material culture consisted of an ocular, corporal, and spatial system of knowing essential to the order of Indigenous ways of being and seeing. Significantly, historical and visual production was a highly valued and respected responsibility assigned to a select few. For instance, the ancient Maya highly regarded scribes for their ability to produce written texts and illustrations, making writing, painting, and sculpting one and the same, highlighting the equal relation between knowledge, power, and visuality.[32] However, through violence, looting, and destruction, European colonizers repudiated Indigenous visuality and knowledge. Such rejection was not merely collateral damage of colonization or a sweeping dismissal but rather consisted of strategic tactics. They ostracized the visual aesthetics of Mesoamerican representation, the proportions of anatomy of the Indigenous bodies depicted, the portrayals of space and the location of objects within that space, and the visual rendering of gods and deities. They rejected this system of representation because the visual language derived from Maya anatomy, space, and perspective located the Indigenous body—not the colonizer's—as a frame of sight.

As Mignolo has written, Spanish dismissal and rejection of Indigenous systems of knowledge was rooted in the Renaissance belief that the Western book was the only repository and disseminator of knowledge and that alphabetical writing indicated civilization and intelligence.[33] Yet, as art historians know, Western scholars locate the origin of history and theory of art as a discipline within the Renaissance, which also coincided with the colonization of the Americas. In *The Lives of Artists* (1550), considered the first written history of Western art, Giorgio Vasari shows that artistic skill during the Renaissance was judged by the mathematical and geometrical accuracy with which artists could "capture" and depict space, perspective, nature, and anatomy. The desire to study and imitate nature attributed godlike status to those who were skillful enough to accomplish such a task: the *artist*.[34]

Renaissance representation simultaneously located the viewer at the center of this system. The notion of "perspective" revolves around the observer who occupies the one and only central position from which space and all its contents are mapped and located. This same notion influenced the measure of proportion, which was located in the human anatomy as the center of the universe, as illustrated in Leonardo da Vinci's *Vitruvius Man*. A mathematical depiction of nature and space allowed the viewer not only to witness a godlike creation, the representation of nature, but to dictate nature and locate him at its center. In sum, at the time of Spanish Conquest, "mastery" of perspective reinforced the status of artist-as-intellectual and the production and recognition of visual art as intellectual work.[35] Thus, in the fifteenth century, the visual conveyed power in political and religious spaces not only by being the standard tool for measuring the world but also by making a claim to the world from the European perspective, effectively situating European man and his ideals of beauty at the center of the universe.

This *mutual* understanding of the power of art and visuality made Mesoamerican visuality a threat to European colonizers for it decentered the European body, perspective, and ways of seeing as universal. European negation and destruction of Mesoamerican systems of visuality was not due to inferiority or nonexistence as we are led to believe by dominant history. On the contrary, *recognition* of the sophisticated visual system of knowledge was effectively an acknowledgment of it as a danger to the colonial project. It was therefore virulently attacked—a violence that has persisted and developed through visual coloniality. Targeting and destroying Indigenous visuality is thus not just an incursion on material objects, sites, styles, or artifacts. It is also a systematic assault on Indigenous peoples, knowledges, and beings, initiated at the moment of conquest in the service of colonization. It makes the way for the imposition of European visuality as the ultimate visual system to aspire to, and then all other attempts dismissed as "derivative." As I discuss in chapter 1, on Mayan art and defiance in Guatemala, this makes the safekeeping, preservation, and new emergence of Indigenous creativity and knowledge a major defiance to visual coloniality. It also encourages us to ask: might the epistemic and ontological power of Indigenous visuality still pose a threat to colonial order? A threat to the US empire?

VISUAL THINGIFICATION

Aimé Césaire equated colonization with "thingification," meaning that colonization requires the commodification and objectification of the colonized into things, or nonhuman objects.[36] This process is one in which the colonizer defines himself (as human) in opposition to the colonized (as nonhuman) to justify his dominance over the latter. To do this, the colonizer must ease his consciousness by *seeing* the colonized as animal in order to then habitually treat the colonized as such. In turn, as Césaire notes, the colonizer "transforms *himself* into an animal," for the only true body that loses its humanity is the one that violently beats, enslaves, dispossesses, exploits, and kills another human.[37] By this logic, the colonizer becomes the true savage of this fabricated and still powerful dichotomy. His idea of humanity is therefore, by default, one of inhumanity. However, to convince himself and the world otherwise, the colonizer remolds the colonized into an image that benefits his economic needs through a series of negations. For example, the colonized are not civilized, moral, good, intelligent, beautiful, or human.[38] It is this multifaceted fictional image, and the real consequences beyond the colonial gaze, that, inspired by Césaire, I call "visual thingification": the colonialist practice of fabricating visual evidence for the dehumanization of the colonized through a series of negations for the purpose of justifying elimination.

The visual thingification of Indigenous and enslaved African peoples was accelerated with the invention of photography in the nineteenth century and projects that aimed to prove racial inferiority through the visual. Its technological nature was put forth as objective and scientific, and, combined with Darwinian evolutionary theories and phrenology studies, contended that racial inferiority could be identified merely by looking at physical traits and skull shape. Soon, photography became a dangerous tool with which to categorize, label, and criminalize colonized peoples and to establish a nonhumanity that aided colonial projects. With the rise of mechanical reproduction, photographic images were disseminated globally. As European travel increased, fueled by a desire to experience and possess the exotic colonial lands, photographic images of untamed landscapes, zoology, botany, and even Indigenous and colonized peoples fulfilled European fantasies of discovery and conquest.[39] Images were displayed, consumed, studied, and examined not only to establish the inferiority of the colonized subject but also to establish the superiority and humanity of the colonizing society.

The visual thingification of Indigenous and enslaved peoples extended from the two-dimensionality of the photograph to the corporeal by way of human zoos, which consisted of the violent coercion and kidnapping of peoples who were held captive and displayed around the world as freaks and animals—a practice that only ended in the 1930s.[40] Human zoos are rooted in a series of displays informed by the nonscientific to racist theories of biological evolution. These range from pre-Enlightenment cabinets of curiosity, a tradition of collecting rare objects, to a fascination with cadavers, anatomy lessons, and public executions in the displays of mortality, to the exhibition of "nations," "mankind," and ethnographic subjects fueling inventions of exoticism and savagery.[41] The conquest of the Americas further fueled a fascination with "missing links," the Darwinian idea of a linear evolution structured like a chain, where one subject displayed the transition to modern human—an idea used as proof of evolutionary hierarchies.[42]

The best-known case in Central America is the kidnapping and exhibition of brother and sister Maximo and Bartola, who were first exhibited in the United States in the 1850s as "The Last Aztec Children." Born in a small village in San Miguel, El Salvador, the children suffered from microcephaly, the neurological condition that causes reduced brain and head size, and dwarfism. Their physical appearance and size were exploited to prove that they were the remaining two "missing links" of a nearly extinct race, and they were exhibited to American and European audiences and offered to scientific communities as objects of study and testing. For four decades, Maximo and Bartola were held captive, obligated to perform as freaks, and were ultimately forced to marry each other to garner further publicity.[43]

The visual thingification of Maximo and Bartola occurred through the fabrication of photographs, promotional material circulated about them, and a forced display of their bodies, which were dressed with supposed Aztec garments. Additionally, a fictitious illustrated narrative published as a pamphlet told the story of their "discovery." The pamphlet visually connected Maximo and Bartola with the ancient Indigenous culture to establish them as the declining and soon extinct race and, by extension, whites as the superior evolved race destined to replace the colonized.[44] As Robert D. Aguirre points out, the children were often depicted in profile: a visual strategy to accentuate anatomical and alleged racial differences that by the 1850s served as "a cue to look for a deviant subject—racial, criminal, or both—within the visual frame."[45] The constant profile-view depiction, along with their juxtaposition with images of archaeological Mayan sculptures and stelae, further associated the children with "a stony, lifeless past while dissociating them from the technological modernity of the viewer."[46] As "stony" and "lifeless," Maximo and Bartola were made into artifacts to convey that they belonged on the lower spectrum of civilization—as animals, monsters, or *things* detached from humanity. The long history of collecting, storing, and exhibiting Indigenous peoples' artifacts, ritual objects, and physical remains continues today in museums, which are often sites for visual thingification.

Characteristics projected onto colonized peoples in the process of visual thingification suggest they are (1) criminal, (2) anachronistic, and (3) monstrous. But these do not remain mere ideas or images; rather, visual thingification materializes the series of negations used to turn humans into things by eliciting very real reactions. Philosopher George Yancy elucidates the nature of this process as a series of mythos, codification, ritual, ontologization, constructivity, stereotyping, and overdetermination.[47] As he describes, the white colonial gaze freezes the colonized body through mythopoetic constructions, projecting onto the colonized body its own fears. Though these are projected fantasies of otherness, the white gaze considers them factual by erasing its role in creating such fantasies. The white imaginary then codifies the colonized body with attributes (evil, dirty, etc., values opposite to those attributed to whiteness: good, pure, etc.). These attributes suggest not only a void of values in the colonized but that the colonized body is an enemy of values, and thus of whiteness.[48] Myths and codes then lead to rituals, through which bodies undergo transformation; that is, the white body physically reacts to seeing the colonized body. Yancy cites the classic trope: white woman sees Black body and clutches purse. Thus, an asymmetrical constructed relation forms between colonizer and colonized, followed by a process of stereotypification where colonizer and colonized become solid types to the colonizer. These types are consumed by colonizers unchangeably and unquestionably through overdetermination, which fixes the colonized body, as Yancy states it, as "something *it is* rather than as something that is *done* to it."[49]

Visual thingification is a violence *done* to Central American people through the fabrication of images and visuality. It is designed to render Central Americans nonhuman, criminal, and monstrous, not only in the imaginary realm but in the physical world. While this may no longer take place through human zoos, as was the case of Maximo and Bartola, visual thingification persists for Central Americans today with the visual fabrication of the *marero* (gang member) and, by extension, of the migrant and refugee. This visual thingification stems from multiple centers of power, including the US and Central American governments. The visual disobedience Central American artists enact to protest migration, criminalization, and captivity, as I discuss in chapters 3 and 4, defy the centuries of fictitious visual narratives fabricated and adopted by governments to *thingify* Central Americans, which cause very real corporal violence against us.

VISUAL EXTRACTIVISM

Extractivism in Latin America, or what is also called neo-extractivism or extractive imperialism, is not only a current problem of late capitalism; rather, it has been a continuous, albeit changing force in the Americas since the sixteenth century, when the search for silver and gold mines motivated European expansion into the Caribbean, Central America, and South America.[50] The resources targeted are usually found in zones inhabited by Indigenous peoples whose relations to the land are disregarded and ignored. Their communities face looting of resources, pollution of water and land, privatization and food scarcity, diseases, and decreased life expectancy.[51] Gómez-Barris theorizes these areas as "extractive zones" and as areas produced by the "extractive view." The "extractive view" is the colonial way of seeing that treats land and resources as attainable commodities, "while also devalorizing the hidden worlds that form the nexus of human and nonhuman multiplicity."[52] She thus points us to the broader phenomenological aspects of extractivism and connects colonial seeing to the facilitation of land and resource theft. As complementary to Gómez-Barris's "extractive view," I here extend my concern with extractivism to the direct theft of Indigenous visual design as yet another resource targeted by extractivism and turned into commodity for profit.

With the phrase *visual extractivism*, I refer to another mechanism of visual coloniality to name the direct robbery of Indigenous visuality, both materially and epistemically. The material type of looting is evidenced by European explorers who stole and looted ritual objects and artistic creations ranging from ceremonial objects, textiles and weavings, jewelry, masks, clothing items or headdresses, tools and weapons, and quotidian objects. With these items, they built private collections and exhibitions and sold rare and valuable objects in markets.[53] This visual extractivism created the foundation for today's richest museum collections and continues to fuel a market economy in the art and museum world. Additionally, an epistemic type of looting under visual extractivism is seen in Western art history. Consider the most famous and admired artists of Western art history, such as Pablo Picasso or Paul Gauguin, who took styles, designs, and objects from Indigenous communities, whose own art was ignored, devalued, or mislabeled as primitive and naive. Yet, when taken by the West, the very same Indigenous visuality was framed as "inspiration" for new artistic movements and styles that were then credited to Western artists who profited with financial and cultural capital. This type of visual extractivism has justified the valorization of Western artworks for massive amounts of money, while imbuing them with historical presence and authority. Entire movements such as "cubism" or "abstraction" are credited to European artists.

Visual extractivism is practiced even by Latin American governments, whose lands are extracted by foreign companies and who find themselves increasingly dependent on foreign investment for the purpose of their tourist economies. In Guatemala, where an (under)estimated six million people are Indigenous (Maya, Garifuna, Xinca, and Afro-descendants), the government fosters its economy by promoting tourism to sacred temples and sites, while closing these spaces that are important for ceremony to Indigenous peoples today. Likewise, it exploits Mayan textiles and weavings as visual bait for foreign travelers, with no permission from, or profits returned to, Maya communities. Weavings and textiles are worth more than money. Their unique designs visually document history, identify specific tribes and identities, encompass preconquest traditions passed on for centuries, and enforce ancestral spiritual connections. As sacred garments, certain Mayan weavings can only be used by elders or spiritual leaders and/or during ceremonies. Maya women have compared the significance of their *trajes* to that of their own child, as it accompanies them everywhere, even in burial after death.[54] Their significance maintains continuity for a Maya diaspora in the United States, as scholar Floridalma Boj Lopez has argued.[55]

When these ancestral visual elements are not exploited for tourist consumption, they are used to target Indigenous peoples and coerce assimilation.[56] In Guatemala, textiles and weavings are a source of discrimination against Maya people, who are ridiculed, humiliated, and verbally abused for preserving ancestral garments and clothing. Ladinos are known to use words like *embueltas* (wrapped-up women) as derogatory terms for Maya women that reduce them to objects. In her reference to the racialization of clothing, Egla Martínez Salazar explains: "This denotes the clothes Maya women wear are not real clothing but pieces of worthless fabric" and belittled as "*unprocessed* fabrics."[57] That the item is considered crude and unrefined, and thus worthless, until it is "processed" and commodified by a Western entity reinforces the perception of Indigenous aesthetics as natural resources that are wasted unless they are extracted and processed by more "civilized" people. Both national and international designers continuously steal Mayan embroideries and patterns to make clothing and accessories (shoes, handbags, belts, and other clothing garments) that sell for hundreds of dollars throughout the United States and Europe. The items are sold as exotic fashionable trends that simultaneously function as souvenirs, mementos, and keepsakes. In the colonial mindset, only then do sacred weavings and patterns yield profit and value in a tourist economy and market.

Just as Indigenous communities are resisting and defending their lands, water, and resources against extractivist corporations all over the Americas, Indigenous communities are also increasingly defending their creative, visual, and aesthetic resources because of their value and significance to life and being. In 2011, Guatemala designer Giovanni Guzmán used sacred K'iche' Maya designs reserved for spiritual male elders for Miss Guatemala in the Miss Universe Beauty Pageant, sparking indignation from the Maya community. That same year, the Navajo Nation sued clothing company Urban Outfitters, which had launched an entire clothing line with the tribe's name, but lost the case in court because they could not prove that the tribe had sufficient prominence. In 2015, two French designers, Antik Batik and Isabel Marant, stole *huipil* designs from the Mixe community, an Indigenous people who reside in Santa Maria Tlahuitoltepec, in the southwestern state of Oaxaca, retailed the garments at $365, and attempted to copyright the design as their own. Currently, Maya women in Guatemala, led by the Asociación Femenina para el Desarrollo de Sacatepéquez (AFEDES; Women's Association for the Development of Sacatepéquez), are fighting national and transnational companies to protect the collective intellectual property of Indigenous peoples and demanding a halt to the theft of their sacred weavings and designs by the Guatemalan government as well as by international fashion designers and sellers in companies and online websites like Etsy.[58]

Naming visual extractivism as yet another mechanism of visual coloniality allows me to more accurately address a type of colonial thieving that has long been obscured under art historical terminology. While the words *appropriation* or *influence* are popular terms in art to address artists' use of other cultures' preexisting objects and images as their own, visual extractivism acknowledges the power abuse and violent repression that comes with visual theft through colonization. Terms like *appropriation* and *influence* may allude to a cultural exchange, but visual extractivism emphasizes the explicit thievery of art and visual systems from Indigenous peoples as yet another resource that, once commoditized, is exploited to yield monetary profits for private entities, megacorporations, and the Western art world. By exposing its colonialist logic and function and explicit thievery, visual extractivism can no longer persist under the innocuous excuse of cultural exchange or artistic influence, which perpetuate uneven power relations, loss, and violence, under the cloak of artistic normalcy.[59]

Visual erasure, visual thingification, and visual extractivism are just a few of the many mechanisms of visual coloniality as it manifests in Central America. Visual erasure names the colonial deletion of Indigenous artistic history and significance to impose colonial standards as superior and unreachable. It is the rewriting of visual history in the service of empire. Visual thingification names the dehumanization and criminalization of people through visual fabrications as a way to justify both violence done to them and their disposability. And visual extractivism names the thievery, that of Indigenous designs and visuality/knowledge in Western art histories, by nation-states, and by non-Indigenous designers. Naming these mechanisms of visual coloniality, which function differently but are entangled within the colonial project, allows me to identify real and tangible consequences beyond abstract theories and thus to contextualize the role of art and decoloniality in this book as more than an attempt at inclusion in art historical canons, and rather as a deliberate stand against visual coloniality as a system of oppression. Acknowledging how visual coloniality works, hides, and affects us, one can begin to make sense of how making art amid colonial violence and negations of our humanity *is* a radical act of defiance.

VISUAL DISOBEDIENCE

In historizing creative actions, gestures, and interventions, such as the ones briefly mentioned thus far and the more than eighty to come in the following chapters, I offer this book as a story of survival and creation in the face of erasure, invisibility, and dehumanization brought on by both colonial violence and colonial ways of seeing. I therefore theorize the artists, actions, and creations in this book within a framework of "visual disobedience" to directly address a liberation movement in which Central Americans use art to expose ongoing colonialism, defy visual coloniality, and reveal the radicalness of our art and visions as we combat death with creation. Three premises of visual disobedience are key.

First, visual disobedience is an act of informed intervention: it is art as praxis. Centuries of colonial legacies and decades of US military intervention and anti-immigrant policies have led to the current sociopolitical context for the artists addressed in this book. It is from their geo and body politics that artists are using every tool at their disposal to take back public spaces, challenge state aggression, expose racist and colonial logics, and condemn ongoing and unresolved injustices. It is especially relevant when we consider that, despite civil wars and counterinsurgency violence in the 1970s through the 1990s, the region now has greater levels of violence than before. This means that there is no postwar Central America just as there is no postcolonial Central America. Artists engaging in visual disobedience do not represent suffering and oppression—they interrupt, expose, condemn, and provide counternarratives and other ways of seeing. Thus, their disobedience is an intervention into reality. While violence as a theme remains constant, it is not as an exoticized subject but rather as testimony to existence and resistance. Visual disobedience thus understands the artists as knowing and capable humans active in liberation efforts.

Second, visual disobedience comprises an all-sensing and questioning existence where the tactile, auditory, and visual coexist. The experimental art practices addressed here in performance, conceptual, installation, and video art comprise a combination of corporal uses of the body, manipulations of objects, physical gestures in space, and a tactile and auditory cognizance that creates and evokes memory through an honoring of the senses. Through the remaining visual images of such acts of visual disobedience, as seen throughout this book, we can now revisit these historical moments that can be repeated but never duplicated. These images here archive visual counternarratives to the hegemonic ones created about Central Americans and thus are in confrontation with visual coloniality. Visual disobedience centers a sensorial existence in its many facets, from the tangible and corporal to the remaining visual images in its aftermath—a fusion of archive and repertoire.

Third, visual disobedience is a mutiny motivated by love for those Frantz Fanon called "the damnés"—the condemned. It is not merely a disorder by colonial subjects for the sake of appropriating the spaces and resources from which it has been excluded—whether the state or the mainstream art world—for that is not an attempt to undo visual coloniality but instead an appropriation in order to benefit from it. Rather, I locate visual disobedience as part of a long revolt against a historical repression that impedes peace, justice, and a dignified way of being. It is a fight against visual thingification, and all the ways in which Central Americans have been placed in a zone of nonhuman. In fact, the vast majority of the creative work and actions analyzed in this book emerged in moments of urgency, shock, and pain upon experiencing or witnessing attacks on Central America's most vulnerable, as was the case for Galindo's *¿Quien puede borrar las huellas?*, and it is precisely that love that allowed rage to manifest; it is love—so integral to a decolonial attitude, as Maldonado-Torres noted—that has pushed the artists here to a visual disobedience.[60]

While the word *disobedience* evokes anger and rage that irrationally leads to insolence, I remind us that in actuality love precedes rage. Love for the *damnés* inspires disobedience of colonial-based structures as a necessary step toward self-love—not a love required from the state but a love required from within and for each other; the very human ability that coloniality attacks. Thus, I locate love at the core of visual disobedience, as Frantz Fanon did on his theorizations on violence, as Chela Sandoval did in her methodology of the oppressed, and as Che Guevara did in his revolutionary motivations.[61] Visual disobedience is motivated by decolonial love.

BOOK STRUCTURE

The chapters in the book center on how Central American artists have been engaging in visual disobedience for three decades against the most pressing manifestations of violence and the attack on the region in a so-called postwar context. While injustice and movements of resistance are many in Central America, I focus on Indigenous genocide, gender-based and anti-LGBTQ violence, displacement and migration, and systematic criminalization and imprisonment. These issues constitute the historical violence of a so-called postwar Central America and best explain the current phenomenon of women and child migrants and their criminalization on a transnational scale.

Chapter 1, "*Semillas*: Art and Indigenous Defiance in Guatemala," asks: What happens when "bad seeds" defy the demands of coloniality and violence enacted on them, and survive and grow? And what happens when they do indeed retaliate through visual disobedience? Guatemala's 1954 coup, backed by the US Central Intelligence Agency (CIA), set the stage for the thirty-six-year-long civil war (1960 to 1996) that resulted in the deaths of more than 200,000 Guatemalans and the disappearance of 40,000 others. Eighty percent of all deaths were of Maya Indigenous peoples. Recent investigations and trials have shown that the military, led by former Guatemalan dictator José Efraín Ríos Montt, directly executed the genocide of Maya people and their children, whom he labeled "bad seeds" to prevent their future retaliation.

This first chapter analyzes the artistic work of Maya Tz'utujil, Maya Kachikel, and Maya Q'eqchi' artists who belong to the generation of Maya children targeted by the military government. Their presence today alone is an act of defiance. Through their performance art, video art, installations, and object-based works, these artists depart from Indigenous episteme to bring notions of spirituality, gender, and earth relations to the forefront of decolonial visual thinking, while connecting the current repression against Maya peoples in the region to the continuity of repression brought on by the Spanish conquest. Therefore, this chapter addresses visual disobedience of Maya artists against the state and against the coloniality of seeing in visual research of Indigenous peoples' culture.

Chapter 2, "A Creative Turn to the Body: Feminist Dissonance and Erotic Autonomy in Central American Art," centers on a postwar historical shift in feminism and feminist art history of Central America. Following the peace accords and efforts for reconciliation in the 1990s, violence against women in the region has been greater than it was during armed conflicts, while countries like Guatemala, Honduras, and El Salvador are among the most dangerous for nonheteronormative and gender nonconforming peoples. At the same time, performance art became a preferred medium in the region, revealing a departure from decades earlier, when the representation of women as revolutionaries and liberators proliferated in the public art aimed for the masses. This chapter asks: How does a creative turn to the body in a postwar context redefine feminism and erotic autonomy in the region? What is revealed when artists bypass the right-/left-wing rhetoric of decades prior and expose the various mechanisms of what Latin American, Indigenous, and women-of-color feminists have shown to be an entanglement between gender and coloniality?

Through a feminist decolonial reading of selected artworks, I show how artists visually and physically theorize, expose, and condemn a systemic gendered violence beyond the physical injury of women, instead exposing the current gendered violence as a historical tool of patriarchy and nation-state that also functions in the service of coloniality. This chapter shows how through visual disobedience, especially in performance art, artists expose and condemn public attacks on women and gender nonconforming people that have functioned to perpetuate fearful submission. This includes rape and forced reproductive control, domestic violence and psychological control in private spaces, government impunity, Eurocentric notions of beauty and sexuality and anti-Blackness, neoliberal workspaces like *maquiladoras* (sweatshops), and the increasing attacks on land and environmental activists. This chapter also addresses artists that defy, and undo, the nation-state through their own embodied erotic autonomy, while denouncing the nation's role in homophobia and transphobia.

The third chapter, "Shifting the Border: Central American Art against the War on Mobility," analyzes artworks that respond to the waves of Central American migration as a result of civil wars, new manifestations of violence, and neoliberal policies. I decenter the traditional focus on the US-Mexico border as a site of migration discourse and show how the conceptual shift of the border now extends down to Mexico-Guatemala, El Salvador–Honduras, Nicaragua–Costa Rica, and even along the "vertical border" that is Mexico. Shifting the border expands an analysis of border art beyond the US-Mexico dichotomy and allows for consideration of the invisibilized migratory passage for Central Americans through the region and Mexico. This journey is often marked by anti-Indigenous and anti-Black tensions, abduction, rape, forced sexual slavery, and the killing and disappearance of Central American migrants, revealing that the migratory dangers begin long before reaching the US-Mexico border.

While criminal violence is understood to be the main cause for mass migration today, in this chapter I analyze artworks that show how these manifestations of criminal violence are directly related to the decades of US intervention and US anti-immigrant policies of the decades prior. The artists I analyze expose the complexities dismissed in the media and lost in numbers and statistics. They center on the physical journeys and landscape of migration, anti-immigrant sentiment within the region, the consequence of migration on families, the architecture of remittances and changes to urban space, memory and map making in migration, unaccompanied child migrants, and other intricacies of Central American migration. Shifting the border takes us back to a site of multiple border cultures and to the visual politics of unequal capitalist exchange of what activist, writer, and educator Harsha Walia calls border imperialism.[62] I show that artists in Central America shift the border in an act of visual disobedience to create countercartographies of migration and recenter our right to freedom of mobility.

In the fourth and final chapter, "'Los Siempre Sospechosos de Todo': Art on Criminalization, Prisons, and Social Cleansing in Central America," I address one of the gravest consequences following US intervention in Central America: the systematic criminalization of Central Americans and their subsequent captivity and annihilation through the idea of the *marero* and the "*illegal* migrant." The criminality of migrants in the United States has been critically addressed by scholars who reveal how prescribed illegality of migrants enforces labor exploitation, global capitalism, and the impediment of solidarity and coalition building by positioning oppressed groups against each other in the fight for who deserves value. These analyses are useful in considering racialized groups in the United States, to which we can include Central American migrants. This becomes evident when Central Americans' worthiness of citizenship protection and human rights is dependent on their not being mistaken for gang members or terrorists, the presumed "real" criminals. This chapter asks: How do artists in the region, through their visual disobedience, expand and challenge the debates around criminality, worth, and citizenship both in the region and in the United States? Specifically, how do artists expose the multiple origins of such criminalization to reveal it as a violence that both precedes and follows migrants reaching the US-Mexico border?

The art in this final chapter reveals that criminality is not ascribed to migrants only upon reaching the US-Mexico border. As I show, from the making of transnational gangs in the United States, to the increase of mass incarceration in the region, a wave of mysterious prison fires that are burning inmates alive, and the construction of mega-prisons, Central American artists theorize illegality and delinquency within a broader colonial agenda of dehumanization. Beyond a critique of anti-immigrant sentiment, artists reveal and expose a carceral logic rooted in coloniality that ties a perpetual criminalization of Central Americans across borders and that is inseparable from the colonial agenda of social cleansing of poor, racialized, and marginalized Central Americans. Thus, I show how collectively their visual disobedience against policing, criminalization, and imprisonment of Central Americans—both within the region and across borders—pushes not for immigration reform, not for selective citizenship, but for an abolition of the carceral logic, the carceral state, and the carceral state's mechanisms of violence.

This book does not pretend to offer a comprehensive art history of Central America. Instead, I proceed from the assertion that when a people are forced into silence, a scream is an act of defiance; when a people are reduced to an image of suffering and victimhood, creating images of oneself is an act of rebellion; and when a people are made invisible through historical erasure, telling one's stories is an act of insurgence. I show how Central American artists have engaged in visual disobedience as an epistemic and ontological practice of defying coloniality and visual coloniality through corporal interventions, manipulations of space and sound, and the subsequent images through which these practices live on in our historical imaginaries. This book conveys the radical and resilient nature of Central American artistic creation as acts of defiance and as essential in our decolonization. While the dominant idea of us revolves around US-centric images of suffering or less-than-human status, this book aims to show how Central Americans see our history, our present, our future, and ourselves. It is written with Central Americans in mind and all whose creative culture, knowledge, and ways of seeing and being are continuously erased through colonization and empire.

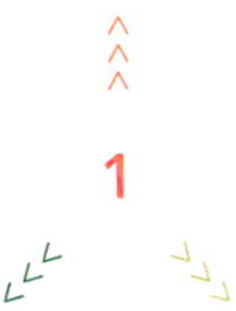

SEMILLAS

Art and Indigenous Defiance in Guatemala

In the capital city of Guatemala, an Indigenous man dressed as an elder from his Maya Tz'utujil community intervened in the chaotic urban space, drawing everyone's attention to his performance, *El grito* (2002) (The scream) (see figure 1.1). Benvenuto Chavajay paced back and forth on the busy sidewalk, amid the fast-paced pedestrians and loud traffic, swinging a *matraca* (a rattle or noisemaker used during processions) around and above his head. With this religious instrument and symbol of Guatemalan identity from his hometown, he echoed a sound his community would recognize from the thirty-six-year-long civil war (1960–96)—gunshots. Meanwhile, the Tz'utujil garment he wore linked the sound with its historical target—the Indigenous body. Projecting this sound into the city and for its pedestrians, he evoked a memory of the armed conflict and all its unresolved injustices, but he did not speak a word. Instead, he transformed a sound associated with war into a visual and corporal scream of denunciation emerging from an Indigenous embodiment and disrupting the silence and invisibility imposed by visual coloniality.

In a country like Guatemala, as in other areas across Latin America where indigenismo was a prevalent political and ideological movement, the visual image of an Indigenous man is not an anomaly. Since its inception in the 1920s and 1930s, indigenismo became a pan–Latin American political and ideological movement through which nation-states theoretically promoted a celebration of Indigeneity, albeit in practice it was mostly as a national symbol in service of mestizo formation.[1] The visual arts were a key platform for its propagation. Art typically entailed figurative depictions of Indigenous peoples to emphasize the country's cultural heritage and traditions over a European influence, and thus co-opted Indigeneity as a claim to authenticity. Meanwhile, discounting their current realities and relegating them to a romantic past, the mestizo-led movement denied Indigenous peoples a contemporary political presence that consequently furthered their marginalization. Art historians have noted indigenismo's entanglements with nationalism and paternalism; its Pan-American reach; its consequences across class, race, and gender; and the institutional museum logics that uphold it.[2] In reality indigenismo was a move away from Indigeneity and Blackness and toward assimilation and whiteness.

Chavajay's physical presence does not abide by the rules of indigenismo but defies them. In a gesture of agency, he chooses his own body as an artistic medium to bypass the traditional figurative depiction of an Indigenous man. He does not offer a subject matter frozen in time to be seen and celebrated, or an idealized figure to legitimize a mestizo nation-state. His intervention is a physical, optical, and sonic interruption into space that enunciates his existence in the present, interfering with historical amnesia and disrupting the temporal disjuncture produced by the legacy of indigenismo. Chavajay's performance can better be understood as a visual disobedience to coloniality in the present. Through his performance he forces a remembrance and confrontation with the largest and most public genocide of Indigenous people in Central America during the twentieth century, the Guatemalan civil war (1960–96).

The Truth and Reconciliation Commission reported that up to 80 percent of deaths during the conflict were of Maya Indigenous peoples, many more of whom were terrorized, tortured, and disappeared.[3] Within that time frame, ex-dictator José Efraín Ríos Montt led a US-backed massacre that resulted in 1,771

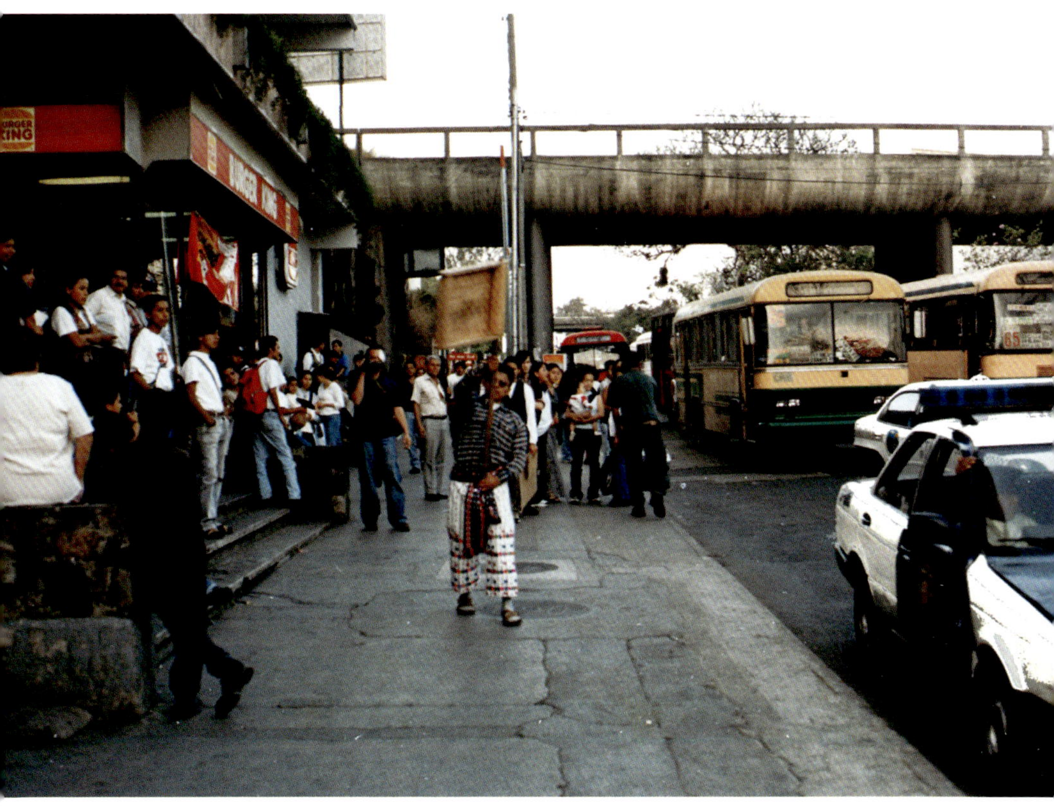

FIGURE 1.1.
Benvenuto Chavajay, *El grito*, 2002, performance. Courtesy of the artist.

Maya Ixil killed and 29,000 displaced over a seventeen-month reign of terror (1982–83). Maya children were explicit military targets for destruction during the war.[4] Often dismissing the assault and bloodshed of Indigenous infants, toddlers, and young children as "unexplainable" and "unthinkable," authorities also rationalized their deaths as unfortunate casualties, or consequential victims, due to their misfortune of being the children of antiestablishment and subversive parents—the military's supposed real targets.[5] Yet, as Egla Martínez Salazar argues, the deaths and killings of Maya children were "not a secondary casualty of state terror, but a clear object of destruction within the context of genocide."[6] In fact, she explains, the state defined Maya babies, toddlers, and children as "bad seeds," spawn of the "internal enemies," a term defined in the 1983 Manual of Counter-subversive War by the Center for Military Studies of the Guatemalan Army as follows:

> All those individuals, groups, and organizations who through illegal actions want to break the established order . . . who following direction from internal communism develop so-called revolutionary war and subversion in the country. Those individuals, groups and organizations that are not communist but that want to break the established order are also considered internal enemies.[7]

For the state, Maya children constituted "internal enemies" by default of their birth, since their Indigeneity was automatically construed by the state as communist and subversive. However, it is worth noting, as Maya Kaqchikel historian Edgar Esquit has written, that liberatory concepts associated with mestizo-led guerrillas of the 1970s–1980s, such as the Kaqchikel words *meb'ail* (*pobreza*/poverty), *poqonal* (*sufrimiento*/suffering), *qawinaq* (*nuestra gente*/ our people), or the Spanish words *superación* (overcoming*)*, *conciencia* (awareness), and *consiente* (conscious), are rooted in Maya epistemologies and precede those revolutionary movements.[8] More telling is the response by a former civil patroller who, when asked by the Comisión para el Esclarecimiento Histórico (CEH; Commission of Historical Clarification) "Why are you killing children?" clarified, "Because those sons of bitches one day will get revenge and fuck us up."[9] Maya children were defined as antiestablishment adversaries for their mere existence as Indigenous peoples and considered a future threat. To be Indigenous and simply exist was a defiance, not just during the civil war but for more than five hundred years.

Chavajay's *El grito* becomes an embodiment of testimony against historical erasure. It is a condemnation brought forth from the rural areas, where most atrocities done to Indigenous peoples were unreported or ignored, into the fast-paced urban city protected from the violence. His scream is a reminder that the wounds of violence remain an agonizing pain in the postwar period and testifies to the persistence of Maya existence. By bringing *El grito* to the urban space, Chavajay creates witnesses out of the urban public. The crowd is forced to hear the sound and recognize his presence—a strategy facilitated by performance, in which audiences participate in the production and reproduction of knowledge by "being there" and forming part of the transmission. *El grito* was a protest shout evoking the thousands of visual and corporal screams that since colonization have testified to and denounced genocide. In the visual archive he creates, there is no peaceful Indigenous body from an ancient civilization, common in a national art that promotes tourism, but rather a dynamic body in the urban space that demands to be heard. Through his visual disobedience, Chavajay simultaneously exposes racist colonial structures of war and offsets Western representations of Indigenous peoples as passive.

Contemporary Maya artists like Chavajay locate the genocide of the Spanish conquest and the twentieth-century genocide as the ongoing violence of a settler state attempting to eliminate Indigenous peoples. Like Chavajay, Antonio Pichillá (Maya Tz'utujil), Ángel Poyón, Fernando Poyón, Marilyn Elany Boror Bor, and Edgar Calel (Maya Kaqchikel), and Sandra Monterroso (Maya Q'ekchi') all belong to a postwar generation of artists who have brought global attention to the Guatemalan contemporary art scene and to a Central American art context more broadly. What do their creative works reveal about the contemporary Indigenous struggles in postwar Guatemala when the subject matter is no longer the emblematic representation of an Indigenous figure promoted by Latin American modernist art but rather self-representations of Indigenous embodiments and knowledges through experimental practices and a decolonial position? Further, how does their art speak to the disregard and attack of Indigenous children, from the civil war to today's Maya children killed, disappeared, and detained at the US-Mexico border? With their interventions, installations, and video art, I show that these artists' works go beyond filling an artistic void in Central American art. Their visual disobedience both defies a state-sanctioned visual language of Indigeneity and condemns the current racial, class, and gender oppression in Guatemala, not as symbolic of contemporary governments or political figures but as a continuity of the conquest and colonization of 1492. In this process, their visual disobedience is an act of self-determination that also Indigenizes Central American art.

EVOKING MEMORY AND HEALING

In her performance *Rakoc Atin* (2008), the artist Sandra Monterroso occupied the plaza in front of the Supreme Court of Guatemala both as a condemnation and as a healing process. During her performance, she used sea salt to write "RAKOC ATIN" in large letters on the ground (see figure 1.2). In Maya Q'ekchi', *rakoc atin* means *hacer justicia*, or "to make justice." Under Ríos Montt's rule it was common practice for military forces to dispose of Indigenous people, sometimes alive, by throwing them from helicopters into the Pacific Ocean. A Defense Intelligence Agency secret message from April 1994 states that the purpose of the strategy was to eliminate evidence of torture and killings by vanishing the bodies.[10] Some returned with the tide, but most bodies were never seen again, impeding a proper burial ceremony and rituals of mourning. By using sea salt, Monterroso condemned the inhumane military practice while simultaneously calling on the significance of salt in many Indigenous rituals and practices for healing and cleansing.

As part of her performance, various intravenous machines, which are used to transfer liquids (blood, medicine, or drugs) into a main artery during a medical treatment, slowly leaked liquid onto the words, dissolving them. This subtle watering down of the phrase *rakoc atin* spoke to the fact that when victims or their families reported crimes of violence in their native languages to police authorities, they often went undocumented due to a lack of translators. The same silencing occurred following the signing of peace accords, when officials sought testimonies to initiate healing and reconciliation processes but lacked translators to communicate in various Indigenous languages. In simulating the disintegration of words with a machine intended to keep people alive and heal them, Monterroso implicated language within the power of coloniality as well as underscored the superficial healing of a failed peace process.

In 2013, Judge Yassmin Barrios gave her historic guilty verdict in a national court to US-backed military dictator Ríos Montt for genocide and crimes against humanity. He was sentenced to eighty years in prison. Ten days later, the Guatemalan Constitutional Court annulled the jury's verdict. It seemed to many that whenever possibilities for justice appeared on the horizon, the racist structures of the governmental institutional systems remained intact, protected through impunity. The series of brave testimonies given by Indigenous men and women who either suffered direct violence under Ríos Montt or lost family members under his rule reopened wounds that were left exposed rather than healed due to the annulment. This makes Monterroso's performance and the location, in front of the Court of Justice, ever more poignant. Her choice

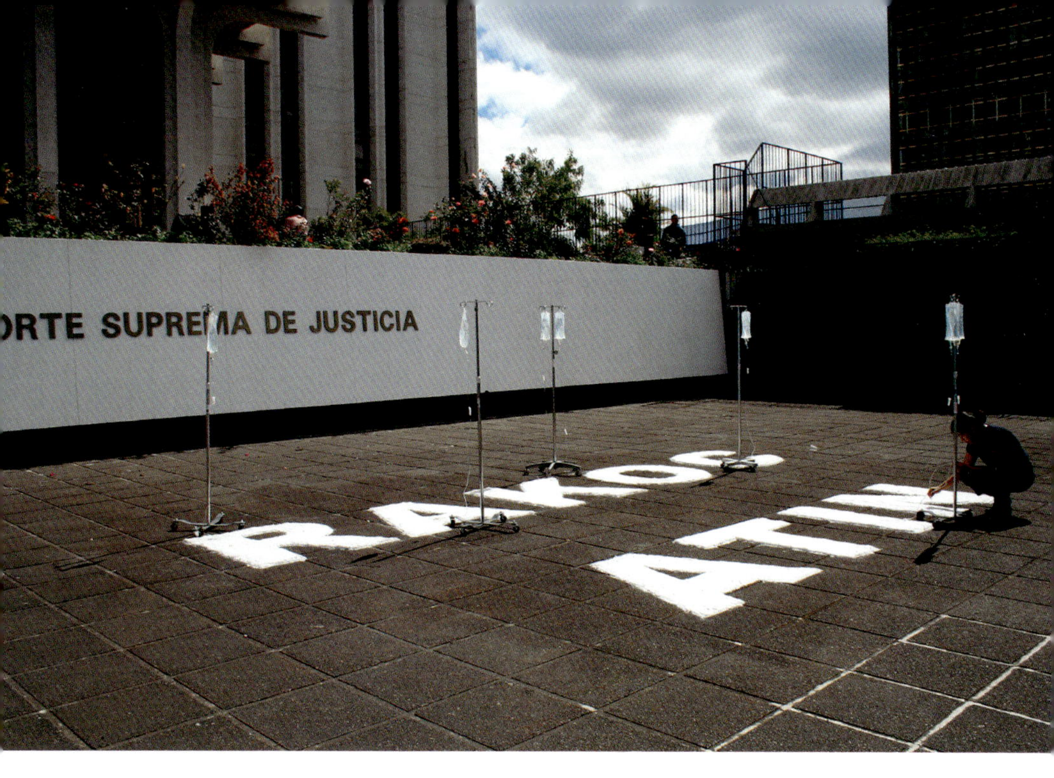

FIGURE 1.2.
Sandra Monterroso, *Rakoc Atin*, 2008, performance. Courtesy of the artist.

of location was already publicly challenging the key judicial institution, condemning its contradictions. It also points toward other institutional failures such as the efforts to establish historical records for healing when diverse Indigenous languages are ignored.

Similar violence was enacted on the Afro-Indigenous Garínagu (plural of Garifuna) in Guatemala, who were also displaced, tortured, disappeared, and killed during the civil war but whose testimonies the CEH did not collect or document. As Scherly Virgill Artiaga notes, despite multimedia announcements asking for testimonials of incidents or grievances in nine Mayan languages (out of twenty-one), none were made in the Garifuna language, leading to the omission of Garifuna testimonies from the official record and exposing anti-Black racism.[11] This is also a result of a long history of anti-Blackness in the region.[12] Through the site specificity of her performance, Monterroso denounced the judiciary's culpability in perpetuating the physical, psychological, and spiritual traumas that come from the erasure of Indigenous victim's testimonies.

While Chavajay and Monterroso use sound, gestures, and the installation of words to expose the failures of urban ladinos and their institutions in properly accounting for Indigenous suffering and healing, artist Ángel Poyón turns directly to the healing of the disappeared and their relatives. During the war, the military conducted numerous massacres in rural and Indigenous communities. In addition to the ocean, they disposed of the victims' bodies in clandestine graves to evade condemnation for their crimes. Maya people were robbed of the details of their loved ones' deaths and unable to practice burial and mourning practices according to their cosmovision. The exhumation of massacre victims has thus been a crucial aspect of reconciliation in postwar Guatemala and one initiated by Maya women. For Maya people, exhumations hold both political and spiritual importance, providing historical information that confirms what they believe happened and offering evidence for state accountability, as well as allowing for proper burial and mourning ceremonies that bring peace for both the dead and the living.[13] But beyond a form for state accountability, Maya women's search for clandestine graves and the disappeared reveals what Maya K'iche' public intellectual, sociologist, and activist Gladys Tzul Tzul describes as a "desire to live," pointing specifically to "the social energy Indigenous women produce that allows them to preserve their memory and defend the land where the dead rest and water is born."[14] This will to survive and persist is tied to Maya relations to land, water, and ancestors.

In 2003, the Fundación de Antropología Forense de Guatemala (FAFG; Forensic Anthropology Foundation of Guatemala) began exhumations in

San Juan Comalapa, where it recovered 220 victims.[15] A few years later, Poyón conceptualized the performance *Letanía* (Litany) (2008) and invited Carlos Poyón, from his Kaqchikel community in the town of Comalapa, to assist in carrying out the action (see figure 1.3). With a machete, a tool used by campesinos for agricultural work, Carlos dug a hole in the ground, creating a portal, or window, into the depths of the earth. With a lighted candle, a jar of water, and a list with hundreds of names of those disappeared during the conflict in Comalapa, Carlos spoke into the pit, communicating with the souls of the disappeared. One by one, he read out their names and posed a series of questions: "what happened to you, what did they do to you, where are you now?"[16] Ángel referred to a Mayan Kaqchikel ritual of calling the names of the deceased whose souls were suspected of still wandering in the realm of the living, encouraging them to transcend into another cosmological dimension.

Originally, Ángel imagined Carlos, who was also an active member of a mobilization that searched for the disappeared and exhumed their cadavers when they were discovered in clandestine graves, would carry out the ritual for his father, who was among the disappeared. His death was a "cold" death, that is, unwarranted and unexpected. Thus, Ángel Poyón offered Carlos the opportunity for a *desahogo*, a moment to vent and relieve pain. Yet Carlos felt he could not ignore the other victims and chose instead to summon a dialogue with all the disappeared from Comalapa. Ángel agreed. With the performance, the artist centered community collectivity in memory and healing.

Chavajay, Monterroso, and Poyón offer gestures of communication that break through a silence. This silence, however, extends beyond the repression of Indigenous peoples under Ríos Montt, who died in 2018 during his retrial. Instead, their acts defy the constraints of visual representation Maya people are relegated to in Western modern art, as they summon sound, voice, and gesture to evoke a collective call for remembrance and justice across centuries of settler colonial violence and coloniality. While performance gained momentum in a postwar context in Guatemala, Chavajay, Monterroso, and Poyón conjure ancient Mayan practices and elements that precede performance art—that center on the body as a vehicle for healing, transmitting knowledge, and seeking justice; and that transcend the corporal to attain the spiritual. They engage experimental forms to create art as well as give continuity to a way of living based on Mayan epistemologies and cosmologies. They depart from these Maya ways of being to offer creative decolonial acts that publicly attack the legacy of coloniality in current governmental, military, and legal institutions. Their embodied acts become a collective critique of visual coloniality and a method of communal testimony and healing.

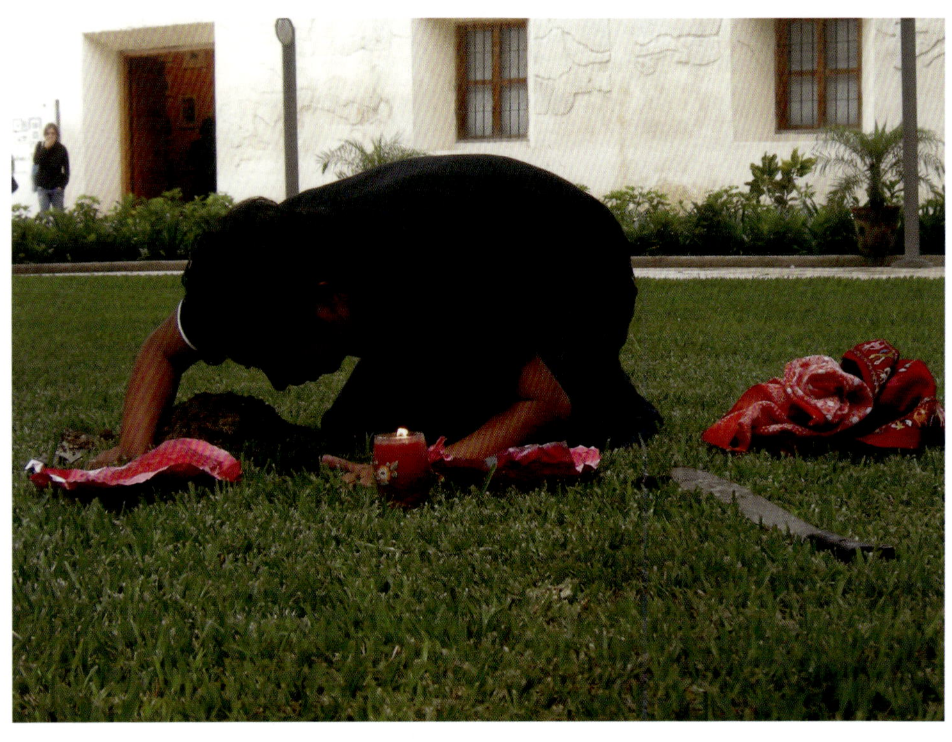

FIGURE 1.3.
Ángel Poyón, *Letanía*, 2008, performance, with the participation of Darío Poyón, son of disappeared father during the repression in Guatemala. Courtesy of the artist.

San Pedro La Laguna is one of several Indigenous towns located at the edge of Lake Atitlán in the department of Sololá, Guatemala.[17] It is home to the Tz'utujil community, one of twenty-one Mayan ethnic groups in the country that made up the ancient Maya civilization. An influx of foreign travelers has turned the town into a tourist site with an overflow of backpackers, hostels, and restaurants run by foreign retirees. Away from the shore, or what art historian Maria Victoria Véliz has called the "downtown" of San Pedro, and up the steep slope of the volcano, tourists become less visible and the Tz'utujil community becomes more present.[18] While the town is known for its strong self-taught artistic community, in particular paintings of quotidian Tz'utujil life in a traditional folkloric style, a favorite among tourists, a new generation deviates from this artistic tradition to engage in practices rooted in Indigenous ways of seeing, and not just as Indigenous subject matter.[19]

Chavajay, who resides in both Guatemala City and San Pedro La Laguna, links the lake's environmental deterioration to the arrival of a foreign modernity. In his La suave chapina series, the artist transforms local rocks, stones, and other objects from Lake Atitlán by attaching plastic straps of the popular Suave Chapina brand of sandal (see figure 1.4). The brand's name is a merger of the words *soft* and *chapina*, the informal name used to refer to a Guatemalan woman. As Chavajay has noted about plastic, "This material marked Guatemalan society, above all the Indigenous world. With its arrival everything changed. Modernity *plasticated* our culture."[20] This brand of sandal became both an inexpensive commodity of desire and an alternative to going barefoot. While the lightweight material of the sandal should project comfort and convenience, Chavajay has replaced the sole of the sandal with the natural rocks from San Pedro La Laguna, bringing forth the weight, heaviness, and plight of the Tz'utujil community. This juxtaposition and relation between materials, in which plastic represents a foreign modernity and the rocks represent the lake and the Tz'utujil people, serve as a critique of environmental destruction from the tourist invasion of San Pedro.

Modernity as "plastification" of Indigenous culture further summons in the artist's own terms what scholars like Argentinian Mexican philosopher of liberation Enrique Düssel and the modernity/coloniality group have noted as the underside of modernity.[21] Düssel locates the beginning of Eurocentric modernity in the discovery and conquest of the Americas in 1492, in which Europe defined a single version of modernity—one elevated as a center among a periphery—and then imposed it onto the world as a global design.

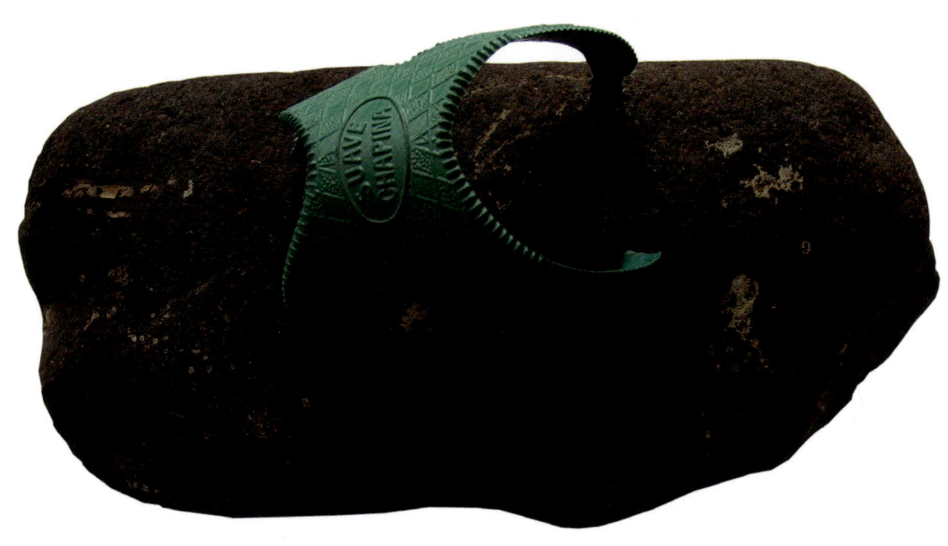

FIGURE 1.4.
Benvenuto Chavajay, La suave chapina series, 2007–8, intervened rock. Courtesy of the artist.

While Europe expanded into other parts of the world as a "center," it required the creation of the opposite side of this binary—the underdeveloped, the backward—which for Düssel constitutes the "second moment" of modernity, or its underside.[22] With the concept of transmodernity, Düssel calls for colonized peoples around the world to express a multiplicity of critiques of modernity. He views this task as necessary to truly complete the project of decolonization. Through his nonfigurative, object-based works, Chavajay responds to Düssel's call and brings forth current political issues of the environment, borders, and migration as the underside of modernity. With La suave chapina series, the artist exposes the "plastification" of Indigenous culture as the underside of European modernity and, importantly, asserts Indigenous resistance and survival. Chavajay maintains a Tz'utujil epistemic connection through the base and sole of the artworks—pieces of earth that have existed for centuries as witness to Tz'utujil journeys.

The stones were infused with a definition of art and the sacred that we can delink from Western definitions of art such as the "found object" or "readymade" (artworks made from material considered to have nonart function, such as discarded or manufactured products). In the Tz'utujil community, the word *art* or *arte* in the Spanish colonial idiom emerged only six decades ago.[23] For artists like Chavajay, the closest equivalent to the meaning of art in Tz'utujil is "the sacred," which applies especially to nature, from the tallest trees to the smallest rocks.[24] This notion reflects a belief and daily praxis in relation with Mother Earth based on respect, sustenance, and reciprocity. Maya relations with nature contrast and challenge the ill treatment and violent disregard of nature prominent in the coloniality of power, capitalism, and Western ways of living—especially as they entail the destruction of Indigenous bodies and sacred lands and plants. Accordingly, the conviction that the sacredness of life in nature's objects is the most accurate definition of art challenges the notion of art as commodity, while maintaining a fundamental spiritual connection to visual culture and life that has survived for more than five hundred years.

Chavajay also uses other sacred materials such as maize, tortillas, and *guacales* (gourd vessels) to address the process of transculturation from the perspective of modernity/coloniality. For instance, in the 2013 exhibition at the Feria Internacional de Arte Contemporáneo in Madrid, Spain, Chavajay submitted a black *mazorca* (corncob) with wooden wings attached to its side as his art piece (see figure 1.5). The work stemmed from Chavajay's personal memory: the first time a plane crossed the skies over San Pedro La Laguna and across Lake Atitlán. He captured the weary reaction of the community, which looked at the sky with a consciousness that this object above all of them marked an upcoming change, one spoken of by the elders and ancestors. This was a "dark consciousness" of Western modernity, as Chavajay sees, which connects the black color of the *maiz* to an arrival of modernity and a dark future, thus linking the impact of colonization in 1492 with ongoing settler colonialism and coloniality. The black *maiz*, already instilled with sacredness and historical and cultural significance tied to life and spirituality for Indigenous communities, is hard to cultivate, making it both sacred and rare. When colonizers came to the Americas in search of riches and wealth, they were shocked to know that Indigenous communities ascribed more value to *maiz*, chocolate, and other natural items than gold, and colonizers belittled this significance as ignorance. Sending *maiz* back to Spain as an art object imbued with cultural value conveys a visual disobedience that reinforces the resistance, persistence, and preservation of Indigenous spiritual and cultural values, despite colonization and coloniality. The arrival of modernity/coloniality did not fully impose its own values, as Indigenous communities have resisted them for centuries through epistemic and visual disobedience.

Meanwhile, the Kaqchikel artist Ángel Poyón, who also makes object-based artworks, conveys the failures of modernity in Guatemala by referencing displacement. Poyón is from the town of San Juan Comalapa, located in the department of Chimaltenango and inhabited by the Indigenous Maya Kaqchikel. It is widely known for a tradition of folklore painting that extends back to the 1940s with the master Andres Curruchiche (1891–1969). As a young boy, Curruchiche worked as a farmer, during which time he acquired an interest in painting objects and local scenes onto feathers, wood, *jícaras* (gourds), and later cloth panels. Once "discovered" by a local priest, he gained international recognition and went on to exhibit in the United States, consequently initiating the artistic tradition in Comalapa, where he taught others his style of painting. Hundreds of artists reside in Comalapa today, including his daughter María Curruchiche, who, along with several women artists, continues painting in the traditional style of Comalapa.[25] While the style is respected in the community, it is also preferred by the state as an acceptable and depoliticized national style representative of a nonthreatening Indigeneity in Guatemala. Yet this governmental exaltation of Comalapa as a nonthreatening artistic community did not spare it from mass disappearances and violence. Ángel Poyón and his brother Fernando Poyón mark a clear departure from the traditional style toward experimentation with conceptual, installation, and performance art.

In *Estudios del fracaso medidos en tiempo y espacio* (Studies on failure measured in time and space) (2008), Ángel Poyón recovers old-fashioned twin-bell alarm clocks, eliminating the numbers as a reference to Western concepts of time and

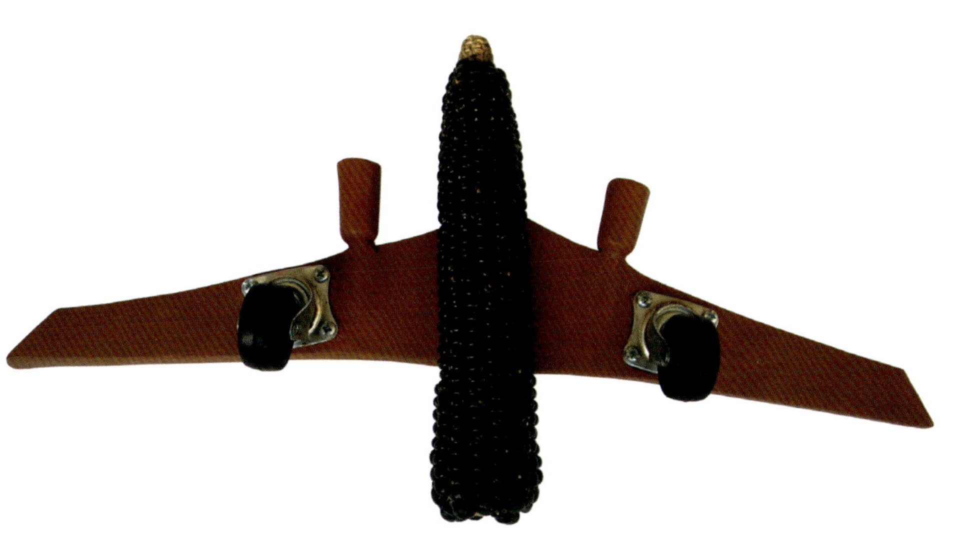

FIGURE 1.5.
Benvenuto Chavajay, *Untitled* (black *mazorca*), 2013, intervened maiz. Courtesy of the artist.

instead depicting in their place paths of movement, migration, and displacement (see figure 1.6). The lines—evoking modernist geometric abstraction styles—offer a contradictory journey, with overlaps, repetitions, and an unclear directionality that proposes an oppositional framework of time and space brought on by modernity's failures. As Rosina Cazali has argued, "these studies suggest a useless pathway, as was the project of modernity."[26] The vintage clocks further evoke an element of nostalgia for the passing of time and movements in space; but in the context of Guatemala, nostalgia is offset by recent memories of forced migration—either rural to urban, or across national borders—as a result of the Guatemalan conflict.

Similar to how maps of the world have located Indigenous lands on the periphery, Poyon's work underscores how concepts of Western time have also located Indigenous peoples in prehistory. In Western modernity, time is a linear chronology of development with a point of "discovery" from which supposed real time begins. An event becomes factual only when located within that Western time frame of development and progress. Anything left out of that chronology, including people and their visions of the world, are deemed backward and incapable of self-actualization. In modernity, history is presented as one large chronology, in contrast to Indigenous concepts of history and time.

Poyón's piece disrupts measurements of time and space associated with Eurocentric modernity by inverting its Western concept of the line. Linda Tuhiwai Smith has noted:

> There is a very specific spatial vocabulary of colonialism which can be assembled around three concepts: 1) the line, 2) the center, and 3) the outside. The "line" is important because it was used to map territory, to survey land, to establish boundaries, and to mark the limits of colonial power. The "center" is important because orientation to the center was an orientation to the system of power. The "outside" is important because it positioned territory and people in an oppositional relationship to the colonial "center."[27]

Poyón's replacement of numbers (representing measurements of time) with broken and undecipherable lines confronts the spatial vocabulary of colonialism. His clocks subvert the line to convey instead movement, migration, and displacement that blur the epicenter of power. Both the sleek shape (the clock's outer form) and the unruly lines (on the inner clock) create a visual juxtaposition that alludes to two coexisting modernities—the former presented as keeper of time, and the latter its underside. Only when space is compartmentalized can it be measured and defined as it has been in Eurocentric modernity, where

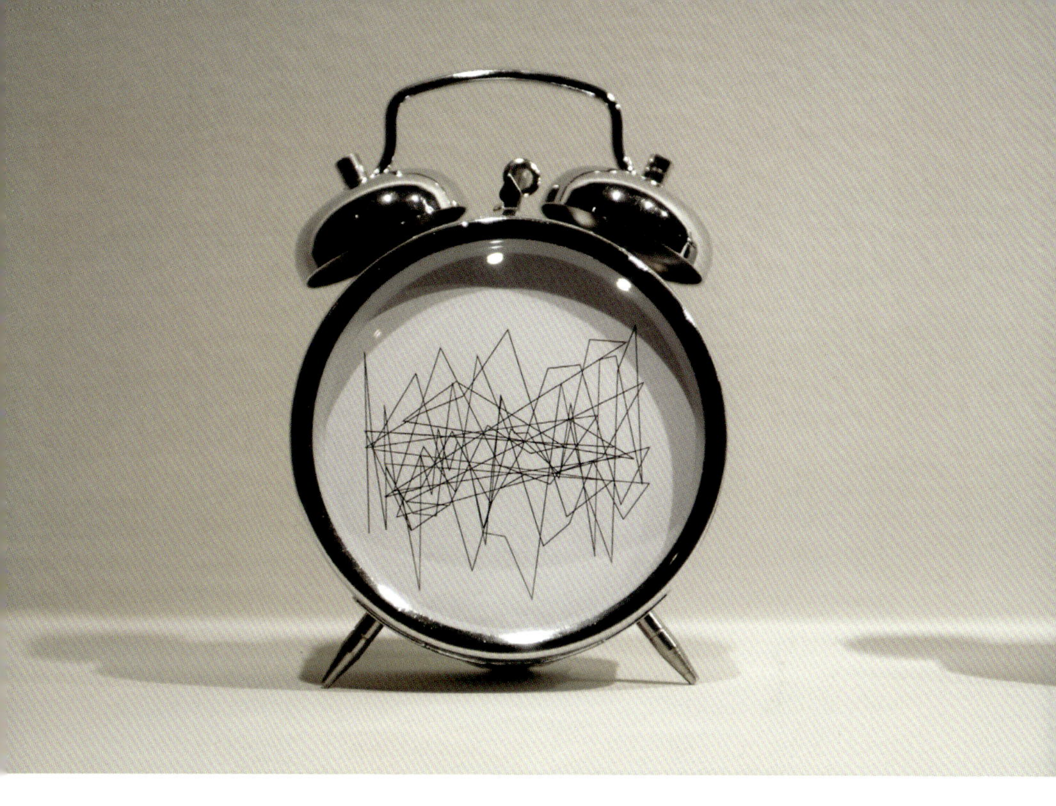

FIGURE 1.6.
Ángel Poyón, *Estudios del fracaso medidos en tiempo y espacio*, 2008, intervened clock. Collection Hugo Quinto and Juan Pablo Lojo. Photograph by Andrés Asturias. Courtesy of the artist.

social activity in relation to space and time produces binaries such as work/home, public/domestic, and city/country. With these concepts of Western time and space, Western modernity has represented and radically transformed Indigenous worldviews in the spatial image of the West, made for the West. Thus, when Indigenous social activity does not fit within these concepts, Western views ascribed notions of laziness to Indigenous peoples. Poyón deliberately disrupts Western modernity by undermining the compartmentalization of Western time as it has been used in the oppression of Indigenous peoples.

Chavajay's La suave chapina series and Ángel Poyón's *Estudios del fracaso medidos en tiempo y espacio* expose the relation between an imposed modernity and its underside: coloniality. Their ways of seeing materialize through a resignification of objects: Chavajay reinscribes onto rocks the Tz'utujil ways of seeing the sacred in the earth, and Poyón challenges concepts of time associated with Western modernity with altered vintage clocks. Curators and historians may be tempted to place these artworks within a legacy of Western definitions of art and art movements, in particular the conceptual art and found-object art initiated in Europe and the United States in the early twentieth century. This type of Western art time line places Euro-American art as a center and point of departure, relegating all else as derivative. But when we center a Tz'utujil geography of reason, Chavajay's objects are not found objects but, as he explains, they are *remembered* objects rooted in Tz'utujil cosmology. They are not "objects" at all but living things—they are nature and therefore sacred. From this point of departure, objects are not art because Chavajay says they are art (as is the logic of conceptual art); they are art because they are nature, sacred, and evidence of Chavajay's way of being and seeing. Both artists defy Western art concepts, Western history, and visual coloniality by conveying the underside of modernity from a Maya Tz'utujil and Maya Kaqchikel perspective. Theirs is a visual disobedience to Western notions of time, space, and history as well as to the figurative representations of Indigenous life customary in their hometowns.

SAFEGUARDING THROUGH VIDEO AND INSTALLATION

Within a long legacy of colonization and visual coloniality, art remains a contentious space for Maya cosmovision, a space in which Maya people both endure colonial violence and enact visual disobedience. It is known that Indigenous artists trained in Western styles of art during the colonial period inconspicuously incorporated symbols and imagery of Indigenous significance unknown to the Spanish colonizers and priests who supervised the works. Thus, while they were forced to adopt Christian religious practices, they also subverted them to incorporate and preserve Indigenous cosmologies.[28] While Maya people continue to fight against social and political injustice, the state profits by promoting a romanticized idea of Indigeneity by privileging towns, sacred landscapes, and ancient sites and temples crucial to Maya cosmovision, creating a cultural commodity for a tourist economy. This was evident during the much-anticipated Baktun 13 on December 21, 2012, which to the Maya people signifies the beginning of a new era for humanity. For the state, the event was an opportunity to profit. The government invested more than US$6 million to lure the more than 200,000 foreign tourists for the official state celebrations at the ancient Maya temple of Tikal. Meanwhile, sacred sites were off-limits to Indigenous peoples, forcing them to celebrate the event, as Maya leader Rigoberta Menchú observed, "in silence [and] in the intimacy" of their spirituality and *cosmovisión*. Only priests and spiritual guides conducting ceremonies were allowed on the Maya sacred temples.[29]

Artists such as Fernando Poyón and Antonio Pichillá bypass figurative depictions to address Maya cosmovision and use installation and video to critically reflect on Christianity's colonizing impacts on Indigenous spirituality today and the continuous safeguarding of Maya cosmovisions. In the fifteen-second video *Contra la pared* (Against the wall) (2006), Maya Kachickel artist Fernando Poyón presents a close-up shot of three Maya women in their traditional dress (see figure 1.7). Poyón frames the lower half of the women's faces while they speak words unheard by viewers. The only sound heard in the background is the classical Catholic hymn "Ave María," which plays throughout the duration of the video. The camera zooms out, never showing the women's faces but merely expanding the screenshot to frame their torsos and present a broken figuration. The women then repeat a gesture customary of the Catholic prayer "I Confess to You." In the Spanish version of this prayer, during the phrase "por mi culpa," one is to repeatedly take the right fist to the heart as a gesture of guilt and remorse. "Por mi culpa, por mi culpa, por mi gran culpa."

Poyón associates this act as being "backed against the wall," as the title indicates. In removing all context and isolating the act of self-blame as the focus of the video, the artist highlights the lack of justification for the confession, conveying the robotic gesture of guilt as an internalized colonialist act. Poyón points to this self-blame, rooted in the imposition of Christianity as a tool of colonization and for slaughtering those who refused conversion, as a forced but also internalized mode of survival. The lack of facial expression or visible eyes and the mechanical manner in which the women repeat the gesture convey a dissociation from its meaning, distinguishing between complete submission and a compromise made to evade death. In this manner, the artist reveals

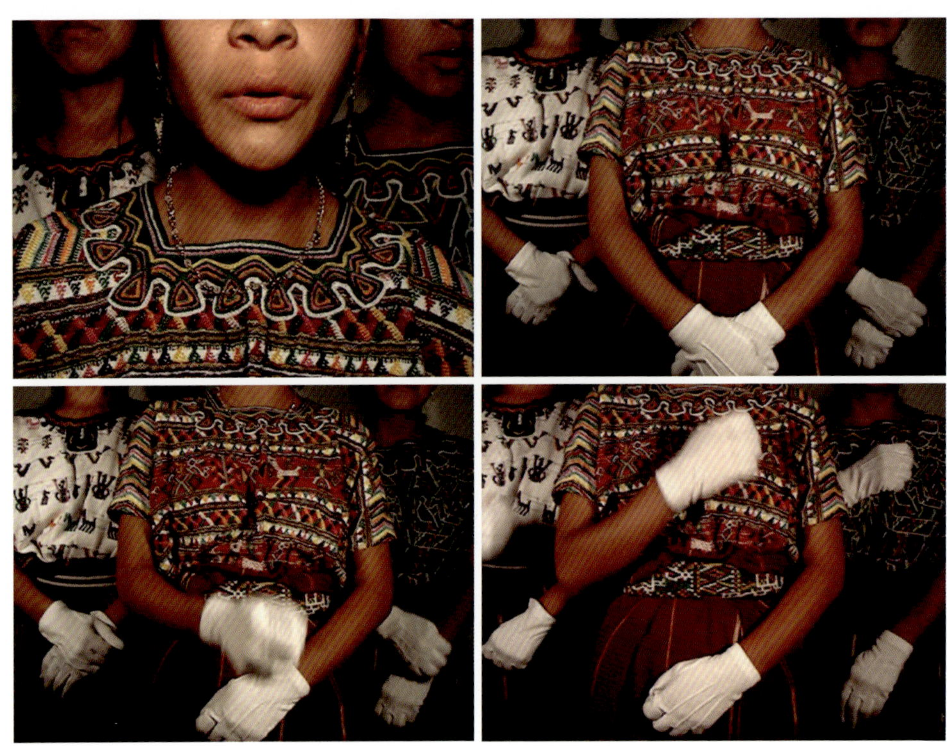

FIGURE 1.7.
Fernando Poyón, *Contra la pared*, 2005, video (stills). Courtesy of the artist.

the role of Christianity from an initial colonization to one that extends into the contemporary, as it manifests through self-blame.

In Central America, governments constantly evade responsibility for the violence Indigenous peoples face—including extreme poverty, severely inadequate educational resources, rape, and genocide—and instead, they attribute blame to notions of ignorance, uncleanliness, and promiscuity in Indigenous peoples, resorting to colonialist racial discourse for impunity. Women in particular often suffer both state and domestic violence in silence, while their perpetrators convince them that they are responsible for "provoking" the violence. This practice of repudiation is echoed with the denial of the genocide. A large portion of the elite population in Guatemala, including former president Otto Pérez Molina and other politicians, refuses to acknowledge that the military agenda to kill hundreds of thousands of Maya Ixil in the 1980s constituted genocide. Fernando Poyón's video *Contra la pared* exposes a colonialist tactic still present today, which was made possible through religious conquests and perpetuated through the state's political system. That is, in refusing to take responsibility for the genocide, the state continues to breed self-blame in Indigenous women for the atrocities committed against their bodies, their families, and their culture.

Artist Antonio Pichillá references the necessary protection of Indigenous cosmologies through artistic practices that involve Tz'utujil textiles, thread, and knots, to safeguard the sacred. In the Tz'utujil community of San Pedro La Laguna, the artist is also known as a spiritual guide called upon by the community to heal individuals on matters of the spirit. Thus, his artistic practice stems explicitly, as he has stated, "from experience, from life, and life is spiritual."[30] Like Chavajay, Pichillá does not claim to make art, since the concepts he works with are already sacred. For Pichillá, art is already there, already made, and already exists in the landscapes, objects, and garments used by the community elders, the candles used in rituals, traditional textiles, and even the thread from which these textiles are made by hand.

In the large-scale installation titled *Ku'kul'kan* (Feathered Serpent) (2011), Pichillá uses massive amounts of red cloth in a sculptural representation of the ancient fire serpent god Quetzalcoatl. The serpentine form is defined by a series of large knots across the wall to simulate movement. *Kahn* is a day in the Mayan calendar represented by the fire serpent. Despite the serpent's negative association in Western thinking, for the Mayan community the fire serpent constitutes one of the strongest energies; thus, Pichillá engages with this serpent energy through sculptural representation. This energy is also evoked in candle sculptures, in which the artist either paints the candles in colors used for rituals or leaves them white, and then manually molds them into knots (or *nudos*), as in the piece *Vida* (Life) (2011) (see figure 1.8). He then unties the knots to represent the process of a shifting energy. In one video performance, the candles are lit and the artist consumes the emanating smoke as an intake of this spiritual energy; in another, the candles burn, with the emanating smoke representing the feathered serpent's energy.

The knot holds symbolic value for Pichillá as both an artist and a spiritual guide, alluding to an individual's problems, or struggles, and their constant *knotting* and *unraveling* as part of the learning process of life. But for the artist, knots are also symbols of Tz'utujil aesthetics and concepts of beauty, as they resemble the braided hair of a Maya woman, traditionally secured with cloth and knots as a sign of attractiveness.[31] Gesture becomes equally important for the artist as he explains the process of creating and unraveling a braid or a knot (like covering and unraveling a bundle) as a continuous cycle of life, which the serpent also represents. In the process, one knot leads to another and another like a cycle of time that intersects states of knowing, being, and the sacred, where an end is actually a beginning.[32] With this idea, Pichillá again refers to the Maya calendar and the Baktun 13 as sources for his *nudos*. While many people inaccurately interpreted the Baktun 13 as a Mayan prediction of apocalypse, it in fact indicates an end to a Mayan era and the beginning of another era rooted in Maya cyclical concepts of time that oppose the linear notions of time in Western thought.

The knots or bundles further allude to the safeguarding of the valuable and the sacred in private domestic spaces. Common in Tz'utujil homes, items of value are hidden in tied bundles, safeguarded in various locations throughout the home or at times on the body. These knots are often made from traditional Tz'utujil textiles and cloth, which the artist used in the work *Lo oculto* (The hidden) (2005) (see figure 1.9). The installation consists of two bundles placed in a triangular shelf conveying a domestic space. The contents inside the bundles are unknown—an intentional critique of the Western tradition of displaying ritual and spiritual objects from Indigenous communities in museums. The politics of museum display imply "accessibility," where the object exhibited is for the visual and epistemic consumption by the viewer. Pichillá deifies this colonial logic by prohibiting visual access to the contents inside the bundle. Instead, the artist willingly presents aspects of Indigenous cosmovision already common for most general audiences, such as the significance of Quetzalcoatl as a Mayan god or the aesthetics of Mayan textiles, both of which have been popularized from anthropological and art historical investigations. The deeper spiritual significance, however, is beyond visual limits, concealed from sight within the bundles.

Safeguarding the sacred is an act of self-preservation and resistance amid a history in which Indigenous cosmovisions and cultural traditions are either

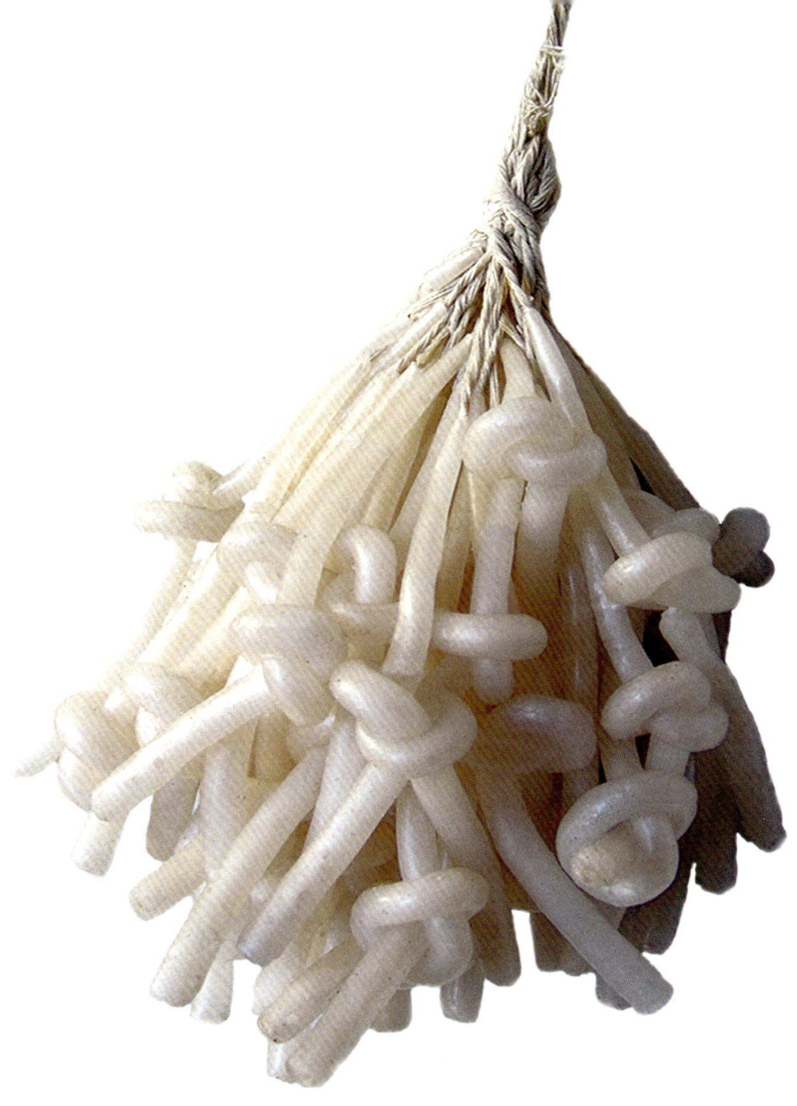

FIGURE 1.8.
Antonio Pichillá, *Vida*, 2011, intervened candles. Courtesy of the artist.

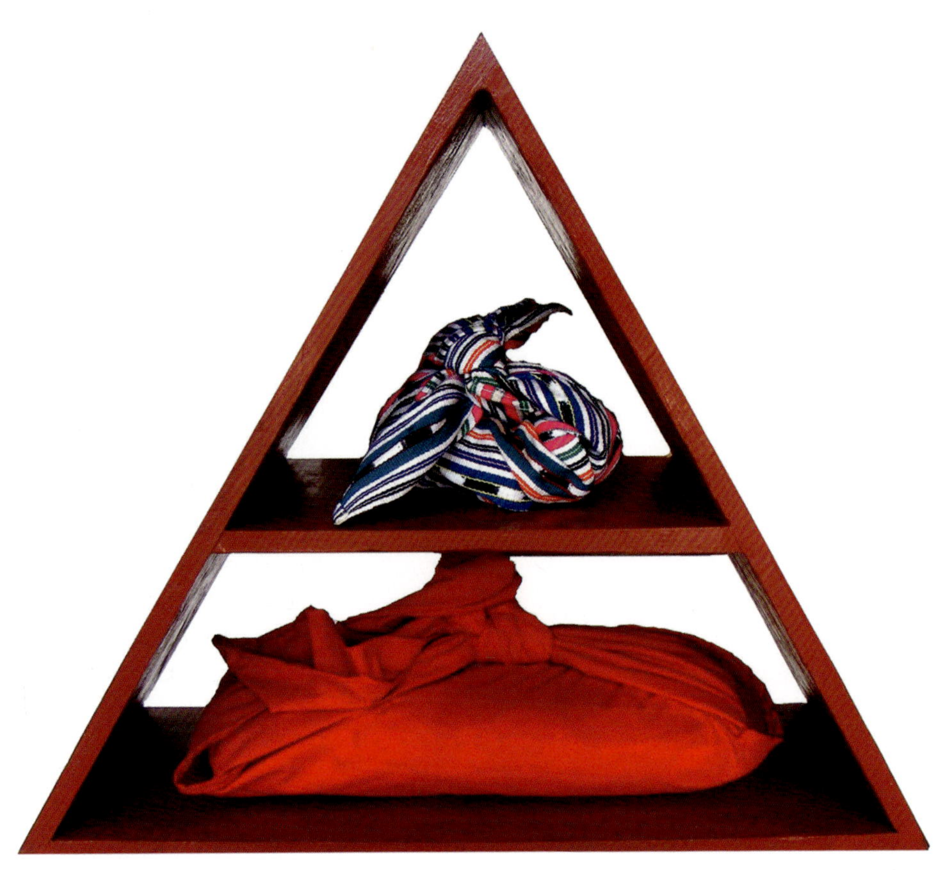

FIGURE 1.9.
Antonio Pichillá, *Lo oculto*, 2005, multimedia installation. Courtesy of the artist.

repressed through Christianity or objectified as subjects of study by non-Indigenous peoples. Fernando Poyón uses video to expose how religion continues to be a colonizing tool for Maya people, entangled with notions of blame and impunity that further prevent justice for Indigenous communities. And Pichillá draws from Tz'utujil notions of the sacred, of time, and of spirituality, while maintaining a clear understanding that there is an unknowable, unseeable, and inaccessible realm of Tz'utujil spirituality not meant for display, a visual disobedience against visual extractivism and visual thingification. Their use of video and installation further defy the desired aesthetics dictated by the state, one that prefers apolitical figurative paintings of village life that depict religious rituals and quotidian scenes for its tourist economy. Not only do the artists refuse to provide expected depictions of Maya bodies for tourist consumption; they also defy the artistic mediums permitted and expected of them so they can expose and condemn ongoing visual coloniality.

RECLAIMING INDIGENEITY

Unlike Chavajay, Pichillá, and the Poyón brothers, artist Sandra Monterroso only became aware of her Mayan roots when, in the late 1990s, her grandmother disclosed a secret at her deathbed. She revealed to the family that she had led an unconventional life (according to societal standards): she had never married, and had had three lovers. As punishment for her transgressions, an overseer had expelled her from the *finca* where she lived along with other workers, and she migrated to the city, where she felt the pressure fueled by racial discrimination to repress her Indigenous culture. She ceased wearing her traditional dress and never uttered a word in Maya Q'ekchi' again, until that moment in her deathbed. Even Monterroso's mother was unaware of this well-kept secret and soon after began a process of family reconciliation by seeking out aunts, siblings, and family members she never knew existed.[33]

Meanwhile, Monterroso experienced a series of what she describes as dreams in the Q'ekchi' language that were indiscernible to her and that increased in frequency. She interpreted her dreams as a sign that her grandmother wished for her granddaughters to recover their Maya identity.[34] Committed to recovering her family and Indigenous past, Monterroso began learning Q'ekchi' and studied the Mayan calendar. She sought to be more knowledgeable of issues affecting the Maya Q'ekchi' community, especially women, and did so through an anthropological lens that situated hybridity and Indigeneity as central issues as she negotiated her own positionality.

For Monterroso, this was an emotional and philosophical catalyst into an exploration of her own identity, fueled by a desire to recover the Maya culture that her grandmother had buried, yet aware that this recovery could be interpreted as an appropriation of a culture she was not born into. In a video performance, *Lix cua rahro/Tus tortillas mi amor* (Your tortillas my love) (2002–4) (see figure 1.10), she takes an initial step in self-decolonization by beginning a dialogue with herself in which her desire for cultural acceptance parallels intimate partner relations. In the video, Monterroso obsessively bites into several ears of corn, spitting out from her mouth and into the pot a mixture of chewed corn with her own saliva. Mixing the *maiz*, which has always held cultural significance for Maya people, and her own bodily fluid, the artist first creates the *masa*. She then enacts the ancient tradition of tortilla making as she fuses gesture and fluids into the staple diet made with the sacred *maiz*. She only disrupts her hypnotic ritual act to recite lines of a poem in Q'ekchi', as a gesture of being with, knowing, and indulging in the metaphors of her grandmother's language.

By presenting a common practice of women in Guatemala and elsewhere (tortilla making), the work raises issues of gender and the desires and compromises of intimate relationships. These issues are a uniting thread in many of Monterroso's early video pieces that address the gendered role of culture preservation—a social responsibility typically attributed to women as keepers and caretakers. *Tus tortillas mi amor* offers an act of intimacy and seduction in the creation of food and sustenance for the artist's love. The desire to seduce extends beyond a romantic partner and toward a seduction of a culture that may be skeptical of the artist's Indigenous identity.

The systemic violence and racial and gendered discrimination that Maya people endure in Guatemala has coerced many into giving up visual signifiers of identity, such as traditional clothing or language, as in the case of Monterroso's grandmother. This is most prevalent among Maya people who migrated to the urban cities because of displacement or war violence in their rural communities or because of the inequality that forces many to seek domestic work in middle- and upper-class ladino households. Racial discrimination intensifies in these exploitative zones.[35] Maya Kaqchikel researcher, teacher, and activist Aura Cumes argued in her doctoral dissertation that servitude is a long-term colonial-patriarchal institution. Beyond an economic system dependent on Indigenous labor, servitude is a form of domination to control the lives of Indigenous peoples. It produces both a social imaginary that insists on viewing Indigenous women as servants and a microcosm of power relations in which the house of employment becomes a private space of domination that synthesizes racial gendered and class relations produced by colonialism and patriarchy. As

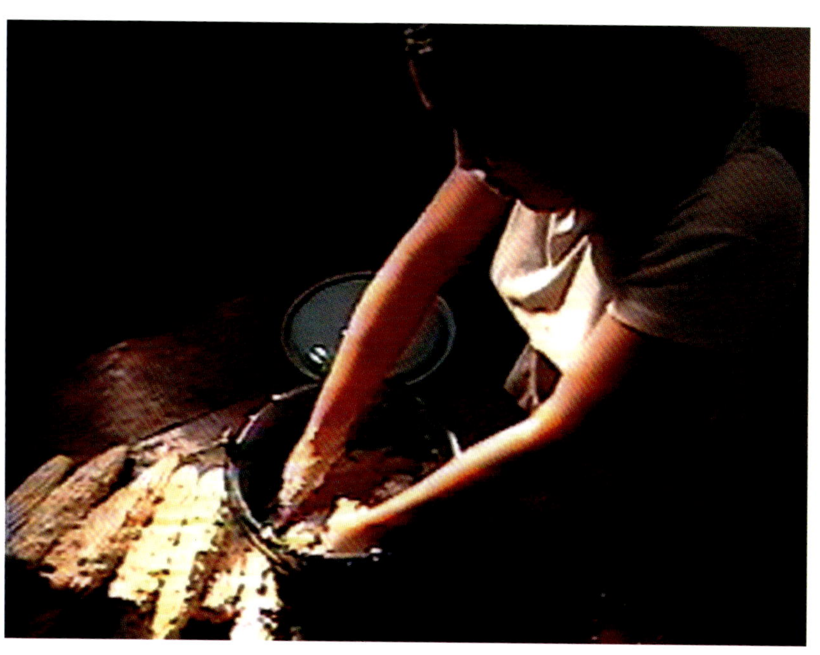

FIGURE 1.10.
Sandra Monterroso, *Lix cua rahro/Tus tortillas mi amor*, 2002–4, video (still). Courtesy of the artist.

Cumes explains, outside the reach of state laws, ruled only by social codes, and secured from state surveillance or policing, the house of employment is a space of danger for Indigenous women.[36]

Maya men and women are particularly targeted for their traditional dress or language in Guatemalan urban spaces, where dominant groups equate Westernized clothes with respectability, honor, "high" culture and status, and Mayan clothing with poverty, backwardness, and a primitive past.[37] As a result, Maya women are especially targets of racist jokes and demeaning abuse for their *trajes* or *huipiles*, which hold profound meaning to their communities. For some, leaving behind these identifiers of Maya identity is a means of survival, as it was for Monterroso's grandmother. For others, holding on to traditional dress and language are daily acts of defiance. Monterroso's videos highlight the significance of repressing and reclaiming Maya identity in a context where thousands have been violently forced and coerced into giving up visible connection to an Indigenous identity through assimilation. This is often done out of fear of discrimination or threat of physical harm. Her work further questions whether identity can be measured or confirmed through visible dress and language or whether a desire to preserve cultural history and knowledge can override visual codes.

Maya Kaqchikel artist Marilyn Elany Boror Bor, born in San Juan Sacatepéquez, extends this concern of cultural loss into the linguistic realm. Her interest in language stems from her parents' choice to not teach their daughter Kaqchickel in order to shield her from the racism she would endure by speaking the language. As a result, Boror felt disconnected from certain aspects of her Maya identity and was constrained in her relationship with her grandmother, who refused to speak to her granddaughter in Spanish. Boror found this was a common experience of many of her generation—those born during the civil war and whose parents experienced the height of anti-Indigenous violence. Because language is connected to Maya cosmovision, a whole generation of Maya people are losing the stories and histories passed on by the elders. To resist this loss of language and identity, Boror began studying Kaqchikel and read dictionaries. One day she encountered a section in Gabriel García Márquez's *One Hundred Years of Solitude* in which the citizens of Macondo begin forgetting everything, including the names of objects, and start to label everyday items to retain their names and avoid falling into an oblivion of disremembering.

Relating Macondo to Guatemala, Boror began a series of urban interventions titled Para no olvidar sus nombres (To not forget their names) in San José, Costa Rica, in 2012 and Guatemala City in 2013. Boror centers Central American cities where Indigenous populations are especially invisibilized through assimilation practices fueled by the type of anti-Indigenous discrimination her parents tried to protect her from. In her interventions, she labels urban objects with both the dominant Indigenous language in each city and its colonial translation in Spanish. Objects labeled range from steps to light posts, benches, public phones, trees, and so on. In her 2012 intervention in San José, she labeled each of the steps on a stairway with "Ma̱né̱gö · subir" (go up) or "já̱wa̱ksa · bajar" (go down), corresponding to the direction of the person walking over them, giving the word first in Cabécar and then in Spanish (see figure 1.11). The language Cabécar belongs to the Cabécar people, an Indigenous people of eastern Costa Rica. This poetic labeling points to the action and use of steps rather than the word *step*, reflecting Boror's interest in neologisms of Indigenous languages. Since certain objects have no name in Mayan and other regional languages, joining existing words to create new words and meanings becomes a poetic action, such as translating *computer* as "weaver of words." The labels also relink the visual and oral dimensions of language, as the artist realized that some Indigenous youth could recite Indigenous words but could not visually recognize or read them. In the stairway intervention, the vanishing effect of the deteriorating labels as they are walked on over time further signals the threat of disappearance of Indigenous languages and cosmovisions.

With her interventions, Boror resists the loss of Indigenous languages to coerced assimilation by reinserting them in spaces where they are mostly negated or repressed, like the urban cities. She forces "Indigenous-ladinos," a term she uses to describe Maya people who are assimilated into ladino culture, to retain the language and reminds the non-Indigenous that the urban space they occupy is still Indigenous land. This differentiation between native and foreigner, as suggested by the Indigenous word and Spanish translation, is a reminder of the ongoing coexistence of both. This idea was further developed in her later work in the installation *Kaqchikel-slash-Kaxlan* (2014). With it, Boror expresses the power and resistance of this coexistence with two unique word stamps: one labeled "KAQCHIKEL" and the other "KAXLAN," which translates to foreigner or nonnative. When pressed on paper, the KAQCHIKEL stamp prints a set of words associated with Indigeneity—INDIGENA, INDIO, ORIGINARIO, NATIVO, INGENUO, INCULTO, DE MODALES RUSTICOS—whereas the KAXLAN stamp prints a set of words corresponding to the colonizer: LADINO(A), ESPAÑOL, NO NUESTRO, CRIOLLO, CASTELLANO, LENGUA EXTRANJERA (see figure 1.12). Boror uses the stamps to create large-scale signs juxtaposing the two words through repetitive and overlapping imprints. The final outcome is the two large-scale words with heavy concentrations and darker tone in the beginning of each word, and sparse stampings producing a lighter tone toward the end. The result is both a saturated and fading

FIGURE 1.11.
Marilyn Elany Boror Bor, Para no olvidar sus nombres series, 2012–13, urban intervention, San José, Costa Rica. Courtesy of the artist.

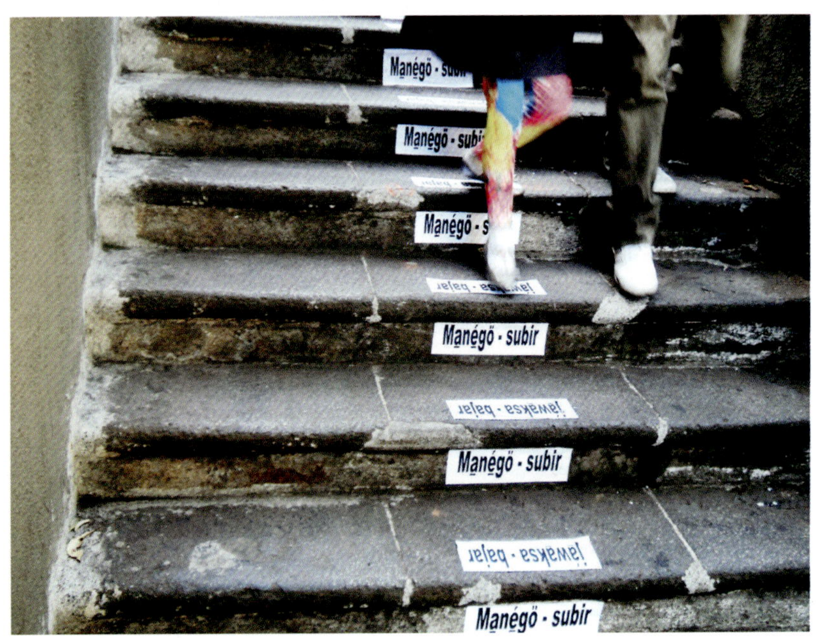

effect that alludes to overlapping cultures, one that colonizes and one that resists colonization (see figure 1.13). Language is the tool of the colonizer but also the decolonizing tool of Maya people who preserve their language and reclaim their Indigeneity.

In these works, Monterroso and Boror enunciate from the experiences of assimilation imposed on them by their relatives' choices: the forsaking of Q'ekchi' identification and culture by Monterroso's grandmother and the refusal to pass on the Kaqchikel language by Boror's parents. While these decisions were painfully felt by both artists as limiting their connection to Maya culture, language, and thus cosmovision, they contextualize these coerced choices as a contemporary colonial violence done onto Maya peoples. These works may not directly reflect the massacres carried out during the Guatemalan civil war, but they take on the painful aftermath of war tactics, intimidation, discrimination, and violence against Maya people and their children that continues through self-censorship, assimilation, and forced disconnections. Yet Monterroso and Boror defy such cultural loss and reclaim their Indigeneity by learning their language and centering Maya cultural recovery as acts of visual disobedience. Like Chavajay, the Poyón brothers, and Pichillá, Monterroso and Boror use art—conceptual, video, performance, and urban interventions—to center their Maya agency. Yet Monterroso and Boror differ from the other artists in that they reflect the struggles of Indigenous people in urban cities rather than rural Maya communities like San Pedro or Comalapa. Collectively, these artists reflect the diversity of experience, struggles, and forms of resisting among Maya people in Guatemala.

THREADS AND ROOTS FOR DISPLACEMENT AND RETURN

In Monterroso's installation *El matador* (2011), a *huipil* stands juxtaposed to a black T-shirt with Milton Glaser's popular logo, I♥NY (see figure 1.14). The two garments are connected via an umbilical cord, which Monterroso uses as a metaphor for human relationships. Though the *huipil* is traditionally made in a variety of colors that pertain to specific ethnic groups, Monterroso presents a black *huipil* as reference to colonial violence, similar to Chavajay's black *mazorca*. The black *huipil* alludes to the paradoxical view of traditional Maya clothing in Guatemala, which on the one hand is celebrated as a signifier of "authentic" Indigenous culture, and on the other is the target of defamation and degradation. Whereas the *huipil* is the epitome of Indigenous identity, history, and ethnic identification, the iconic I♥NY T-shirt draws in notions of a world center, tourism, US patriotism, consumerism, and Western popular culture.

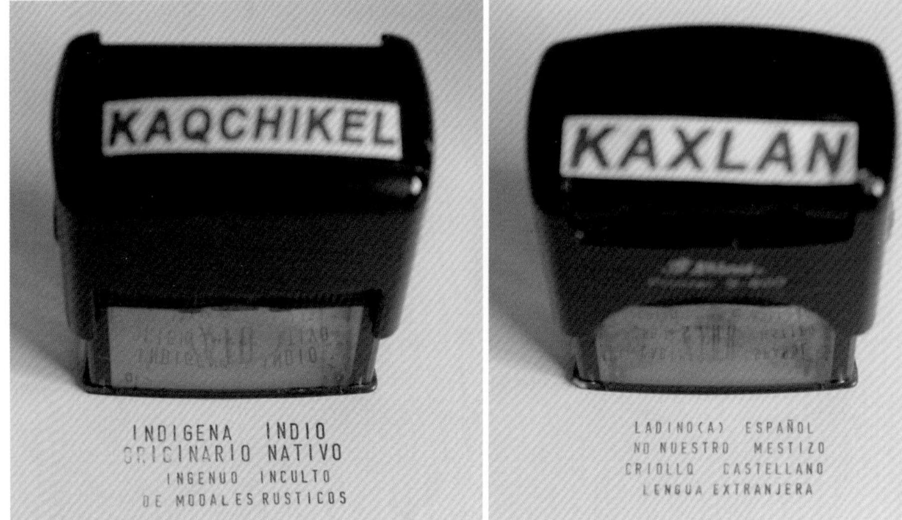

FIGURE 1.12.
Marilyn Elany Boror Bor, *Kaqchikel-Slash-Kaxlan*, 2014, stamps with ink on paper. Courtesy of the artist.

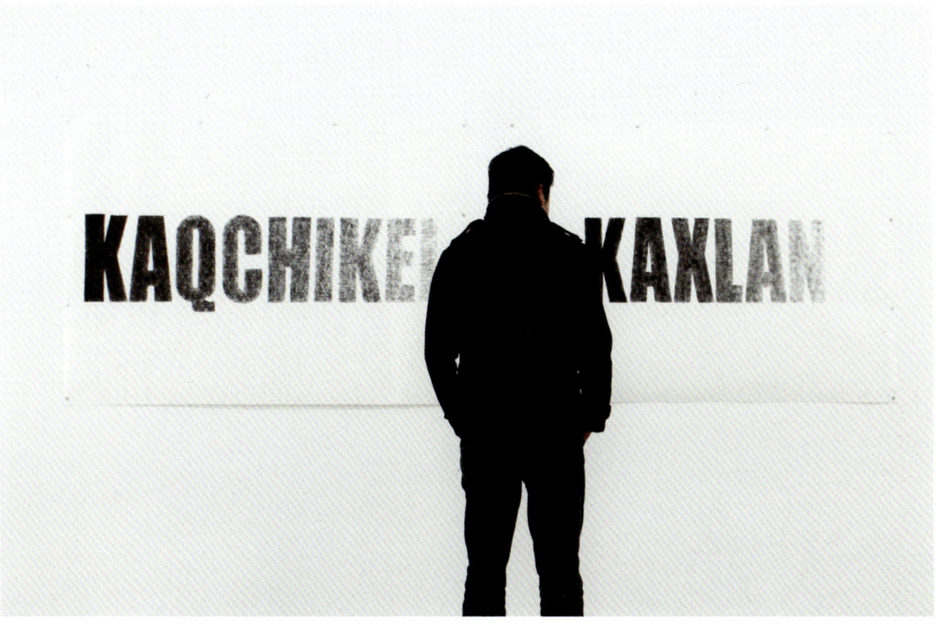

FIGURE 1.13.
Marilyn Elany Boror Bor, *Kaqchikel-Slash-Kaxlan*, 2014, ink on paper, installation view. Courtesy of the artist.

FIGURE 1.14.
Sandra Monterroso, *El matador*, 2011, multimedia installation. Courtesy of the artist.

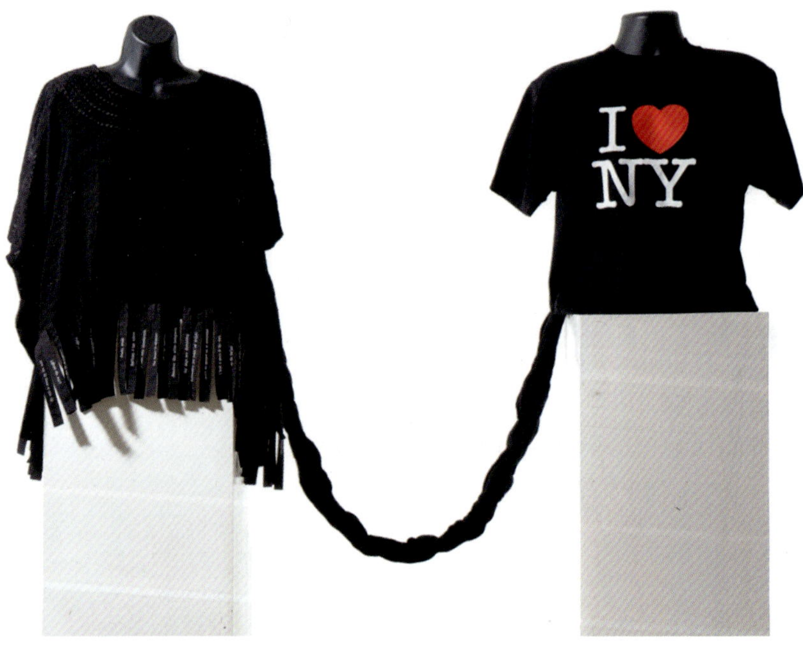

The garments thus stand in opposition: the T-shirt's symbolism of a world led by imperialism and consumption, and the *huipil*'s evocation of centuries of Indigenous resistance. Together, the black *huipil* and the black T-shirt, connected through the umbilical cord, convey two interdependent sides of modernity. The umbilical cord further summons a contested relation for the artist with the contemporary art world. Given that New York City is an important center for art, artists from Central America were typically excluded from participating in this desirable global circuit of creative production. Moreover, the *huipil* in the installation is unique to Valparaíso, her grandmother's Indigenous hometown. In this way, the umbilical cord also highlights the artist's Mayan roots and her artistic identity bound together and inseparable, even if in constant struggle.

Monterroso's installation further asks that we consider the push and pull of forces that lead to mass Mayan migration and result in transnational communities, increasingly on the rise since the wave of wars in Central America. As new Maya communities form in cities in the Global North, the *huipil* takes on a deeper meaning of Maya resistance. Wearing traditional dress in US cities defies the notion of cultural loss through a preservation of Mayan visual codes and further contests the homogenization of Maya people into Latino categories, making a Mayan diaspora presence visible.[38] This is especially relevant for youth of the Mayan diaspora in the United States, for whom traditional Maya clothing remains a visual connection to their specific ethnic groups and the lands and histories their parents left behind.

Maya Kaqchikel artist Edgar Calel points to the ancestral culture and knowledge Indigenous migrants take with them as acts of resistance to cultural loss, and which extend beyond the *huipil*. In his diptych photograph *B'atz constelaciones de saberes* (Constellations of knowledges fabric) (2015), a frontal and back-view self-portrait of the artist reveals him standing amid a corn field (see figures 1.15 and 1.16). The top half of the composition is dominated by the blue sky, while the bottom half is engulfed by the rustic golden corn stalk. Connecting the earth and sky, Calel stands in the center with arms to his side and stares directly at the viewer with a stoic expression. The back-view photograph reveals his jet-black long hair tucked inside a sweater that echoes the blue color of the sky. Across the sweater's fabric, the twenty-one Maya ethnic groups in Guatemala are hand-sewn in different-colored thread.

For Calel, traditional Maya clothing holds significance but is expensive, and it is often mostly worn by women. Some Maya people, like himself, cannot afford to own a *huipil*. In fact, the sweater Calel wears in the photographs is a second-hand garment sent from the United States to Guatemala, as are most of the clothes his community wears. The sweater, gifted to him by his father to

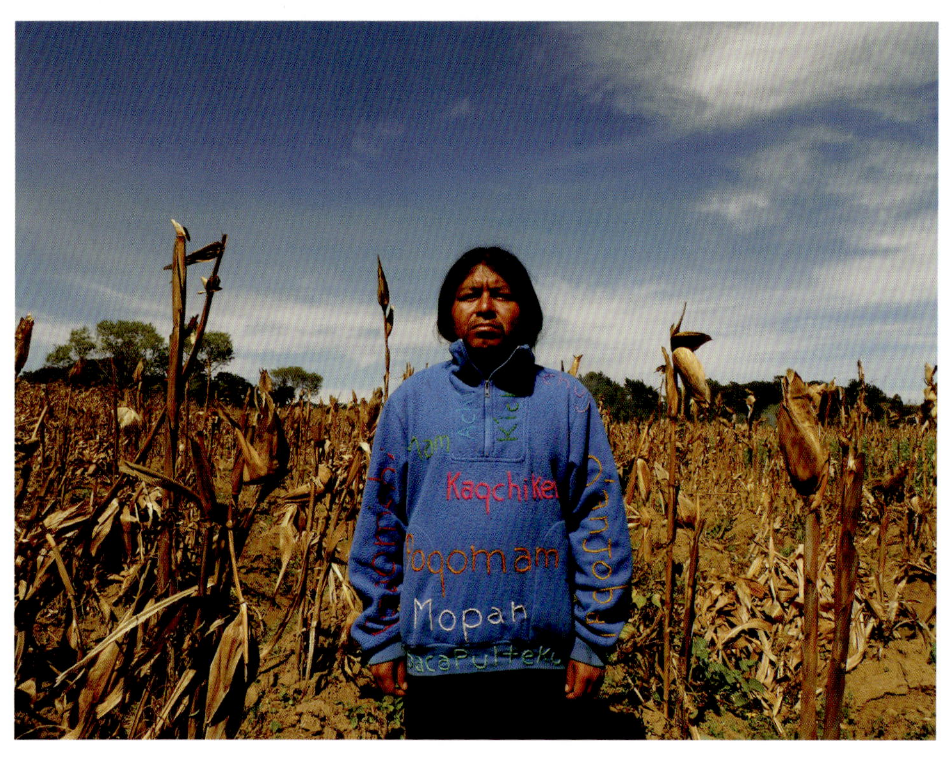

FIGURE 1.15.
Edgar Calel, *B'atz constelaciones de saberes*, 2015, diptych photograph, front view. © Edgar Calel. Courtesy of the artist.

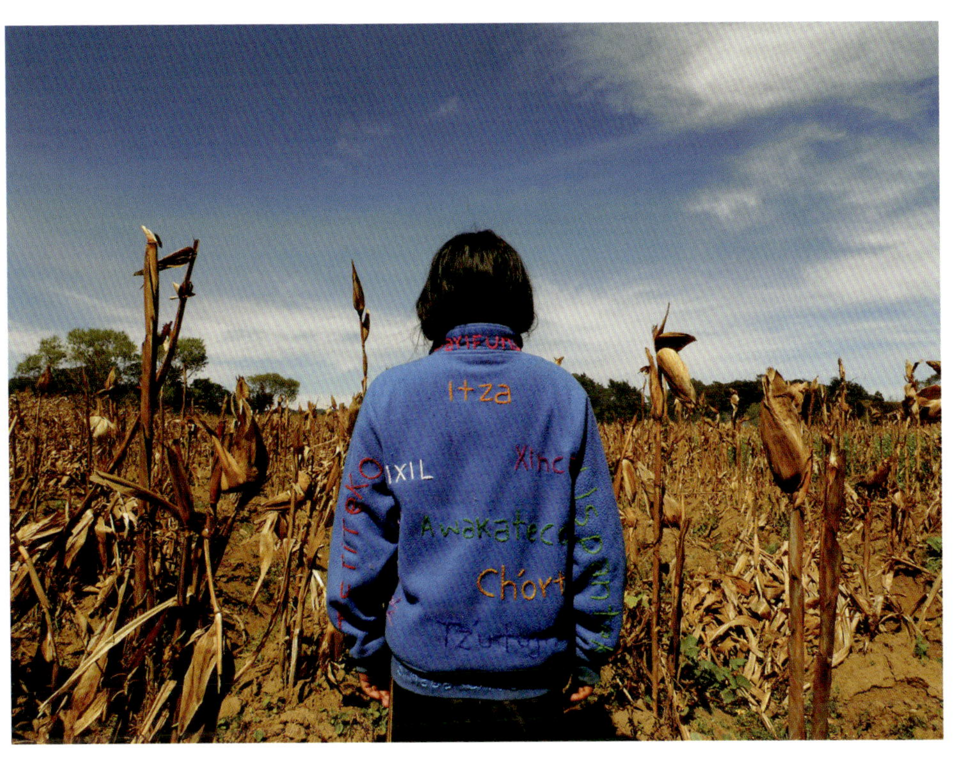

FIGURE 1.16.
Edgar Calel, *B'atz constelaciones de saberes*, 2015, diptych photograph, back view. © Edgar Calel. Courtesy of the artist.

protect him from the cold temperature of the highlands, is a garment that migrated from north to south. If the threads of the *huipil* metaphorically carry the stories and histories of the ancestors in their designs, what of the many like himself who are not able to cover their bodies with these revered vestments either for financial reasons or, as in Monterroso's and Boror's cases, due to coerced assimilation practices? For those who migrate north but their *huipiles* stay in the South, do they not still carry the histories of their ancestors on their skin and in their minds and spirits?

B'atz constelaciones de saberes is a visual reminder that each Indigenous community has its own language that structures its own cosmovision and that is carried epistemically and ontologically as well. Maya cosmovision offers unique ways of healing, mourning, remembering, resisting, safeguarding, and learning, as we have seen with the works discussed so far, and collectively they formulate a pluriverse of Maya ways of being. Calel does not own a *huipil*, but he honors the twenty-one Maya communities as "a constellation of knowledges." Like the sweater gifted to him by his father, this constellation of Maya knowledges protects and warms his body like an ancestral embrace, which the artist suggests all Indigenous migrants take with them wherever their journey takes them.

Calel's meditations on the ancestral knowledge carried by Indigenous migrants are rooted in his experiences with travel outside his Maya Kaqchikel community. Calel was the first person in his family to ever leave his hometown of Comalapa when he traveled to Nicaragua to attend EspIRA/ESPORA, the art school for Central American artists directed by artist Patricia Belli.[39] Among the new encounters with other Central American young artists, Calel was intrigued by the preliminary question students asked of each other, *¿De dónde sos?* (Where are you from?). This common question, which had not been asked of him before, led Calel into a deep contemplation about the nature and effects of mobility, movement, displacement, and migration on Indigenous identities. Though his migration was temporary, it led him to ask: what components of ourselves stay behind, and what components of ourselves migrate with us?

In his video performance *At nu jukukempe* (I drag you with me) (2016), a scene opens to a view of a horizontal dirt path in a woodsy area of the Guatemalan highlands, with the sound of birds chirping and the atmospheric mountainous backdrop in the distance (see figures 1.17 and 1.18). From the right side of the screen the artist emerges into view as he walks across the frame. A nest-shaped mask made of *maiz* roots covers his entire face, while in his arms he carries a bundle of flowers. When his back becomes visible, he reveals a small tree tied and secured from its root to his long, braided hair. The sound of the tree's branches and leaves dragging against the dirt intensifies as he continues uphill until he disappears from view.

For Calel, the act of walking uphill represents the motion of a life's voyage. The tree he drags with him is the culmination of knowledge, experiences, encounters, and places he has traversed. Despite its uprootedness, the tree also carries the inherited histories and knowledge of his family and ancestors. Wherever he goes, he metaphorically "drags" this ancestral richness with him, adding to it what he collects from his own journey. The nest-shaped mask covering his face is made with the sacred *maiz* roots because, as he explains, words are like roots; he plants them wherever he goes when he speaks. Calel's performance affirms that a single body, like a seed, can penetrate new spaces and create new meanings, in the way migrants do. It can do so without dislodging from its spiritual umbilical cord and while securing Indigenous futures.

Monterroso and Calel experienced mobility through artistic opportunity and thus were able to return home. But their works speak to broader ideas of physical and cultural uprootings, displacement, and disconnection, which manifest in unique ways for Maya migrants. Already dispossessed of land through settler colonialism, Maya people are forced into either rural-to-urban migration or across northern borders for better opportunities but where they are vulnerable to exploitation, violence, and death. The death and disappearances of Maya child migrants have increased especially since 2014 and the "unaccompanied minor crisis." Seven-year-old Jakelin Caal, eight-year-old Félix Gómez Alonzo, sixteen-year-old Juan de León Gutiérrez, sixteen-year-old Carlos Hernández, and two-year-old Wilmer Josué Ramírez Vásquez are five Maya children migrants who died between 2018 and 2019 either during detainment or following release from border control custody. The names of others who died continue to emerge. Because they are homogenized as Latino or Central American migrants, they are not recognized as Maya Indigenous. And because of an inability to report abuses when detained due to lack of Maya-language translators, the uproar over and condemnation of Indigenous children's deaths is not as loud as it should be. The artists, however, evade the figurative representation of wounded migrant bodies to condemn Indigenous displacement or forced migration, as is often circulated in the media, and instead highlight the strength and connectedness Indigenous migrants carry with them. Through either the materiality and threads of the *huipil* or traditional ancestral knowledges, Monterroso and Calel call upon inherited cosmovision and centuries of Maya existence to address the acts of resistance that Maya migrants enact. Their visual disobedience contests the rootless and ahistorical notions

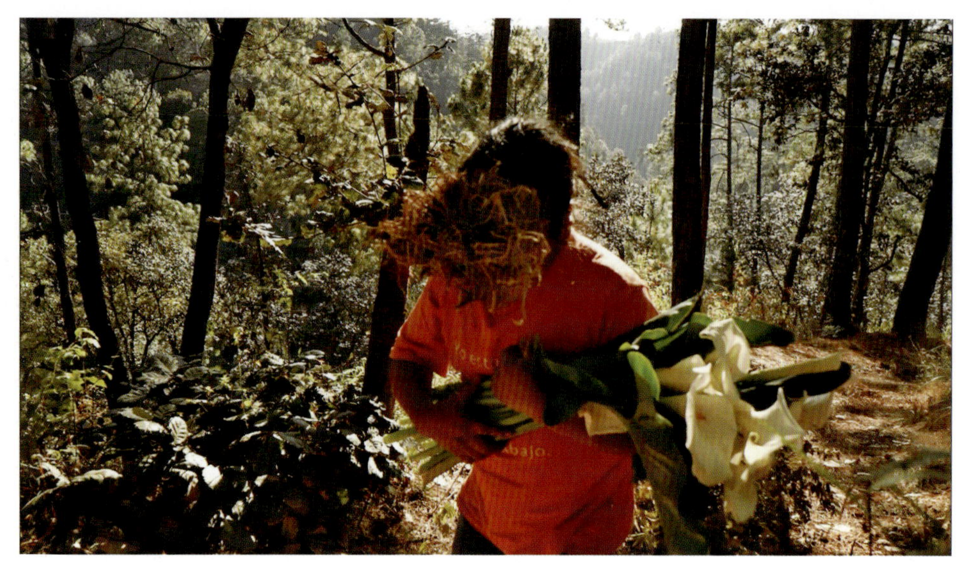

FIGURE 1.17.
Edgar Calel, *At nu jukukempe*, 2016, video (still, at 00:29). © Edgar Calel. Courtesy of the artist.

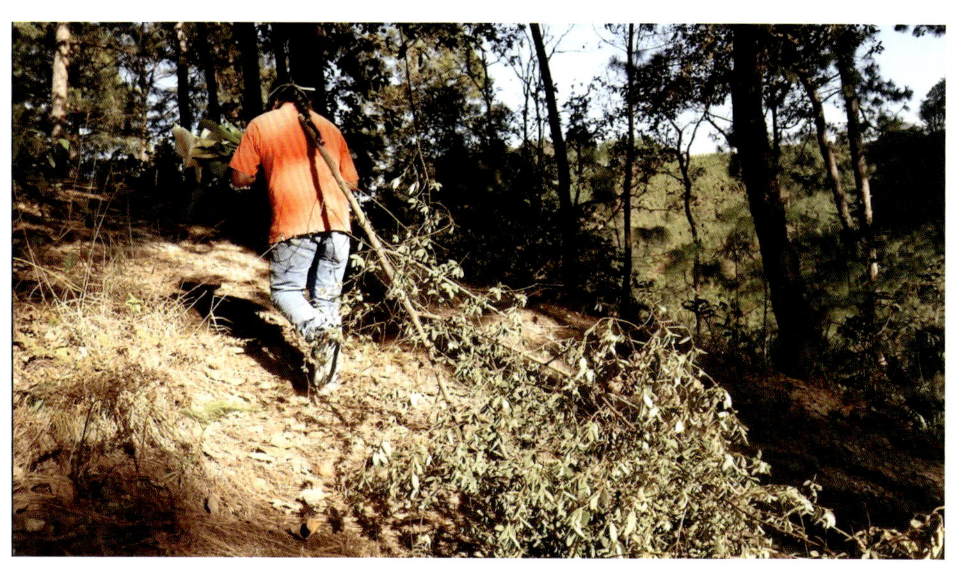

FIGURE 1.18.
Edgar Calel, *At nu jukukempe*, 2016, video (still, at 2:07). © Edgar Calel. Courtesy of the artist.

ascribed to Indigenous migrants and the erasure of Indigeneity entailed in imperial border policies.

SEEDS OF INDIGENOUS RESISTANCE

When the Guatemalan military labeled a generation of Maya children "bad seeds" to justify their elimination, it took every step of brutal violence to end their lives, to impede their growth, to keep them underground and out of sight. Yet, as has been the case since colonization, Maya people contest this colonial logic by resisting and existing; living is always already a defiance. Some so-called bad seeds grew anyway, and some became artists. These artists use their bodies in public spaces to expose hidden sounds, language, and memories of the disappeared during the armed conflict and turn them into decolonial gestures of healing. They create object-based works to expose the hidden underside of modernity, revealing Maya views and experiences of history, time, and space that precede art historical labels. Some bring light to the hidden function of coloniality in contemporary religion and in impeding justice for Indigenous peoples. Others reveal an ongoing defiance through self-preservation and safeguarding the spiritual. They address an array of experiences from rural violence, forced assimilation, migration, and the importance of language and ancestral memories. My argument, therefore, is not just that they exist but that they theorize, defy, historicize, and create from a decolonial standpoint—engaging the very capabilities visual coloniality denies to Central America people and particularly Indigenous peoples. Through visual disobedience they offer intellectual understandings of history, existence, and decolonial resistance creatively materialized through the ancestral knowledges inherited within their corporal embodiments.

While I here analyzed selected works of Maya Indigenous artists in Guatemala, there are many more also worthy of analysis who belong to that generation. Because Maya people in Guatemala were targets of the most public genocide of Indigenous people in Central America during the twentieth century, Maya artists in Guatemala are among the most visible, prolific, and visually defiant, and therefore the focus of this chapter. Yet Indigenous communities throughout the region are vast and diverse. They include the Garífuna, Xinca, and twenty-three different Maya groups in Guatemala; the Lenca, Pech, Tawahka, Xicaque, Maya Ch'ortí, Misquito, and Garífuna peoples in Honduras; the Lenca, Kakawira, and Pipil in El Salvador; the Rama, Mayagna and Miskitu peoples in Nicaragua; the Yucatec Maya, Mopan Maya, Q'eqchi' Maya, and Garifuna in Belize; the Kuna and the Ngobe-Bugle (Guaymi) people in Panama; and the Boruca, Bribri, Cabécar, Guaymí, Huetar, Maleku, Matambú, and Térraba in Costa Rica, to name a few.[40] Though often made invisible through historical erasure or lack of recognition by governments, the Indigenous population in Central America remains strong. A regional history of visual disobedience from their individual and collective perspectives is key to ongoing Indigenous decolonization efforts and to a delinking from Western art histories and visual coloniality. The artists I've written about here are already paving the way.

Chavajay, the Poyón brothers, Pichillá, Monterroso, Boror, and Calel draw from Mayan epistemologies and cosmologies to disobey a colonialist history of negation and extermination. They defy not only the historical amnesia of colonial and imperial powers but also their mechanics of visual coloniality. While engaging in experimental art practices, they depart from Mayan epistemologies and cosmologies to reinsert, reinscribe, reconnect, and revalidate a Mayan visual episteme that has been dismissed and silenced through visual coloniality and thus Indigenize Central American art.

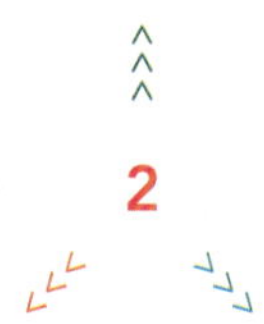

A Creative Turn to the Body

Feminist Dissonance and Erotic Autonomy in Central American Art

Performance artist Regina José Galindo entered a small, undecorated, gray space and sat on a chair in the center of the room. She lifted her black dress, exposing her leg, while holding a small sharp knife in her hand. She concentrated for a moment and then began to slowly carve on the flesh of her thigh, where droplets of blood slowly revealed each cut, eventually spelling "PERRA" (bitch). Between incisions, Galindo's hand and thigh shook slightly, and she took the occasional deep breath, revealing a struggle with pain despite her steady and focused concentration. She never looked away. Once the word *perra* was fully visible in blood, the artist covered her leg with the dress, stood up, and calmly walked away (see figure 2.1).

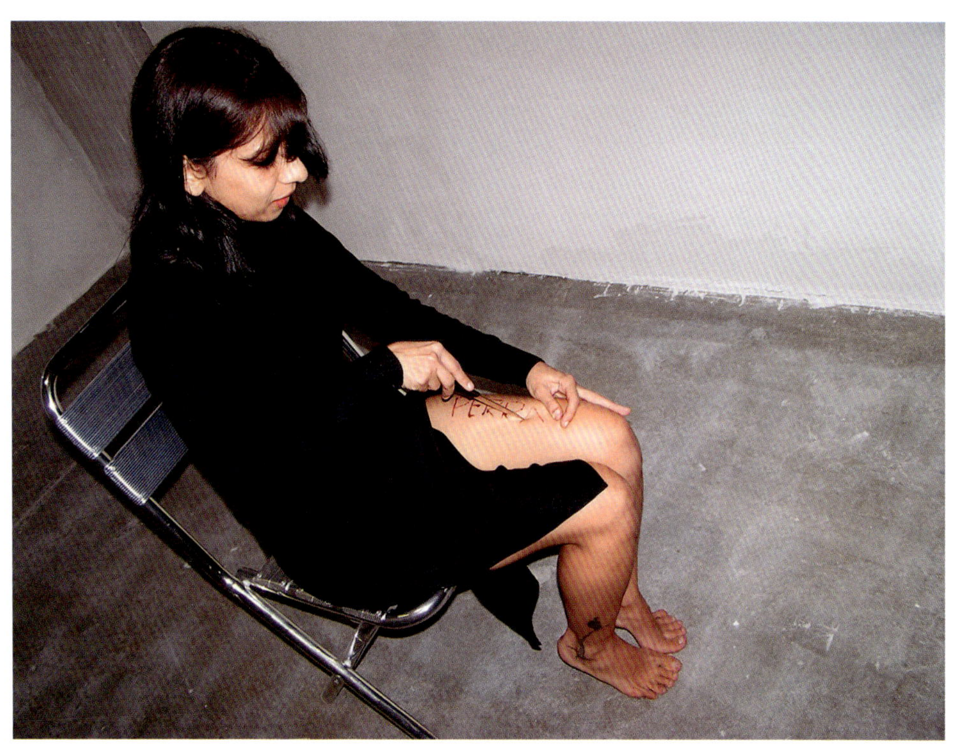

FIGURE 2.1.
Regina José Galindo, *Perra*, 2005, performance. Courtesy of the artist.

The iconic performance *Perra* (2005) demonstrates a stark departure from the artistic representation of women during years of armed conflict when the empowered Central American woman was a popular subject matter in public art. Imagery of female self-determination, idolized martyrs, and charismatic leaders became an emblematic tool of consciousness raising, particularly during civil wars in Guatemala, El Salvador, and following the Sandinista Revolution in Nicaragua. In such leftist revolutionary feminist depictions, the ideal progressive woman could tactically carry a child in one arm while holding a firearm in the other.[1] Eventually, a regional feminist visual culture in the 1970s and 1980s centered the heroic, autonomous, revolutionary woman and was aimed at the masses. Posters and murals ranged from scenes of insurrection to health and social campaigns, many relying on women to uphold and materialize socialist objectives for a liberated society. How, then, following peace accords and efforts for reconciliation in the 1990s, do images and art such as Galindo's *Perra* more acutely represent a postwar reality for women in Central America, when violence against women is actually greater than it was during armed conflict?

Postwar artists in Central America, as I discuss in this chapter, reveal a shift in feminist art history of the region. Yet I first caution, along with art historian Andrea Giunta, against automatically equating art made by self-identified women as feminist art. In Latin America, she reminds us, artists have negotiated different categories related to their historical and political contexts: those who identify as feminist artists; those who identify as women artists addressing feminine themes; and those who identify solely as "artist," thereby distancing themselves from any explicitly gendered identity or political agenda, even when it can be interpreted as such. Understanding these fluid categories of identification used by Latin American artists, and Central American artists in particular, allows us to consider the varied temporal, geographical, and historical locations of enunciation, along with intersecting subjectivities.[2] Additionally, it reminds us that fear of patriarchal repercussion in art spheres is still very real. Yet, as Giunta asserts, reading artworks through the lens of gender will reveal feminist concerns, prompting us feminist art historians to analyze, historize, and theorize "that which normative and patriarchal history declassifies and invisibilizes."[3]

In identifying feminist concerns in the region, it is equally important to recognize the heterogeneity of feminist movements. In her 1984 canonical speech to Western feminists, "The Master's Tools Will Never Dismantle the Master's House," Audre Lorde discouraged a tolerance of differences and instead advocated an acknowledgment of them as a powerful tool for community, being, and embarking in change. "Difference is the raw and powerful connection from which our personal power is forged," she stated. "Without community there is no liberation, only the most vulnerable and temporary armistice between an individual and her oppression. But community must not mean a shedding of our differences, nor the pathetic pretense that these differences do not exist."[4] Lorde's poignant words for feminists are equally relevant in the Central American feminist context, where to assume a hegemonic feminist perspective, or a denial of class, race, or sexual orientation differences, would only impede true feminist possibilities for antipatriarchal futures. Together, the artists I discuss here reveal a spectrum of feminist concerns brought on by multiple differences and intersectionalities—race, class, gender, sexuality—even within a collective discourse of feminism in the region. This warns us against the myth of natural allyship between feminists and encourages us to recognize the real anti-poor, anti-Black, anti-Indigenous, and anti-LGTBQ realities within feminist movements as ongoing struggles.

In considering gender as a lens in the postwar Central American art context, I argue that artists increasingly bypass the right-/left-wing rhetoric of decades prior and expose the various mechanisms of what Latin American, Indigenous, and women-of-color feminists have shown to be an entanglement between gender and coloniality. Feminists of color like M. Jacqui Alexander, Chandra Talpade Mohanty, and Gayatri Chakravorty Spivak recognized that Western feminist discourse is a hegemonic view that not only excludes the realities of women in the Global South but relegates them to roles of victimhood and powerlessness, thus in turn presenting Western feminism as modern and liberated.[5] Maria Lugones and Hortense J. Spillers specifically address how in the project of colonialism, enslaved and colonized women were not only racialized but also gendered into a hierarchical structure that produced the conditions for their ongoing oppression, now understood as the coloniality of gender.[6] From this understanding that race, class, gender, and sexuality are linked and shaped by colonialism, capitalism, neoliberalism, and imperialism, feminists in the Global South, such as Lorena Cabnal, Aura Cumes, Silvia Rivera Cusicanqui, Julieta Paredes Carvajal, and Gladys Tzul Tzul, among others, assert one cannot consider these as separate or isolated categories of analysis but as an interlocked system of oppression that in turn gives way to other forms of resistance. This resistance is an anticolonial, antipatriarchal, and antiheteronormative feminism from Abya Yala.[7]

It is at this juncture of hemispheric decolonial feminism that I look to artists who expose the coloniality of gender as part of the contemporary conditions and realities of Central Americans. I ask, what role does a creative turn to the body as medium play in exposing coloniality and forming new decolonial feminisms in art? How does such art offer a broader understanding of a violence tied to the mass displacement of Central American women, nonheteronormative people, and nonbinary people who seek asylum at the US-Mexico border?

While gender-based violence, or *femicide*—the systematic killing of women for being women—is popularly noted as a migratory cause, and indeed it is, these artists challenge the oversimplified use of the term as a phenomenon inherent only to the Global South. Instead, they unravel how heteropatriarchal culture and misogyny are embedded in the multiple structures of violence and policing that target women and nonheteronormative and gender-nonconforming people in Central America. They also expose systems of oppression within the region, such as anti-Indigenous and anti-Black violence. Thus, in combating intersectional oppressive systems, Central American artists also point us to the context of displacement and migration for thousands of women and nonbinary or nonheteronormative people. In doing so, they further demonstrate the most popular artistic medium in the region for social political art and activism that emerged in a postwar context—the body.

A POSTWAR TURN TO THE BODY

The creative turn to the body in Central America paralleled the emergence of action art in the 1960s and 1970s in Chile, Brazil, Argentina, and other countries in the Americas that experienced substantial state repression.[8] In these geopolitical contexts, artists took back and embodied public spaces to confront the state. Such practices are distinct from the opposition to the art institution, evidenced in the emergence of Euro-US performance art practice. Artist and scholar Coco Fusco reminds us that for Latin America the state has been experienced as "harsh, if not excessively physical" due to the forced disappearances, military and police brutality, and repression of opposition voices.[9] Moreover, underscoring the link between historical, social, and individual traumatic experiences, art historian Kristine Stiles notes that artists use their bodies as a creative form that gives testimony to the incomprehensibility of tragedy.[10] Similar to other parts of the Americas, war in Central America provoked an artistic exploration of the fragility and strength of the human body as it sought to reconcile with the state culture of death—one that specifically relied on a visual coloniality through the display of vulnerable, tortured, and disposed bodies.

A turn to the body through performance and intervention art can be understood as an agentive act against the state. This creative turn follows intense decades of governmental repression, making the Central American body a site of protest, dissidence, testimony, healing, intervention, remembering, and memory making.[11] Such political embodiment aligns with Diana Taylor's observations of performance art in the Americas as political acts of being "presente/present" in the face of political repression. These acts are imbued with epistemic and ontological reflections on participatory and relational recognition to the more contemporary struggles across the hemisphere.[12] In the isthmus, performance art was further supported by the vast artistic initiatives that emerged in the 1990s and encouraged reflection, analysis, and new strategies to deal with the fragmentation, isolation, and stereotypical notion of Central America in the aftermath of war.[13] Guatemala specifically became a catalyst for emerging performance artists in the late 1990s due to its abundance of artist collectives.[14] The festival Octubre Azul (2000) distinctively influenced a generation of artists who took to public space to reconcile with memories of military presence and public massacres that occurred in the streets and plazas only a few years prior.[15] Of that generation, Guatemalan artist Aníbal López, who later went by his identification number, "A1-53167," became one of the most influential performance and intervention artists in the postwar region.

A range of artists across the region began to address the systematization of violence and social control of the body enforced by the state. In *Matemática sustractiva* (Subtractive mathematics) (2001), Guatemalan artist Isabel Ruiz drew a total of forty-five thousand lines onto the exterior wall of a red building, each representing the number of victims during the country's thirty-six-year war (see figure 2.2). With the tally marks, which are commonly used to count ongoing results (as in the score of a sports game), Ruiz highlights the numeric politics of military violence, where military gain equates civilian loss. A simple gesture, drawing a white line in a public space, becomes both a denunciation of the disappeared at the hands of the military and a recognition of the thousands whose void remains unrecognized by the state.

Some artists increasingly juxtaposed their own bodies with other symbolic material as a metaphorical way to expose and condemn the brutalities of the state and the realities of quotidian life. In *No necesitamos más papel* (We don't need any more paper) (2011), Salvadoran performance artist Alexia Miranda read the Universal Declaration of Human Rights out loud (see figure 2.3). After reading each article, she tore each sheet and pinched her body with clips to show a consensus among Central Americans that no peace accord or formal agreement has ended or reduced violence in the region. She exposes the superficiality of bureaucratic documents that fail to protect human rights.

For Salvadoran artist Natalia Domínguez, the materiality of trash bags points to the normalcy of gang violence. In her performance *Atuendo* (Attire) (2010), the artist partially covered her nude body in plastic trash bags during a procession along Boulevard Constitución while holding a flag made of the same material (see figure 2.4). The trash bags reference a then-recent gang dispute that led to an incinerated bus, killing all passengers inside. The victims'

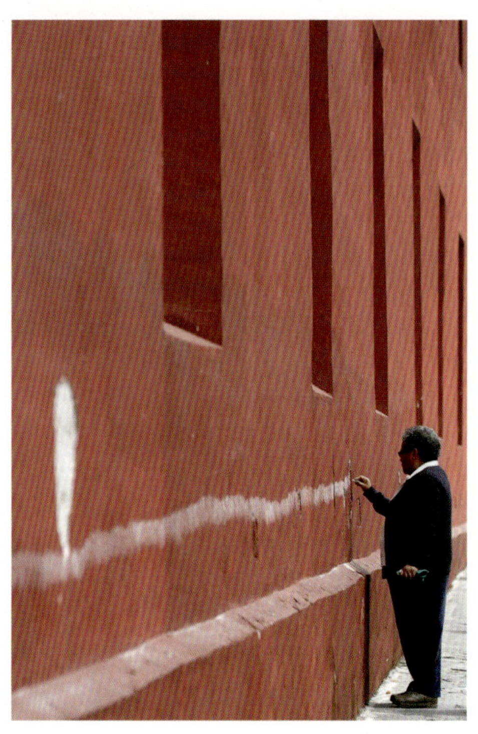

FIGURE 2.2.

Isabel Ruiz, *Matemática sustractiva*, 2001, performance. Photo by Carlos Sebastián for *Horror Vacui* exhibition. Image courtesy of Rosina Cazali.

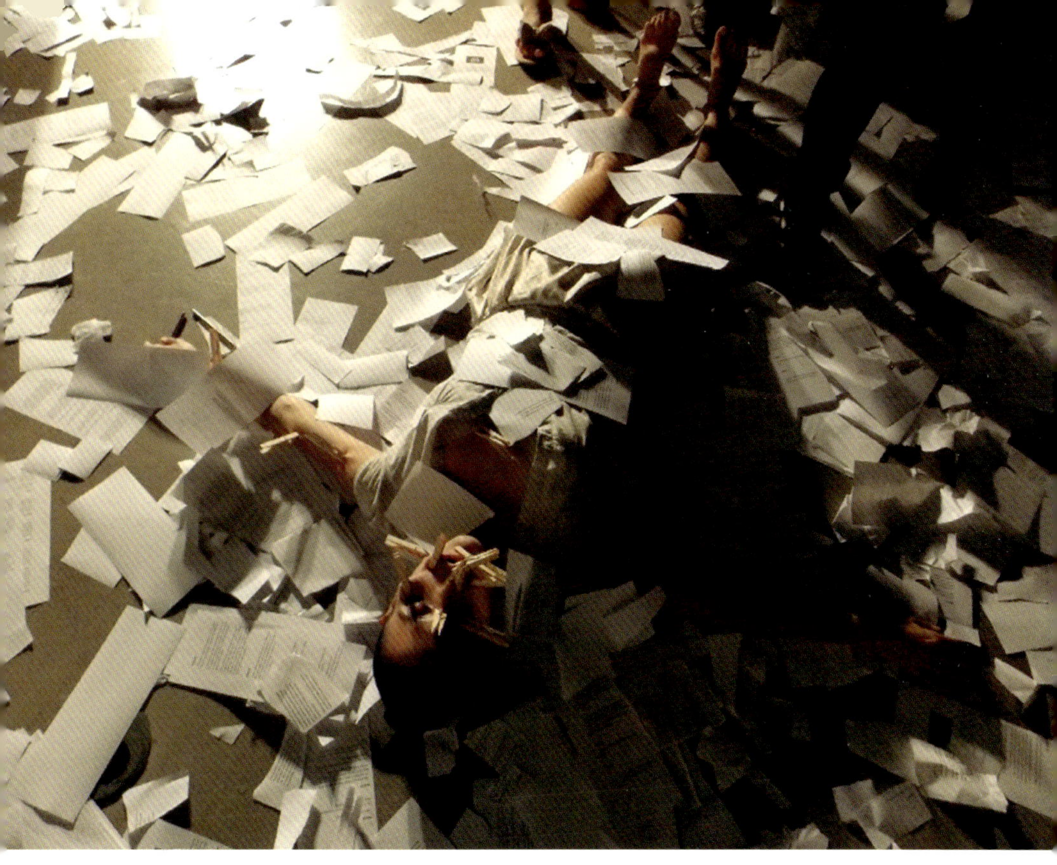

FIGURE 2.3.
Alexia Miranda, *No necesitamos más papel*, 2011, performance. Courtesy of the artist.

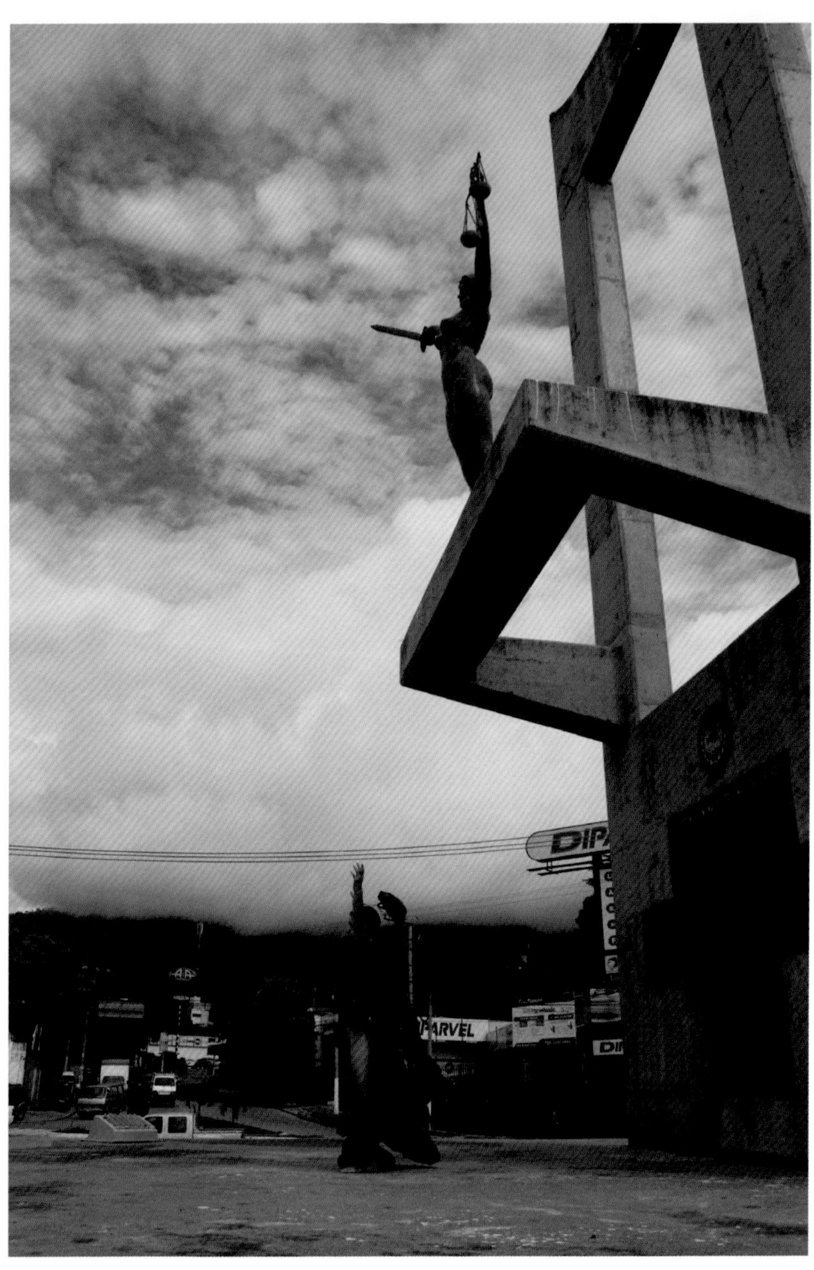

FIGURE 2.4.
Natalia Domínguez, *Atuendo*, 2010, performance. Photograph by Dalia Chévez. Image Courtesy of the artist Natalia Dominguez.

unrecognizable bodies were placed in the same black bags used to dispose of garbage. Domínguez's procession concluded at the Monument to the Constitution (also known as "La Chulona"), erected during the peace accord process to honor the constitution and a future period of peace in El Salvador. Wrapped in a symbol of human disposability, her corporal presence exposed the symbolic failure of national monuments.

In Honduras, Jorge Oquelí addressed the failure of the nation in his performance *Honduras* (2010), for which he excavated a grave-like hole on university grounds and filled it with muddy water (see figure 2.5). For more than an hour, breathing only through a discrete straw, the artist submerged himself in the ditch, evoking a death scene.[16] With his plunged head and body and the title of the performance, the artist pointed to both an escape of the senses that can occur when witnessing overwhelming violence and a criminology process that leaves bodies exposed for visual consumption pending slow police investigations. Across Guatemala, El Salvador, and Honduras, as these artists reveal, the use of the body through performance art exposes the incompetence of the state while centering the corporal losses of such failures: human lives.

It is likewise significant and worth noting that postwar Central American performance art was predominantly led by women artists. In addition to addressing the state, the turn to the body also facilitated an analysis, reflection, and protest of issues previously overshadowed by the collective atrocities of war, such as the specificities of being a woman or nonheteronormative in a patriarchal society where violence is not just a casualty of armed conflict but an everyday experience endured in both public and private spaces. These creative acts did not center the role of women within idealized visual tropes of revolution. Rather, by bringing forth concerns pertaining to misogyny and patriarchy, while centering their own bodies, artists began disrupting notions of femininity and normative behaviors to expose ongoing violence beyond the left-/right-wing politics of the nation-state.

In one of the region's earlier iconic performances, *Pantalones para los días de regla* (Pants for period days) (1996), Costa Rican artist Priscilla Monge used her own body as a medium to intervene in public spaces in defiance of the gendered social boundaries found in the private and public spheres (see figure 2.6). She performed a casual day in the urban city of San José, during which she ran errands and made an occasional call in a public phone booth. Monge wore a pantsuit made of sanitary napkins, and she was menstruating at the time, thus slowly revealing her bodily function as the menstrual blood spread. Otherwise, the artist did nothing out of the ordinary. With her wardrobe choice and what it revealed, Monge disrupts the static female image as pure, clean, and submissive

FIGURE 2.5.
Jorge Oquelí, *Honduras*, 2010, performance. Courtesy of the artist.

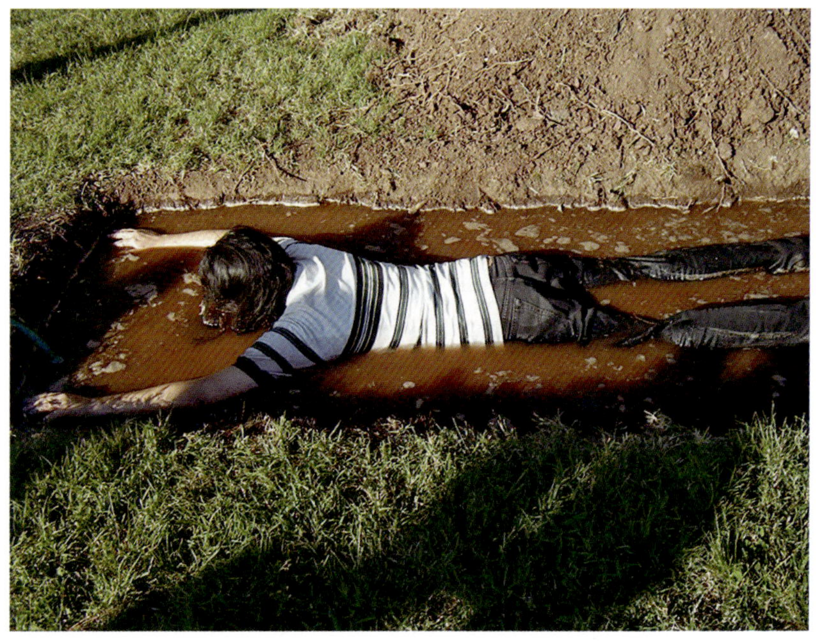

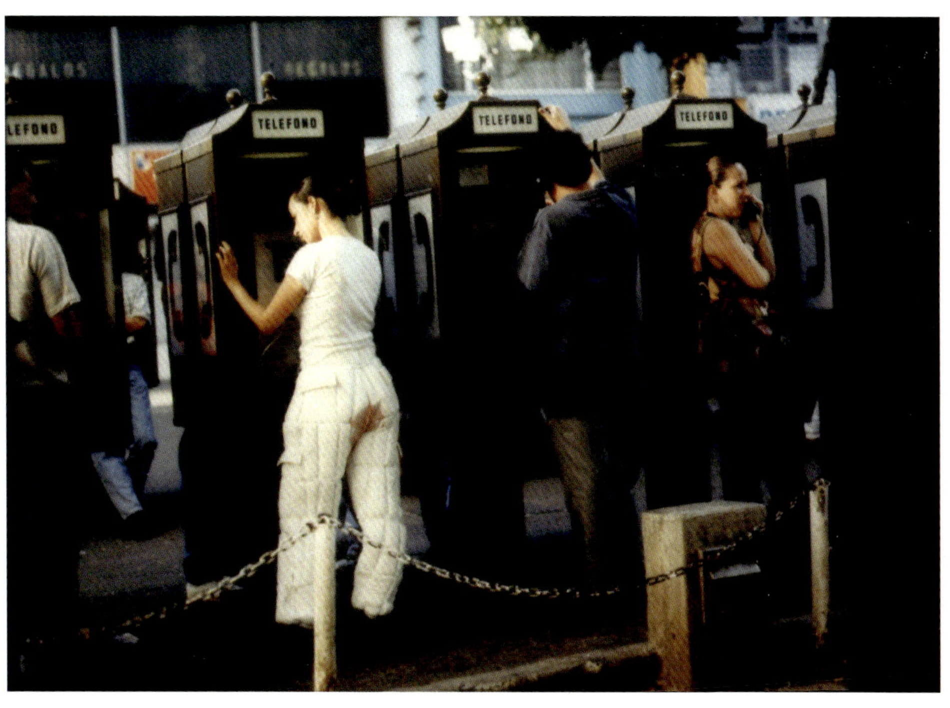

FIGURE 2.6.
Priscilla Monge, *Pantalones para los días de regla*, 1996, performance. Courtesy of the artist.

by making visible a bodily function characterized under patriarchal society as unhygienic, dirty, disgraceful, and thus a function to be concealed in the private sphere. Her performance effectively questions the limits of normalized patriarchal behavior. She further disobeys the role of women in Eurocentric and patriarchal art, in which the female body, especially the nude, is considered acceptable subject matter as a passive object of beauty for the male gaze.[17] Trespassing the line between private and public, internal and external, social and antisocial, in much of her art the artist exposes the ambiguity between violence and the feminine, questioning the limits of normalized patriarchal behavior.

Such performances create scenarios that question and challenge audience reactions. In *Pantalones para los días de regla*, the majority of viewers responded with horror and fear. Men asked they not be photographed in the performance documentation because they felt "embarrassed," and some women ran to inform Monge that the menstruation blood had seeped through her pants so that she would run from public view.[18] Thus Monge exposes the abjection the public experiences at the horror of witnessing, and being confronted by, the artist's corporal, if also mundane, reality. Bulgarian scholar Julia Kristeva describes abjection as that liminal space that does not respect borders, that blurs the inside and outside and the socially acceptable and unacceptable, that divides life and death, and that can evoke desire and repulsion. This sense of the abject as significant to Monge during her performance is evidenced through her juxtaposition of the violent and the feminine. Like other bodily fluids (urine, tears), menstrual blood traverses the interior/exterior divide of the body, a function that is symbolic of both life and death. Nonetheless, it is perceived as waste by the public, thus inducing repulsion. As scholar Leticia Alvarado has shown, there is political power in artists who embrace negative affect and use abject performance as a strategy of resistance and of imagining futures outside the mainstream.[19] Monge defies the normative rules of disgust and shameful obscurity by publicly, visually, and corporally engaging in quotidian acts without concern, as if already moving through that alternative future.

With its use of nudity, bodily liquids, and a defiance of the borders of corporal limits, performance art became a tool in postwar Central American art to defy the unspoken rules of the private and public divide in terms of women's suffering and oppression. This turn to the body facilitated a new form of feminism for postwar artists, which occurred in parallel with the rise of gender-based violence and gave way to new types of visual disobedience that use creative embodied defiance to blur the private and the public, the living and the dead, and to undo cultures of silence.

DISMANTLING THE PRIVATE/PUBLIC DIVIDE OF FEMICIDE

There is great impunity in Central America, meaning gender-based violence and its colonial legacy are institutionalized by the state when governments and police authorities uphold their subordination of women and fail to investigate gender-based crimes. Returning to the performance that opens this chapter, Galindo's enactment of embodied defiance calls attention to a common practice in Central America, in which perpetrators dispose of their victims' bodies after having carved the motive for their attack onto their victim's flesh. Numerous bodies throughout the region are found raped and murdered but also tortured, mutilated, and/or decapitated, revealing a specific aesthetics of violence toward Central American women. The word *perra*, which translates to "female dog" or "bitch," is often used as a derogatory accusation that a woman is "loose," as in promiscuous. Thus, when a cadaver is found in public displaying the word, it is clear that her life was taken as a punishment for her sexual agency, condemning her as impure and unworthy for not conforming to colonial notions of feminine purity. Galindo's self-inflicted incision, and the blood that seeps to the surface of her body as a result, is a condemnation of the everyday criminalization of women even when they are targets of violence. It alludes to the fact that women are criminalized not only by the perpetrators but also often by authorities who justify the violence against them as provoked and warranting reprimand.

In a postwar context, violence in general has increased in Central America, but the killing of women in particular has placed the region on the map as one of the most dangerous places for women in the Western hemisphere. From the 1970s through the 1980s, the term *femicide* came to define the systematic killing of women by men *because* they are women. Some scholars use the term in Spanish, *feminicidio*, to acknowledge the response, theorization, and modification of this term from women in the South, who are both affected by and have long been at the forefront of exposing and combating multiple forms of violence against women, thus decentering the unidirectional North-South geopolitics of knowledge.[20] To further acknowledge the politics of translation across Latin America, some feminist scholars theorize translocalities/*translocalidades* to account for the flow "of bodies, texts, capital, and theories in between North/South, and to reflect the mobile epistemologies they inspire" as a feminist act.[21] I suggest that like these feminist scholars and activists from across the hemisphere, Central American artists battle the extreme gender violence in the region while creating their own epistemes through embodied acts and images that circulate in these flows of translation. In this case through their visual disobedience, they unpack and condemn femicide and impunity in the region and its facilitating mechanisms from the realm of the domestic to media communications and judicial spaces.

Because one-third of femicides result from domestic violence, some artists pay special attention to the private aspects of interpersonal violence.[22] In the late 1990s, Priscilla Monge created a series of three video art works titled Lecciones (Lessons). The first video, *Lección no. 1: Lección de maquillaje* (Lesson no. 1: Makeup lesson) (1998), opens to a man entering a room where a woman, played by Monge's sister, sits on a chair in profile view (see figure 2.7). In the backdrop, a dark melodramatic musical score intensifies the eerie mood. Facing the cameras, the man explains that the viewer will now learn useful makeup techniques that can be applied for day or night. As he rationalizes that cosmetics facilitate beauty and a healthy appearance, he takes the woman's face and applies powder, blush, and eye shadow. At one point he briskly strokes the woman's mouth creating a phallic image with his finger as he violently smudges color outside the lines of her lips. Like her other videos, Monge concludes this work with an unexpected twist. As the man reiterates that makeup is important to "conceal all imperfections and defects," the woman turns to fully face the camera, revealing a black eye, and the marks of domestic violence.

In Central America, domestic violence, including rape, is often framed by authorities as "traditional cultural behavior" and projected as "normal" for impoverished, uneducated people. Rosa Linda Fregoso and Cynthia L. Bejarano note that framing interpersonal violence as private and cultural rather than public and political reinforces the gendered hierarchies of colonialism. They quote Gayle Binion to explain that "it renders women subject to the control of patriarchal familial authorities, such as the father or brother, with the understating that family matters are private and therefore beyond the scope of government authority and intervention."[23] Monge's video defies this private and public divide by contextualizing domestic violence within a greater patriarchal and colonial system of regulation and control over women's bodies. She addresses interpersonal violence but does so through a critique of the imposition for standards of beauty onto women through media such as infomercials and telenovelas. In the video, the man is more concerned with her physical transformation to disguise her defects and make her aesthetically desirable than with assisting her. Monge shows how the imposition of beauty standards that uphold gender norms simultaneously becomes a tool to conceal the physical and psychological assaults that come with domestic violence.

In Central America, authorities often fail to properly investigate domestic violence matters, not only because they view it as a matter left to the husband

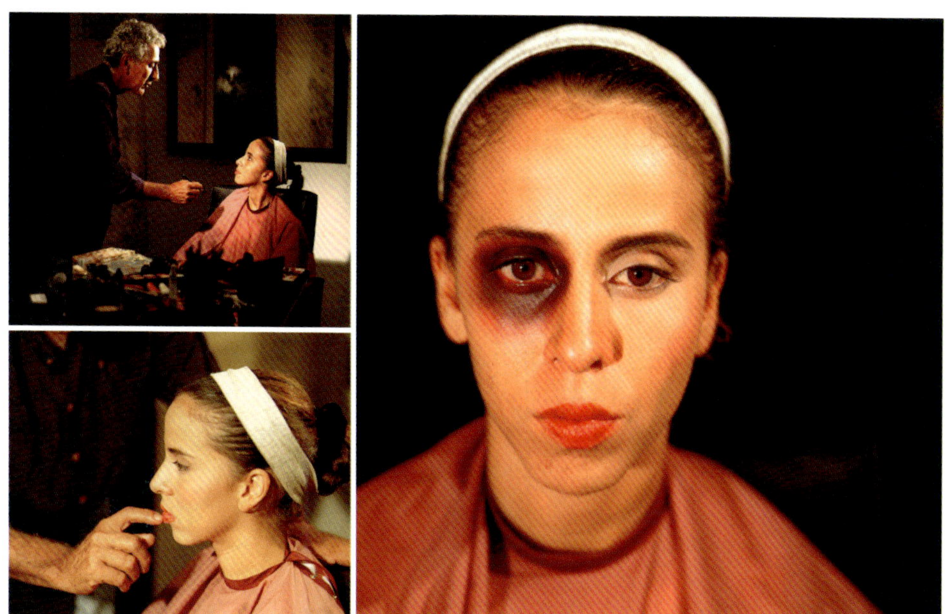

FIGURE 2.7.
Priscilla Monge, *Lección no. 1: Lección de maquillaje*, 1998, video (stills). Courtesy of the artist.

but because of the assumption that the victim somehow provoked or deserved the aggression. Instead of properly investigating the motives for their assaults or death, police and prosecutors question the victim's "character" by citing their assumed choices, acquaintances, or even fashion choices as reasons for their deaths, placing the blame on the victim.[24] Such was the case with Claudina Isabel Velásquez Paiz, a nineteen-year-old law student who was found raped and beaten, with two gunshots to the head. Authorities failed to conduct a proper investigation, which included a failure to analyze fluids found on her body, a failure to conduct forensic analysis, and a refusal to fingerprint the main suspect even after he voluntarily made a statement that provided sufficient evidence for an arrest. Instead, investigators labeled Claudina a "nobody" based on the fact that she was wearing a belly-button ring and sandals.[25] Authorities viewed her fashion choices as an indicator of her indecency, which they weighed more heavily than the actual evidence against a perpetrator, and thus held her responsible for her own death. The ease with which the authorities condoned her aggravated death further revealed they accept rape, beating, and shooting as a reasonable punishment. The vagueness and lack of accountability in media reports of femicide often contribute to this same victim-blaming framing.

In one of her earliest performances, Regina José Galindo used her body to contest the desensitizing of sexual assault and aggression reported in the media. In *El dolor de un pañuelo* (The pain of a handkerchief) (1999), Galindo appeared blindfolded with her wrists tied to a vertical bed while various newspaper projections covered her nude body (see figure 2.8). Each projection consisted of newspaper headlines that reported systematic attacks on women in Guatemala, with captions such as "Treinta violaciones en sólo dos meses" (Thirty rapes in only two months), "Violaciones sexuales deben ser tipificadas" (Sexual violations should be typified), and "Asesinan a mujer, dejan cuerpo en Planes de Minerva" (Woman assassinated, body left in Planes de Minerva). The rails on the side of the bed onto which Galindo was bound in her performance, and the simplicity of the sheets and bed, evoked a clinical setting rather than the traditional comfort or domestic connotations of a bed. The position of her body, centered and upfront with arms akimbo, counters sleep or rest as intended functions and instead presents her body as an experimental subject. The blindfold over her eyes prohibits her sight and engagement with her surroundings, and this impedes control over what is to occur to her body. Is this a restrained body on the verge of physical violence or a postcrime corpse prepared for autopsy?

In contrast to the revolving headlines, the static and sterile aesthetic of her body and its position on the bed suggest a certain repetition. The media headline and the minor details that differentiate one crime from another and one

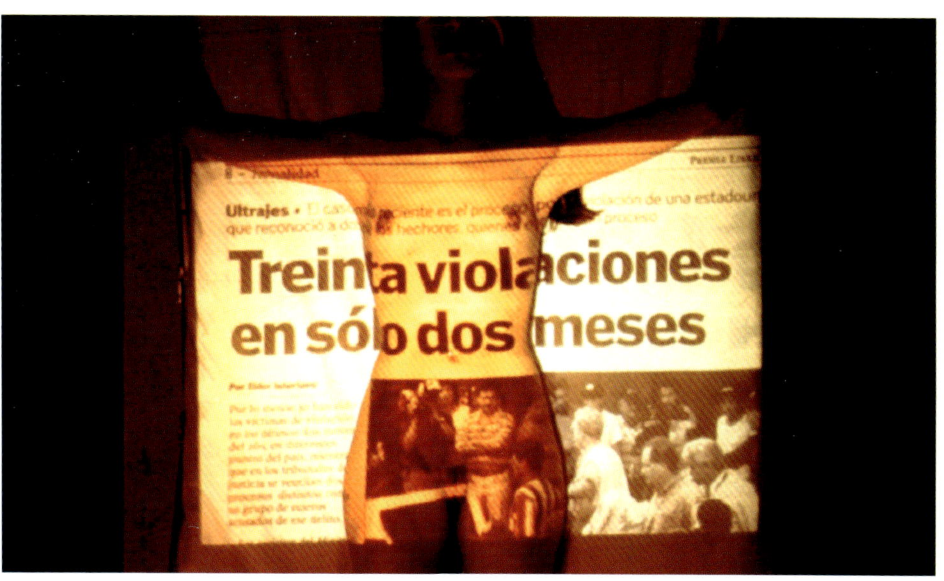

FIGURE. 2.8.
Regina José Galindo, *El dolor de un pañuelo*, 1999, performance. Courtesy of the artist.

victim from another may vary, but the constant mechanical projection points to the endless assembly of bodies and headlines and a continuity of crimes. Yet, if the viewer focuses on the projection first, the inverse occurs: *from* the perpetual production of headlines, the artist's body emerges to disrupt its continuity and consequential desensitization. Her physical body materializes from the text to challenge the reduction of raped and murdered women to depersonalized headlines and statistics. This act simultaneously conjures the notion that crimes against women are expected and normal, or mere unfortunate events. Galindo's performance challenges the role of the media in covering and reporting gender violence in Guatemala as it uncritically propels a sense of normalcy and/or impunity that is systematic in colonial structures of gender.

Feminicide is epidemic in Central America today, with rates even surpassing those of Mexico, which typically receives more attention. Studies reveal that rates in Guatemala, Honduras, and El Salvador, home to the majority of artists I discuss here, are among the highest in the world.[26] Data from 2017 to 2019 reveal these countries are among the world's highest in homicide, extortion, and sexual violence rates, which are still gravely underreported.[27] Impunity prevails in Central America as the state further institutionalizes gender-based violence through law and policy. In one study, Cecilia Menjívar and Shannon Drysdale Walsh examine legal codes in Guatemala and offer various examples of how judges counter laws made to protect women from violence by arguing such laws are "unconstitutional" relative to other laws that were previously designed to protect men. For instance, a judge will deny a woman's request for a restraining order against an abusive husband on the grounds that doing so would violate existing property laws that favor the male as owner of the house.[28] Yet laws that criminalize women are strictly enforced. In El Salvador, for instance, a woman can receive a thirty-year prison sentence for homicide under current anti-abortion laws, even if the pregnancy was a result of rape or incest, and even if the pregnancy termination was due to miscarriage or physical trauma.[29] Salvadoran Maira Veronica Figueroa served fifteen years in prison after she suffered a miscarriage and hospital staff reported her to authorities on suspicion of abortion. She was only released in 2018 due to the work of activists who are challenging the anti-abortion laws. One such activist, Teodora Vasquez, served one-third of a thirty-six-year sentence after she gave birth to a stillborn baby in 2008. In the documentary *Fly So Far* (2021), Swiss Salvadoran director Celina Escher follows Vasquez's homicide conviction, her eventual release due to international pressure, and her transformation into an activist in defense of women worldwide imprisoned for having had a miscarriage.[30]

In *Perra,* Lecciones, and *Dolor de un pañuelo,* Galindo and Monge bring viewers into the private and inaccessible spaces of femicide to turn them into witnesses. Regarding *Perra,* Lillian G. Mengesha observes that "we are given a sense that we are seeing what is not meant to be seen, in a place that is not meant for the public eye—which is perhaps the very reason why we must not turn away from the action."[31] Galindo's oeuvre, in particular, is the largest and most consistent in Central America to expose the structural systems, steeped in coloniality, that generate femicide.[32] Galindo does not claim to be or represent a victim of femicide but rather materializes with her own flesh the ghosts of women who even in death are denied visibility, witness, and justice. Galindo thus disrupts the pervasiveness attributed to gender violence in Central America by detouring from numbers and statistics and centering her body as a site of intervention to reveal the deeper structure of feminicide, as a decolonial disobedience against the patriarchy.

HONORING WOMEN'S LABOR TO CONTEST NEOLIBERAL VIOLENCE

A site of violence for women in postwar Central America emerged with the implementation of the Central America–Dominican Republic Free Trade Agreement (CAFTA-DR), an expansion of the North American Free Trade Agreement (NAFTA) to the Dominican Republic and Central American countries (Guatemala, El Salvador, Honduras, Costa Rica, and Nicaragua). As with NAFTA in Mexico, CAFTA proved detrimental to the economic and social state of the region. While private and transnational corporations received immeasurable power, even over Central American governments, the livelihood of citizens drastically deteriorated. Unemployment, labor abuse, poor working conditions, low wages and benefits, and environmental deregulation increased and displaced rural Central Americans from their homes and sources of income. As in many other Latin American countries, a proliferation of *maquiladoras* (sweatshops) in the 1990s as a result of this neoliberal model generated conditions for increased exploitation, violence, and violation of the rights of women workers; maquiladoras have become a less visible but equally dangerous site of gendered violence in postwar Central America. Threats and aggression extend beyond the confines of workspaces. For instance, during their commutes to and from work, women are raped, murdered, or simply disappeared. Maquiladoras are notorious for the danger they pose to women of all ages. Yet, as a result of their structural position in the global economy, women are often forced to take the risk. Frequently, when their lifeless bodies are found, authorities label these women as "sexual subjects lacking value, worth, and respectability" for seeking employment away from home and during late hours.[33]

The Honduran collective Artería has actively exposed the connection between femicide and labor conditions by centering and honoring the labor of women in their interventions. In *ZIP 504, un país cinco estrellas* (ZIP 504, a five-star country) (2001–5), the collective interviewed women on their working conditions and commissioned them to make 2,500 small white T-shirts as part of the art piece for distribution in exhibitions and public interventions. The small T-shirts consisted of a logo, "ZIP 504," the acronym for Free Trade Zones and the number code dialed to reach someone in Honduras (see figure 2.9). Printed on the T-shirt labels was a poem that read: "Wash my soul with cold water, machine dry, that with time you don't consume my fibers. Iron out my fears at medium temperature, but don't iron out my faith. 100% human. Care instructions inside." With the label, the collective reinforced the human aspect of labor often disregarded in a system of neoliberal and neocolonizing policies centered more on cheap labor, production, and exportation than on the livelihood of its workers. It also acknowledges economic inequalities as a continuous form of violence in the region. The products were thus presented as material witness of neoliberalism and neocolonialism. The collective traveled to various Latin American cities, including Tegucigalpa, Cuenca, La Havana, and San José, where members handed out flyers in the streets, announcing the arrival of an exotic product that could be obtained free of charge. In each of the cities in which *ZIP 504* was distributed, the Collective Artería also held a series of lectures, debates, and public interventions with social workers, philosophers, and economists.

In a similar way, Salvadoran artist Dalia Chévez condemns the rise of industrialization in El Salvador that led to an increase in sweatshops and a diminishment in the artisanal work of many Salvadorans. While the Collective Artería collaborated with women sweatshop workers for their interventions, Chévez hired artisans from Ilobasco to address shared concerns. Ilobasco is a municipality in the Cabañas department of El Salvador that is well known for generations of artisans who produce a range of clay-based ceramics purchased by locals and international tourists alike. Especially popular are the clay "miniatures," no bigger than two inches, that depict Salvadorans in quotidian activities. Yet, like other artisan towns with a history of *artesania* (handcraft) production, such as San Sebastián in San Vicente, known for textile production (hammocks, blankets, tablecloths, etc.), Ilobasco faces the threat of economic displacement and cultural loss from the rise of industrialized mass production in the country. To bring attention to the displacement of monetary and cultural capital and how it affects women, Chévez created *Falso-Franca*

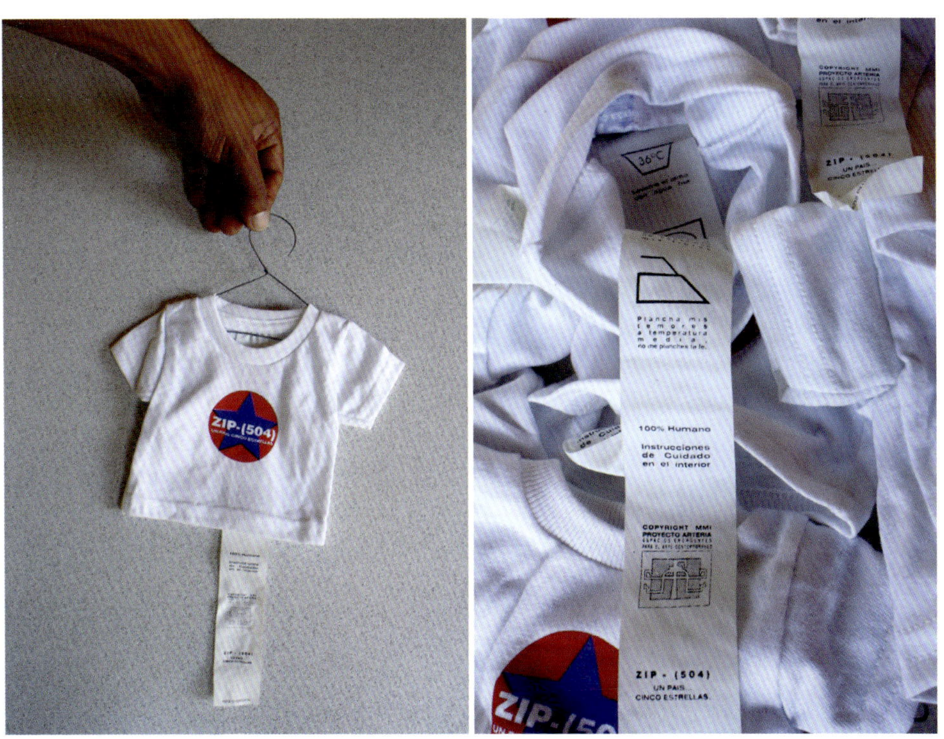

FIGURE 2.9.
Colectivo Artería, *ZIP 504, un país cinco estrellas*, 2001–5, small T-shirts and varied interventions. Courtesy of Adán Vallecillo.

(2007), for which she hired artisans from Ilobasco to produce a large quantity of miniatures that she then painted by hand. The miniatures she commissioned all re-create women sweatshop workers (see figure 2.10). She installed the miniatures over a brick-and-mortar base, subverting the traditional polished exhibition display stands and making further visual reference to cheap, manual labor. The miniatures, arranged in a series of rows, convey the inside of a textile sweatshop. All the women stand in front of sewing machines. In the center an isolated figure represents the overseer, a man who monitors and controls the women's bodies and their production.

By hand painting different features, hair colors, and dress of the many otherwise identical miniatures, the artist rejects the loss of individuality that comes with mass production, where the demand for workers and their disposability and easy replacement disregard the personal narratives, struggles, and lives of each female worker (see figure 2.11). She also directly points to the panoptic system of surveillance for women workers in maquiladoras, where the only male figure, the overseer, is the sole power exerting control over a mass number of women, and under whose monitoring abuses against women workers persist. This figure can be understood as a contemporary manifestation of the landowner overseeing the control of labor and production of the enslaved person, when colonized women were gendered according to a hierarchical structure that ensured a racialized and classed order. Chévez placed a surveillance camera over the installation so that the entire piece would be recorded and displayed on a monitor on the other side of an adjacent wall, capturing not only the installation of miniatures but also the audience viewers who approach to gaze over the work. The viewer thus also becomes a reference, not only as witness but as consumer of such labor products, and thus complicit.

Works like *ZIP 504, un país cinco estrellas* and *Falso-Franca* combine object-based work, art actions, and research to reveal how violations of a woman's bodily integrity involve systemic and structural forces and a multiplicity of factors and intersecting logics—in this case, how neocolonial and neoliberal policies reinforce gendered divisions of labor and gendered violence in Central America. This is especially true for women trapped at the bottom of a racialized socioeconomic pyramid firmly rooted in colonialism. Through these artworks, the artists bring attention to extractive labor practices and the commodification of impoverished women in Central America who are worth less to a country than the cheap material goods they are hired to produce. By centering their labor and exposing their realities through engagement, research, and creative production, the Collective Artería and Chévez honor these women as integral to society and life.

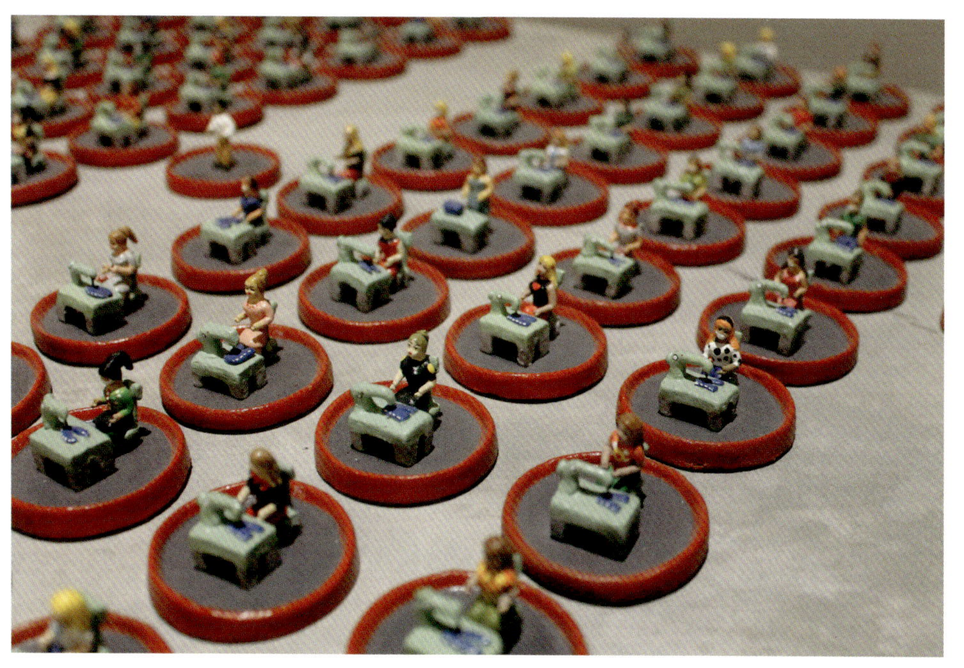

FIGURE 2.10.
Dalia Chévez, *Falso-Franca*, 2007, multimedia installation. Courtesy of the artist.

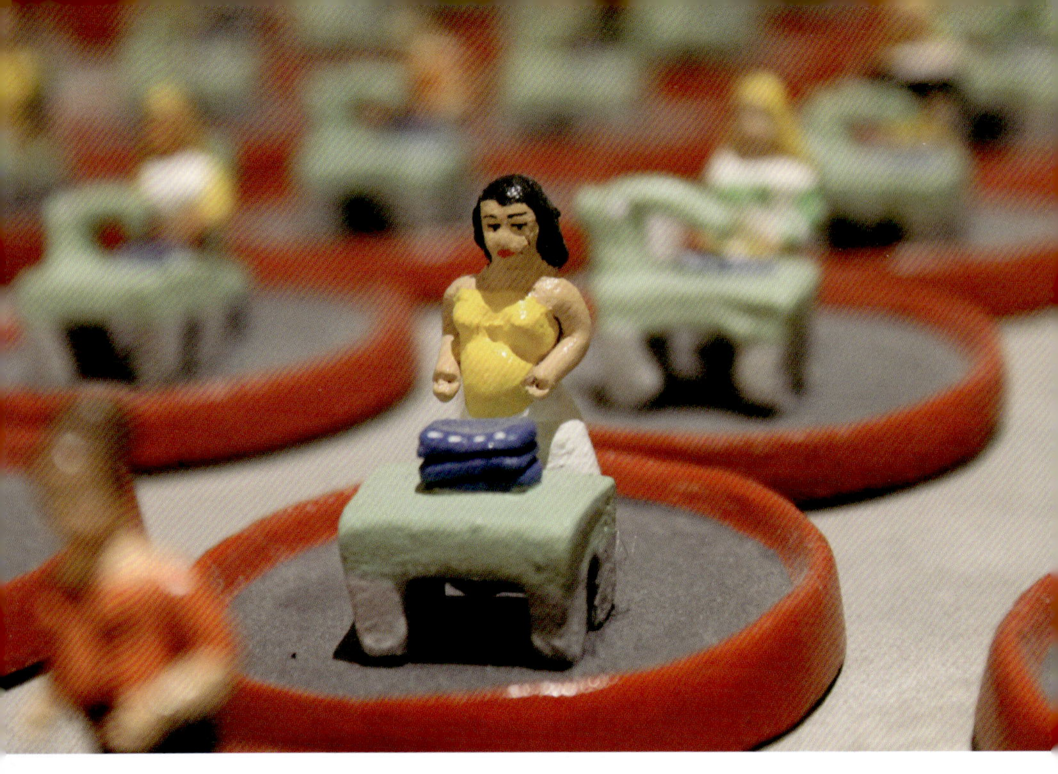

FIGURE 2.11.
Dalia Chévez, *Falso-Franca* (detail), 2007, multimedia installation. Courtesy of the artist.

PHYSICAL AND ENVIRONMENTAL PLUNDER AS FEMINIST CONCERNS

In a room located in the Edificio de Correos in Guatemala City, Galindo lay nude on a bed for an hour as people entered the room and found her restrained. She was eight months pregnant at the time of this performance. As she lay on her back, her legs and arms were spread opened and tied to the corners of the bed with umbilical cords around her wrists and ankles (see figure 2.12). The position reflected the exact way that soldiers restrained and raped Indigenous pregnant women in Guatemala during the civil war. This performance, titled *Mientras, ellos siguen libre* (Meanwhile, they remain free) (2007), is known for critiquing previous military regime tactics in Guatemala. Gang rape, sexual slavery, mutilation, and torture were forms of terror used against women during state counterinsurgency in Guatemala, El Salvador, Nicaragua, and Honduras, as military repression and patriarchal culture were mutually constituting forces.[34] However, *Mientras, ellos siguen libre* extends beyond a critique of military practices during the war to directly confront a racialized gendered violence: the rape of pregnant Indigenous women enacted for the purpose of inducing forced abortions and miscarriages—to eliminate what the military officially coined "bad seeds," a practice elaborated on in the previous chapter.

According to the Commission of Historical Clarification, the majority of rape victims during the thirty-six-year-long war were Indigenous.[35] Countless testimonies recount how pregnant Maya women were raped, tortured, their bellies stomped on, and in some cases their fetuses ripped directly from their wombs.[36] The umbilical cords, which Galindo purchased illegally from clandestine abortion clinics, symbolically reference a documented military ploy to eliminate Indigenous children through the violation of women. The control of a person's reproductive abilities, such as forced sterilization, is an old and favorite strategy of settler colonial nation-states, a violence it directs toward Black and Indigenous peoples. As scholar Inés Hernández-Avila has noted about Indigenous women across the hemisphere, "it is because of sex, that she is hunted down and slaughtered, in fact, singled out, because she has the potential through childbirth to assure the continuance of the people."[37] Galindo's performance does more than critique a 1980s military tactic, and to limit the culpability of such violence to the previous regime alone is to ignore the historical roots in colonialism that sanctioned that military regime to enact such atrocities. With *Mientras, ellos siguen libres* Galindo reveals that the problem extends to the termination of life and to reproduction as a centuries-old and ongoing tool of colonization.

FIGURE 2.12.
Regina José Galindo, *Mientras, ellos siguen libre*, 2007, performance. Courtesy of the artist.

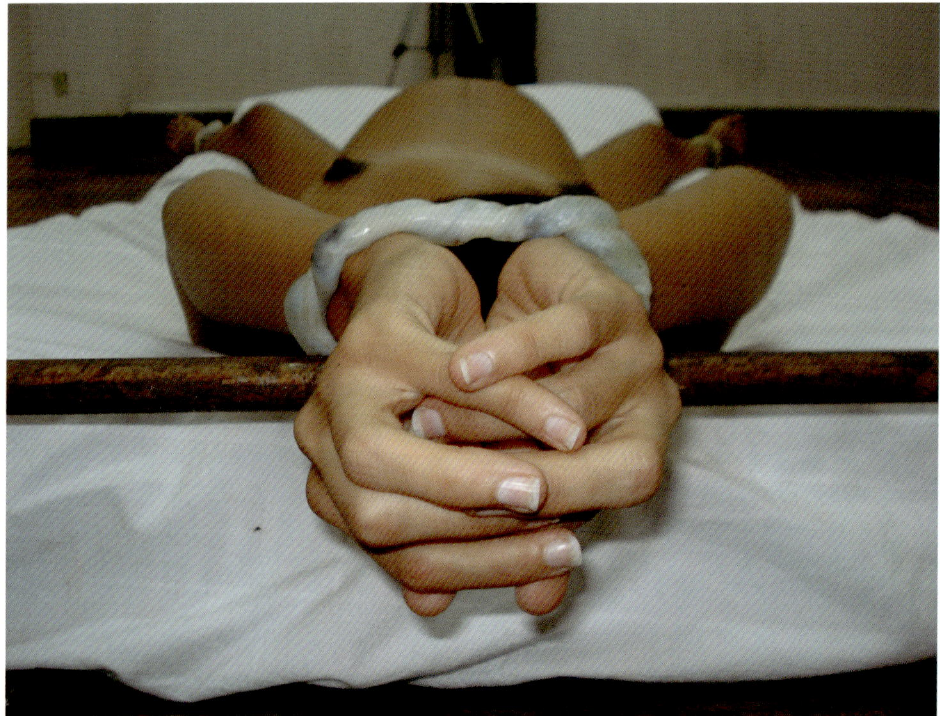

Galindo reminds us that sexual violence is a historic colonial tool that is still used against Central American women, and rape continues to be its most violent manifestation. Nelson Maldonado-Torres locates the practices of rape and murder within the "non-ethics of war." For Maldonado-Torres, the treatment of enslaved and colonized peoples did not have to adhere to the "ethics" of war applied to European societies; in fact, their existence was relegated to a perpetual state of war, a coloniality of being, in which war practices were naturalized.[38] "While in war there is murder and rape, in the hell of the colonial world murder and rape become day to day occurrences and menaces," Maldonado-Torres explains.[39] Controlling a woman's body, her sexuality, her pleasure, and her reproductive abilities and choices, including through forced sterilization, can be seen as the perpetuation of war and of the ways race and gender fit within the coloniality of being. The logic of rape, as a naturalized practice of war for subjugated peoples, also can be seen with the pillage of Native land in the Americas. Land also assures the continuance of Native peoples and has been condemned to a perpetual state of war and rape. From the colonial perspective, women's bodies and Native lands are seen as inherently violable and conquerable; thus, the pillage of Native land in Central America is also a feminist concern. Artists draw these connections between environmental extractivism and the practices for war.

In her work, Honduran artist Lucy Argueta condemns the criminalization of human rights activists in Central America amid political corruption sanctioned by US governments and corporations as a result of CAFTA-DR. Her work is even more relevant considering the assassination of beloved and respected Indigenous environmental leader Berta Cáseres on March 3, 2016. Cáseres's assassination was a direct result of the US-backed coup in 2009 and the escalating violation of the rights of Indigenous peoples in Honduras, as well as the repressive tactics, including assassination, used against those who speak against extractivism. The repression after the coup specially targets campesinos and activists who defend their land rights against foreign multinational corporations. In her video and installation *Merma* (2012), which translates to "loss, deterioration, or diminishment," Argueta places soiled, deteriorated clothes over white sheets on the floor (see figure 2.13). Pants, shirts, and jackets partly covered in dirt appear like archaeological artifacts deteriorated with time. For Argueta, the violent repression that emerged in Honduras after the 2009 coup echoed the aesthetics of violence that dominated in the 1980s when US-funded counterinsurgency groups perpetrated killings and disappearances. The artist visited clandestine graves that continue to be discovered in Honduras today and observed that the only remains of the decomposed bodies were often the clothing victims wore at the moment of their assassinations, which become the only identifiable markers for family members to claim the deceased.

To connect postwar repression to the 1980s violence, Argueta purchased used clothing that showcased 1980s style and buried the garments in clandestine graves. After a month, she returned to unearth the garments, which by then had taken different material form and resembled exhumed cadavers. The only light shining on the clothes, centered in a dark room, emanated from the video installation displayed on a center wall. The video shows a remote location in Honduras that juxtaposes the serene sound of whistling winds and chirping birds in the background with the meticulous excavation in the earth and the sound of shovels digging into the soil and brushes sweeping away the dirt. What becomes evident in the video is the missing presence of people, which alludes to the loss of the human body. Argueta's *Merma* denounces the criminalization and assassination of campesinos and Indigenous peoples who dare defend their land against government-sponsored corporations. With the work, the artist condemns the repression against Indigenous peoples and workers of the land, the same people Berta Cáceres defended for years before her assassination.[40] Today's violation and killing of Central American women, water and land defenders, is a continuation of colonial practices that functioned to eliminate a population and control their lands. Both women and land are were framed as violable.

The 2019 performance *El agua se volvió oro, el rio se volvió oro, el oro se volvió azul* (The water turned gold, the river turned gold, the gold turned blue), by Sandra Monterroso, first took place at the Ex Teresa Arte Actual Museum in Mexico City and two months later in Guatemala (see figure 2.14). The performance functioned as a healing ritual for the sacred rivers wounded by extractivism, specifically the construction of Oxec hydroelectric plants on the Oxec and Cahabón rivers that sustain life in the northern area of Guatemala. Alta Verepaz, where Monterroso's family resides, is located in this area, which is inhabited by the Maya Q'eqchi'. There, extractivist companies are granted permits despite lacking, and preventing, consultation with the local communities that will be affected by the militarization of the river and its contamination. Such extractivist projects disrupt the communities' relations to land and water as well as exacerbate the damages and vulnerability already caused by the climate crisis in the region. The Ixil community was among the most affected by Hurricane Iota and Eta in 2020, which destroyed homes and crops and displaced tens of thousands across the region. Even when such projects generate electricity, it does not benefit the local communities, which are only met with intimidation, repression, or imprisonment. Bernardo Caal Xool, Maya Q'echi'

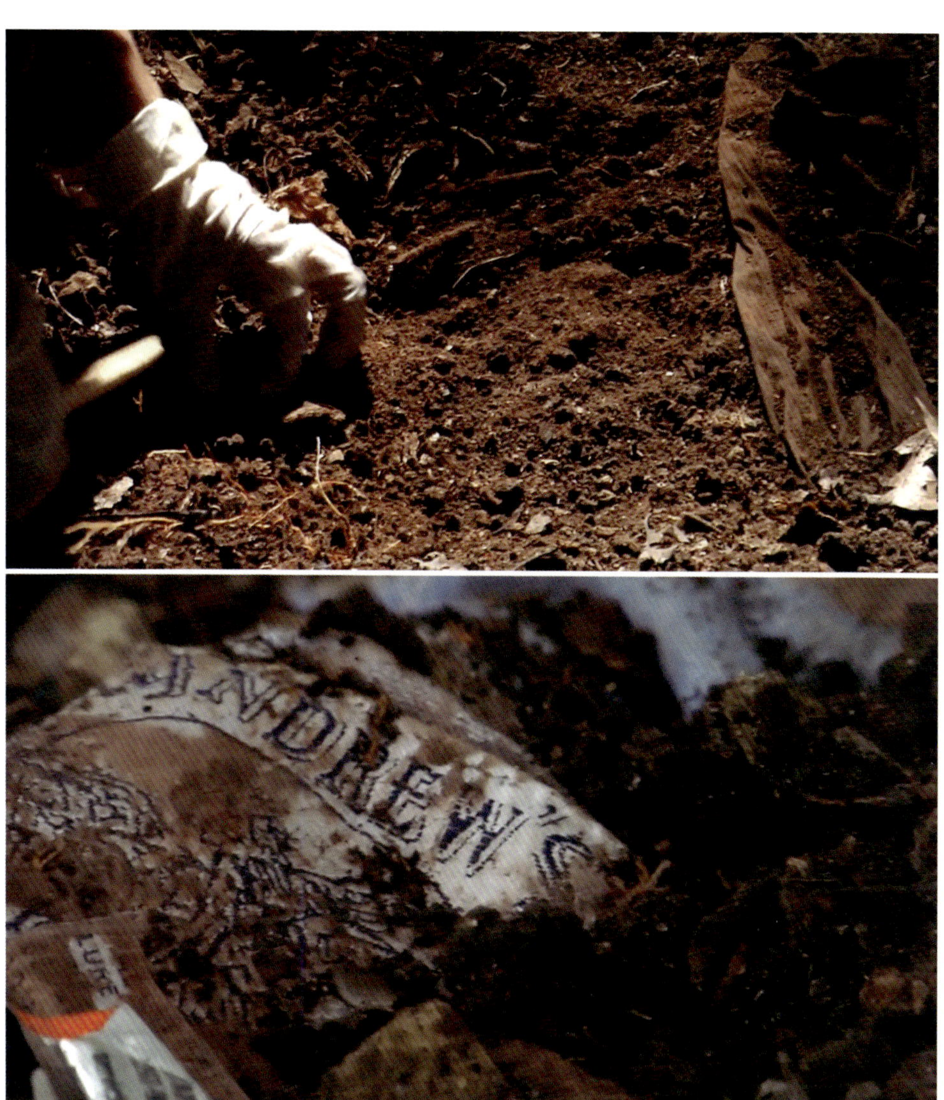

FIGURE 2.13.
Lucy Argueta, *Merma*, 2012, video (stills) and multimedia installation. Courtesy of the artist.

teacher, land defender, and leader, filed a series of injunctions against the Oxec hydroelectric project for failing to consult with local Indigenous communities. After high courts sided with Caal, he was falsely arrested in retaliation under bogus accusations and sentenced to seven years and three months of prison. In 2020, Amnesty International declared Bernardo Caal Xool a prisoner of conscience, and while he was released in 2022 on good behavior, he remains convicted of a crime he did not commit. This context has led scholar Giovanni Batz to describe megaprojects in Guatemala as "the 'new invasion' with three previous invasions consist[ing] of Spanish Colonization, the creation of plantations at the end of the 19th century and early 20th century, and the thirty-six-year civil war (1960–1996)."[41]

For the performance, Monterroso purchased fifty-three *huipiles* from Alta Verepaz. Drawing on the Maya importance of weaving textiles as a form of resistance to centuries of colonization and visual extractivism through the theft of Indigenous knowledge and cultural productions, Monterroso color-dyed the textiles with indigo blue, a ritual rooted in Maya customs, to represent the color of the sacred river. She then sewed them together as one, resulting in a mosaic of blue *huipiles*. The new large *huipil* hung from the ceiling of the Ex Teresa and cascaded downward like a waterfall toward Monterroso, who lay on the floor. The artist associated this singular huipil with the healing powers and feminine energy of the goddess Ixchel (goddess of the moon, love, medicine, and textiles). It functioned as a healing cloth over the wounded river represented by the artist's body. As the large *huipil* cascaded over her body, she evoked a prayer for the healing of the river spirit. Drawing on feminine energies of her ancestors, the weaver women who produced the textiles, and the goddess Ixchel, Monterroso connects the Indigenous female body with sacred water, sacred textiles, and healing spirituality as a counter to the extractivist violence perpetrated against Indigenous territories and people.

When placed in dialogue, these performances correlate the rape of the body and the rape of the land under colonial practice. The attacks on women's reproduction, through violent eliminationist practices, and the related attacks on the land through violent extractivist policies are rooted in colonial attempts to end the continuation of a people in order to claim their lands. The attack of water and land defenders in Central America is also a feminist concern, for the violation of land is rooted in the same violation of women's bodies since the moment of conquest.

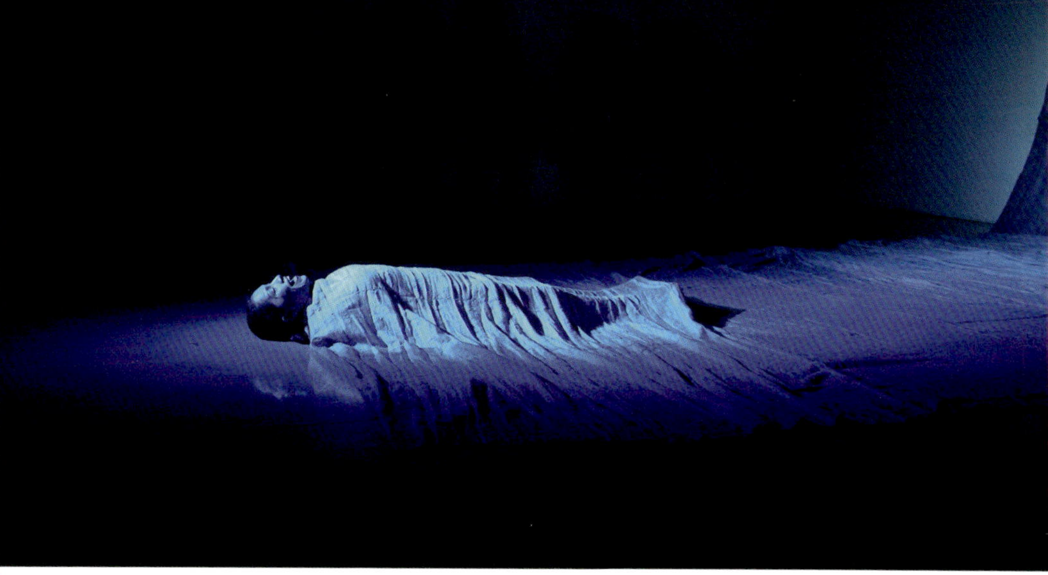

FIGURE 2.14.
Sandra Monterroso, *El agua se volvió oro, el rio se volvió oro, el oro se volvió azul*, 2019, performance. Courtesy of the artist.

CONFRONTING ANTI-BLACKNESS AND COLONIAL BEAUTY STANDARDS

Critiquing colonial standards of beauty was practically an untouched topic in art before and during the years of conflict, when the main concern was related to representing a type: revolutionary woman, campesina, victim, martyr, and so on. In the postwar context, especially with the emergence of performance art, wherein the artist's own body became the canvas, artists began to address the Western standards of beauty imposed on women in the Global South as feminist concerns. This allowed for an exploration of the violent psychological and corporal consequences for women in a patriarchal society through anti-Black racism and relatedly through body shaming, resulting in body dysmorphia and often dangerous body modification. Instead of viewing these concerns as unrelated to the brutality of the state or as outside the rise of gender-based violence in a postwar context, artists began to link unreachable beauty standards rooted in colonial notions of beauty to imperial nations and the intricacies of capitalist consumption, patriarchy, and white supremacy. The focus on the body in performance art specifically allowed for self-referential experiences and an exploration of the violence women endure due to the colonial and Western canons of beauty upheld in a misogynist society.

Belizean artist Katie Numi Usher has consistently addressed body shaming and the anti-Blackness embedded in Latin American and Western beauty standards though her art. For her performance *#GRUB* (2017), which took place at the Image Factory in Belize, Usher invited people who have personally shamed her in person and via social media platforms, like Facebook, to a fancy social dinner (see figure 2.15). A dining table was decorated in a white lace tablecloth, and the artist wore a formal Sunday church hat. The plates, however, lacked food, and once inspected closely depicted close-up shots of the artist stuffing food in her face. Usher then proceeded to eat a meal in front of the audience as she offered a confessional monologue recounting her relation to food and the earliest memories of body shaming, recalling that "over" and "weight" were the first words she remembers from her pediatrician. She narrates the various forms of invisibility she experienced due to her body weight as an invisible subject of sexual desire and simultaneously as a visible target of anti-Black aggression. Both by sharing a personal narrative and doing so while eating and seemingly enjoying a meal, Usher confronts her body shamers with an unapologetic enjoyment of food and with personal insights into her own journey that culminate in self-acceptance.

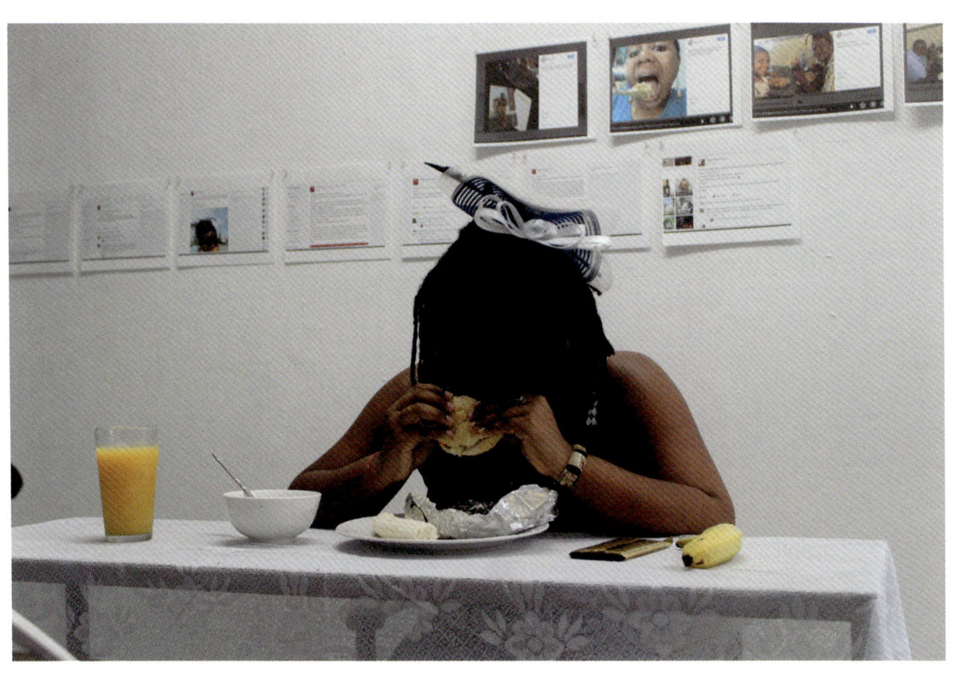

FIGURE 2.15.
Katie Numi Usher, *#GRUB*, 2017, performance. Photograph by Briheda Haylock and Yasser Musa. Image courtesy of the artist.

Along with Black feminist scholars and writers like Audre Lorde, Sylvia Wynter, and Lorgia García-Peña, activists and journalists have also long exposed issues of identity, race, and colonial legacies for Afro–Latin American and Afro-Latinx women. For instance, Dash Harris, who is Black Panamanian, and Janel Martinez, born to Black Garifuna Honduran parents and raised in the Bronx, are two Afro–Central Americans who use media and digital platforms to expose the myth of mestizaje as a white supremacist project that perpetuates invisibility and oppression of Afro-descendants in Latin America and Afro-Latinx people in the United States. Among their projects are Harris's docuseries, *Negro: A Docu-Series about Latinx Identity* (2010), and Martinez's "Ain't I Latina?" (2013), a digital space for content about Afro-Latinas.

Usher, also conscious of racist logics of mestizaje, and the exoticization and oversexualization of the Black female body, places her own experience as one deeply rooted in the colonial history of the enslavement of Black women. She began exploring the white colonial and white supremacist roots that link body shaming and anti-Blackness in Latin America. This became even more pronounced when she moved to Mérida, Mexico, where anti-Black racism intersected with classist perceptions of Black bodies. For her performance series Facing the Music (2008), Usher wore white T-shirts with common Mexican sayings, such as "un frijol en el arroz" (a bean in the rice), that exposed anti-Black sentiments in Mexico and Latin America. She then intervened in public spaces connected to colonial power, such as the Cathedral, City Hall, and the Casa de Montejo, a colonial house that belonged to the Spanish colonizers of the Yucatán Peninsula. Usher confronted structures of colonial power that existed because of enslaved forced labor of Black and Indigenous peoples.

One of the performances in this series, *Trabajas como negra para vivir como güera* (You work like a Black woman to live like a white woman) (2008), stems from the racist sayings throughout Mexico that uphold racial hierarchies by associating and reducing Black people to laboring bodies, while exalting whiteness to leisure and privilege (see figure 2.16). As Usher strolled through public spaces wearing a white T-shirt with the phrase on the front, viewers were confronted with an oppositional message on the back of her shirt: "Still you can't thot walk like me." Usher referenced a popular term and song of the time in rap and hip-hop music. "Thot" emerged as a derogatory word for promiscuous racialized poor women, which Usher reclaimed as sexual empowerment. She confronts her viewers with the hypocrisy of Western society that perpetuates anti-Blackness yet still desires to consume and appropriate Black culture.

In *Trabajas como negra para vivir como güera*, Usher further evokes two strategies of translating Blackness as theorized by Lorgia García-Peña.[42] With

FIGURE 2.16.
Katie Numi Usher, *Trabajas como negra para vivir como güera*, from Facing the Music series, 2008, performance. Image courtesy of the artist.

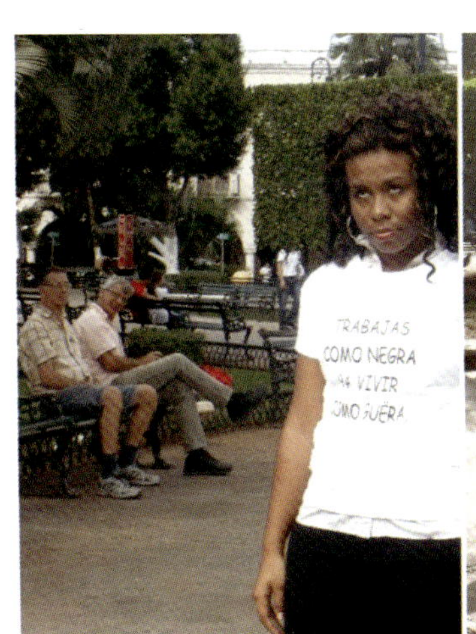

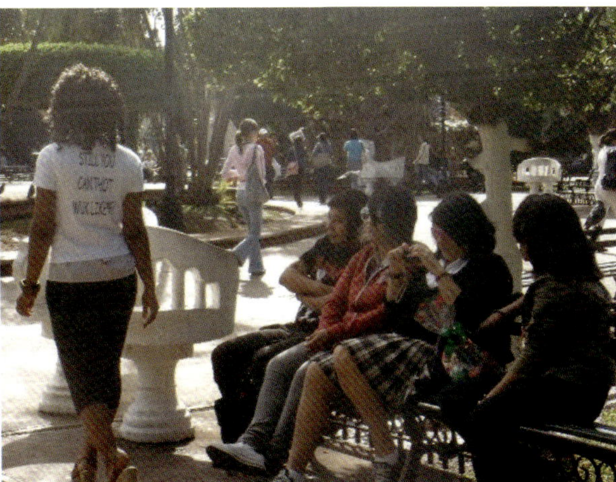

the "thot" reference, the artist engages hegemonic Blackness to become visible to the world through belonging and solidarity as a Black person, but as a Garifuna-Creole Belizean woman in Mexico, the "trabajas como negra" speaks to the localized experience of Black Central Americans within the Latin American context of anti-Blackness. Thus, her performance reveals what García-Peña calls the contra*diction* of Black Latinidad when race intersects with citizenship, migration, and nation.[43] As García-Peña reminds us, "translating blackness is only the first step, to be seen as a Global South person in the world requires the audience to reach beyond the universalizing hegemonic symbol and ask questions about the specifics. To translate blackness can lead to contest exclusion and demand Black belonging, protection, and rights within the nation."[44] In this manner, Ushers contests the broad consumption and appropriation of Black culture but further reveals the intricacies of being Black, Creole Garifuna, woman, noncitizen, and artist.

Like Usher in Belize, Panamanian artist Maria Raquel Cochez creates paintings, videos, installations, and performance art with autoreferential and biographical accounts of her personal experience with eating disorders, self-esteem, and body dysmorphia. A recent study on the relation between beauty standards and the rise of anorexia in Panama City found that for the majority of young women the ideal beauty type is a thin woman with blue eyes, blonde hair, Mediterranean skin color, and a height of five foot nine—characteristics that do not represent the physical appearance of women in Panama and instead exalt Western ideals of whiteness.[45] The authors trace a direct correlation between the pressures for women to conform to these ideals and the rise of anorexia. They note these pressures are experienced in a series of spaces—including the family, school, and platonic friendships—imposed by intimate partners and relationships, and accompanied by a psychological rejection of the self. They argue young women who endure these pressures are victims of symbolic violence.[46] Cochez offers a personal journey of such violence. In her early work with canvas paintings, Cochez presented isolated moments depicting the artist binge eating and addressing her complex relationship with food. As her medium changed, her work became more intimate, referencing medical procedures to modify her body that culminated in a three-part, nonchronological performance series.

In *Live Performance No. 1*, *Live Performance No. 2*, and *Live Performance No. 3* (2006–9), Cochez relinquished all control over to the camera and invited the viewer into a personal and emotional journey that included body modification surgery (see figure 2.17). The video performances documented specific surgeries the artist underwent, including gastric lap band removal surgery after complications from one hundred pounds of weight loss, breast reconstruction and silicone implant surgery after feeling ashamed over her breasts, and gastric bypass surgery. The documentation includes scenes of the artist being prepped for the surgery, the surgeons' hands penetrating her open body, the medical instruments before and during the surgery, and her unconscious, recovering postsurgery body. As Cochez states, her work investigates the "psychology behind the forming of beauty ideals in childhood, the cultural differences in beauty canons and their subjectivity, the self-harm involved in distorted conceptions of the body, the sexual dynamic surrounding bodies not currently celebrated in the media, and the impact that distorted relationships with food can have on all of these premises."[47] The artist also exposes and resists the secrecy in which this usually happens. Cochez challenges the traditional canons of beauty that have long been the subject of Western art and instead exposes the cost of that canon on women's minds, spirits, and bodies as violence from which beauty industries profit.

The extremes of secrecy and plastic surgery are the subject of another performance by Regina José Galindo, in which she relates underground plastic surgery to the whore/virgin dichotomy that is especially dominant in Latin America, imposed through colonialism and upheld through Christianity. In the video performance *Himenoplastia* (2004), the artist undergoes a clandestine but popular operation in which doctors surgically reconstruct her hymen (see figure 2.18). The performance was later exhibited in video form at the 2005 Venice Biennial, where she was awarded the Golden Lion award in the category "Artist under 30." Galindo conceived the idea for the performance after watching a television commercial advertising the surgical procedure to restore a woman's virginity, an advertisement she had previously seen in paper format. The surgical procedures are often conducted in hidden environments with unsanitary tools, resulting in complications that can lead to death. Galindo herself experienced uncontrolled bleeding after her surgery/performance and had to be taken to her gynecologist, who then checked her into a hospital for a medical emergency.

Like a cosmetic product or gym membership, hymen reconstruction surgeries are sold to Guatemalan women via print and television media with the argument that restoring their virginity will better increase their chance of marriage and bring about higher social status. Yet sex traffickers who abduct and sexually abuse young girls also use this surgery so they can charge higher prices for "virgin girls." While Galindo was fortunate to receive appropriate medical attention, countless women and young girls suffer grave consequences, including death, after their operations. Galindo subjects her own body to the surgery to show how the gendered colonial system pushes women to extreme surgeries

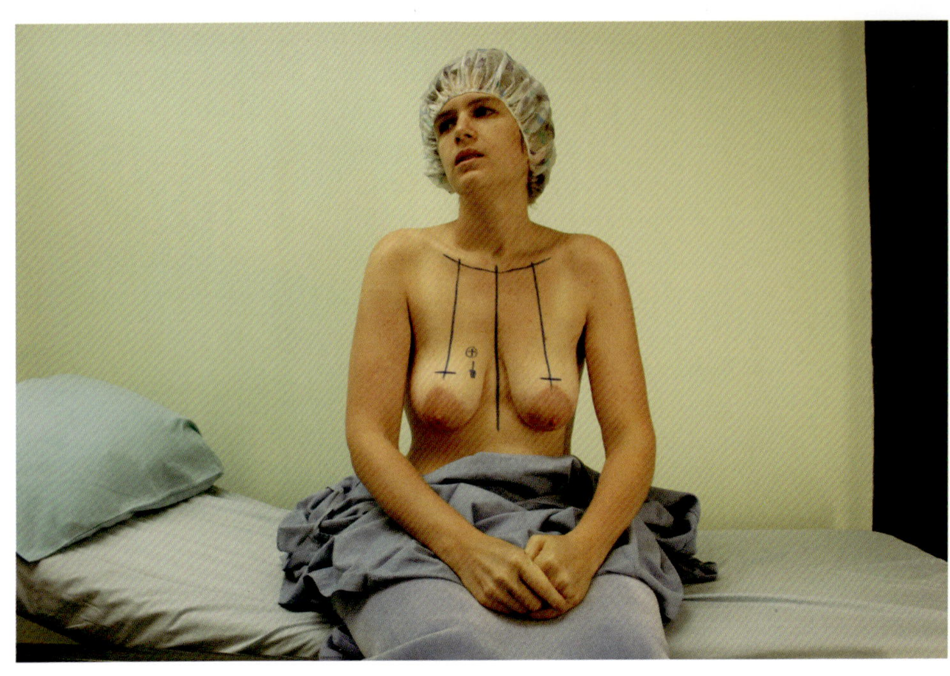

FIGURE 2.17.
Maria Raquel Cochez, *Live Performance No. 3*, 2009, performance. Courtesy of the artist.

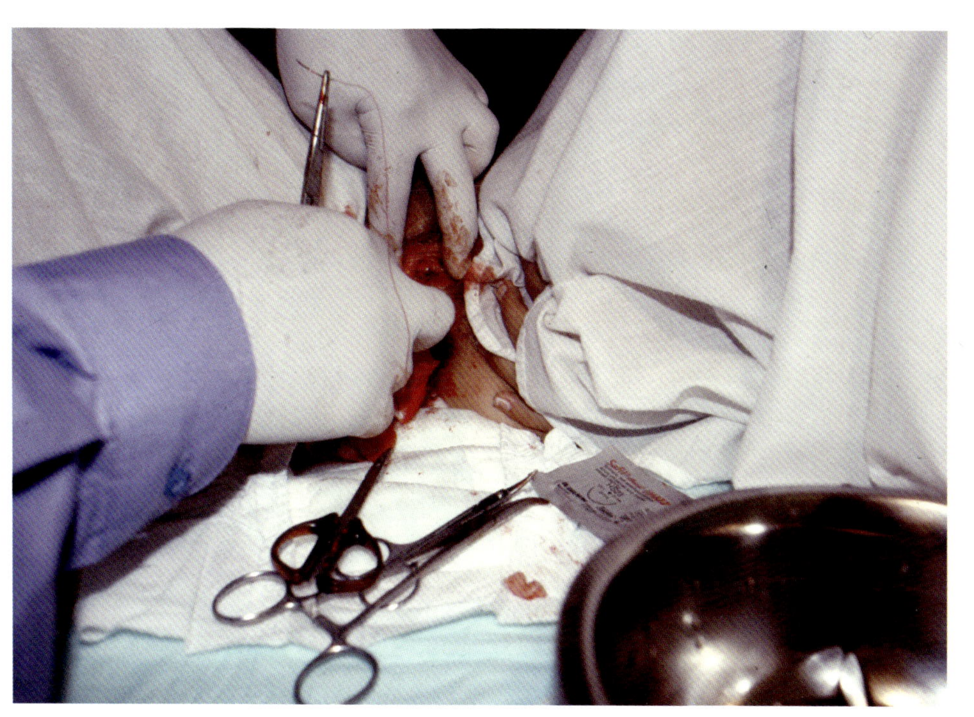

FIGURE 2.18.
Regina José Galindo, *Himenoplastia*, 2004, performance. Courtesy of the artist.

that endanger their lives to encourage sexuality for the service of men in a patriarchal system, while simultaneously punishing women for ideas of promiscuity as in *Perra*. In both cases, sexual pleasure and desire do not belong to, nor are they for, women but rather exist only for men.

Artists like Usher, Cochez, and Galindo are contesting the normalcy of Western beauty standards and exposing their roots in patriarchy, colonialism, and white supremacy. They collectively bring forth the ways colonial notions of beauty, bodies, and desire are also embedded and espoused through visual coloniality. Though their critiques extend beyond the state and toward a colonization of beauty and aesthetics and anti-Black racism, they reveal how these systems function collaboratively in a patriarchal nation-state to perpetuate psychological violence against women, which benefits capitalist-driven beauty industries in the service of white supremacy.

EROTIC AUTONOMY AGAINST THE NATION

In a culture of silence against human rights violations, amplified through cis-heteronormative attitudes and policies, proclaiming erotic autonomy and exposing the colonial roots of misogyny and heteropatriarchy amounts to visual disobedience against the nation-state. Afro-Caribbean scholar and activist M. Jacqui Alexander has noted in her work on the Bahamas that in the state's conflation of heterosexuality with citizenship, erotic autonomy is perceived as a threat and corruption to the nation. She explains that "because loyalty to the nation as citizen is perennially colonized within reproduction and heterosexuality, erotic autonomy brings with it the potential of undoing the nation entirely."[48] Consequently, the nation creates nonreproductive noncitizens who according to its views and laws violate the codes of morality, decency, and loyalty to the nation by "choice." These noncitizens are thus presented as threats not only to the nation but to the hetero-nuclear family, and are thus criminalized and subject to surveillance, policing, and punishment. Such colonial and heteropatriarchal views on sexual and gender identity in Central America facilitate high levels of violence against LGBTQ people, which contributes to the large number of LGBTQ asylum seekers at the US-Mexico border.

In response, artists from across Central America and its diaspora—including US-based Nicaraguan Patricia Villalobos, Canadian Guatemalan Naufus Ramírez-Figueroa, Costa Rican Roberto Guerrero, Salvadoran artist Nadia, and US Guatemalan Alex Donis, among others—are challenging the coloniality of gender and sexuality in the region and thus redefining feminist politics in postwar Central America. US-based Guatemalan artist Martin Wannam and Nicaraguan artist Elyla (Fredman Barahona) especially engage in erotic autonomy in their visual disobedience that aims to undo the nation. In his performance *Hueco* (2019), Martin Wannam walked with a radio in hand to the center of the Plaza Mayor de la Constitución in Guatemala City (see figure 2.19). He played the national hymn at full volume and stood in allegiance with his right hand over his heart while facing the National Palace and the Metropolitan Cathedral. After a few minutes, Wannam removed his white shirt and a male figure approached him from behind with a knife. He began to carve incisions over Wannam's left shoulder until blood emerged and the word "Hueco" became visible on the flesh. After the hymn concluded, Wannam put his shirt back on and walked away.

In dialogue with Galindo's performance *Perra*, described at the introduction of this chapter, Wannam's performance connects the violence done onto LGBTQ people in Central America with the similarly violent and misogynist practice in femicide of carving the motive for a murder onto the victim's body. The literal translation of *hueco* is "hole" or "gap," but in Guatemala it is used derogatorily against effeminate gay men to imply a vaginal cavity, and it has been found carved on the bodies of victims of hate crimes. Such was the case of eighteen-year-old LGBTQ activist José Roberto Díaz, whose lifeless body was found tortured with the word *hueco*, and other homophobic slurs, cut into his abdomen. But for Wannam, whose performance takes place in a public setting, the action is both a confrontation of the state's complicity in propagating deaths of LGBTQ people and an appropriation of the word as a gesture of indignation and pride.

Wannam rehabilitates images and words associated with *cuir* shaming, nonbelonging, expulsion, and clandestine killings to rebrand them as acts of agency, empowerment, and self-love. His performance demonstrates an act of "disidentification," which José Esteban Muñoz theorizes as a "survival strategy" by people whose identity is formed in response to cultural logics that sustain state power, such as heteronormativity, white supremacy, and misogyny.[49] Queer and racialized people must negotiate their existence in a world where the majority attempts to erase, punish, and eliminate those who do not fit or conform to normative citizenship. Through disidentification, minority subjects do not fully identify with or reject dominant ideology. Rather, they "work on and against it," inverting and subverting its cultural codes as they aim to "transform a cultural logic from within" with their insertion.[50] Through *Hueco*, Wannam enacts a survival strategy that exposes national culpability in facilitating violence and impunity but more importantly takes a visual code—a term associated with penetrability and state-sanctioned hate and violence—and recodes it with his own corporal agency.

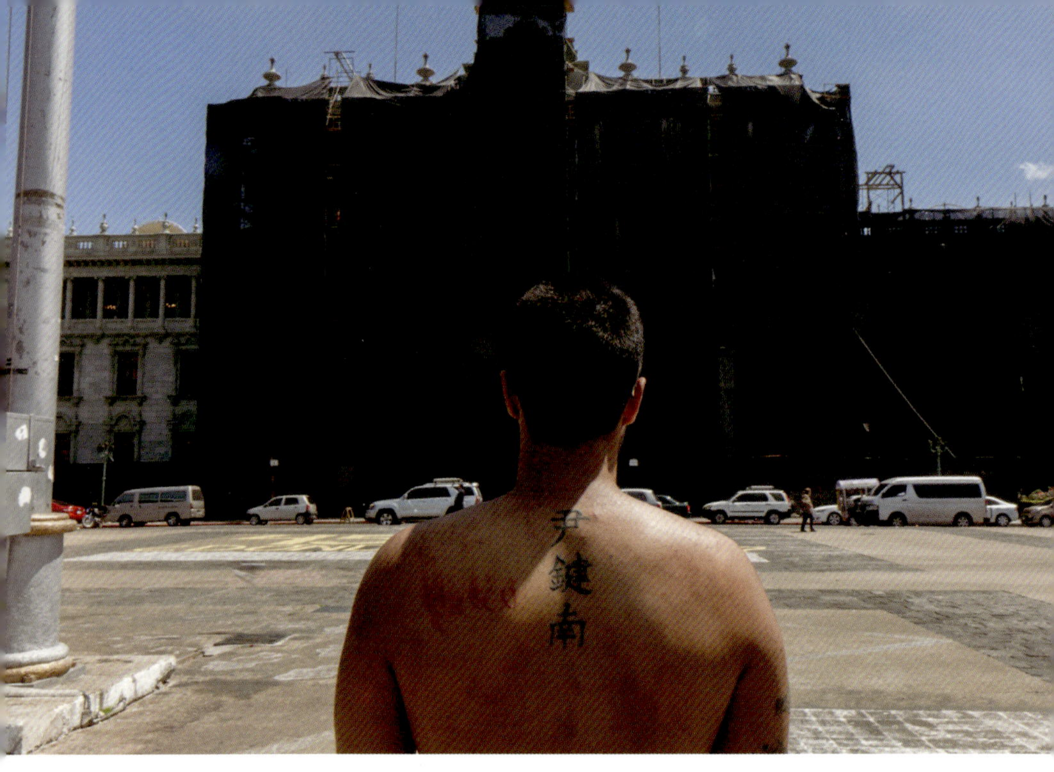

FIGURE 2.19.
Martin Wannam, *Hueco*, 2019, performance. Courtesy of the artist.

This visual disobedience further echoes what Xhercis Méndez and Yomaira C. Figueroa condemn within decolonial discourse as the equating of femininity with penetrability and dehumanization as a violence of enslavement and colonialism done to men of color. As they explain, "Dehumanization here is (over)coded as the 'humiliating' possibility of being penetrated, a condition that has been 'naturalized' as permanently attached to female bodies. Indeed, it is the 'naturalized' penetrability of female bodies that supposedly makes our bodies more susceptible to rape."[51] They thus warn against the implication that men, or human men, should be "impenetrable" since it negates the possibilities for nonnormative sexualities, gender nonconforming people, and counters the "making of new humanity," a key project of decoloniality.[52] Wannam counters and reverses the stigma of penetrability of men as feminine and less than human by appropriating the word *hueco* as a symbol of pride, resistance, and existence.

Wannam's oeuvre brings attention to the normalcy of violent crimes against LGBTQ people in Central America, where, according to a 2020 Human Rights Watch report, LGBTQ people are especially vulnerable in the Northern Triangle.[53] Honduras, for example, has the highest rate of murders of transgender people in the world.[54] Historian and activist Suyapa G. Portillo Villeda has noted the correlation between the Barack Obama administration's support of the 2009 Honduran coup d'état and a rise in crimes against LGBTQ people in Honduras.[55] While not popularized yet in Central America, in some countries, such as Mexico and Argentina, the word *transfemicide* is increasingly used to describe the rampant killing of transgendered people because their gender identity or expression differs from what they were assigned at birth. Trans and gender nonconforming Central Americans are especially vulnerable in the region when they are unable to assimilate into heteronormativity and are thus targets of attacks. Aggression, discrimination, and violence occur in a multiplicity of social spaces, including domestic life, education, and employment.

Impunity for such crimes is high in Central America because LGBTQ people are often unable to report violence to police either because they are dismissed due to their gender and sexual expression or because the state and police authorities are the perpetrators. Loopholes or direct homophobic and transphobic clauses in laws often place LGBTQ people in danger and exclude them from protection. El Salvador, Guatemala, and Honduras do not allow transgender people to change their names on identification cards, making them vulnerable when they must present themselves. In Guatemala, officials claim trans women are not protected under femicide laws because they do not consider them "biological women."[56] Substantial testimonies attest to the authorities' homophobic and transphobic responses that validate the attacks as necessary or question the victim's humanity altogether.[57] A case that received international attention was that of Salvadoran Camila "Aurora" Díaz Córdova, who was deported by Immigration and Customs Enforcement (ICE) in 2019 despite seeking asylum in the United States due to transphobic attacks. Just a year after her deportation back to El Salvador, Díaz Córdova was picked up by three police officers, assaulted in the car, and thrown out of the moving vehicle. She died from her injuries. The conviction of the police officers a year later marked the first conviction for homicide of a transgendered person in El Salvador's history, though the state still failed to acknowledge the murder as a hate crime.

In response to Central American nations' complicity and a deliberate lack of accountability, Wannam initiated the series THEY (2018–19), for which he researched and collected data on violent attacks against and deaths of LGBTQ people in Central America and the Caribbean. The title of each of the large-scale photographs he produced consists of a victim's name along with the location and date of when and where the body was found, inserted below the photographs as the only reference to the crime. For Wannam, it is imperative to acknowledge the murders are hate crimes while highlighting the sexual dissidence of the victim as celebrated and loved.

The photograph titled *Paulina Marrot, zona 1 Centro, 15 de febrero del 2006, Guatemala* focuses on Paulina, who after a night of dancing was shot to death by strangers in a car. Soon after, Sulma Alegrai Robles, a trans woman, LGBTQ activist, and the main witness to the shooting, was beaten and tortured and killed in her own home. Wannam displays four handguns as a reference to the shooting but engulfs them in black and silver glitter against a colorful background of cartoon unicorns. In another example, *Daniela Pacheco, Hospital General, 1 de noviembre del 2012, Guatemala*, the artist references Daniela, a trans woman who was found dead with a fractured cranium and her body restrained (see figure 2.20). In the photograph, a shirtless gender-nonconforming body holds their hands in a gesture of prayer. Their white acrylic nails come to a point and their fingers and palms are wrapped and tied with red string. And in *Jorge Steven López, Barrio Guavete, 13 de noviembre del 2009, Puerto Rico*, Wannam honors the memory of Jorge, whose teen body was found decapitated, dismembered, and partially burned. A nude and burned male doll is crucified against a celestial background of white clouds and a blue sky, and a halo crowns his head.

In the majority of these cases, authorities refuse to acknowledge homophobia and transphobia as motives in the killings. Wannam incorporates enough visual and textual references to distinguish the murders as hate crimes, while an abundance of bright colors, glitter, and imagery summon a queer aesthetic in honor of the victims' sexual and gender identities. This aesthetic aims to minimize the sensationalization of violence done to the victims by offering an honoring and celebration of the victims' ways of being and loving in this world. For Wannam, queer existence will continue to prevail over death and open possibilities for other ways of being.

In the Central American context, heteropatriarchy is a tool of coloniality used by the state to facilitate the elimination of those outside colonial categories of gender and sexuality. Wannam's exposure and reference to the systemic violence that LGBTQ Central Americans endure is a visual disobedience to the nation-state that is eager to expunge sexual dissidents from its national narratives and sanctions their physical elimination. The consequences are explicitly seen at the US-Mexico border, where between January 2007 and November 2017 at least 2,253 LGBTQ migrants sought asylum in the United States. More than half were from the Northern Triangle.[58] On August 10, 2017, the first LGBTQ caravan of migrants known as "Caravana Trans Gay" arrived in Nogales, Mexico, at the Arizona-Mexico border to seek asylum in the United States. All were Central American, and many similar caravans followed. Wannam's visual disobedience explicitly addresses a broader context of expulsion and forced displacement that is violently correlated to border imperialism.

COCHÓN-ING EL NUEVO HOMBRE

Nicaraguan artist Fredman Barahona, better known as Elyla, a fusion of *El-y-la* that translates to "he and she" (pronouns are they/them), began doing actions that consisted of dressing and undressing in gender nonconforming clothing at street intersections. Influenced by their theater and activist background, these early actions were a way for the artist to work through and understand their own gender identity and sexual expression. Yet, after attending the Central American art school EspIRA/ESPORA from 2011 to 2013, peers identified and encouraged Elyla's interventions as performance art, which the artist embraced. Soon after, in 2014 Elyla was invited to participate with an inaugural piece for the XI Biennial of Nicaragua. The artist proposed a performance titled *Solo Fantasía* (Just fantasy) that would entail Elyla walking in procession through the historic Avenida Bolívar in high heels and an elaborate dress that incorporated inverted symbols of the nation as a critique of the aesthetics the Daniel Ortega–Rosario Murillo government imposed on the public spaces of Nicaragua. However, only four hours before the scheduled performance, Elyla was notified that the vice president and first lady, Rosario Murillo, had ordered the halt of the performance and the expulsion of the artist from the biennial. The artist, however, proceeded with the banned action, which became a catalyst for

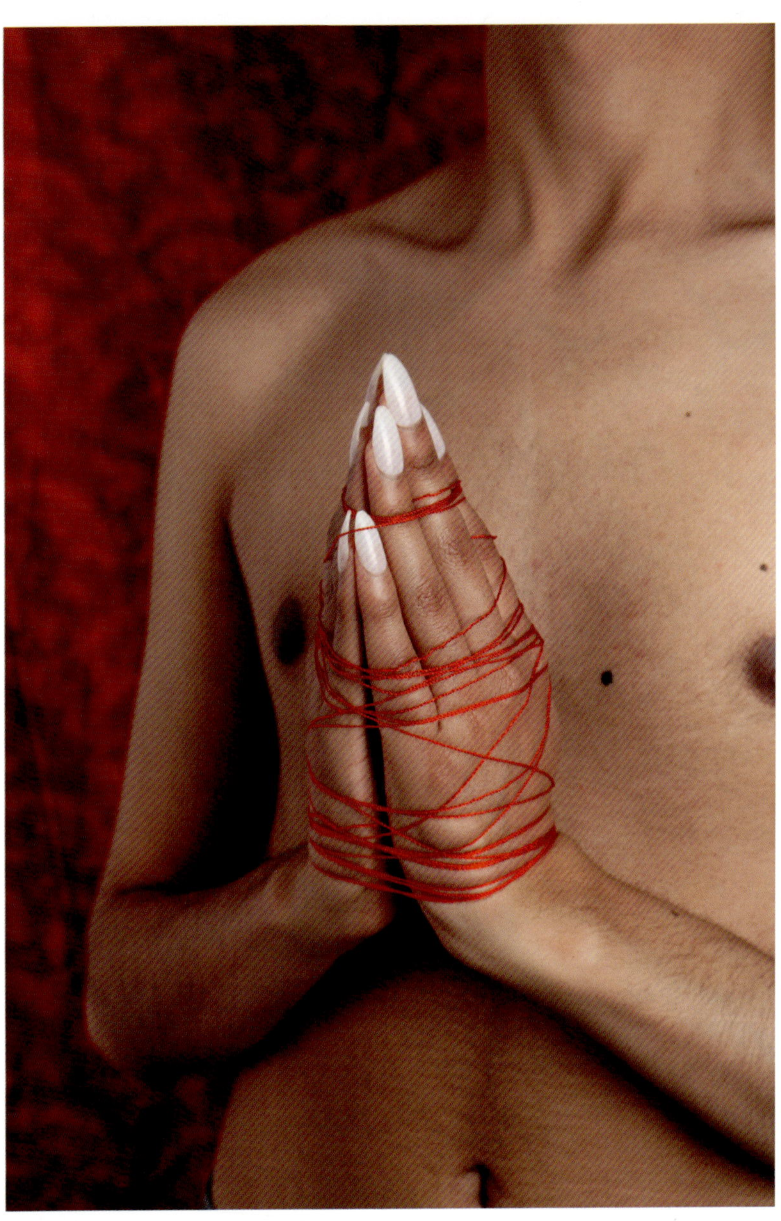

FIGURE 2.20.
Martin Wannam, *Daniela Pacheco, hospital general, 1 de noviembre del 2012, Guatemala*, from THEY series, 2018–19, photograph. Courtesy of the artist.

a series of performances that disrupt and disobey the heteronormative narratives of Nicaragua as a revolutionary nation-state.

Elyla identifies as both a *cochón*, which in Central America refers to an effeminate or homosexual man, and a *transvesti*, which the artist frames as a decolonial embodiment of sexual and gender dissidence that dismantles heteronormativity and its patriarchal and colonial logics. Through *transvestimo* Elyla explicitly exalts *lo cuir* in Sandinismo as an insubordination to the myth of "el nuevo hombre" (the new man). Originally proposed by leftist revolutionaries such as José Martí and Ernesto "Che" Guevara, the idea of el nuevo hombre was upheld by the Sandinista Revolution and political party. Yet for Elyla and others, the idea of el nuevo hombre is rooted in patriarchal ideas that discount women and sexual dissidents.[59]

In *Somos una patria* (We are a homeland) (2014), the artist produces a self-portrait of themself accompanied by two national heroes: poet Rubén Darío in blue to the left, and revolutionary Augusto Sandino to the right (see figure 2.21). Wearing a full beard and a see-through red dress, Elyla leans over Darío's legs, with an arm resting over Sandino's right knee, conveying the intimacy of a familial portrait. All figures pose and stare directly into the camera, and the brown sheet erected as a backdrop alludes to a carefully choreographed studio portrait. Yet, with their presence, Elyla disrupts the heteronormative idea of the nuclear family perpetuated by the Ortega campaign for Nicaraguan identity formation, which claims all in the nation to be "sons" of Dario and Sandino. The implication is that all sons will eventually be fathers of the nation, thus upholding the heteropatriarchal designs of the nation-state, a normalcy Elyla subverts with their gender-nonconforming body and presence.

Having grown up in a Sandinista family, Elyla does not here criticize the legacy of Sandino and revolutionary goals of a liberated society but rather asserts that there is no true liberation if patriarchy and heteronormativity remain pillars of the nation. Equating national loyalty and the descendants of revolutionary greatness with a male heir reproduces a heteronormative masculinity that excludes women, gender-nonconforming people, and trans people from the myth of a revolutionary Nicaragua, despite their crucial involvement in the revolution. Many feminists attribute their political activism to their participation in the Sandinista Revolution even though organizing around gay and lesbian rights in the 1980s was not favored and met with hostility.[60] Sexual dissidence did not fit within the idea of the left nuevo hombre then, and it remained so decades later with homophobic and transphobic law and policies.[61]

While there have been recent moves toward LGBTQ rights and visibility in Nicaragua, political scientist Karen Kampwirth views these advancements as

FIGURE 2.21.
Elyla (Fredman Barahona), *Somos una patria*, 2014, photograph. Courtesy of the artist.

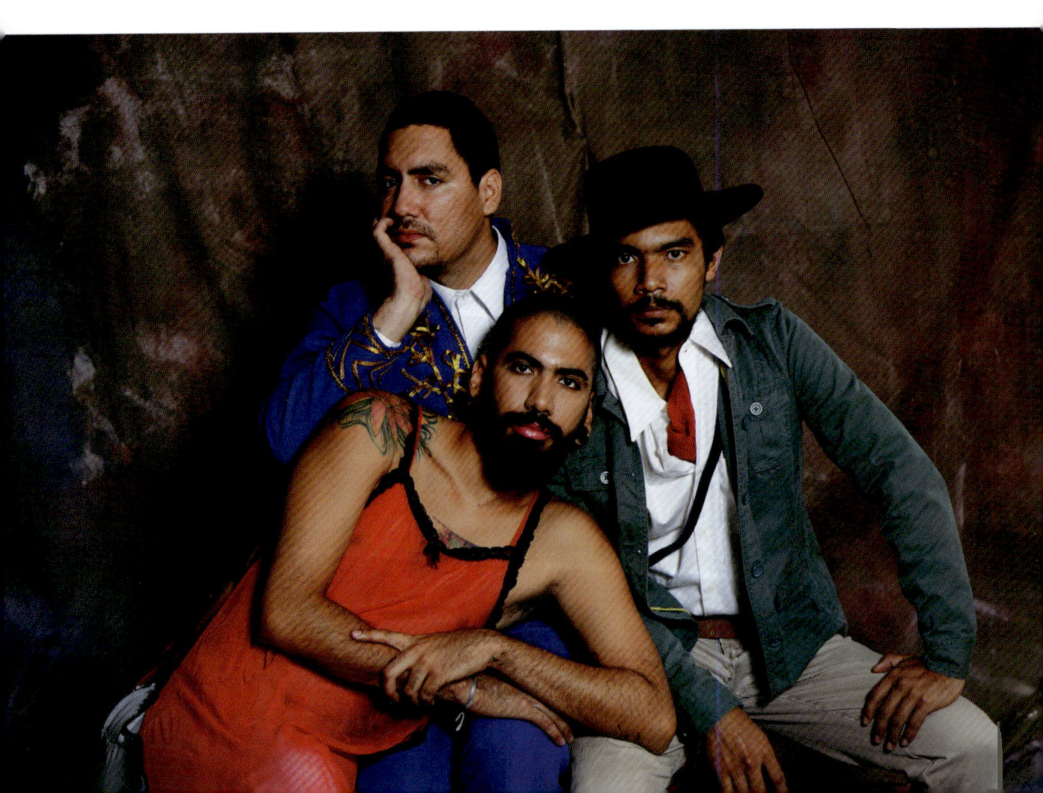

the co-optation by the Frente Sandinista de Liberación Nacional (FSLN; Sandinista National Liberation Front) of sexual diversity politics originally proposed and fought for by feminist groups and activists between 1980 and 2007. McGee and Kampwirth describe the co-optation as a strategy to weaken the power of feminist organizations and as a form of pinkwashing.[62] Macarena Gómez-Barris further addresses the recent wave of progressive governments throughout Latin America that use the language of decolonization to mobilize, only later to repeat the same oppressive and authoritarian practices they initially aimed to eliminate.[63] In this context, and applicable to Nicaragua, creative resistance in all its forms, particularly from Indigenous, Afro, and queer feminists, offers ways to move "beyond the pink tide," as Gómez-Barris suggests, and toward alternative decolonial futurities. With a long history of activism, including as cofounder of the activist organization Operación Queer, Elyla is familiar with the erasure of sexual dissidents and *cuir* bodies within political organizations and has thus turned to performative interventions as a way to undo the patriarchal idea of the nation and posit queer futurities for Nicaragua.

Four years after Elyla's banned performance, Nicaragua experienced the deadliest manifestations since the end of the civil war when the FSLN, led by Daniel Ortega, triumphed over the Anastasio Somoza Debayle dictatorship. Since 2007, Ortega has remained president of Nicaragua, and in 2016 he consolidated his power by making the first lady, Rosario Murillo, his vice president. What began as discontent in response to Ortega's proposed social security reforms in 2018 escalated to broader protests against the Ortega government, its hold on power, and its plans to build an interoceanic canal that would displace Afro and Indigenous communities. As demonstrations increased in size and numbers, the Ortega government responded by cracking down on protesters with beatings and incarceration, resulting in 325 deaths and more than 500 detained, ironically simulating the Somoza dictatorship he helped topple decades earlier. During the manifestations, first lady and vice president Murillo taunted protesters by comparing them to tiny little ants eager to accuse her of any crime. It was a reference to a poem she previously wrote titled "Tengo miedo de tanta realidad," which expressed her fear of rodents, and in particular ants, which she described as tiny beings with small thoughts, agendas, and consciousness. When she publicly compared them to ants, protestors countered her analogy by adopting the ant as a symbol of resistance and collective dissidence.

According to Elyla, who was among the protestors, there was a realization that the struggle would be for the long haul.[64] Understanding the futility in seeking recognition within the nation-state, Elyla began a series of performances in public spaces that explicitly conveyed disdain for both the patriarchy of the revolution and the neoliberal politics of the Ortega/Murillo government, both of which invisibilize a queer existence. That same year, Elyla initiated a two-part performance titled *Yo (no) tengo miedo de tanta realidad* (I am [not] afraid of so much reality) (2018–19) in San Francisco, California, where the artist resided after leaving Nicaragua due to death threats (see figure 2.22). The second part was performed the following year in Mexico City. In both performances, the artist walked in procession to the Nicaraguan embassies, where they released three hundred ants at the embassy doorsteps. Simultaneously, the artist recited the names of students, activists, and campesinos killed during protests. In the first performance, Elyla wore a black corset, high heels, and other items that exposed a body fully covered in red. In the second, a similar outfit and wig in blue revealed their body covered in white. In personifying each pair of colors, black/red adopted by the Sandinistas and blue/white adopted by Ortega's government, the artist critiques both political spectrums for the continuous erasure of queer existence. Meanwhile Elyla counters Murillo's metaphoric words with three hundred physical and real ants, which metonymically represent the nearly three hundred protestors killed by that time (students, sexual dissidents, and campesinos).

In these performances, Elyla's *cochón* body in *transvestismo* exists as a visual disobedience to the ocular signifiers of both political spectrums that, despite claims for liberation, remain rooted in heteropatriarchy, homophobia, transphobia, and a neoliberal agenda. With the visual image of a seminude red body in wig and heels, the artist further enacts a visual and corporal dissidence to the nation that places sexual deviants outside the purview of citizenship and rights. Elyla's *cochón* and *transvesti* body offers an antithesis to the nuevo hombre as a heteropatriarchal design for the nation-state; it is a body that exists despite the nation and is incomprehensible to the nation. This type of feminism is a far stretch from the images of women holding babies and rifles that came to represent feminist empowerment for the Sandinista Revolution. This type of feminist visual disobedience threatens to undo the nation.

While speaking to a specific Nicaraguan context, Elyla's performances also align with a hemispheric trend of recognizing and calling out the superficiality of visibility and recognition politics of LGBTQ rights as insufficient when the nation-state remains anchored in colonial categories of gender and sexuality. For instance, in the Chilean and Argentinian context, Joseph Pierce describes similar *cuir*, trans, and *transvesti* resistance as embodying the "monstrous." Pierce explains, "The travesti as monster becomes a method of corporeal dissidence that challenges the symbolic and political order as a parody of the social contract and a critique of the false promise of state-sanctioned protections

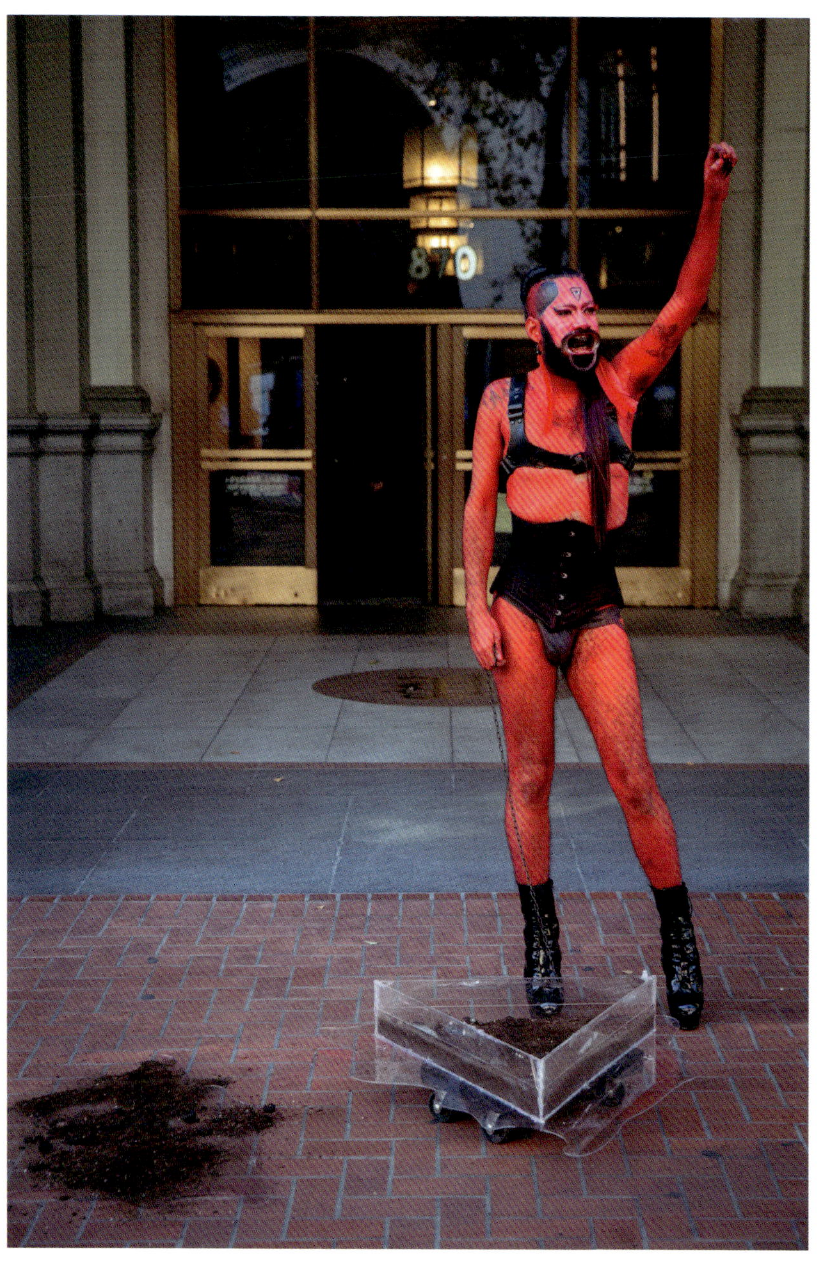

FIGURE 2.22.
Elyla (Fredman Barahona), *Yo (no) tengo miedo de tanta realidad*, 2018–19, performance. Courtesy of the artist.

for marginalized subjects."[65] Comparably, Gómez-Barris proposes "the sexual underground" as a uniquely Latin American space, "for political change that is organized by the logics of cuir sociality and trans embodiment," one incomprehensible to or absorbed by the nation-state.[66] We can view Elyla's visual disobedience to Nicaragua as part of this broader hemispheric move of *cuir*-ing dissidence across the Americas that does not seek absorption into the nation-state and that stems from a queer dissidence that "rejects the here and now" and asserts a world otherwise.[67]

COLLECTIVE DECOLONIAL FEMINISMS

The rise of performance art in postwar Central America gave way to experimentation with the body in ways that facilitate a critical inquiry into gender-based violence, its many manifestations, and its roots in the coloniality of gender. In this chapter I have addressed a few of the many issues artists are exposing, condemning, and challenging through their bodies, collaborations, and remaining images. These include feminicide and impunity, interpersonal violence, neoliberal and enduring colonial violence against women, rape of body and lands, anti-Indigenous and anti-Black racism, Western canons of beauty and body image, and homophobia and transphobia. Unlike the limited left-/right-wing framework of decades earlier, in which the liberation of Central American women relied on class-based models, these artists reveal that feminism in Central America today includes intersecting oppressions tied to anti-Indigenous and anti-Black racism, patriarchy, misogyny, and visual coloniality. They have thus expanded the parameters of a feminist aesthetics from decades earlier with a feminist visual disobedience centered on embodied agency that is both antipatriarchal and anticolonial.

These artists' visual disobedience should be considered as part of a broader redefining of feminist movements in Central America. Feminist mobilization across the region has led to a growing body of political collectives and organizations committed to the feminist concerns taken up by the artists discussed. For instance, Colectiva Feminista en El Salvador aims to dismantle toxic masculinity and oppression of women by working with youth, women, and men and organizing public interventions of dissent for sexual reproductive rights, an end to femicide, empowerment and economic autonomy for women, and feminist environmental justice. Based in Honduras, Red Lesbica Cattrachas is a feminist lesbian collective dedicated to investigating and disseminating information in defense of human rights for the LGBTQ community. Operación Queer, a collective based in Nicaragua made up of artists, activists, and academics, produces interdisciplinary and transfeminist projects to address an intersection of exclusions in the region, including based on gender, age, ableism, ethnicity, and economic status, among others. Mayan, Garifuna, and Mestiza trans women in Guatemala collectively organized Red Multicultural de Mujeres Trans de Guatemala (REDMMUTRANS) in response to the abuse Indigenous women endure, thus promoting empowerment and self-protection from gender and ethnic violence. These are just a few of many feminist activist organizations across the region that fight against the interlocking oppressions women and nonheteronormative people face.

This anticolonial, anti-imperialist, and antipatriarchal feminist dissidence in Central America is one completely erased in the US media and overshadowed by the images of women asylum seekers at the border that render them helpless victims or culpable for the violence they flee. Such reduction of Central American migrants who are framed as inherently violent and uncivilized, and thus a threat to the nation, is especially used against women refugees to deny them asylum in the United States. From an analysis of the feminist visual disobedience I address here, however, one sees a more comprehensive and critical context for the current realities of Central American women that have forced many to migrate. Yet the gender violence Central American women flee is not solely a Central American issue. Central American immigrant women and asylum seekers are deemed disposable, violable, and detainable on US soil precisely because there is already a long history of such practices in the United States. The United States' own impunity and disregard for the disappearance and murders of Native women, and its history of forced sterilization of women of color, reveal that feminicide and migration are interrelated issues across the hemisphere. The postwar feminism of Central American artists speaks to a broader system of coloniality that crosses borders; thus, Central American migration, as I discuss in the next chapter, is not just a Central American issue but requires a hemispheric and transnational disobedience of colonial borders.

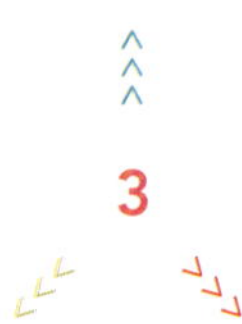

SHIFTING THE BORDER

Central American Art against the War on Mobility

In the first stage of an autopsy, a pathologist makes a *Y*-shaped incision on the deceased body that travels from the shoulders, to the sternum, over the abdomen, and down to the pubis. This *Y*-shaped map on the body allows access into the breastplate for removal of the body's main organs—heart, lungs, liver, stomach, and spleen. After the cause and time of death are determined, the organs are placed back into the body and the *Y* incision is sewn up, leaving visible marks on the corpse. For his performance *Líneas de referencia* (Reference lines) (2009), Salvadoran artist Mauricio Esquivel had the *Y*-shaped autopsy incision tattooed onto his body (see figure 3.1). With this marking he referenced both the foreseeable fate of most poor youth in Central America, where homicide

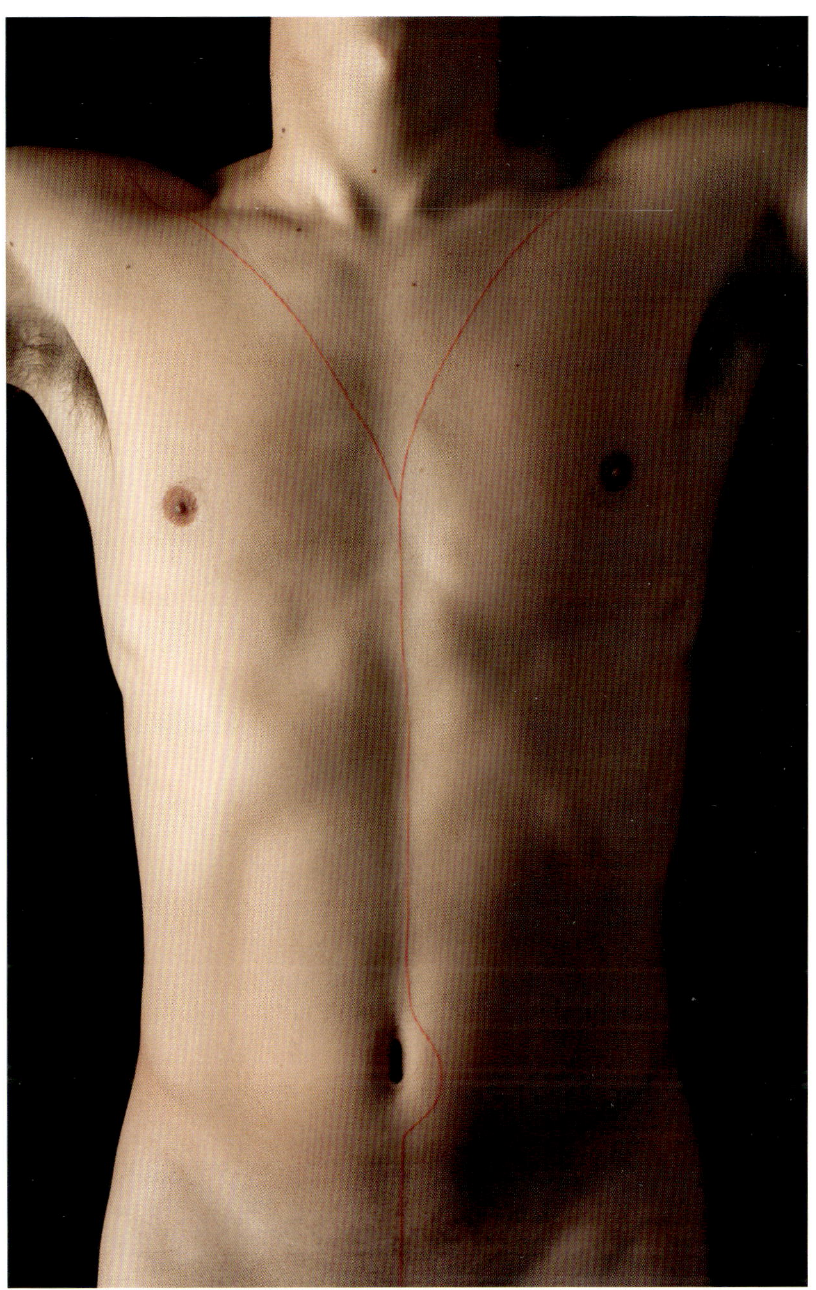

FIGURE 3.1.
Mauricio Esquivel, *Líneas de referencia*, 2009, performance. Courtesy of the artist.

rates are among the highest in the Western Hemisphere, and an anticipation of his own demise.

The permanent marking also evokes a wider context of imperial and colonial violence that propels the forced mass migration of Central Americans, including the migrant bodies returned to the region as corpses, those who return alive but maimed in the process, and those who never make it to their destinations and simply disappear. In colonization, incisions, known as borders, are similarly drawn onto land and violently enforced. They facilitate access to and extraction of the land's vital organs (oil, gold, silver, water, and people), while additional cuts (binaries such as safe/unsafe, civilized/uncivilized, and us/them) further ensure domination. Existing communities, cultures, and ecologies are disregarded, removed, or subjugated. Unlike the deceased body, in colonization the land is alive when it is gutted. Thus, with his performance Esquivel reminds us that dividing lines displace, violate, and colonize, metaphorically connecting migration, death, and colonial legacies to an existing border regime.

Whether physically, mentally, or metaphorically, the visual imaginary in Latin American or Latinx art around the border situates its geographical location at the nexus of the United States and Mexico, where, as Gloria Anzaldúa once poetically wrote, "the Third World grates against the first and bleeds."[1] That geopolitical line has since come to embody a geocorporal lesion, "una herida abierta," or a site-specific wound popularly evoked in various ways by artists and writers. For Robert D. Hernández, the "U-S///Mexico" border, beyond a nation-state framework, is a "geospatial manifestation of a long history of racialized and gendered colonial violence" rooted in coloniality, emphasizing the systemic historical violence that creates and maintains such a wound.[2] For Harsha Walia, this border results from a constellation of collaborative factors, driven by contemporary global capitalism, that together produce the current "border imperialism" we live under—displacement, migration, racialization, criminalization, and exploitation.[3]

Coloniality and settler violence, neoliberal policies, and global imperial authorities reveal that the border is neither static nor stationary but what some scholars and activists describe as "moving," "stretching," or "elastic." The outsourcing of border management tactics to other nations, including through the training of police forces, surveillance technologies, and weapons supplies, reveals the geopolitical border as a wide-reaching spatial and temporal border regime. While the US-Mexico border continues to represent "una herida abierta," what happens if we shift the border and begin at a different wound? How would centering a different wound reconfigure the US-centric visual discourse constructed around Central Americans, and how could it reshape the aesthetics of border art in Latinx visual culture?

The artworks in this chapter engage in what I describe as "shifting the border"—an act of visual disobedience that decenters the US-Mexico border, showing it is not the only site of border violence and revealing the progression of displacement and migration due to global capitalism and coloniality for Central Americans. The artworks in this chapter suggest that for Central Americans the wound begins elsewhere. With their paintings, performative actions, installations, and videos, artists shift the US-Mexico border down to El Salvador and Honduras, to Nicaragua and Costa Rica, to Guatemala and Mexico, and beyond, in an act of what Hernández has called "cartographic disobedience."[4] Shifting the border takes us back to Central America—to imperial intervention and forced displacement, and to the way migration shapes landscapes and architecture. Shifting the border takes us back to a site of multiple border cultures and to the visual politics of unequal capitalist exchange. Ultimately, by shifting the border, I argue, Central American artists locate migration beyond the US-Mexico border to reveal empires' spatial logics of movement control—a war on mobility.[5]

SURVIVING WAR VIOLENCE AND RIVER BORDERS

The postwar violence Central Americans flee in the present is a direct result of US intervention and military funding and training in the 1970s and 1980s, though US administrations systematically forget or deny this fact.[6] In addition to the long trajectory of intervention in the isthmus the United States had already established, the US government directly fomented those decades of civil war with millions of dollars of economic support to right-wing governments and dictators, fueling wars in El Salvador and Guatemala and counterinsurgency training and repression in Nicaragua and Honduras.[7] As the 1984 Iran-Contra Scandal revealed, the Ronald Reagan administration illegally and secretly supplied weapons to right-wing paramilitaries in Central America, which orchestrated a wave of human rights violations and atrocities. The administration facilitated the training of Central American militaries in torture techniques at the School of the Americas in Georgia that resulted in the "death squads" that terrorized the region.[8] The death squads tortured, disappeared, and murdered thousands of Central Americans and, between 1974 and 1996, forced millions to migrate within the region and beyond.

While art produced in Central America at that time mostly testified to the atrocities of US intervention, it also connected war with displacement, border violence, and the war on mobility. The most famous painting in El Salvador, *El Sumpul* (1984), was created by artist Carlos Cañas as homage to the victims of one of the worst massacres fueled by US military intervention of the time, at the Sumpul River—a natural border between El Salvador and Honduras (see figure 3.2). On the day of the massacre, May 13, 1980, US-funded Salvadoran paramilitary groups attacked villages, incinerated homes, and assassinated their inhabitants.[9] Hundreds of Salvadoran campesinos fled to the Sumpul River toward their only escape route and in the hopes of seeking refuge in Honduras. Yet Honduran soldiers on the other side of the river prevented their entry due to years of anti-immigrant sentiment between the two nations. With soldiers attacking on both sides of the river, six hundred men, women, and children died, either drowned in the river currents or assassinated by soldiers, leaving behind a massacre scene later memorialized by Cañas's painting. A pallet of purples and blue depict the gloomy and grim scene where a pile of bodies evokes a mountainous landscape. A nude child symbolizes innocence, and the red flowers are interpreted as hopeful signs for the future.

By shifting the border and revisiting this national tragedy beyond the context of civil war, the painting not only commemorates a national massacre but further testifies to and condemns border coloniality, the attack on the freedom of mobility, and the logic of disposability. Emblematic of the US-funded war, *El Sumpul* reveals how border violence took place for Central Americans before the refugee crisis at the US-Mexico border, in which national defense of a territorial demarcation came at the cost of hundreds of people slaughtered, drowned, shot, and stabbed to ensure they existed neither in El Salvador nor in Honduras. The massacre was not only a consequence of US military intervention but also a result of the colonial logic that justifies border sites as nonhuman zones for racialized and gendered peoples who are first forced to be on the move, and then whose movement is punished with death. This colonial border logic was further corroborated a year later in March 1981, when thousands more attempted to cross the Lempa River into Honduras to escape military repression and were similarly shot at by both Salvadoran and Honduran soldiers.

Despite these multiple massacres at rivers and borders within the Central American region, many were able to pass through. By the end of the 1980s, it is estimated that 230,000 Central Americans lived "illegally" in Honduras, since the border further ascribes illegality onto those forced to cross it. Many other Salvadorans migrated to Belize, Guatemala, and Nicaragua; Guatemalans fled to Belize; and Salvadorans and Nicaraguans migrated to Costa Rica. By 1989

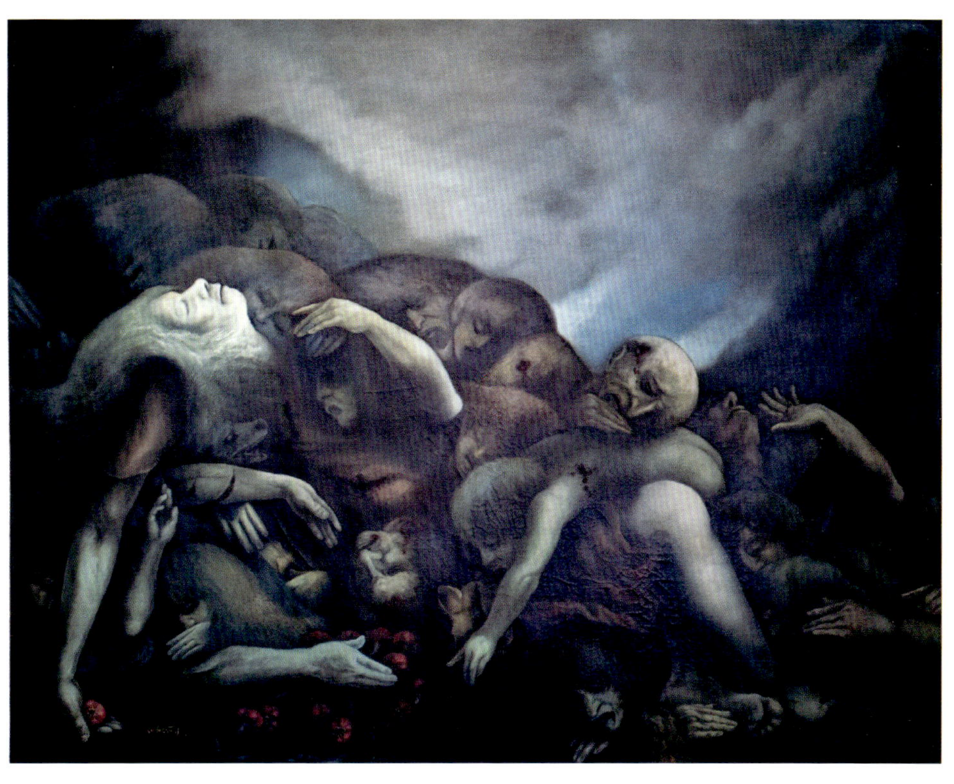

FIGURE 3.2.
Carlos Cañas, *El Sumpul*, 1984, oil on canvas. Colección Museo de Arte de El Salvador. Image courtesy of Museo de Arte de El Salvador.

the Costa Rican government claimed that 290,000 Salvadorans and Nicaraguans lived undocumented in the country.[10] The large refugee population of Central Americans within Central American borders was mostly made known through the work of the Office of the United Nations High Commissioner for Refugees (UNHCR), an estimated one hundred international nongovernmental organizations (NGOs), and the six hundred grassroots NGOs that operated in the region and aimed to make visible the plight of refugees within Central America.[11] These organizations confronted governments that imposed financial restrictions, paramilitary groups that attacked refugee camps, and politicians who feared refugees would drain resources, compete for jobs, and include "rebels" who could destabilize the nation.[12] Politicians pushed to isolate refugees into military-patrolled areas in rural outskirts and limited their movement, leading to the creation of concentration-type camps. From one of the largest refugee camps in Honduras, located in Mesa Grande, visual testimonials by Central American refugees to the dispossession and displacement as a result of US intervention are only recently emerging.

In 2017, a donation of embroideries made by Central American refugees was given to the Museo de la Palabra y Imagen (MuPI) in El Salvador, which is now known as the largest archive of visual and media material documenting Salvadoran history. Like the Chilean *arpilleras* (patchwork tapestries) that denounced dictator Augusto Pinochet's repression, Salvadoran women and child refugees in the Mesa Grande camp visually testified on small cloths or empty cornmeal sacks to the violence and displacement their communities experienced.[13] The embroideries typically depict scenes of camp life and the military repression they fled. Often, they include sewn messages, and many depict the river as a site of border violence. One embroidery depicts a group of people along a river border (see figure 3.3). The top register of the embroidery illustrates a military helicopter and air planes with flames below; beneath is a procession of men, women, and children—some carrying infants—who walk away from the burning villages. They carry sacks full of the only possessions they are able to salvage. Beneath them, bodies float in the river currents, figures swim across the river with children on their backs, and in some cases a head surfaces over the water or a single hand reaches for help. The text beneath reads: "This is the story us campesinos have lived, where many brothers drowned due to the repression."

In another embroidery, the text reads: "Due to heavy bombardment in our *cantones*, we had to flee and seek refuge in another country, leaving behind the rest who drowned in the river." Those "left behind" are depicted in a river between two mountains, where two figures float on top of sacks, two small heads appear slightly above water, and one outstretched hand symbolizes a last attempt

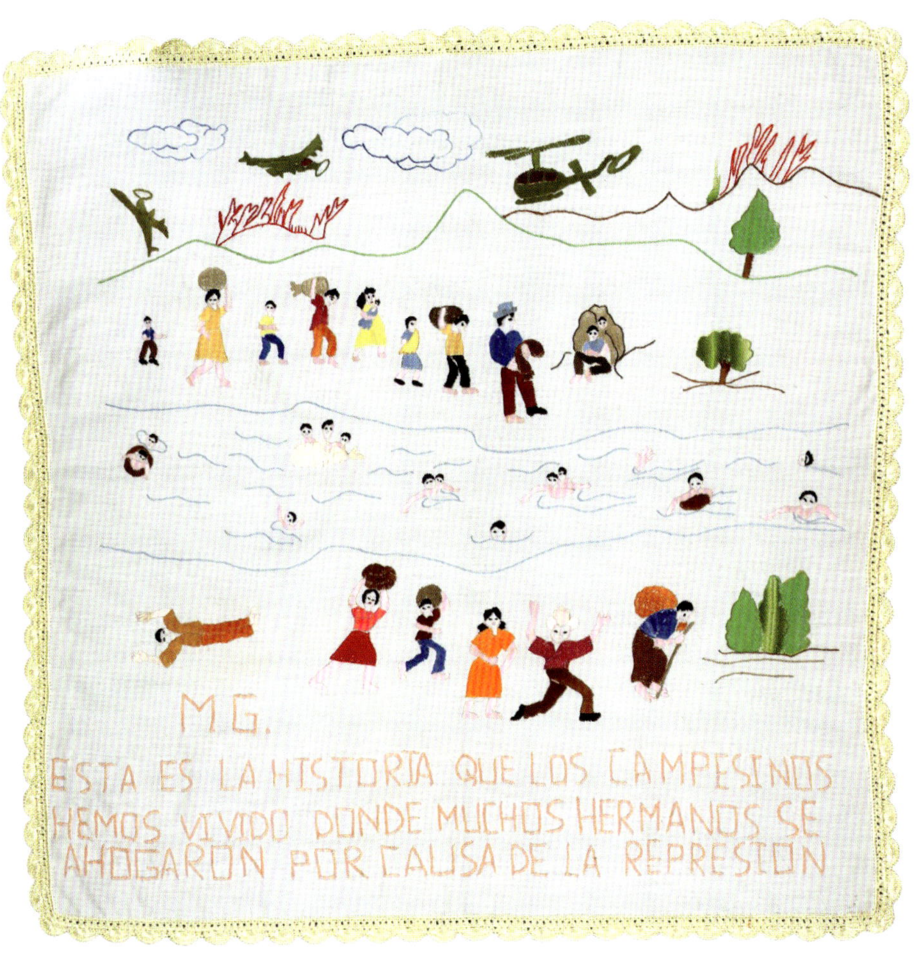

FIGURE 3.3.
Artist unknown, *Untitled* (Mesa Grande *arpillera*), ca. 1980s, embroidery. Colección Bordadoras de Memorias, Museo de la Palabra y la Imagen. Image courtesy of Carlos Henriquez Consalvi.

at survival as the figure drowns underneath the water. At the riverbanks, soldiers appear with weapons and are standing over dead bodies, while others are positioned on the mountain. Above them, military helicopters and planes hover over the scene and drop silver bombs. In the top left corner, a jagged red line represents fire, and on the other side of the river a partially nude figure lies on the ground while two others flee. A child attempts to climb a tree to escape a similar fate.

From their memories, women and children visually testify and convey the vivid scenes of military repression, internal migration and displacement, and rivers as sites of border violence. Hand-stitched and with the accuracy of memory, the embroideries depict simplified figures, like a drawing with no contour, and reveal a bird's-eye perspective over entire areas that capture Central American topography, corporal details, and military helicopters and planes. The "us" in the text positions the embroideries as representing a collective Central American campesino history in defiance of dominant histories written by victors, intellectuals, or the state. In a way, the embroideries precede by decades the similar images we see in the dominant media today of Central American migrants crossing or drowning in the Rio Grande—except these embroideries are made in defiance to border regimes, as they are testimonies of survival and not the visual spectacles of gaze and consumption that dominate the media today. They help us shift the border to reveal an initial location of border violence and the agency of those who survive it, and, like Cañas's *El Sumpul*, expose the logic of coloniality at the border as interconnected with the US military repression that fueled the prior decades of civil war that Central Americans fled. Their creative works function as alternative forms of mapping: that is, as historical maps of border violence and spatialized immobility that locate the human lives forced into the depths of the river.

EXPOSING ANTI-IMMIGRATION AND ANTI-BLACKNESS IN THE BORDER REGIME

Under border imperialism, the state's securitization of the border controls and orders the flow of migration. By positioning itself as a victim, the state criminalizes immigrants as the perpetrators, invaders, and deviants who not only trespass but violate the state with their penetration.[14] This happens at the US-Mexico border as well as with other Central American borders, as the previously discussed works have shown. But what about the immigrant life outside the protected, or imprisoned, space of refugee camps? What about those who manage to enter a nation where they are not isolated as the protected victim but criminalized as the deviant trespasser?

Costa Rican artist Guillermo "Habacuc" Vargas's performances and interventions center on the multiple migration populations within the isthmus. His multimedia installation *Exposition #1* (2007)—his most controversial piece—was exhibited at the Gallery Códice in Managua, Nicaragua. The installation consisted of six symbolic elements: (1) the sound of a Sandinista hymn played in reverse; (2) an incense burner burning 175 rocks of crack cocaine and an ounce of marijuana; (3) a sick dog from the streets tied to a short leash inside the gallery; (4) instructions not to feed or free the dog, which the artist named "Natividad"; (5) a text reading "eres lo que lees" (you are what you read), written on the gallery wall in dry dog food; and 6) responses to the installation, which accumulated during the three days of the exhibition from mass media communications systems, including television, newspapers, internet blogs, cell phones, texting, YouTube, et cetera. Immediately after the exhibition closed, rumors of the dog's death during the exhibition spread through the media and ignited global outrage (see figure 3.4).

Though the dog's death was never confirmed, Habacuc was accused of animal cruelty and profiting from the suffering of a defenseless dog. Attacks and protests ranged from global-wide petitions demanding an end to the artist's participation in national/regional/international art events, to threats of violence, even against his life. As global protestors demanded justice for Natividad the dog, at all cost to the artist, Habacuc documented the reactions on his blog, which also included extensive documentation on the notorious case of an immigrant youth named Natividad Leopoldo Canda Mairena, after whom he had named the dog.

Canda Mairena's case was the central subject matter of the installation. He was an impoverished thirteen-year-old Nicaraguan immigrant who sought work opportunities in Costa Rica to support his family. When his attempts to secure a job and transcend Costa Rica's hostile anti-immigrant environment failed, he broke into a warehouse to steal for survival. Warehouse security guards spotted him and released two Rottweilers, who attacked him. As his screams echoed in the night, a growing crowd of neighbors quickly arrived at the scene, followed by the police and the media. Yet, rather than intervening, and instead following the owner's orders not to shoot the dogs, the police and all the spectators simply watched as the Rottweilers mauled Canda Mairena for an entire hour. His death and the inaction by witnesses and police were captured on video.

FIGURE 3.4.
Guillermo "Habacuc" Vargas, *Exposition #1* (dog), 2007, multimedia installation. Courtesy of the artist.

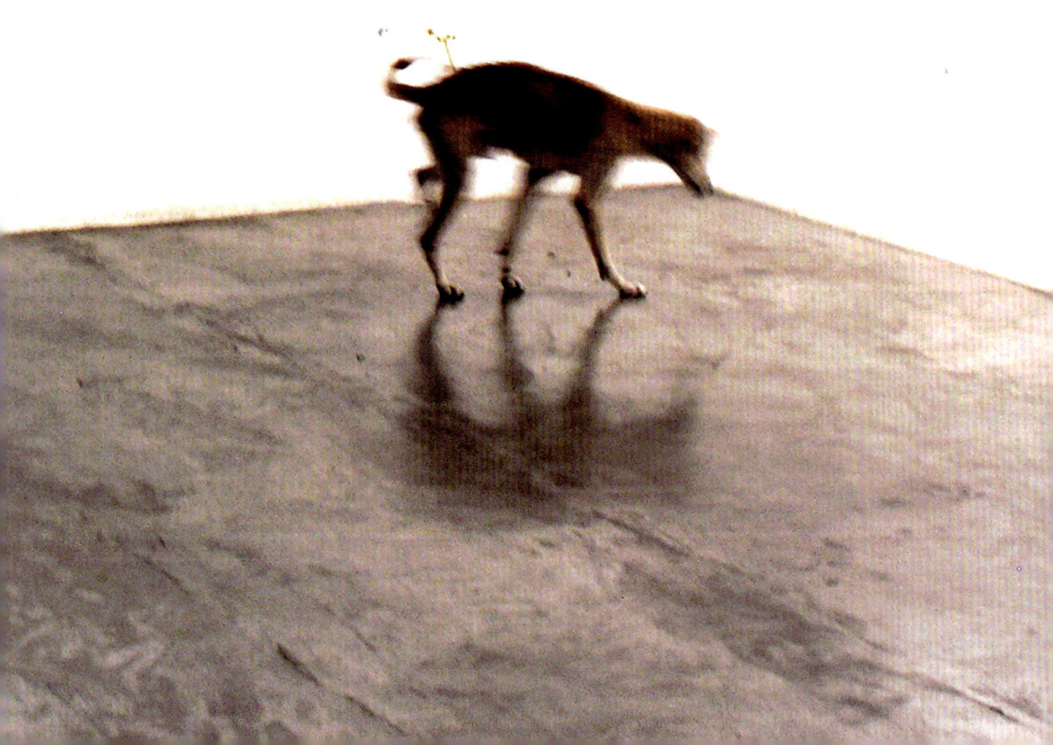

The case of Natividad Canda Mairena brought to light the history of racial and class tensions between Nicaraguans and Costa Ricans, which had begun with the influx of undocumented Nicaraguan immigrants into the country at the start of the nineteenth century, and which Habacuc highlighted with his installation. Canda Mairena's life was perceived as disposable by many Costa Ricans because of his immigrant status and the anti-immigrant hatred in the country. Following his death, the Costa Rican media presented the Rottweilers as heroes, applauding the dogs for "effectively" eliminating the "Nicaraguan problem."[15] Commercials advertised Rottweilers for half price, offering to throw in a free "Nica" (the appellative given to Nicaraguans) in order to test the dog's efficiency. Some even proposed replacing the Costa Rican border patrols with Rottweilers, as they proved more capable of eliminating immigrants than the border guards. Others proposed that the Rottweiler be celebrated as the new national hero and that historical monuments of Juan Santamaria (the country's official national hero) be replaced with statues of Rottweilers. Dog food was advertised as "Nica food."[16] The historical roots of the anti-immigrant tension Habacuc exposed, however, date back to colonization, postindependence, and border disputes over the San Juan River—another border river.[17] Habacuc exposes the "vida de perro" that Nicaraguan immigrants are forced to endure in Costa Rica and the hypocrisy of a global society that is more enraged over the rumored death of a dog in a gallery than the public torture and death of a Nicaraguan immigrant youth.[18]

In a later intervention titled *Rostros vivos* (Living faces) (2016), Habacuc turned the focus toward Nicaragua's anti-immigrant stance, specifically its anti-Black racism in Peñas Blancas, the border post between Nicaragua and Costa Rica. The night before the 2016 presidential election in Nicaragua, Habacuc covered the streets of Managua with posters displaying the faces of Black immigrants (see figures 3.5 and 3.6). With the collaboration of photographer Julia Murillo, the artist photographed twelve Haitian and African refugees in Peñas Blancas, creating large-scale black-and-white portraits. In what the artist calls a "photographic intervention in public spaces," three hundred posters were plastered on walls, polls, and trees all over Managua. The faces belonged to a group of three thousand refugees from Haiti, the Republic of Congo, Togo, Ghana, and Senegal. They represent a wave of migrants fleeing unbearable economic conditions and seeking refuge and work opportunities in the United States. Their journeys begin by crossing the sea, resume in Brazil, and continue through South American countries and into Central America as a path toward Mexico and eventually the United States. Along this journey they cross multiple borders and landscapes and undergo a number of dangers, exploitations, illness, and assault.[19]

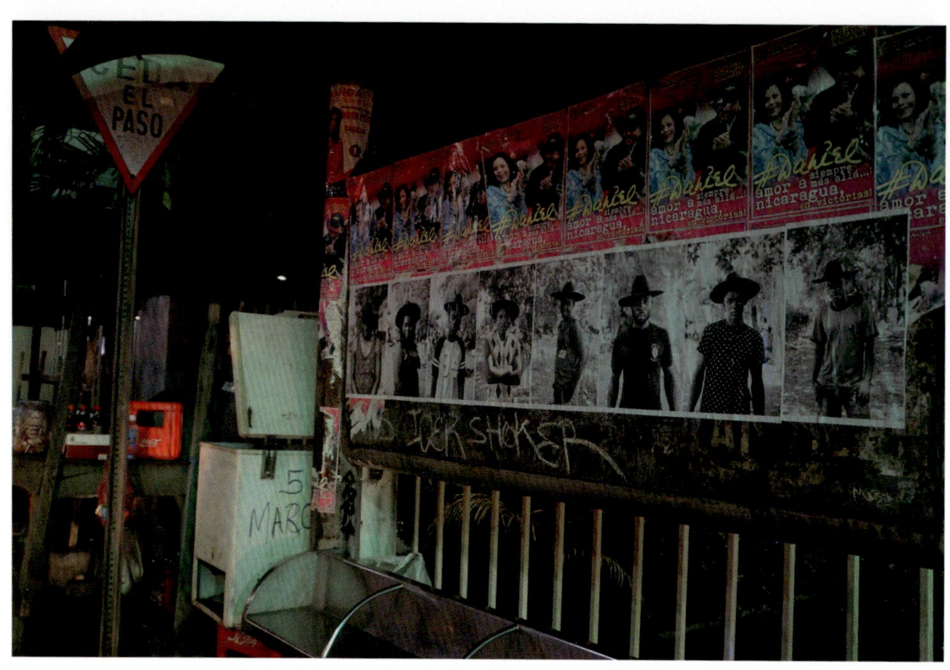

FIGURE 3.5.
Guillermo "Habacuc" Vargas, *Rostros vivos*, 2016, urban intervention. Courtesy of the artist.

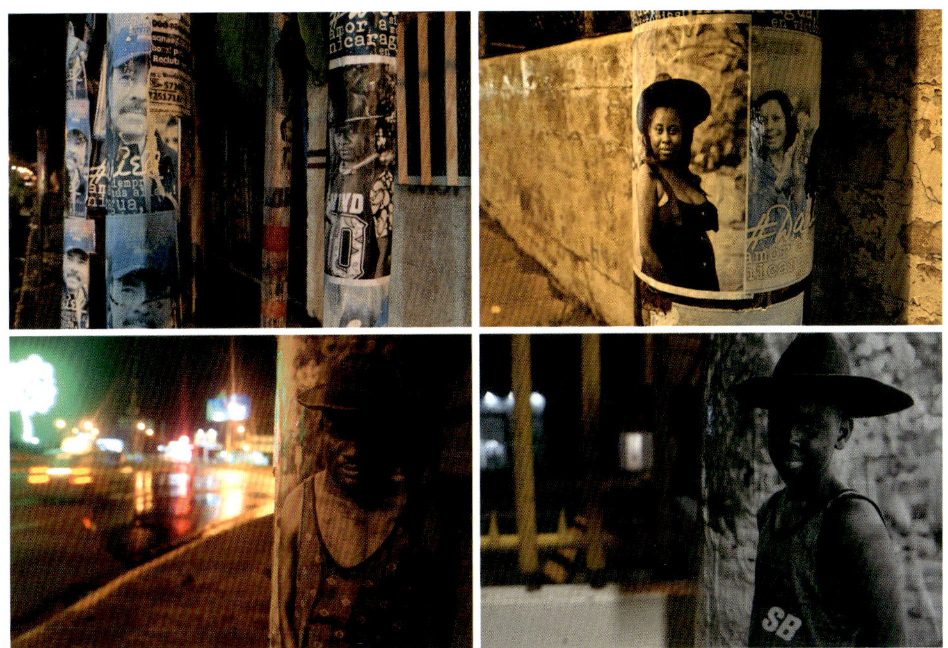

FIGURE 3.6.
Guillermo "Habacuc" Vargas, *Rostros vivos* (details), 2016, urban intervention. Courtesy of the artist.

Yet, even after surviving such a voyage, hundreds to thousands of migrants—which include men, women, pregnant women, and children—find themselves trapped in Peñas Blancas, the border between Costa Rica and Nicaragua.

Since 2015, the Nicaraguan government, led by former Sandinista revolutionary Daniel Ortega, has officially closed its border to these migrants and refugees, deeming them—along with terrorists, drug traffickers, and human traffickers—as threats to national security. Unable to move forward, migrants were forced to live in temporary camps at the border, with no access to food, clean water, or clothing. Temporary tents failed to keep out the tropical rains, creating wet, unsanitary conditions that fomented several illnesses, like diarrhea, especially among the children.[20] With no money or food, hunger and desperation led several migrant men to plead with border agents and implore President Ortega to grant them permission to cross through Nicaragua, clarifying and insisting that their destinations were not in Nicaragua but in the United States, where they believed work opportunities awaited them. The Nicaragua government responded with military troops and border guards to block migrants from crossing and at points dispersed them with tear gas. It further declared that anyone offering aid to the refugees would be guilty of aiding human smugglers, criminalizing anyone who showed compassion for the men, women, and children.

Refugees became even more vulnerable to coyotes and smugglers, who promised to find alternative routes but often abandoned them after taking their money. In the Rio Sapoá, ten Haitians drowned after being deserted by a coyote, their bodies washed away in the Nicaraguan lake. Many others died crossing the river or in the mountains. They were vulnerable to labor exploitation, human trafficking, and modern-day slavery. In September 2017, at a ceremony in Managua celebrating the anniversary of the armed forces, the Nicaraguan army's commander-in-chief, General Julio César Avilés, stated that in the fight against illegal migration, a total of 4,579 migrants were detained, the vast majority of whom came from countries in Africa and the Middle East.[21]

For *Rostros vivos*, Habacuc placed the iconic Sandino hat over the head of each refugee, who gazes directly at the viewer. The iconic hat is a popular symbol that represents Augusto César Sandino (1895–1934), the leader who gave his name to the Sandinistas, the revolutionary group that toppled the Somoza dictatorship in 1979 and is now a political party. The simple hat silhouette can be found in murals, posters, and other visual material across the country.[22] By placing the iconic hat on each refugee portrait, the artist directly critiques the Sandinista government led by Daniel Ortega, who was originally a leader of the Sandinista National Liberation Front (FSLN) and who has maintained his presidency in Nicaragua since 2006. With the Sandino hat, the artist visually exposed the contradictions of a revolutionary government whose motto states, "Christian, Socialist, and in Solidarity," while it publicly closed its borders to hundreds of displaced Black refugees. The intervention was done the night before the 2016 election, in which Ortega was up for reelection. The photographic intervention was designed to coexist and contest the political propaganda that saturated the streets of Managua the night before elections. The next morning, as Nicaraguans headed to the ballots, they were confronted with the faces of the hundreds to thousands of human beings its government excluded, criminalized, and invisibilized. Habacuc inserted, at least visually, the Black faces and bodies ignored by the state and did so in defiance of the war on their freedom of mobility.

Habacuc's evaluation of social and political hypocrisy in *Exposition #1* and *Rostros vivos* exposes the anti-immigrant sentiment in two Central American nations, Costa Rica and Nicaragua. In the first, he exposes spectacle diversion and citizen passivity in both the media and the art world. His installation visualized the institutionalized domination that cultivates and maintains submissive viewers, as no one countered the artist's instructions not to feed the dog, nor did anyone disobey the warehouse owner's orders to not stop the Rottweilers. In both Natividad cases, rather than act to change a situation, fear of breaching gallery conventions, passivity, apathy, and a callous lack of concern enabled inaction and delayed reaction. So-called protest and activism on behalf of the two Natividads only materialized at the safe distance of virtual space: in the media where protest immediately transmogrified into a spectacle of self-righteous blame and accusation against the artist, all of which detracted from individual culpability.[23]

In *Rostros vivos*, the artist critiques a government that failed to uphold the revolutionary ideals of its leader and martyr, Sandino, exposing an anti-immigrant system of failed utopias and promises, where neither the left nor the right addresses or fixes new forms of violence against the most marginalized people in the region. Specifically, he connects anti-immigrant xenophobia and anti-Blackness as jointly embedded in border regimes. Harsha Walia reminds us that anti-Blackness is embedded in US migration politics, rooted in the logic of transatlantic slavery and where Texas militias composed of slave owners prevented Black people's escape to Mexico.[24] Yet, Habacuc reminds us, the anti-Blackness of border imperialism exists in Central America as well, and Latin America more broadly. Six years later the United States was reminded of this when, in September 2022, images of border agents on horseback using unnecessary force to prevent Haitian migrants from crossing the Rio Grande circulated in the mainstream media, evoking images of slavery. Both *Exposition #1* and *Rostros vivos* reveal that border policing and racial violence extend beyond the territorial limits of a border and manifest within and throughout the nation-state in Central America.

ENDURING THE VERTICAL BORDER

For those Central Americans who head north, before arriving at the US-Mexico border they must first survive Mexico. Though the nation was a significant transit zone during the waves of migration resulting from the civil wars and conflicts of the 1970s and 1980s, the levels of danger skyrocketed in the postwar period. The rise of violence against Central American migrants became especially evident in the 1990s, when the United States turned its attention to national security issues that were exacerbated by the events of September 11, 2001, in New York. Under the rhetoric of fighting terrorism and organized crime to halt the flow of drugs, arms, and people, the United States placed extra pressure on Mexico to enforce its border tactics—a process of border externalization. Also in 2001, then-president of Mexico Vicente Fox (2000–2006) implemented the national security project El Plan Sur.[25] In the following years, a series of policy adaptations and additions transformed migratory control in Mexico to increase Central American deportation.[26] Later, in 2014, President Enrique Peña Nieto announced the Plan Frontera Sur in response to the increased number of unaccompanied Central American children and US pressures on Mexico. Rather than protect migrants and their right to seek asylum, Plan Frontera Sur increased institutional violence against Central American migrants.[27]

Mexico implemented multiple immigration stations along its southern border to control migration, ensuring that detection, detainment, and deportation could take place at any point on Mexico's terrain, not just at the Mexico-Guatemala border.[28] From 2007 to 2016, the increasing numbers of migrant detentions were no longer concentrated at the southern border region (Campeche, Chiapas, Quintana Roo, and Tabasco) but equally increased in the central and northern regions of Mexico.[29] This vertical expansion of migration control from the southern Mexico-Guatemala border to the northern US-Mexico border reinforced the notion of Mexico as a "vertical border."[30] That is, the entire nation is a violent border for Central American migrants.

As a vertical border, Mexico fulfills its role as immigration enforcer, pushing migrants to find more dangerous routes that expose them to the risk of organized crime, forced labor, sexual slavery, and death.[31] Now Mexico is the most dangerous country for Central American migrants, with mass deportations, more than 20,000 migrant abductions per year, up to 120,000 migrants missing from 2006 to 2015, an estimated 24,000 bodies buried in unmarked graves, and 40,000 unidentified bodies found in public morgues.[32] Despite these dangers, migration from Central America and through Mexico has drastically increased since 2014. By 2018–21 it was estimated that 407,000 people left the Northern Triangle annually, though these numbers are an undercount, for in 2021 alone the US Border Patrol encountered 684,000 migrants from Honduras, Guatemala, and El Salvador at the US-Mexico border.[33]

In her performance and sculptural piece *Móvil* (Mobile)(2010), Galindo focused on the unequal power relation Central Americans experience as they pass through Mexico (see figure 3.7). Exhibited in Mexico City at the Museo Universitario de Arte Contemporáneo (MUAC), the artist lay inside a closed, metal coffin on a stretcher trolley as spectators were allowed to move the coffin around the gallery space as they wished. What began as slight movements became aggressive and jagged manipulations in space. Audience members forcefully thrust the coffin into the crowd or empty space, dragged it in circular motions, and slammed it into a chair and wall with complete disregard for the body inside. The uneven power between the spectators' control of the coffin and the artist's vulnerability echoes the volatility Central American migrants endure when crossing the vertical border, where their bodies are subjected to abuse by gangs, cartels, corrupt Mexican authorities, and the political system's impunity.[34] Moreover, Galindo's body, while secured inside the coffin, metaphorically charted a terrain of unpredictability and violence enforced under the b/ordering logic of social control, a terrifying embodiment the artist understood could only pale in comparison to the actual experience of migrants trapped in the vertical border.

Yet Galindo and others also exalt the resilience, bravery, poetics of migration, and dignity that come with survival through the Mexico passage. In a work titled *Survival Course for Men and Women Who Will Journey Illegally to the U.S.* (2007) (see figure 3.8), Galindo fueled migrants' superhuman strength by training them for survival along their journey through the vertical border. Galindo found a Guatemala-based professional smuggler (or coyote) who was planning on guiding ten Guatemalans, half of them women, through Mexico and into the United States. With the collaboration of a coyote and an instructor of extreme sports, the course taught skills in fire making, map reading, navigation by sun and stars, first aid skills, and self-defense. Participants were also taught how to find water sources and edible bugs and plants to keep them

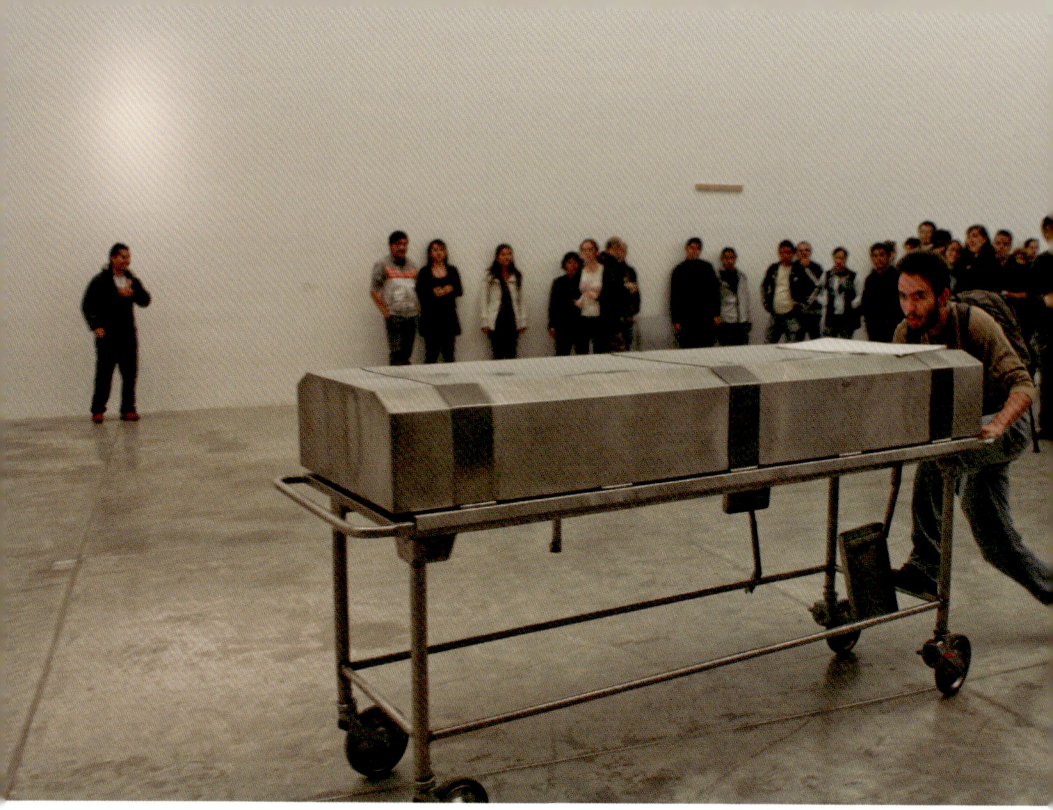

FIGURE 3.7.
Regina José Galindo, *Móvil*, 2010, performance. Courtesy of the artist.

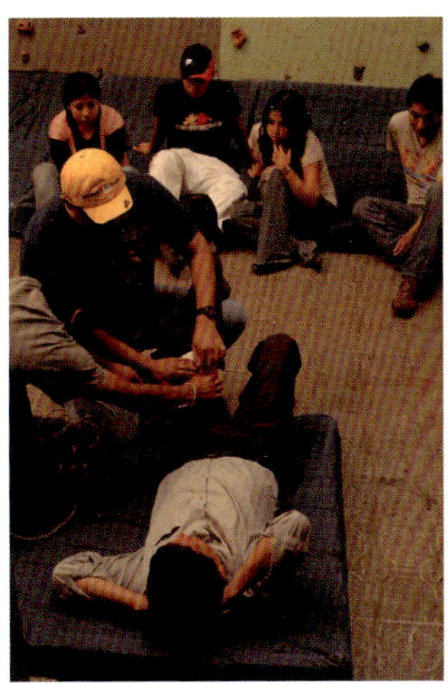
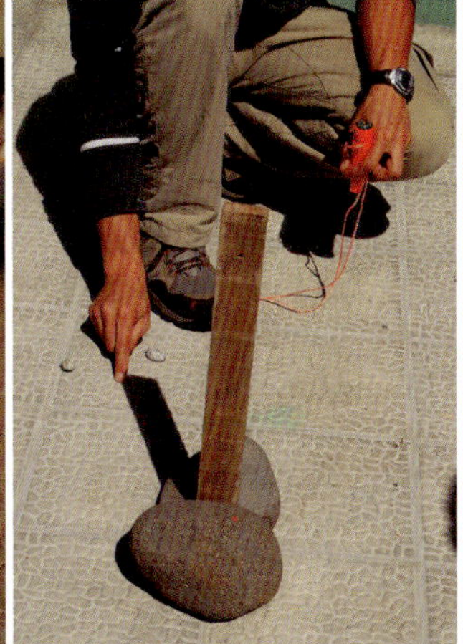
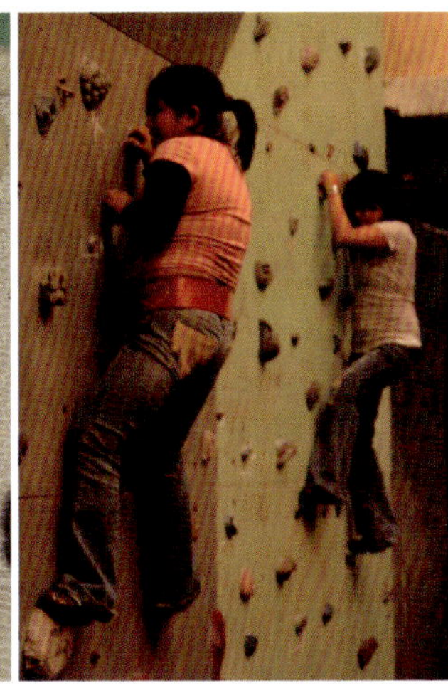

FIGURE 3.8.
Regina José Galindo, *Survival Course for Men and Women Who Will Journey Illegally to the U.S.*, 2007, action. Courtesy of the artist.

alive. All participants were taught rock climbing and rappelling in an obstacle course and were compensated with money to use during their journey.

Galindo's project was designed to aid the women migrants, whose probability of being raped, kidnapped, sexually assaulted, or trapped into sexual slavery while crossing the vertical border was extremely high. The perpetrators of such crimes are other migrants, gangs, bandits, coyotes, or Mexican authorities and officials, meaning that any percentage is a low estimate, since women cannot always report rape to Mexican authorities, who deport them or, at times, are the very culprits of their sexual assault. In Galindo's action, the women were taught how to hide condoms and birth control pills in their waistbands to prevent pregnancy in the likely event of rape. They were also advised to pass as HIV-positive Guatemalan sex workers in order to deter rapists. With *Survival Course*, Galindo reminds us that migrant survival is a form of art and defiance of the vertical border and the war on mobility. While exposing injustices, *Survival Course* shifts the framework from continuous victimhood to the mental and physical challenges migrants endure along the vertical border, equal to that of the most honored athletes, heroines, and warriors.

Móvil and *Survival Course* highlight migrant experiences through the vertical border and beyond the horizontality of the US-Mexico and the Mexico-Guatemala borders. These performative actions locate the body as corporal evidence of the externalization of border practices and its threat to migrant lives.[35] As the United States continues to outsource border policing strategies to Mexico, as more recently seen with the "Remain in Mexico" policy of 2018, it is able to control and manage migratory routes before the point of entry at the US-Mexico border. It does so through logistical, financial, and political support, or in exchange for aid, ultimately placing the burden on other countries, with the goal of reducing access to asylum and increasing dangers for migrants. Galindo's actions are a reminder of both the physical harm of such policies and the ongoing physical resistance to the violent spatial logics of mobility control.

MAPPING EMBODIED AND POETIC LINES

Central American artists turn away from representational victimhood and destitution to produce visual counternarratives that defy the visual thingification of visual coloniality, that is, the colonialist practice of fabricating visual evidence for the dehumanization of the colonized through a series of negations. In the past few years, the images of Central American migrants along the vertical border have become one of the most consumed visual spectacles disseminated by dominant media outlets. Photojournalists depict bodies found in unmarked graves, either throughout Mexico when left behind by cartels or in the desert as migrants embark on ever more dangerous paths to avoid border patrols. News stories of migrants' bodies found starved, dehydrated, asphyxiated, or deceased inside cargo trains and trucks are also common, revealing the dangers and risks migrants endure. In 2011, authorities found 210 migrants, mostly from Central America, packed so tightly inside a truck that they had to remain standing for the entire duration of their journey.[36] In 2015, Mexican authorities found another 68 undocumented Central American migrants in the state of Veracruz who were abandoned in the cargo compartment of two trucks. They had been inside for more than ten hours in scorching heat, among them fifteen children and ten women. In June 2022, heat exhaustion was the cause of death for 53 migrants whose bodies were found trapped in a semi-trailer near San Antonio, Texas, in what is described as the "deadliest tragedy" of migrant deaths in American history.[37] The majority were from El Salvador, Guatemala, and Honduras.

Others are photographed in rivers, as in the recent famous case of Salvadorans Óscar Alberto Martínez Ramírez and his twenty-four-month-old daughter Valeria, who drowned in desperation in the Rio Grande in 2019. Images like the photograph on the *Time* magazine cover of a crying two-year-old Honduran girl separated from her mother by the border patrol are the dominant visual imaginary of Central American migrants, which reveal the realities of sacrifice, risk, and violence migrants face, albeit often at the cost of their dignity and humanity. Highlighting a migrant's *strength* is a subversive act artists engage in against governments and media that continue to render migrants in headlines and images as eternally weak, marginal victims or at the opposite extreme, as dangerous invasive masses.

Salvadoran artist Ronald Morán shifts the imagery of Central American migration from violated body to freedom of mobility as a human right. This shift points us to the poetic process of migrants' movement. For Morán, poetic visual lines become the metaphor for the pathways, journeys, and trails of Central American migrants, as seen in his video *Breve cuestionamiento que traspasa el estado material* (Brief questioning that goes beyond the material state) (2009) (see figure 3.9). In a series of photographs, a single line—the residue of an airplane against a blue sky, the ripple a boat left behind in the water, or a man-made path from a bird's-eye view—crosses from one side of the frame to the other, representing three different geographies of migratory paths. These bifurcated frames create simple and beautiful abstract compositions that represent three ways migration can take its course—by plane, by boat, or by foot. We do not see the machinery or bodies in motion but rather the physical traces left

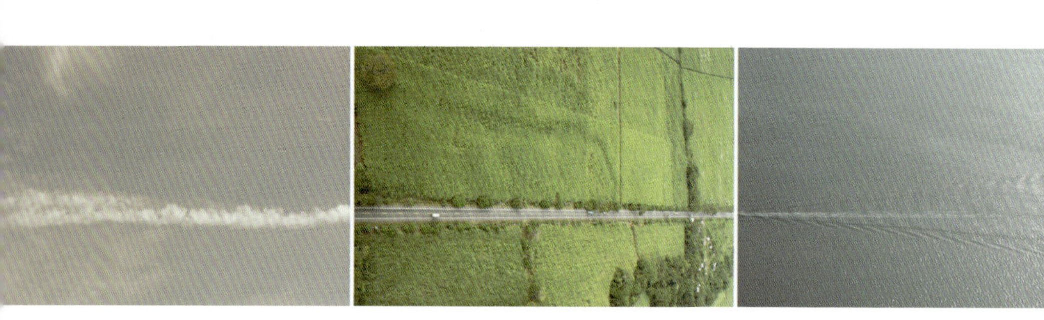

FIGURE 3.9.
Ronald Morán, *Breve cuestionamiento que traspasa el estado material*, 2009, video (stills). Courtesy of the artist.

behind: a path that was made where there was no path before. While from a distance the landscape offers a vision of these journeys, in the video installation each image blurs into the other, transposing the idea of the individual journey onto a greater concept of migration as a historical human phenomenon of continuity. A melodic tune sets the stage for viewer reflection as the continuous line creates a hypnotic sensation of contemplation. There are no human figures in this work, and despite our awareness of the pain and violence implicated in migration, Morán instead conveys landscapes—ocean, sky, and land—as witnesses to these journeys. We imagine the many paths taken, the many destinations reached, and the many dreams of better futures that initiate each journey.

Morán further expands the idea of the line in migration to the concept of the labyrinth in his large-scale installation titled *Brevedad inmaterial* (Immaterial brevity) (2009) (see figure 3.10). The interactive large-scale installation was set in the pitch-black high-ceiling galleries of the Museo Ex Teresa Arte Actual in Mexico City as part of an exhibition featuring six of Morán's works around the theme of migration. A black light reveals a collection of strings in the shape of a labyrinth. Unlike a maze, which has multiple possible courses, a labyrinth is unicursal, with one single path to the exit. Morán draws on the labyrinth's ancient symbolism as a man-made geometric network of paths with no clear exit route, which according to ancient Greek mythology was designed to cause confusion, disorientation, and entrapment. He presents the labyrinth as a poetic metaphor for the migratory journey; the migrant phenomenological experience is the basis of this artistic work. Viewers were invited to enter and navigate the space, to find their path and journey, and to become aware of their bodies. The lack of walls in this labyrinth allowed viewers to see others in their journeys, making spatial relations to others ghostly visible, just as migrants are always linked to the people and communities they leave behind and those they move toward.

Morán's labyrinth installation invites viewers to ask: How do Central American migrants account for uncharted lands and the dangers, setbacks, and time negotiated by exhaustion or injury? How do they *know* how to get north? Rarely are actual maps accessible or reliable, as the migratory journey is never one singular path or experience. The same path will yield unexpected circumstances that make it shorter or longer and thus unpredictable. Obstacles such as Mexican authorities, thieves, cartels, and even injuries, exhaustion, or a search for resources cause deviations, deterrence, and temporal pauses. Time cannot be predicted, nor can life be guaranteed. Morán's installation connects migration to a contemplative and embodied mapping and system of knowing. In the installation's darkness, external factors are removed and all sensorial consciousness centers on the act of walking, in the contemplative decisions of choosing where to turn next,

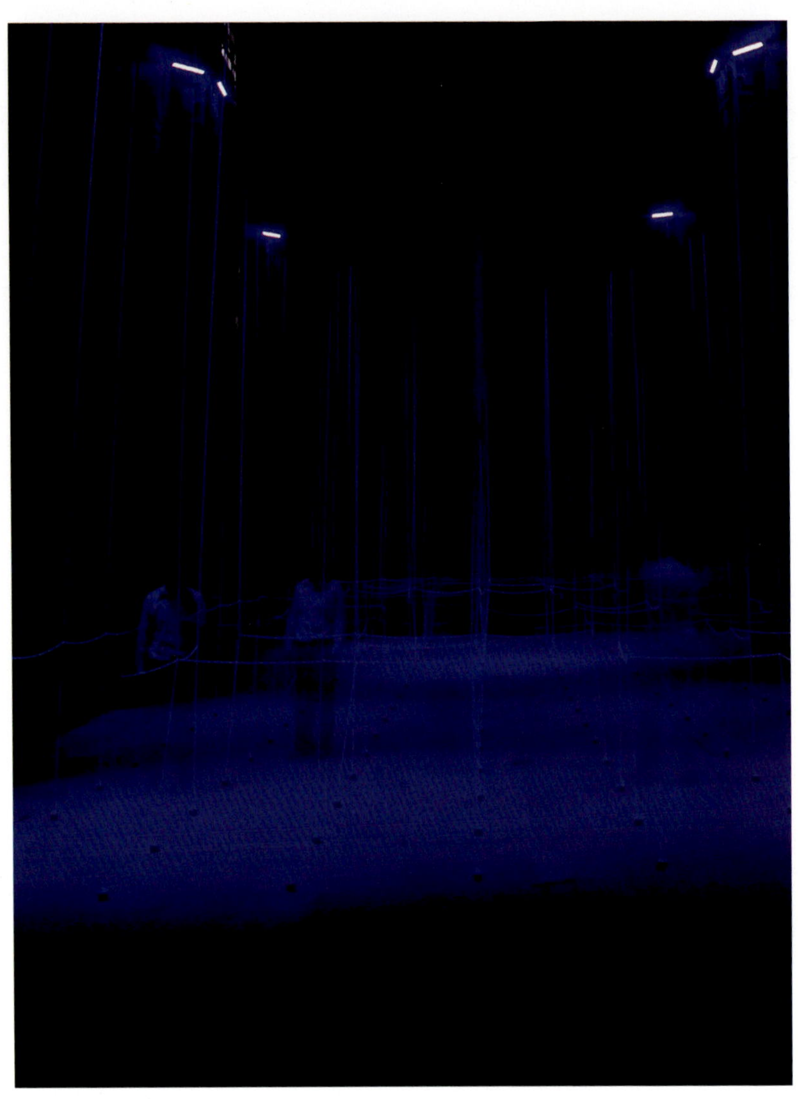

FIGURE 3.10.
Ronald Morán, *Brevedad inmaterial*, 2009, multimedia installation. Courtesy of the artist.

and in not forgetting the traces of one's path so as to maintain awareness of location. The unclear path of a labyrinth parallels the experience of Central American migrants, who, though unfamiliar with the terrain of a foreign nation and without knowledge of a safe passage, must somehow trust they will find their way to their destination and that they will intuitively follow the one safe exit route—that is, they must trust in their bodies to lead them.

Like Morán, the US-based Salvadoran artist Guadalupe Maravilla (formerly known as Irvin Morazán) has used poetic lines to evoke migratory embodied mapping. For *Requiem for My Border Crossing* (2018), Maravilla draws from his own experience as a child migrant (see figure 3.11). At eight years old, he was sent from El Salvador with a coyote to reunite with his parents, who had migrated before him and were waiting for him in New York. Interested in remapping his father's and his own migratory journey through Mexico, the artist visited the different sites where he stopped. He conducted research in each location and came across scans of sixteenth-century manuscripts that depicted crossing routes, with footprints, rivers, and mountains—preconquest mappings. The preconquest maps reminded the artist of a Salvadoran child's game that he often played during his migratory journey called Tripa Chuca. In the game, children take turns connecting pairs of the same numbers across a sheet of paper with a pencil line but without intersection or grazing other lines or other numbers. The possibility of avoiding touching another line or number becomes more difficult, and the child is forced to create long routes around the paper to reach the number, until it can no longer be done. The remaining image is a configuration of lines that resemble an intestinal tract, thus the game's name: *tripa chuca* (dirty tripes, with "chuca" as the slang Salvadoran word for dirty).

Maravilla fuses the iconography from preconquest maps with the game he played as a child migrant, connecting the creativity, improvisation, and play of the game with preconquest systems of mapping and that of the migratory journey of Central Americans. By playing the game with undocumented immigrants, Deferred Action for Childhood Arrivals (DACA) recipients, and others from immigrant communities, the artist evokes the mapping process of migration as nonlinear and improvisational, and as a historical phenomenon and human right. The twisted, improvisational lines more accurately represent the unpredictable paths migrants take. Studies have shown that what commonly may be referred to as a migrant's linear journey north is in fact sideways, circular, and against the linearity of time, as there are sometimes setbacks that force migrants to find alternative paths. These observations show that migrants' maps are oral and embodied.[38]

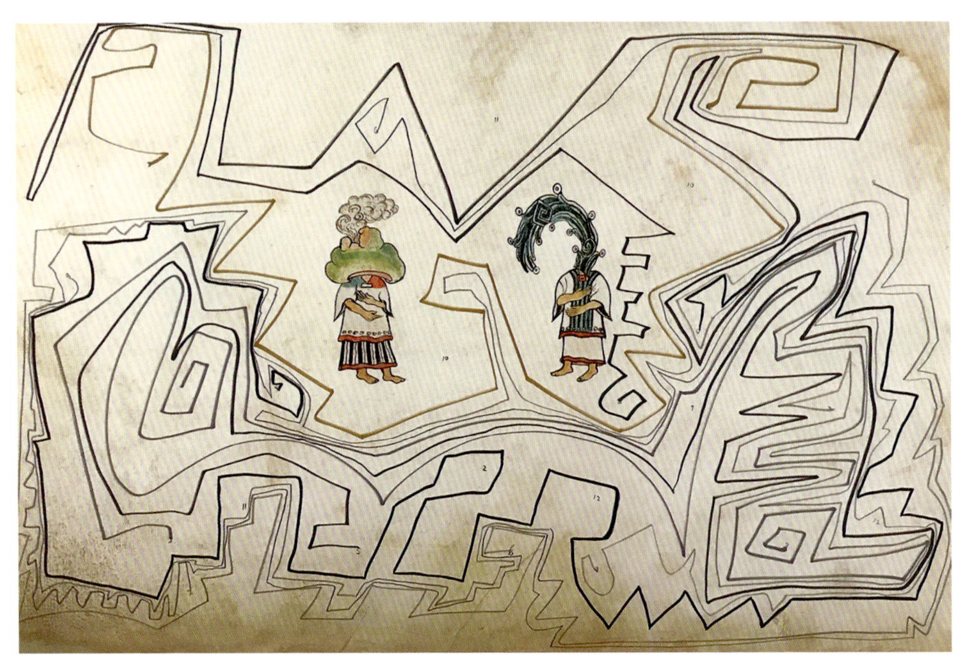

FIGURE 3.11.
Guadalupe Maravilla, *Requiem for My Border Crossing*, 2018, inkjet print with graphite pencil and ink. Courtesy of the artist.

In both Morán's and Maravilla's projects, the migratory journey of Central Americans is poetically conveyed with lines that move, navigate, and are produced and improvised by migrants to conceptually disobey both the visual imagery of destitution that dominates the imaginary of Central American migration and the linear mapping of state maps that do not accurately account for migrants' creativity and collectivity. Morán's installation highlights the unpredictability of the migratory path using the idea of the labyrinth and the phenomenological experience of finding one's way. By playing Tripa Chuca, Maravilla exalts migrant collective mapmaking as a creative and joyful act of knowledge making. Both Morán and Maravilla point to the embodied system of knowledge that migrants create along their journeys. Migrants inherit and transfer cultural and embodied epistemes uniquely made by migrants for migrants, relying on the shared knowledge to create a path for their migration.[39] By focusing on these epistemes, Morán and Maravilla contravene the visual image of migrant misery and their visual thingification with creative resilience. As these artists remind us, shifting the border demands we imagine alternative ways of mapping migrants' shifting paths, their improvisational navigations, and how routes are made, preserved, and transferred between migrants in defiance of border coloniality.

Thus far the selected artworks reveal the complexity of Central American migration and border coloniality *before* arrival at the US-Mexico border. From internal river borders as sites of violence during the civil war, to the concentration-type camps within the region, to the discriminatory practices and racism toward migrants and refugees within, and the power dynamics along the vertical border, Central American artists defy the reductive narratives of Central American migration that begin with deprivation and victimhood at the US-Mexico border. Central American artists also demand we consider the aftermath of migration and ask what other consequences are revealed to us when we shift the border. What of those left behind?

PRESERVING CONNECTIVITY AMID FAMILY SEPARATION

In his video installation *Migrar es siempre cuestión de espacio* (Migration is always a question of space) (2007), Salvadoran artist Walterio Iraheta displays what appears to be a still photograph of a group of Guatemalan Mayan youth against a rural background. Boys and girls of different ages pose together with smiles, shyness, and silliness, evoking friendship and camaraderie as in a typical cohort or class picture at school. During the duration of the video, slowly and one at a time figures disappear from the photograph until only an empty, ghostly, eerie backdrop remains (see figure 3.12). The missing youth highlight the disintegration of community, in this case by young people who migrate not only across national borders but from rural to urban spaces in search of a better life. The video ends with no trace of the individuals, providing the sense of nostalgia, emptiness, and a desire to recover memories. The photographed group was from a Mayan community from the town Plan de Sánchez, Rabinal, Baja Verapaz, Guatemala, where migration numbers are especially high. Though the sepia-toned photograph suggests a past moment captured in time, the artist predicts a futuristic reality for the young community. The video speaks not only to this banishing of bodies that migrate but to those left behind and their communities, who are faced with the painful void of separation.

Central American artists like Iraheta are increasingly addressing one of the worst consequences of migration on Central American life since the first wave of mass migration in the 1970s through 1990s as a result of civil wars—family separation. While artists and Central American scholars have addressed the issue for some time, the Donald J. Trump administration's "family separation policy" and the images of detained children on US soil drew greater attention to it. By shifting the border, however, these artists remind us that family separation takes place even before arriving at the US-Mexico border, when migrants are forced to leave their families behind to survive the neoliberal and colonial policies that make a dignified life in their home countries impossible. Anti-immigrant critics often vilify migrants for either leaving their families or taking the journey with their children, accusing them of being irresponsible and unfit parents. Yet the systemic violence in the region gives them no choice.

For her book *Sacrificing Families*, sociologist Leisy J. Abrego conducted extensive interviews with Salvadoran transnational families that bring to light the complex reasons parents leave their families to migrate north, such as civil war, economic instability, persecution, and even gendered expectations of parenting duties. As she shows, they migrate to ensure their children's survival because, despite exhausting every possible option, "the United States represents the final available measure to achieve success as parents."[40] Often this means ensuring the safety and well-being of their families with basic necessities. Abrego counters the inaccurate perception of family abandonment to reveal the deep sense of family duty, love, and responsibility that leads migrants to migrate without their children.

Salvadoran artist Catalina del Cid uses drawing and installation to show how monetary allowances have become symbolic of transnational parenting, or what is described as "parenting from afar through remittances."[41] Drawing is del Cid's preferred medium, but she transfers the aesthetics of one of her

FIGURE 3.12.
Walterio Iraheta, *Migrar es siempre cuestión de espacio*, 2007, video (stills). Courtesy of the artist.

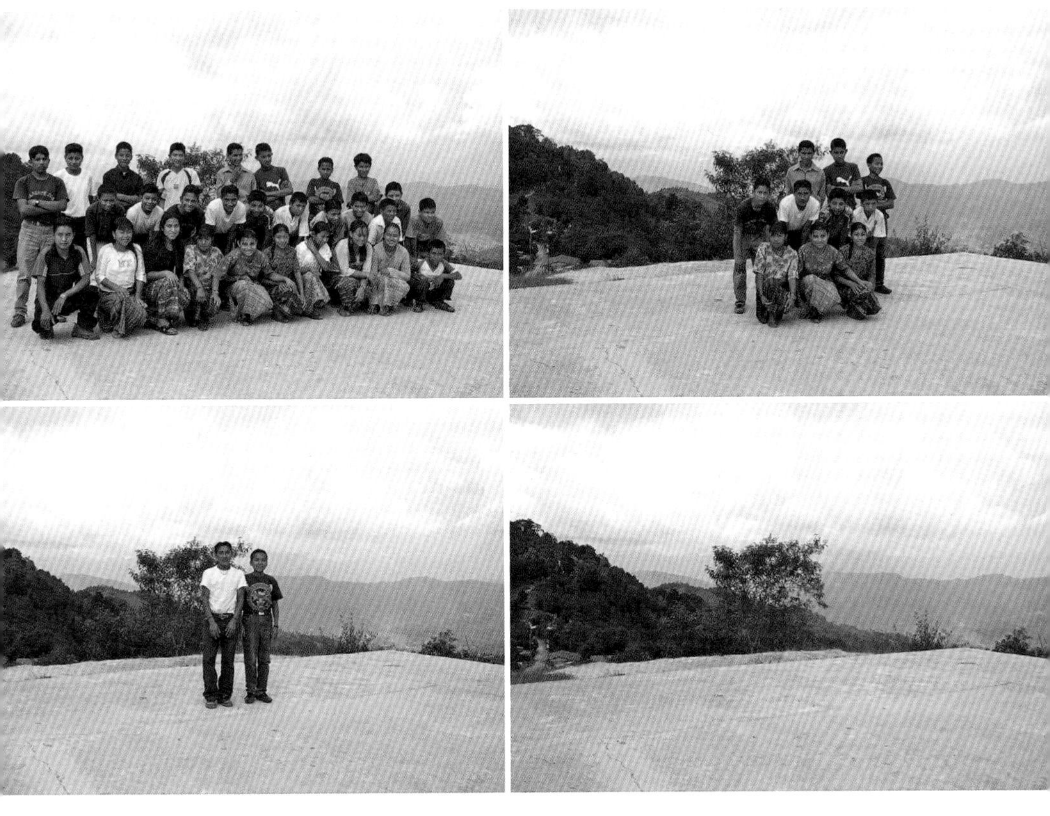

drawings (indicated by the white base and thick black outline) to an installation titled *Electrodomésticos + Regalos = Amor* (Electrical appliances + gifts = love) (2012) (see figure 3.13). The installation displays a low-cost entertainment center typically found in Salvadoran homes where family members send remittances. Like a memorial, the piece of furniture holds valuable gifts migrant parents send to their children, such as a television, a small stereo sound system, or toys from popular movies, like the Buzz Lightyear doll depicted to the top right of the television, the ET doll to the left, or fashion items like the Adidas shoes on the lower left side of the stereo. The toys or shoes, seemingly meant for children, are here depicted as sacred items for display, perhaps used only on special occasions, resulting in a piece of furniture that resembles a shrine full of relics. The framed photograph of the mother and two daughters opposite a framed Sacred Heart Christ further evokes the fusion of holy reverence for the family and gratitude but also serves as a site of prayer, indicating the fear, worries, and emotional precarity that separated families endure.

Del Cid points to the emotional value ascribed to electrometric items and gifts because from a distance they are often the only way migrant parents can convey their love. The items signify a better life of comfort for their children when parents are unable to be near them. It further indicates how migrant parents often confess their guilt and sorrow for their absence from their children, and it simultaneously alludes to the children who sometimes express resentment and rebellious behavior for what they see as their parents' abandonment. The installation, more than representing a modest piece of furniture in a typical home, serves as evidence of the emotional traumas between separated families and their struggles to maintain loving connections despite the distance brought on by forced migration. Yet these gifts also represent a financial struggle parents spare their children from knowing.

As a result of migration, up to 40 percent of Salvadoran children live in single- or no-parent households.[42] Some parents are fortunate enough to make it to the United States and establish jobs that, despite exploitative conditions and pay, allow them to send remittances back home to their children and families in Central America. They also must save to pay off a debt anywhere from US$8,000 to US$10,000, which is the average cost for an unauthorized trip with a coyote, and which most migrants have to borrow from family or friends and pay off once they arrive in the United States. Additionally, the bureaucratic costs of applying for residency, protected status, or citizenship in the United States require high fees for paperwork and lawyers, which often depletes migrants' funds. The money sent back is often barely enough to cover basic living costs and in some cases education for their children, though this is

FIGURE 3.13.
Catalina del Cid, *Electrodomésticos + Regalos = Amor*, 2012, multimedia installation. Courtesy of the artist.

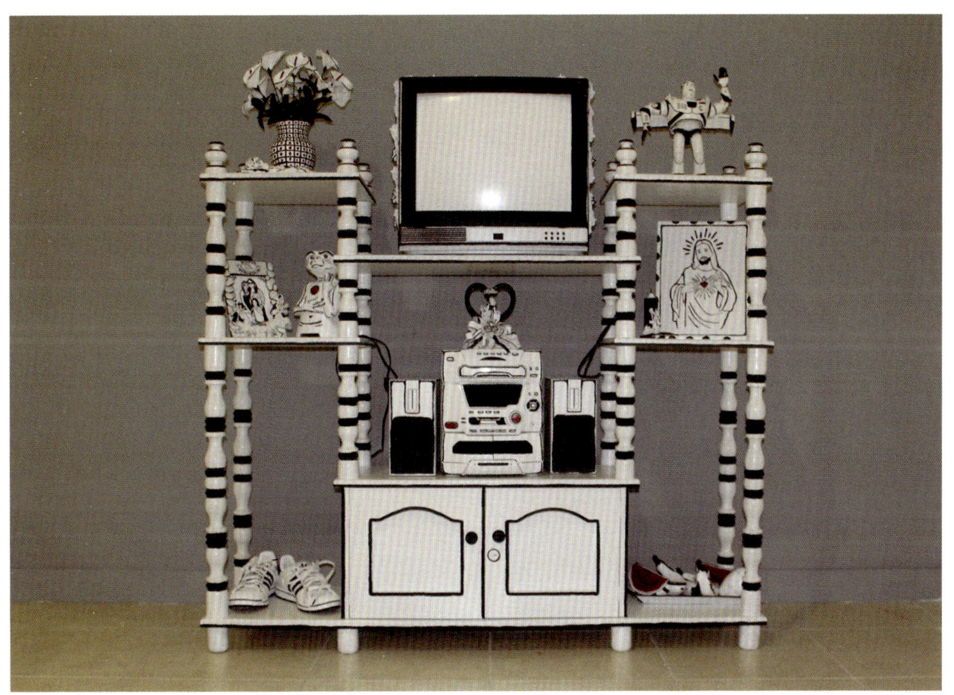

not always possible, as emergency expenses are unpredictable.[43] Studies show the amount of debt that migrants accumulate in the United States due to the illegality ascribed to them reduces the amount of money sent home, leaving families left behind either barely surviving or at times worse off than before.[44] Yet remittances have become the economic backbone of Central American countries, which rely heavily on the money sent by migrants in the United States. Del Cid reminds us that monetary and material gifts are often a strenuous effort migrant parents make to maintain loving connections with their children left behind.

Other artists, such as Myra Barraza, further consider family separation from the perspective of those left behind who long to reconnect with their loved ones. For her public action *Un saludo desde la hermana república de El Salvador* (Greetings from the sister republic of El Salvador) (2006), Barraza set up a table at the Parque Libertad in San Salvador's historic center, where she offered passersby the opportunity to send a message to their family members who migrated to the United States. The probability of finding interested volunteers was not low, considering that four out of ten Salvadoran children have a parent residing in the United States as a result of migration.[45] Barraza offered volunteers the opportunity to write their names and their families' names on a white balloon with the destinations where the migrated family members live as well as personalized or prepared messages such as "love" or "peace" (see figure 3.14). Volunteers released these balloons into the sky in a symbolic gesture of trust that the message would make it to their loved ones, just as they had to trust that their loved ones would reach their destinations safely when they first departed on the migratory journey. Like the fragile balloon, easily pushed off its course by a gust of wind, the migrant represents uncertainty for separated family members but also hopes and dreams. Through video, illustration, installation, and action, Iraheta, del Cid, and Barraza shift the border and center the emotional consequence of family separation for those left behind. Their works highlight the love and efforts to preserve family connectedness by those forcibly displaced and thus shift the negative narratives around migrant parents to acts of love and resilience.

MAPPING REMITTANCE ECONOMIES

Over the past few decades, remittance practices have altered the visual landscape of the region. With his photographic project *Faraway Brother Style* (2008–10), artist Walterio Iraheta demonstrates how the ultimate symbol of migrant success—building a casita (a home)—transforms the aesthetics of Central

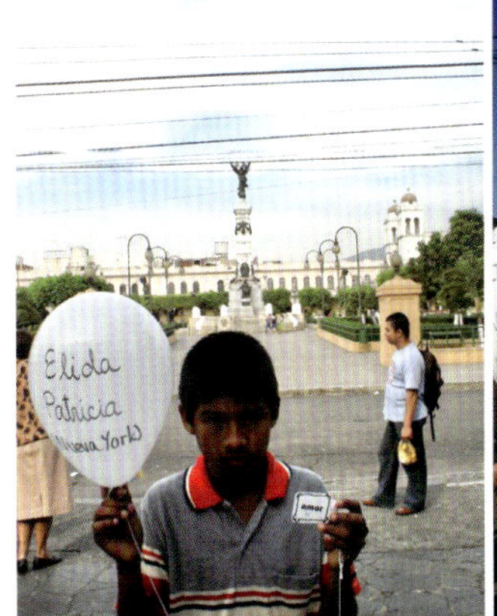

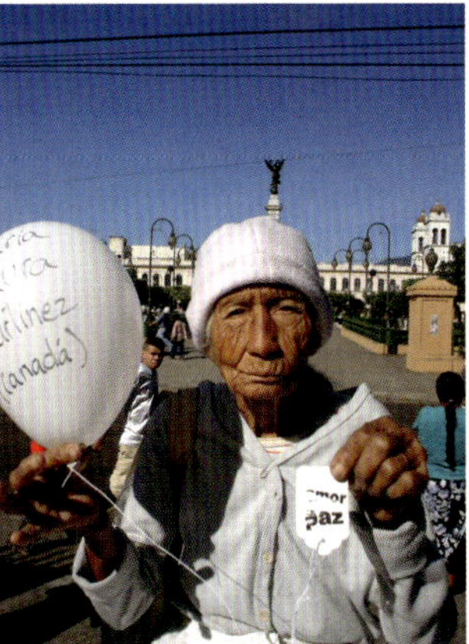

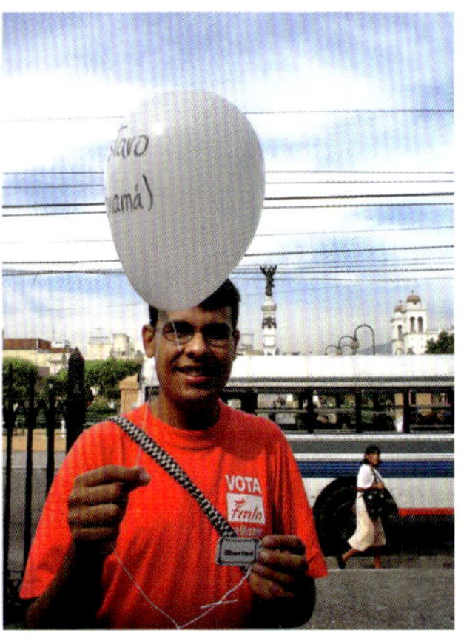

FIGURE 3.14.
Myra Barraza, *Un saludo desde la hermana república de El Salvador*, 2006, action. Courtesy of the artist.

American rural areas toward a transnational architectural style (see figure 3.15). The project is a photographic study of homes funded by remittances throughout Guatemala, El Salvador, and Honduras. Migrants in the United States design these homes from a distance. They send instructions to build dream homes with typical Latin American bold colors in their rural hometowns but with the elaborate and decadent fusion of styles seen in US homes and/or in US popular culture. The artist refers to them as portraits, for each home represents the desires of migrants and, moreover, is a symbol of migrant success and the justification for the sacrifices brought on by their migration.[46] The homes depart from traditional styles to represent a mixture of the classical, baroque, and kitsch. They include multiple floors, ornate baroque-like decor, and even Greek columns, creating what the artist has called a new "Estilo hermano lejano" or "Faraway brother style" of architecture. *Hermano lejano* is the term used for Salvadorans who have migrated to the United States, but the title is also a parody of prestigious publishers like Taschen and Phaidon, which have produced architectural compilations that highlight international trends with titles such as *London Style*, *New York Style*, and *Paris Style*.[47]

The increase in control by gangs in rural areas (discussed in the following chapter) has forced many families to abandon their homes for safety, either to other parts of the country or to the United States to reunify with their families. As a result, several of the remittance houses are abandoned, leaving the appearance of ghostly mansions throughout the Central American terrain. In other cases, since progress is contingent on the migrants' financial stability, certain unforeseen events such as layoffs or sickness can cause long pauses in construction, revealing a capricious temporal building process. With the liberty to build at one's own pace, and dependent on the remittances and vision of the migrant from afar, Iraheta has also referred to these new structures as "buildings without architects." From up-close details of homes to bird's-eye views of villages, Iraheta captures the visual contrast between humble Central American residencies and the eclectic and elaborated styles in the architecture of remittances.

The dependence on remittances is tied to a capitalist system in which imperial investors continue colonizing practices over Central American wealth (lands, resources, and labor).[48] From the golden age of foreign investment in Central America during the 1950s and 1960s, to the shift away from agriculture and toward elite companies investing in shopping malls, banking, tourism, and hotels, the economic structure of Central America has affected land uses and prices and led the isthmus to become one of the most consumer-driven regions in the Americas. The new economic structure has reinforced the position of the ruling elite, who continue to increase their wealth through the exploitation

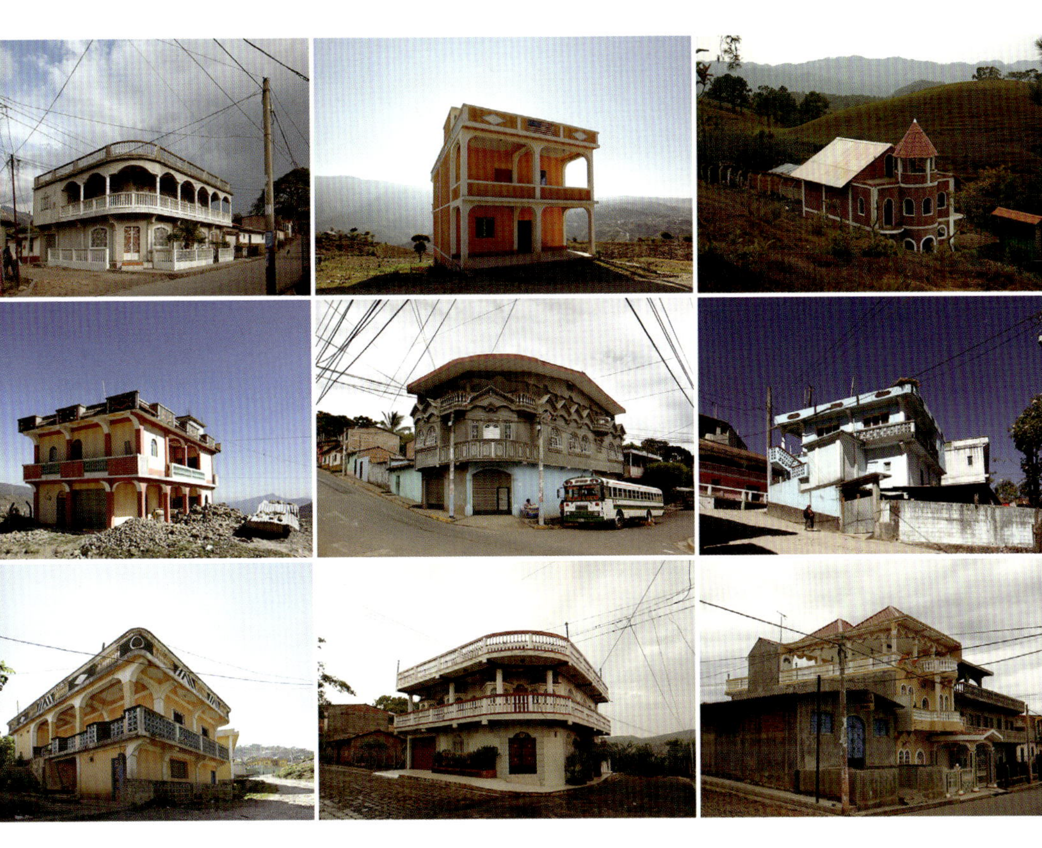

FIGURE 3.15.
Walterio Iraheta, *Faraway Brother Style*, 2008–10, photographs. Courtesy of the artist.

of the poor, and there is increased international interest in the region by those who see it as a growing consumer market. Yet this economic structure does not support access to water, food, or energy services for the poor. Central American governments have benefited by co-opting migrants' remittances to create the illusion of development and social mobility through what scholar José Luis Rocha calls the "Wal-Martization of the poor."[49] Those previously unable to participate in consumerist practices are now the main targets for companies who cater to remittance recipients, for whom consumption at fast food restaurants and shopping malls represents development and social mobility.

In response to the co-optation of migrant remittances by governments, artist Simón Vega offers a visual opposition to Iraheta's architecture of remittances. Using cardboard boxes, wood, plastic, and other discarded items, Vega fuses brands and logos associated with Global North consumption with the structure of a shopping mall. His installation *Shanty Mall* (2006) references the increase in large shopping mall structures and how the shopping centers—markers of foreign products and capitalism—are improvised like the shanty homes throughout the region, which are typically makeshift habitats among the poorest sections of Latin America (see figure 3.16). The structure points to those unable to build their own homes but who nonetheless fuel the rising consumption culture in Central America. Vega alludes to consumption by the poor with the remnants of Kentucky Fried Chicken (KFC) and McDonald's packaging and ripped cardboard boxes that constitute the unstable structure. In using solely discarded items, he points to Central American consumption of US culture as a superficial aid to the social inequalities of the country, and its negative impact on the environment—the foundation of the structure is built on precarity and exploitation. These works also address the social relations these cities produce.[50] Installations representing shopping malls as sites of congregation and consumption evoke the marketplaces and pyramids of ancient civilizations that once held social and political value, pointing to the shifting structure and social dynamics resulting from colonial legacies.

Leading businesses in Central America, whose wealth is facilitated by an increase in sales to remittance recipients, benefit from migrants without having to increase wages for Central American employees. As their wealth increases, while employment decreases, companies create a new dependency model that is contingent on migration and exploitation of migrants' labor in the United States. Other examples include airplane companies that benefit from migrants' travel to and from Central America, as evidenced by the drastic wealth increase of Central American airlines like TACA. In 1990, the airline

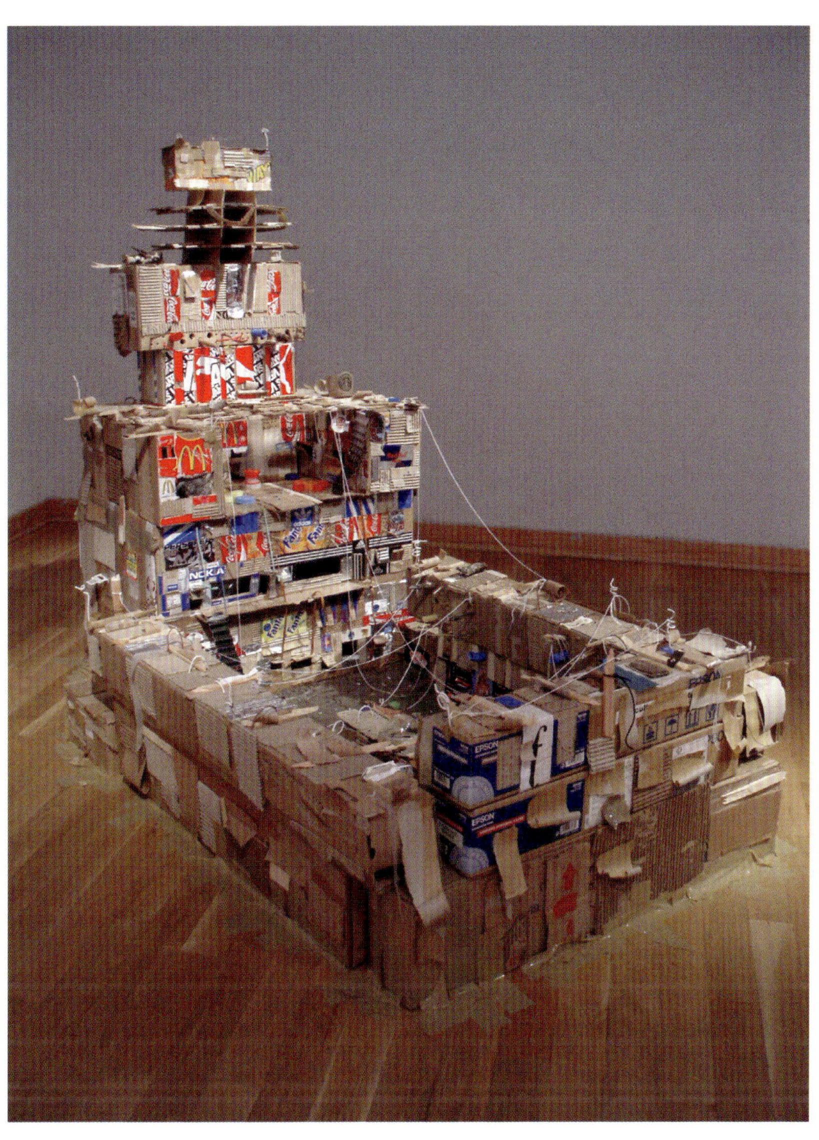

FIGURE 3.16.
Simón Vega, *Shanty Mall*, 2006, multimedia installation. Courtesy of the artist.

transported 123,000 people between the United States and El Salvador alone, which multiplied ten times over by 2004, when it transported more than 1.3 million people.[51] Likewise, telephone companies make large profits from remittance recipients, as telephone communication is a key method of maintaining connections from a distance, especially for families with children. As the leading provider for Central America, the Mexican telecommunication corporation América Móvil is one of the biggest corporations in the world and number one in Latin America.[52] Despite a third of the population living on less than a dollar a day, one out of every seven Central Americans is an América Móvil consumer.[53] As Rocha explains, Central America is "Nokia and Motorola territory."[54]

With his sculptural installation *Remesa Republic* (Remittance republic) (2007), Honduran artist Adán Vallecillo references the hegemony of remittance transfer companies in Central America such as the American company Western Union (see figure 3.17). Abstracting the iconic Western Union logo and colors, Vallecillo constructs a flag-like installation that juxtaposes black on one side and yellow on the other, with a spirit level (an instrument used to determine evenness on a surface) as the spine and handle. The artist draws on visual familiarity, with no need for figuration, for most Central Americans will easily associate black and yellow with the Western Union logo. Remittance transfer companies like Western Union surpass the profits made from telecommunications and air travel. With slogans like "connecting families around the world" and "sending so much more than money," the company advertises itself as the missing link that facilitates a system of migration, labor, and remittances, thus connecting transnational families and facilitating the ultimate goal of migrants who have sacrificed so much. Yet this facilitation comes at a cost that migrants must absorb and that further profits the company. Along with fees for the money transfers and for currency exchange, in a four-year span (2002–6) Western Union obtained US$17.9 billion in gross receipts and US$3.72 million in net income, with 84 percent from remittance clients.[55] Fittingly, Vallecillo replaces the common "banana republic" label associated with Central America with "remesa republic," reflected in the title, suggesting that the former colonial agro-export model of international banana companies, like United Fruit Company, is now merely replaced with a neoliberal remittance-based economic model.

Esquivel returns to the metaphorical line to expose how dollarization relies on migration and remittances yet is designed to benefit the financial autocracy. His series titled Líneas de desplazamiento (Lines of displacement) (2009–14) points to El Salvador's adoption of the US dollar in a bi-monetary system that

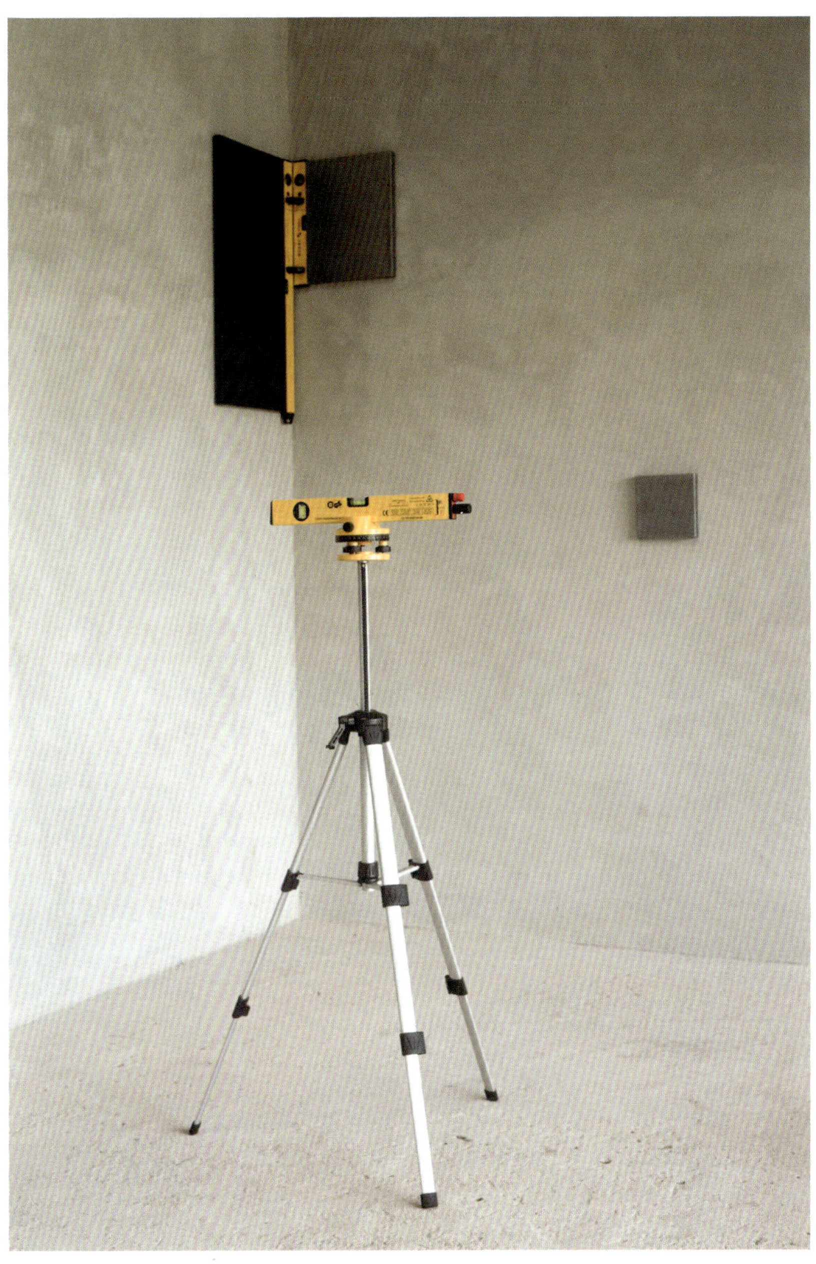

FIGURE 3.17.
Adán Vallecillo, *Remesa Republic*, 2007, multimedia installation. Courtesy of the artist.

was supposed to facilitate remittance transfers, but that ultimately displaced the national coin, *el colon*, for the imperial currency, here the US quarter (see figure 3.18). Scholars observe that the dollarization of El Salvador allowed the ruling class to profit off the alienation of the Salvadoran people, and the people's response to that alienation is often migration and remittances.[56] Remittances deposited in banks privatized in the 1990s created reserves that guarantee international loans for elites through the International Monetary Fund, the World Bank, and the Inter-American Development Bank.[57] The elite then privatized services, such as telecommunication and transportation, forcing Salvadorans to pay more for these services with the remittances their families send. Meanwhile, the majority, who can no longer use the land for life-sustaining production, must "export" themselves to send remittances to their families.[58]

In Líneas de desplazamiento, Esquivel laboriously deguts the US quarter, echoing the degutting in his *Líneas de referencia* performance, which introduced this chapter, by cutting out the eagle from its center, thereby devaluing the coin. The liberated eagles are then arranged in the form of a map representing Central America and Mexico, dispersing into the United States (see figure 3.19). With the series, Esquivel exposes the role of remittance practices within the context of global capitalism and border imperialism. He conjures the line as a border beyond a static geographical location, or one singular wound, to one that affects movements, currency, migration, and diaspora. From the imagery of cutting the body to cutting the coin, Esquivel takes control of the line to show how colonizing lines shape Central American lives, taking the idea of the border line beyond a one-dimensional figure to reveal the unrepresentable, unmappable, nonlinear ways that remittances, migration, and diaspora are connected. Collectively, with photography and object-based interventions, Iraheta, Vallecillo, and Esquivel map remittances beyond measurement in numbers and commodities to highlight new and simultaneously emergent forms of life, networks, and forms of resistance.

TOWARD COUNTERCARTOGRAPHIES OF MIGRATION

As the artworks highlighted here demonstrate, shifting the border is an act of visual disobedience that alters our temporal, geographical, and embodied perceptions of war, migration, mobility, mapping, families, architecture, and economies. Shifting the border implies a temporal gesture, and as such we cannot divorce the US-backed war and repression of the 1970s and 1980s from the mass migration occurring today. It further demands a perceptual shift in

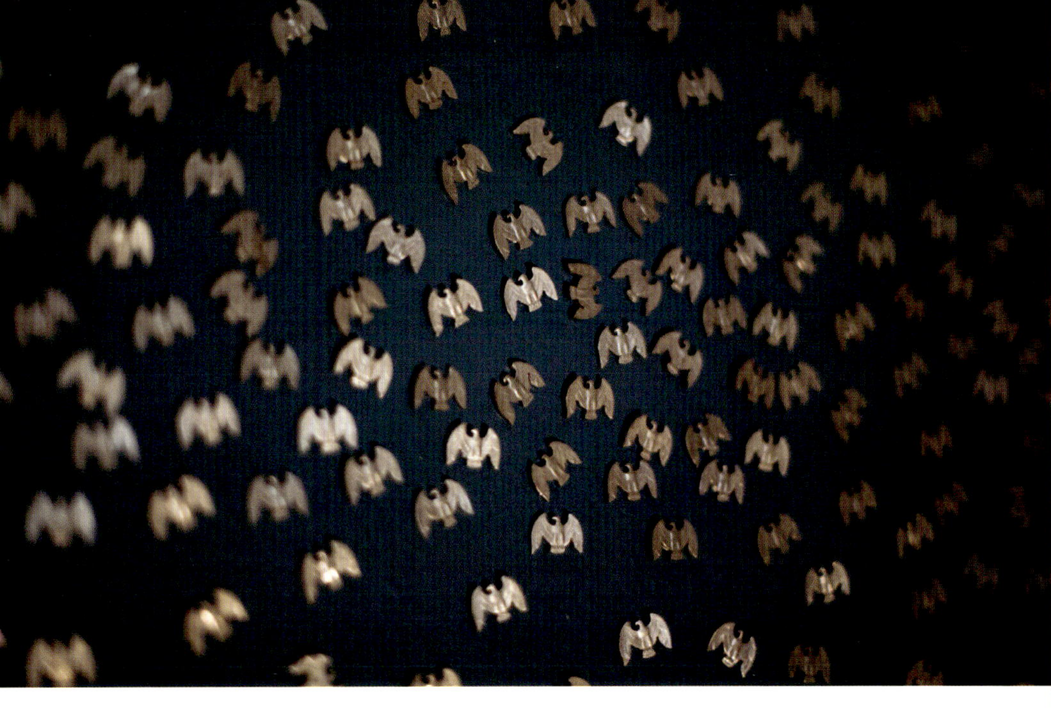

FIGURE 3.18.
Mauricio Esquivel, Líneas de desplazamiento series (coins), 2009–14, intervened coins and multimedia installation. Courtesy of the artist.

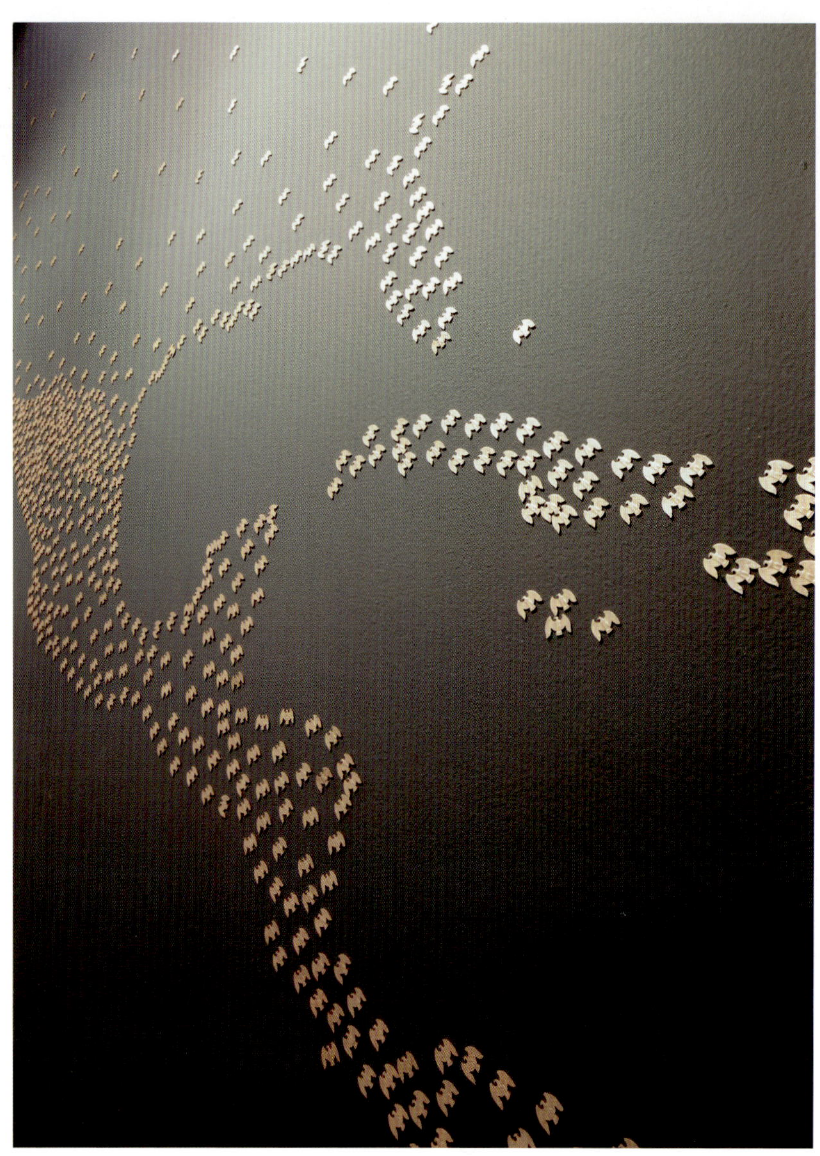

FIGURE 3.19.
Mauricio Esquivel, Líneas de desplazamiento series (map), 2009–14, intervened coins and multimedia installation. Courtesy of the artist.

accountability, including recognizing the complicity of Central American governments and the social hypocrisy of nations that criminalize and police migrants. This reveals that border coloniality exists not only at the US-Mexico border but also within the isthmus, where anti-immigrant and anti-Black sentiment also manifest. Shifting the border calls into question the anti-immigrant media framings that paint Central American migrant parents as unfit, uncaring, and responsible for the separation of their families, when in reality migration is the only option for survival. Moreover, shifting the border demands we rethink the economies of migration within the broader capitalist and neoliberalist system, which, unlike Central American migrants, is allowed and encouraged to cross borders.

Importantly, shifting the border opens possibilities for recentering migrants' phenomenological experiences of migration and to connect these experiences to embodied epistemes. Mapping systems usually ignore embodied experience over a singular colonial and imperial gaze, yet these artists demand their reconceptualization. They defy the visual coloniality around the migrant body, which typically is only made visible when it evidences the aftermath of migration and border coloniality, by instead highlighting their dreams, creativity, and humanity. Their visual disobedience centers the improvisational and creative play in generating and transferring knowledge systems of navigation rooted in phenomenological experience and ingenuity.

Ultimately, these various acts of shifting the border culminate in a countermapping of migration by Central American artists. They don't use the same language of the state to claim authenticity or accuracy in mapping territories but rather use a creative language that bypasses colonial strategies of mapping by centering bodies, networks, and spaces as intervention. This cartographic disobedience undermines the border regime's colonizing lines by relying on the embodied, oral, sensorial, intuitive, familial, and poetic ways that migrants navigate territories and defy colonially imposed borders. Their connections between land, bodies, and mobility reflect a community that resists border imperialism even before crossing borders in their own countries. They reveal to us that migrants are their own cartographers, who produce other ways of knowing and mapping, and survive a logic of disposability and the overall war on mobility. They don't mark territories but instead recenter the human freedom of mobility.

By shifting the border, these artists collectively illuminate a much more complex phenomenon of Central American migration than the narrow anti-immigrant rhetoric and reductive images espoused by the US government. But how can shifting the border complicate other issues deeply associated with the migratory experience of Central Americans, such as their systematic criminalization? How does a visual disobedience go beyond condemning the detention of Central American migrants at the US-Mexico border to instead connect illegality, citizenship, and social cleansing in a transnational manner that extends beyond the US-Mexico border and into a broader carceral logic as a colonial practice of dehumanization?

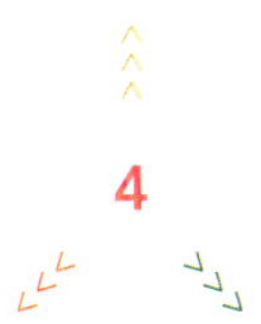

"LOS SIEMPRE SOSPECHOSOS DE TODO"

Art on Criminalization, Prisons, and Social Cleansing in Central America

Los que ampliaron el Canal de Panamá
los que repararon la flota del Pacífico
en las bases de California,
los que se pudrieron en las cárceles de Guatemala,
México, Honduras, Nicaragua
por ladrones, por contrabandistas, por estafadores,
por hambrientos
los siempre sospechosos de todo,
los que llenaron los bares y los burdeles
de todos los puertos y las capitales de la zona

los sembradores de maíz en plena selva extranjera,
los reyes de la página roja,
los que nunca sabe nadie de dónde son,
los mejores artesanos del mundo,
los que fueron cosidos a balazos
al cruzar la frontera,
los que murieron de paludismo
o de las picaduras del escorpión o la barba amarilla
en el infierno de las bananeras,
los que lloraron borrachos por el himno nacional
bajo el ciclón del Pacífico o la nieve del norte,
los arrimados, los mendigos, los marihuaneros,
los guanacos hijos de la gran puta,
los que apenitas pudieron regresar,
los que tuvieron un poco más de suerte,
los eternos indocumentados,
los hacelotodo, los vendelotodo, los comelotodo,
los primeros en sacar el cuchillo,
los tristes más tristes del mundo,
mis compatriotas,
mis hermanos.
ROQUE DALTON, "Poema de amor" (emphasis added)

In 1974, Salvadoran revolutionary poet Roque Dalton (1935–75) wrote a "Love Poem" to the Salvadoran people.[1] Critiquing the exploitation and criminalization of Salvadorans under US imperialism, he describes them as the most tragic, unknown, rotten, exploited, foreign, drunk, violent, and saddest people—and, lovingly, his brothers. Many in the Salvadoran diaspora recognize the poem as a type of anthem, yet it is Dalton's phrases such as "los eternos indocumentados" (the eternally undocumented) or "los siempre sospechosos de todo" (the ever suspected ones), comparable to Frantz Fanon's "the wretched of the earth," that reflect a condition Central Americans face across borders—systematic criminalization.[2] While Dalton attributed the phrase to a pre-neoliberal and prerevolutionary Central American labor force enduring exploitation in the banana plantations or while building the Panama Canal or repairing the Pacific fleet, these phrases continue to find resonance for Central Americans in a postwar and neoliberal context in which, as artist Victor "Crack" Rodriguez describes, to be young and poor is to be criminal.

More recently, the phrase "los siempre sospechosos de todo" was adopted as the name for an art collective in El Salvador that formed in response to the unfounded arrest of twenty-one-year-old Daniel Alemán. On January 10, 2017, Daniel was detained and arrested by police with no cause or reason while playing basketball with his friends in the neighborhood of Alta Vista, Ilopango, El Salvador. When the family publicly demanded answers about the charges and his whereabouts, authorities added bogus charges that ranged from drug possession and intention to distribute, to extortion and membership in a criminal organization. The police presented no evidence for any of the charges. Understanding that Daniel's case would soon be lost in the system and he would be forgotten and disappeared like countless other Salvadoran and Central American youth, Daniel's sister, artist Tatiana Alemán, began a campaign via Twitter and soon was joined by local youth and young artists. Victor "Crack" Rodriguez, well known for a performance in which he ate his ballot at the polls during the 2016 Salvadoran presidential elections as a critique of politicians' hunger for power and corruption and was detained for it, joined Alemán to lead the collective.[3]

The collective's interventions are known to fuse humor and political critique of the judicial system in Central America. In several actions, members dressed in white T-shirts, shorts, and long socks—the clothing typically given to those arrested and detained. At times they were restrained with plastic ties or handcuffs, and they carried megaphones as they read poetry or denounced police brutality and corruption that targets young people. They walked in procession from iconic sites, through public streets, and to police headquarters, where they gathered with arms interlaced in the manner that inmates are transferred from one place to another. They thus disrupted public spaces with the signifiers of captivity.

In an action titled *Poleas* (Pulleys) from October 2017, members simulated a Salvadoran judicial system that exploits and benefits from the criminalization of the poor (see figure 4.1). Members dressed in white as detainees attempted to balance on unicycles. Meanwhile, with the same yellow rope tied around their necks to symbolize their captivity and sentencing, they sustained a hammock in which a member representing the judicial system comfortably lay. Other members further carried the weight of the hammock and the person relaxing in it, pointing to a network of officials that make the exploitation possible. All concealed their identities behind Mexican wrestler masks in a reference to impunity and cover-up. The action took place in front of the entrance to the courts in El Salvador, where the security barrier displayed white banners with the phrase "Culpable por ser joven" (Guilty of being young) and the faces

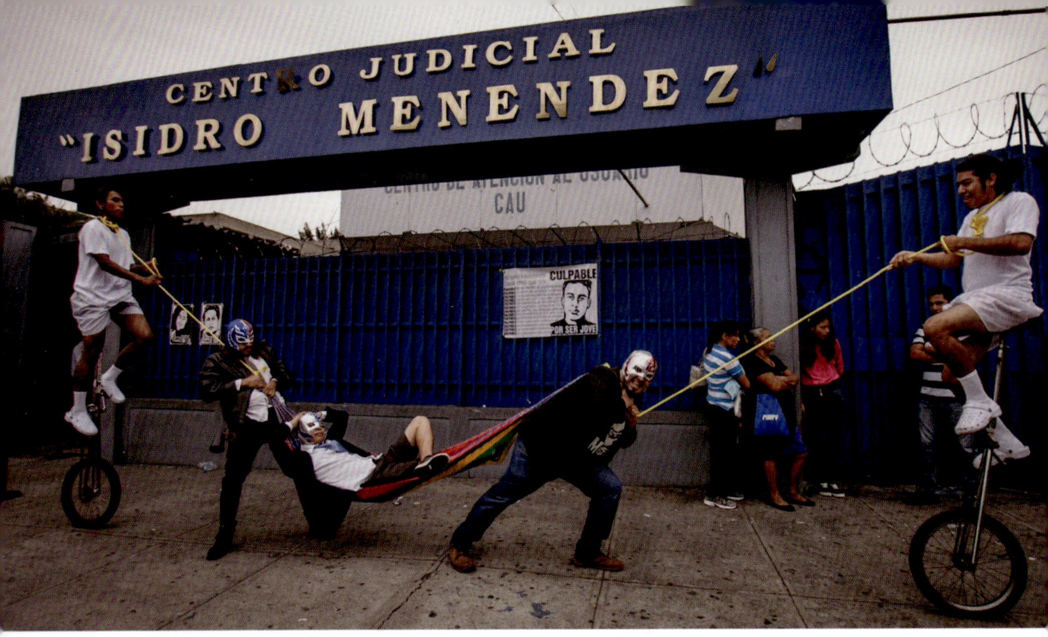

FIGURE 4.1.
Los Siempre Sospechosos de Todo, *Poleas*, 2017, intervention. Photograph by Salvador Melendez. Image courtesy of Salvador Melendez/Revista Factum.

of Daniel Alemán and others. The main banner listed the actual structural reasons why poor youth are equated with guilt. They included "GUILTY for being a member of a poor family," "GUILTY for living in a gang conflict zone," "GUILTY because we lost identity in 1932," and "GUILTY for the breach of peace accords," among others.[4] With humor and spectacle, the artists drew in family members who witnessed and interpreted the performances and began to share their own experiences, opening opportunities for healing. With the visibility the collective brought to the case of arrested youth Daniel Alemán, Daniel was eventually released, though police retaliation forced him to leave the country in exile. Others are not so lucky.

Daniel's arrest is emblematic of the state's weaponization of anti-gang policies that target poor youth to spread fear, keep people subdued, and maintain control through political repression, all under the auspices of eliminating gang and criminal organizations. A series of policies under El Plan Mano Dura (The Firm/Iron Fist Plan) implemented in 2003, for instance, followed by Plan Súper Mano Dura (The Super Firm/Iron Fist Plan) in 2006, and Ley antimaras (Anti-gang law), consisted of area sweeps, police and military patrols, and arrests of *suspected* gang-affiliated youth. Arrests were based solely on physical traits, which was later ruled unconstitutional, but persists.[5] Following Plan Mano Dura, police harassment and detention of poor people on suspicion of gang membership became a daily routine that has led to mass incarceration under deplorable conditions and other human rights violations. These policies that purportedly aimed to eliminate unlawful activity in practice do little more than criminalize poor youth.

In March 2022, figures drastically multiplied when the president of El Salvador, Nayib Bukele, in response to a spike in gang homicides, issued a "state of exception" that increased sweeps and arbitrary arrests with the additional suspension of citizen rights to assemble and to due process. Bukele continues to renew his state of exemption, which was aimed to be temporary. It resulted in fifty-five thousand arrests in the first seven months, with three thousand complaints of human rights violations, and protests by families of innocent detainees who disappear in the system.[6] By January 31, 2023, Bukele inaugurated a new "mega-prison," which he calls the Terrorism Confinement Center, aimed to be the largest in the Americas and to hold captive the massive numbers of arrested people.[7] As Jorge Cuéllar explains, "Bukele's state of exception has produced the very emergency it aims to resolve, relying on the deep-seated punitive culture that has made every Salvadoran *a suspect*."[8]

High incarceration rates are also seen across Central America. According to a 2018 report on the world prison population, Nicaragua had the largest increase in prison population in all the Americas over a three-year period with a rise of 61 percent.[9] In the isthmus, Belize and Panama—two countries with large Black populations—are among the countries with the highest prison population rates, with El Salvador holding the number one spot.[10] In 2018, El Salvador held the second-highest prison population *globally*, beat out only by the United States, which holds the highest prison rate in the world.[11] Since the year 2000, Central America experienced a 77 percent growth in the prison population, with El Salvador and Panama still among the countries with the highest prison population rates by 2020.[12] Thus, it isn't unreasonable to ask: is there a correlation between the state's criminalization of youth in the region and the illegality placed on Central American migrants in the United States?

The criminalization of undocumented people is connected to the larger history of mass incarceration in the United States. Patrisia Macías-Rojas has shown how prison overcrowding due to the US war on crime against people of color became an incentive to convict immigrants of felonies.[13] Making migrants more easily deportable as felons also impedes or further complicates their return. Thus, migrants with no criminal record are coerced into assuming culpability for a felony, and those who are deported and return are automatically criminalized. Others have shown how criminalizing racialized peoples further impedes solidarity and coalition building by positioning oppressed groups against each other in the fight for who deserves value. That is, *value*, understood as *citizenship* and all the social worth it assumes, is linked to the devaluation of another, as Lisa Marie Cacho has argued.[14]

Some scholars and activists therefore reject striving to expand access to citizenship, given its function to reinforce violence against nonnormative people.[15] Framing Central American refugees as deserving of citizenship protection and human rights often depends on proving they are not gang members or terrorists, that is, the "real" criminals. In other words, the fight for citizenship is often dependent on the presumption of criminality and guilt of one group rather than the presumption of innocence or asylum as human rights claim. Meanwhile, the prison abolitionist Dylan Rodríguez has argued that incarceration, beyond the concrete shape it takes through jails, prisons, or detention centers, is a logic and method of dominance. This regime of dominance materializes in forms such as apartheid, military occupation, the reservation, the plantation, and the border.[16] Since carceral logic reveals the underside of the New World, prison abolition is a necessary project of Black and Indigenous liberation, anticolonialism, and decolonization.

As I show in this chapter, Central American artists engage discourses on illegality, worth, and citizenship in a transnational manner. Beyond a critique of anti-immigrant sentiment, they expose a carceral logic rooted in coloniality that perpetuates the criminalization of Central Americans across borders and that is inseparable from the colonial agenda of social cleansing of poor, racialized, and marginalized people. Collectively, their visual disobedience directed against the policing, criminalization, and imprisonment of Central Americans—both within the region and across borders—contributes less to advocacy for immigration reform and more to the urgency of a global prison abolitionist movement.

THE MAKING AND VISUAL CONSUMPTION OF THE *MARERO*

In the 1980s, as a result of the US-funded civil war, Los Angeles became home to the second-largest population of Salvadorans in the world after the capital city of San Salvador. Recently arrived children settled in the city, attended barrio schools, and came to develop an "American" lifestyle, language, and culture. Some children's memories of the war remained painful but faint, while others were too young to have any recollection of their native country. As citizens of barrios, with inadequate schools, little to no educational and economic resources, and racist institutional structures, some of these youth joined local gangs and faced further exposure to violence fueled by poverty and policing.

This violence reached new levels during the Los Angeles Riots of 1992, when law enforcement accused Latino youth and gangs of looting and violent activities. A series of anti-gang laws followed that allowed minors to be charged as adults, sentencing many who committed petty crimes with felony charges. Legislation such as Proposition 184 of 1994, known as the "three strikes and you are out" law, and an increase of anti-immigration laws augmented jail time and deportation of both citizens and noncitizens, resulting in the expulsion of twenty thousand criminalized youth to Central America.[17] Many had no family or home awaiting them, and often no memories of the landscape or the people.

With their "American" accents and nostalgia for the fast-paced urban cities they were forced to leave behind, the recently arrived youth found themselves in a region still recovering from decades of civil war, one that neither welcomed them nor felt like home. At times, the only connections they made were with other gang members, or *maras*. Many found solace in the fraternity and solidarity of gangs, but the experience of extreme poverty led many newly arrived to immigrate back to the United States, where they still held ties to family and community. In this social process of international migration, the interchange of symbols and materials keeps migrants and nonmigrants connected, forming a network or community. Gangs whose members engaged in circular transnational migration between cities like Los Angeles and rural towns throughout

Central America constituted such transnational communities. The most well-known examples are La Mara Salvatrucha (MS-13) and 18th Street Gang—the two most dominant rival gangs in Central America.[18] This transnational phenomenon of gangs led Juan Carlos Narváez Gutiérrez to note that a gang dispute initiated in the West Lake area of Los Angeles can easily end with five deaths in the stadium of Cuscatlán in the capital of El Salvador.[19]

While the US media and government overlook the US role in the making of transnational gangs, emphasizing only their illegality for the purpose of fueling anti-immigrant fear and hate, Central American artists address through a different lens the phenomenon that has so deeply shaped the postwar region and that to date is used to justify massive imprisonment. Well-known Salvadoran artist Danny Zavaleta grounds the emergence of transnational gangs as a direct consequence of the US-funded war. In *Retrato hablado* (Speaking portrait) (2009), Zavaleta disrupts the hegemonic narratives that dehistoricize the rise of gangs in the region. For the piece, he interviewed MS-13 gang member Carlos Portillo, who offered the artist personal letters, documents, and photographs during their conversations. With the material collected, Zavaleta created a photo album of Portillo's life that visually narrated Portillo's journey of displacement, gang membership, and deportations (see figure 4.2).

The album and narrative begin with photographs of Portillo's involvement at age fourteen in the Salvadoran military forces. The forced recruitment of children into the military was common, but Portillo enlisted as a volunteer informant to gather information that would help the guerillas.[20] Once the military discovered him, he was forced to seek political exile in the United States. Photographs then show his arrival in the MacArthur Park area of Los Angeles, where a large concentration of recently arrived Central American migrants resided and still do.[21] Like many Central American inner-city youths, Portillo needed protection from local Mexican-American gangs and as a result joined MS-13. He eventually spent time in prison—an experience illuminated in the album by love letters from his girlfriend and pictures mailed by his niece. Due to the anti-immigrant and anti-gang policies at the time, Portillo was deported along with thousands of youths back to El Salvador, where he remained an active member of the MS-13 gang and facilitated a transnational gang community.[22] Although the civil war had ceased, he returned to a new manifestation of the violence he fled as a child.

Anthropologist Elana Zilberg has observed that in postwar Central America the unpatriotic image of a leftist subversive from the 1980s was replaced by the new marked and criminalized body, now manifested in the *marero*.[23] The same national enemy rhetoric that governments used during the conflict

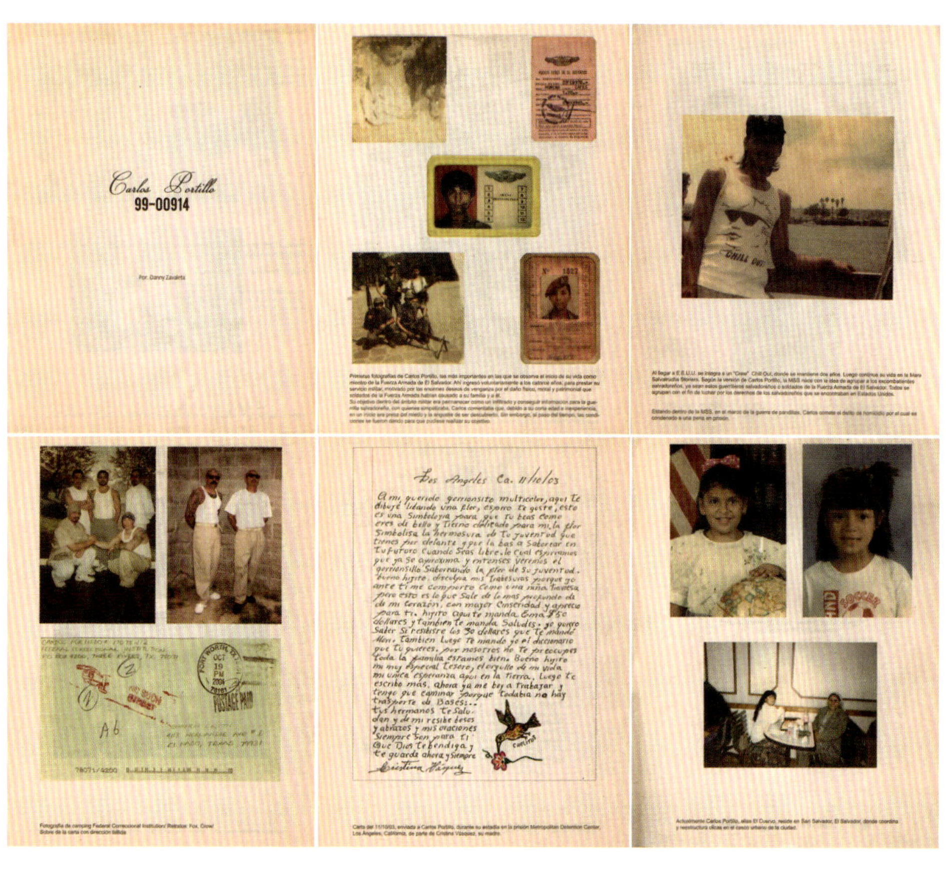

FIGURE 4.2.
Danny Zavaleta, *Retrato hablando*, 2009, book. Courtesy of the artist.

period was then directed toward gangs and criminalized youth to propagate the narrative of Central Americans as a transnational and global threat and as inherently criminal. Central American governments declared war against the "region's enemy," and in 2013 the US government declared the notorious gang Mara Salvatrucha 13 a "transnational criminal organization" that poses a danger to the region, the United States, and the world.[24] Gang members' bodies are now found murdered just like death squad victims during the 1980s, often displaying the same torture techniques taught by the School of the Americas during the armed conflict. The Salvadoran gang has come to function as what Zilberg calls a "dialectical image" that embodies a "doble-cara": an act of mimesis to replace the body of violence from the civil war and more recently that of the state police.[25] Now the war is fought against the criminalized, like Portillo.

Challenging notions of Portillo as innately criminal, Zavaleta emphasizes Portillo's humanity through a diary-like glimpse into his intimate experiences and relations, showing how his life was shaped by US intervention in Central America and anti-immigrant policies in the United States. Zavaleta exposes the carceral logic of dehumanization behind Portillo's criminalization and the ongoing violence he must navigate across borders. When *Retrato hablado* is exhibited, viewers are encouraged to take and keep a copy of the album. Viewers take legal documents, photographs, and prison letters from Portillo's mother, his girlfriend, and his niece that illustrate the personal journey of not just a "marero" but a human being, a son, an uncle, and a partner. Though Portillo is now widely seen as a perpetrator of violence who controls and terrorizes rural towns and urban streets, Zavaleta reminds the viewer that this individual's criminalized experience started with a US imperial logic and violence that set him up for further criminalization in the region. That is, before becoming a perpetrator of violence, he was a victim of US imperial dominance.

With *Retrato hablado*, Zavaleta counters visual thingification—the colonialist practice of fabricating visual evidence for the negation and dehumanization of the colonized, justifying violence against those subjects—as applied to criminalized youth. The visual thingification of criminalized Central Americans is rooted in a broader history of visual coloniality that aims to strip poor racialized people's humanity and negate their rights to freedom, existence, and citizenship. The *marero*, as a postwar Central American criminal image, has become an object of interest in social science and cultural studies as well as in Hollywood films.[26] Part of the fascination with looking at Central American gangs is their physical appearance: racialized bodies notorious for tattoos that sometimes cover the entire face. Foreign photographers have entered neighborhoods and prisons to photograph Central American gangs, echoing nineteenth-century colonialist explorations, in which Europeans traveled to "uncivilized" lands to capture the essence of supposedly inferior beings. Today's glamorized portraits of imprisoned Central American gang members travel in exhibitions and are gazed at in similar fashion. The Central American gang member becomes yet another violent and simultaneously exotic creature—an object of study that draws the gaze to see and perpetuate the criminality of Central American bodies. *Retrato hablado* disrupts the visual thingification of Portillo by taking back Portillo's agency over his image and his narratives, which reveal personal accounts of violence to expose the carceral logic and systems that conscribe him in a cycle of violence, criminalization, and dehumanization. The work is, as the title implies, a portrait that speaks back and thus defies the US and Central American government narratives on gangs as well as the visual coloniality of the *marero* image.

CRIMINALITY AND FEAR SPATIALIZED

In addition to intimate narratives that emphasize the individual experience of violence, artists also address how a carceral logic has shaped urban experience in postwar Central America. Abolitionists and scholars such as Ruth Wilson Gilmore developed the field of carceral geographies to address the social spaces of incarceration, what Michel Foucault described as carceral circles, that like ripples of water extend prison disciplinary techniques out into society.[27] Such studies make connections between prison, immigration, and surveillance and recognize "the carceral" as spatial, emplaced, mobile, embodied, and affective, offering a critical understanding of the criminalization of migrants.[28] But how do artists theorize and understand a carceral spatiality tied to the rise of transnational gang culture and the state's criminalization of marginalized people within Central America? Public space is important to gang visual culture, as is the idea of performing identity in the streets, but the concept of "streets" does not merely imply an exterior place outside one's home. For gang members, home *is* the streets. It is a social space where members congregate, make a visual presence, claim a city, make financial transactions, confront law enforcement, and, often, succumb to violent deaths. The idea of "growing up in the streets" implies a different sense and experience of the city and home. It implies a spatial understanding of the *barrio*, the ghetto, or the hood and a blurring of the private and the public.

To show how the city of San Salvador has been transformed and criminalized as a result of transnational gang presence and the authorities that target them, Zavaleta created his most recognized artwork, *El tur* (The tour) (2006) (see figure 4.3). In the now iconic work, the artist uses a graffiti style to intervene into a tourist map of San Salvador using signs and symbols to mark various destinations. On the left, in pink, the word *Disneylandia* locates la Zona Rosa with its upscale shopping centers and clubs that cater to the Salvadoran elite. The image of the armed police references the growth of the private security business that protects certain communities from others. The number 18 stands in for the 18th Street Gang, and hand signs form an *M* for the Mara Salvatrucha gang. On the far right, against red bloodstains, the phrase *Soya City* marks the municipality of Soyapango, Zavaleta's hometown and one of the most notorious areas for gang activities.

With *El tur*, Zavaleta points to how the inscribed city and body can create new social boundaries and reconfigure territories and spaces. Through graffiti, or writing on walls, MS-13 members and other gangs have visually reshaped the landscape of cities like Los Angeles as well as cities and towns within Central America, such as Tegucigalpa, Guatemala City, Managua, and others. In addition to marking territory, tagging constitutes an artistic war for space and can be understood as a performative and embodied behavior. To write is to establish a presence. Like a soldier in war, the taggers clandestinely mark the gang's boundaries through identifiable letters and symbols (like the "MS-13" letters in written variations, or depicted MS-13 hand signs) in addition to members' names, often their own. This is further evidenced in Simón Vega's *Ciudad encajada* (2001), an installation that replicates the visual war of graffiti on a neighborhood, illustrating how the visual markings are then used by authorities to identify a space as lawless (see figure 4.4). Made from cardboard boxes, the installation (which translates to "boxed city") plays on the idea of marking territories and enclosing spaces, where breaking rules of inclusion and exclusion within these spaces and rules can result in visual and physical wars. Each box depicts the typical graffiti found on houses in residential neighborhoods. Viewers interact in the installation by rearranging the boxes and thus reflecting on the unstable nature of urban neighborhoods. The installation further resonates with the overpopulation of the city and the struggle for space and resources.

Displaced Central American urban youth must negotiate these criminalized, unstable, and safe or prohibited urban spaces to survive. Factors such as visual boundaries, marked identities, and even the presence of rival gangs and law enforcement dictate a member's movement through the city and further alter the phenomenological experience of urban space. While the visual alterations of space are enacted through graffiti, as Zavaleta's work shows, a performative characteristic is also conveyed—an act of transfer that is a means of survival. A performative walk through the streets can also be a tactical war

FIGURE 4.3.
Danny Zavaleta, *El tur*, 2006, intervened map. Courtesy of the artist.

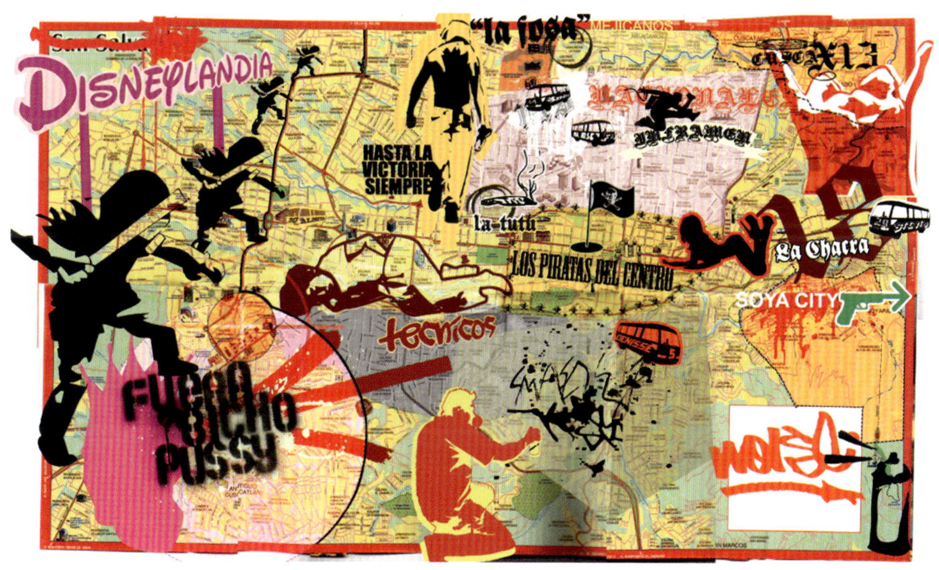

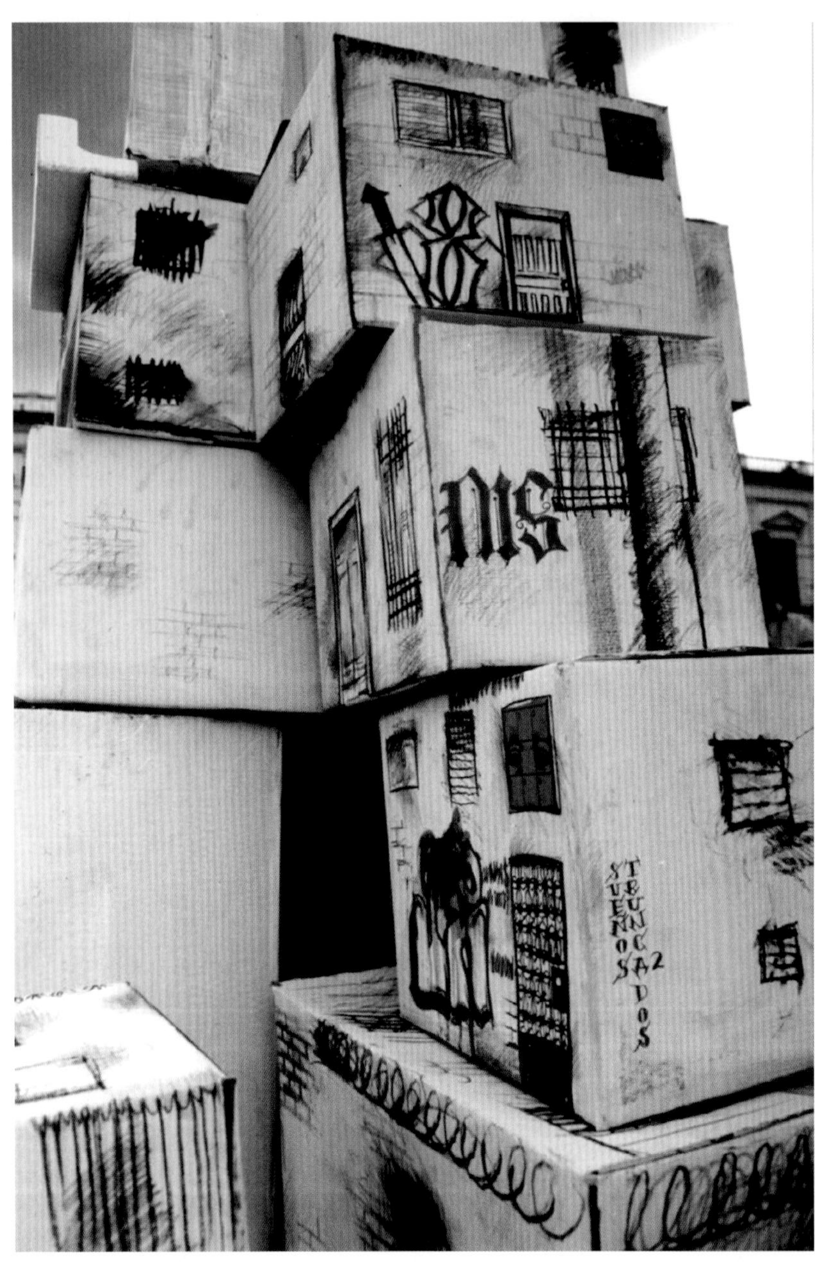

FIGURE 4.4.
Simón Vega, *Ciudad encajada*, 2001, multimedia installation. Courtesy of the artist.

strategy, a gesture meant to be seen by others and to create an imaginary trace or a boundary with which to claim spatial ownership. Michel de Certeau reminds us of the pedestrian speech act: "The act of walking is to the urban system what the speech act is to language or to the statements uttered. . . . It is a process of *appropriation* of the topographical system on the part of the pedestrian. . . . It is a spatial acting-out of the place . . . and it implies *relations* among differentiated positions. . . . It thus seems possible to give a preliminary definition of walking as a space of enunciation."[29] De Certeau's walking *as a space of enunciation*, in addition to Diana Taylor's notion of *repertoire*, helps elucidate that, as transnational identities, the city or the rural are performative spaces in which acts of transfer communicate knowledge and identity, incorporating and addressing all citizens.[30]

As seen in *Shanty Mall* (see figure 3.16), this altered urban space of a postwar El Salvador has led artist Simón Vega to engage with the social production of public space, especially the city of San Salvador. His works consider urban structures, houses, and malls and include transportation systems, such as public bus routes. Re-creating these spaces in his installations, he highlights the elements of quotidian life central to Salvadorans as they navigate the city. The region also has experienced the increasing criminalization of private and domestic spaces by the security industry. In his installation *Vigilantes invertidos* (Inverted vigilantes) (2001), Vega points to the fact that security and surveillance have become an obsession in a fearful country, one that security companies exploit for profit as security guards and surveillance cameras are now a popular commodity that only a few can afford (see figure 4.5). Using discarded items, his installations re-create the humble dwellings found throughout Central America and include an exaggerated amount of security cameras, stitched together from cardboard and tape. Vega exposes how the fear instilled during the conflict by media and governments that claimed to "protect" civilians from dangers of the leftist guerrillas is now used to sell protection from the threat of gangs and criminals. He thus critiques a society so fueled with paranoia and fear that it willingly submits to constant surveillance and imprisonment, transforming into a panopticon society—the ideal model of modern social organization for what Foucault called the "disciplinary society."[31] The same fear of criminality makes prisoners out of civilians. However, in opposition to the high-technology surveillance art that has emerged in the contemporary art world, which makes use of computers, surveillance machinery, biotechnology, and more, Vega uses the discarded items from shanty towns where cameras are stitched together from cardboard scarcely attached with tape, thus contrasting the First World panopticon society with the tropical world.[32]

When surveillance technology is inaccessible, barbed wire offers a practical alternative to security. In *Cuadros de costumbres* (Customs paintings) (2015), Guatemalan artist Jorge de León used barbed wire to create an enclosed space within a public space, in this case the central park in San Salvador's historic center—a site of intense crime and violence (see figure 4.6). For the work, de León created a cage-like structure constructed out of slabs of wood and barbed wire. Inside the structure, a mattress and small table made up a habitable space where a person resided. Placed over walls and rooftop, the sharp edges and intervals were designed to ward off intrusion. The steel fencing wire, along with the surveillance camera, have become another element of urban aesthetics in the region. Like Vega, de León connects the function of barbed wire as a protective security strategy to the criminalization of space and self-containment. It is only within a barbed wire structure that a person inside is able to confidently check their phone without fear of it being stolen or to just read a book and relax while in a public park. The structure's resemblance to a cage further alludes to the irony of Central American self-captivity aimed at producing a sense of security within criminalized spaces and is simultaneously a reference to the cages in the north awaiting those who flee such spaces.

Honduran, US-based artist Alma Leiva, who migrated as a teenager from San Pedro Sula, known as the deadliest city in Honduras, condemns how violence inevitably aids in the criminalization of domestic spaces, where violence and terror also lead to self-confinement within the home. Titled Celda (2010), or cell, her photographic installation series re-creates interiors of humble Honduran houses, in which public spaces of leisure and play are forced inside the home as a precautionary measure from the looming violence outside (see figure 4.7). The series is based on investigative observations of Honduran dwellings and expresses a domestic aesthetic that includes bright wall colors, religious iconography, minimal furniture, dirt or cement floors, cardboard walls, and popular patterns and drapes. Decorative details vary, such as the occasional inclusion of intimate altars with religious candles next to photographs of family members who possibly migrated north. These private domestic spaces are disrupted with the absurd penetration of large-scale public sites, such as an entire soccer field, a children's playground, a park birthday party, or even the beach, speaking to the danger of public social life.

The compositional framing of the photographs positions viewers with the same intruding presence, as if walking into an empty home. The absence of inhabitants leads one to question whether we see the ghostly remnants of a home after a direct threat, which many families at the border claim. Everything seems left exactly in its place, with the appearance of an archaeological find, leading

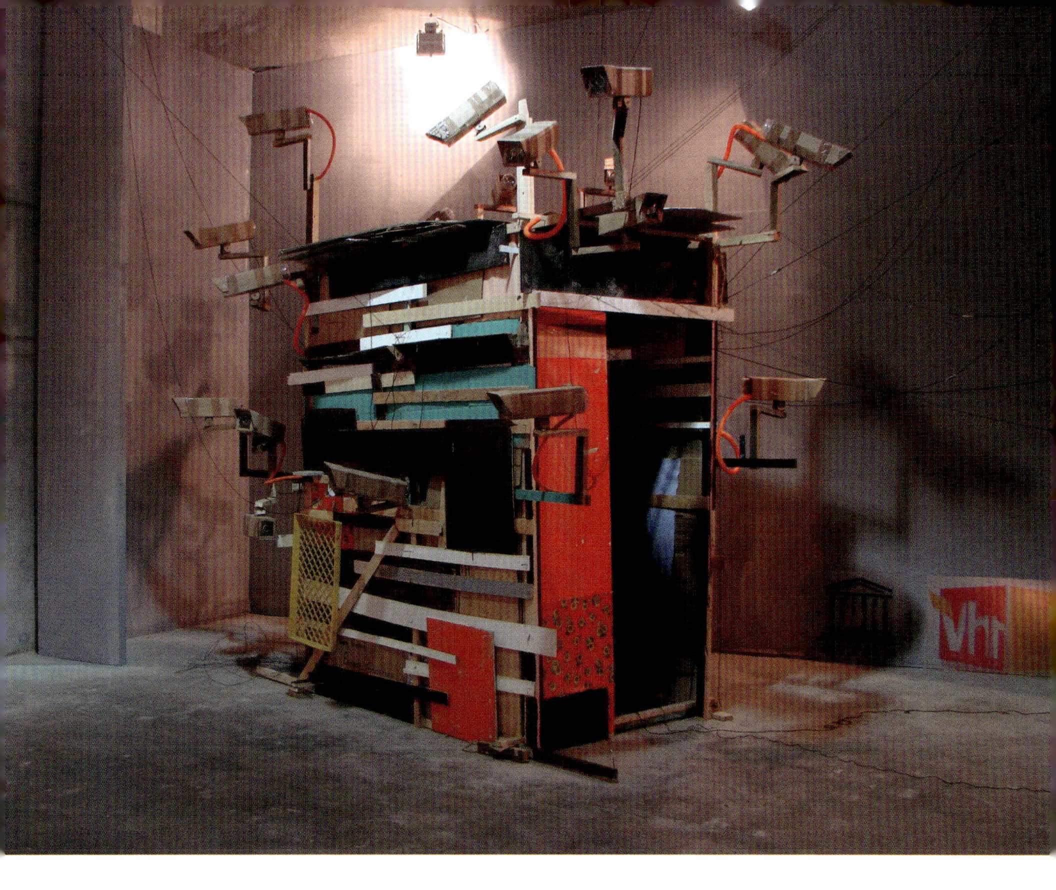

FIGURE 4.5.
Simón Vega, *Vigilantes invertidos*, 2001, multimedia installation. Courtesy of the artist.

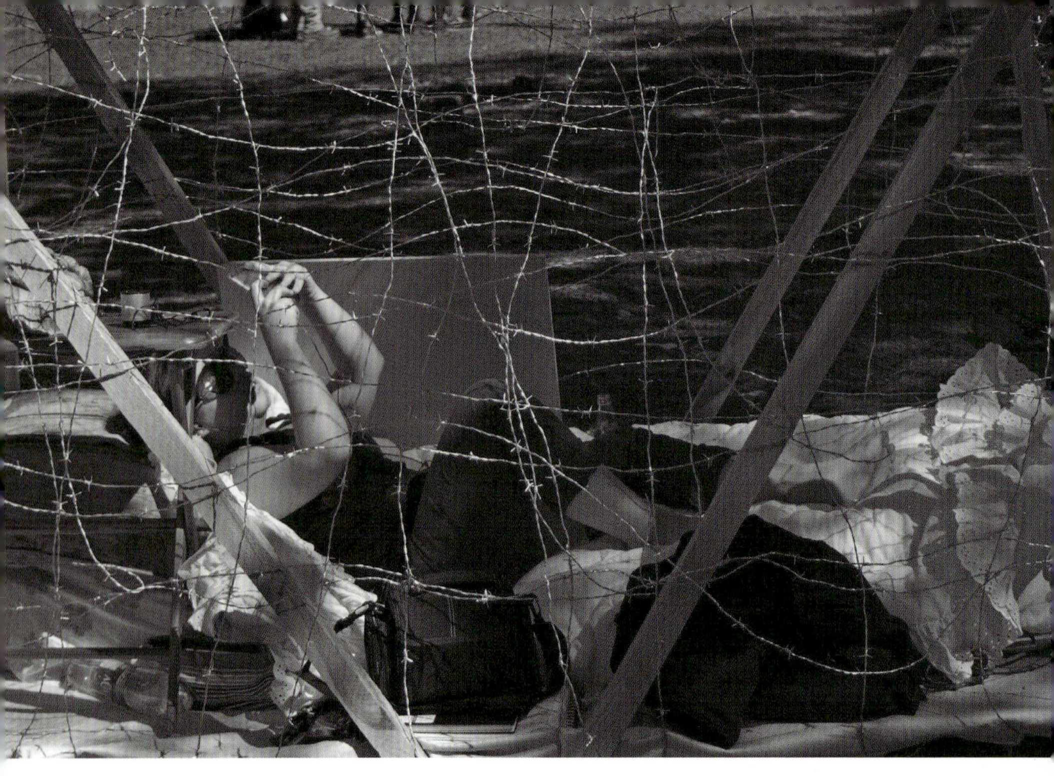

FIGURE 4.6.
Jorge de León, *Cuadros de costumbres*, 2015, performance. Forma y Sustancia, festival internacional de performance. Documentation by Alexander Fields for archive RACA, with the collaboration of Nora Perez. Image courtesy of the artist.

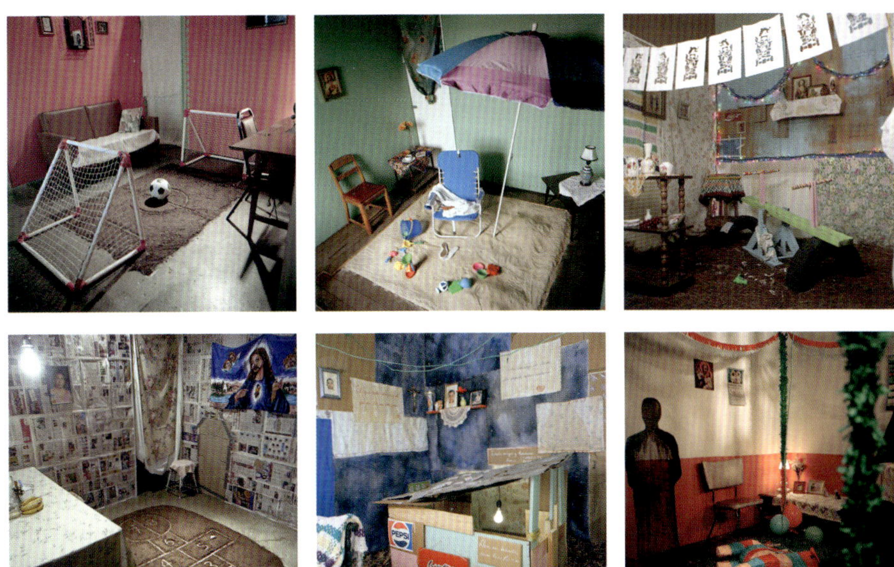

FIGURE 4.7.
Alma Leiva, Celda series, 2010, multimedia installation and photographs. Courtesy of the artist.

one to imagine what life meant within these walls, within such a cell. When Central American migrants arrive at the border, they have nothing with them but the clothes on their backs. Media footage paints the image of rootless wanderers with no past, no social networks, and thus no history. Leiva's installations invite viewers to think of all that was left behind—the humble possessions, the sites of family gatherings and memory making, a safe haven simultaneously morphed into a prison. Because her cells reference specific murder cases that she researches with documentation, they also serve as memorial sites.[33]

The aforementioned examples reveal creative understandings of how criminality and fear manifest in social, public, and domestic spaces in Central America. Zavaleta, Vega, de León, and Leiva show that the criminalization of Central Americans goes beyond the body, extending into the spaces people navigate, reside in, and rest in, that is, spaces they call home. Importantly, the criminalization of space enables fear and behaviors informed by self-censorship, self-restraint, self-discipline, and self-confinement that are unconsciously but willingly performed. Collectively they expose how the logics of carceral power and dominance within Central America further produce a carceral spatiality that leads to performing an already criminalized body.

RACE CRIMINALIZED

The practice of criminalizing everyday people is now a well-known reality in Central America. The criminalization of activists, women, Indigenous people, Afro-descendants, the LGBTQ community, campesinos, and working-class people is commonplace and reveals that the state does not merely assign criminality based on suspected gang affiliation but historically extends it to the racialized, gendered, poor, and marginalized. Abolitionists question the idea of "mass" in the commonly used phrase *mass incarceration*, for it is not large homogeneous multitudes of people that are indiscriminately incarcerated; in fact, the technologies of incarceration historically target, profile, and criminalize racialized, gendered, and colonized peoples.[34] The racialized and poor of Central America are arrested on suspicion of gang affiliation, not the wealthy white elite, despite the latter's criminal behavior and activities. Yet incarceration has been a state-sanctioned strategy across the Americas to stop potential rebellions, uprisings, or movement organizing of those it considers to be a threat to the nation.[35] It reveals that nation-states are threatened by the liberation and empowerment of those whom they oppress and subjugate in order to maintain power and wealth—the racialized and poor. These entanglements between visuality, culture, policy, and racialized criminalization are also increasingly exposed by artists.

In *Targets of Manifest Destiny* (2010) (see figure 4.8), US-based Náhuat Pipil artist Alicia Maria Siu, a Honduran Salvadoran residing in the United States, retrieves a historical moment in El Salvador to expose the deeply rooted criminalization of Indigenous peoples. Siu looks back to the 1932 massacre, in which up to thirty thousand Indigenous Náhuatl Pipil men and boys were executed under military orders of General Maximiliano Hernández Martínez.[36] Under the rhetoric of impeding communist takeover, the state categorized Indigenous men as communist and criminal. Yet "communist" was used interchangeably with "peasant," and "peasant" was understood to refer to "Indian."[37] Anyone with Indigenous features or wearing the typical campesino attire (white shirt and white pants) was accused, criminalized, and killed in mass public executions to halt collective organizing and uprisings against the state. The majority killed were Indigenous peoples who protested the theft of their Native lands by the owners of coffee plantations. However, the strong racial tensions between Native people and the elite ladino population were rooted in centuries of invasion and occupation, which made it more an Indigenous and anticolonial revolt than a communist one, as it is popularly referred to.[38] The mass killing, now known as La Matanza (The Killing), spread a wave of fear among Indigenous peoples living in the country.

Siu acquired the photograph of a Pipil man from a prisoner camp in Izalco, El Salvador, where he was detained for questioning by the Salvadoran military government under accusation of communist activities and then executed. The side profile and marked torso indicate the common position of mug shots and highlight his Indigenous features, associating the criminal with Indigeneity. Over each figure, the artist superimposes common racist labels taken from newspapers, in both English and Spanish, that were used to describe Indigenous people at that time. Labels, which she encloses in quotation marks, include "indian," "communist," "rebel," "savage," "virus infested," and "social cancer." These phrases continue to be used both to dehumanize people and to justify violence against them. With the textual and the visual composition, Siu points to the mechanism of visual thingifcation in the project of visual coloniality and its use in criminalizing Indigenous peoples. As the title suggests, the artist references the ideology of "manifest destiny" as the backbone of US government efforts to expand and colonize lands and displace and dispose of peoples. As a result of La Matanza, Indigenous peoples also lost land rights. Some were taken by landowners upon the jailing or killing of their workers, or

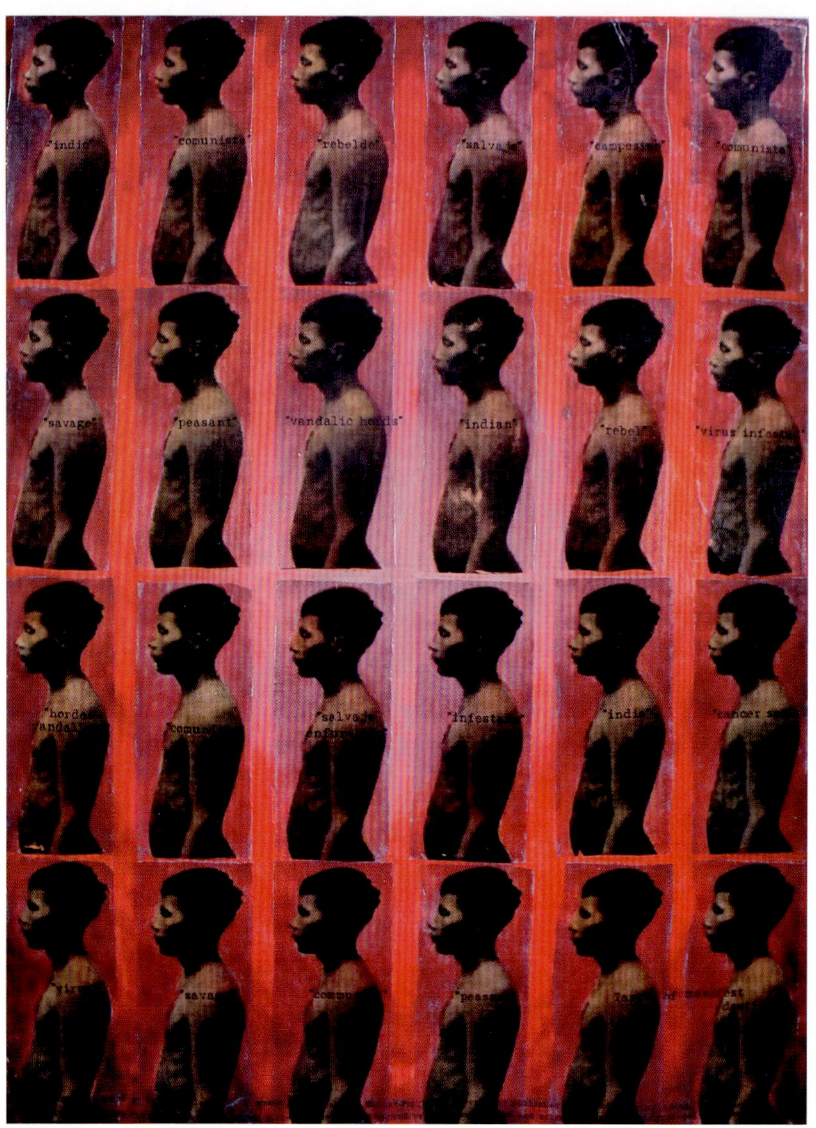

FIGURE 4.8.
Alicia Maria Siu, *Targets of Manifest Destiny*, 2010. Acrylic and mixed media. Courtesy of the artist Alicia Maria Siu Bernal.

in some cases the victims' widowed wives were forced to trade their land deeds for modest sums of food for their children.[39]

Costa Rican artist Marton Robinson also draws from the early history of photography in the visual thingification of racialized peoples and connects this violence to contemporary surveillance and criminalization of Afro-descendants, as in his video piece *Slot Machine* (2020) (see figure 4.9). A slot machine is a gambling device that functions when a player pulls a lever to activate reels that spin and come to a stop according to chance, revealing a combination of symbols. When matching symbols line up in the horizontal segments, the player wins. While traditionally, symbols consist of numbers, card suits, or pictured fruits, Robinson's slot machine instead displays various versions of the artist's full-body portrait with slight variations. His poses include front, side, and back view and reference the nineteenth-century Joseph T. Zealy daguerreotype photographs that depicted enslaved peoples as objects of gaze and ethnographic specimens of racial inferiority.[40] Following eugenics and phrenology ideals, these were also used as visual evidence of criminality.

The wardrobe variation in *Slot Machine* further contextualizes visual technologies to racialization and criminalization in the twenty-first century. The various hoodies seen on the artist are a nod to the garment associated with racial profiling and police killings of innocent Black boys and men in the United States, a long history that more recently became global when captured on cell phone videos and dispersed on social media. On some occasions, Robinson is seen wearing undergarments or is partially or fully nude, as he alternates between past and present temporalities in the spinning reels. In a constant roulette of images, displayed no more than a second each, viewers witness a fast-changing combination of the artist portraits resembling mug shots in which viewers can only briefly capture glimpses of the figure. The result is an anxious anticipation, like waiting for a slot machine, dictated by chance, to rest and display the final combination.

Yet, amid these glimpses, one additional accessory worn by the artist occasionally punctuates the viewers' gaze—a "Cocorí" mask. Written in 1947 by Joaquín Gutiérrez, *Cocorí* was a children's book that centered on an Afro–Costa Rican boy named Cocorí living in the jungle on the Caribbean coast. Depicted in a racialized and caricatured manner, the child is presented as uncivilized, dirty, and inferior, in contrast to his protagonist, a white girl who arrives by boat to the coast, with whom Cocorí becomes enamored, and who in the narrative symbolizes the European arrival of modernity to Costa Rica. The book was required reading for Costa Rican schoolchildren, and, similar to its Mexican counterpart, "Memín Pinguín," Gutiérrez's Cocorí character has been

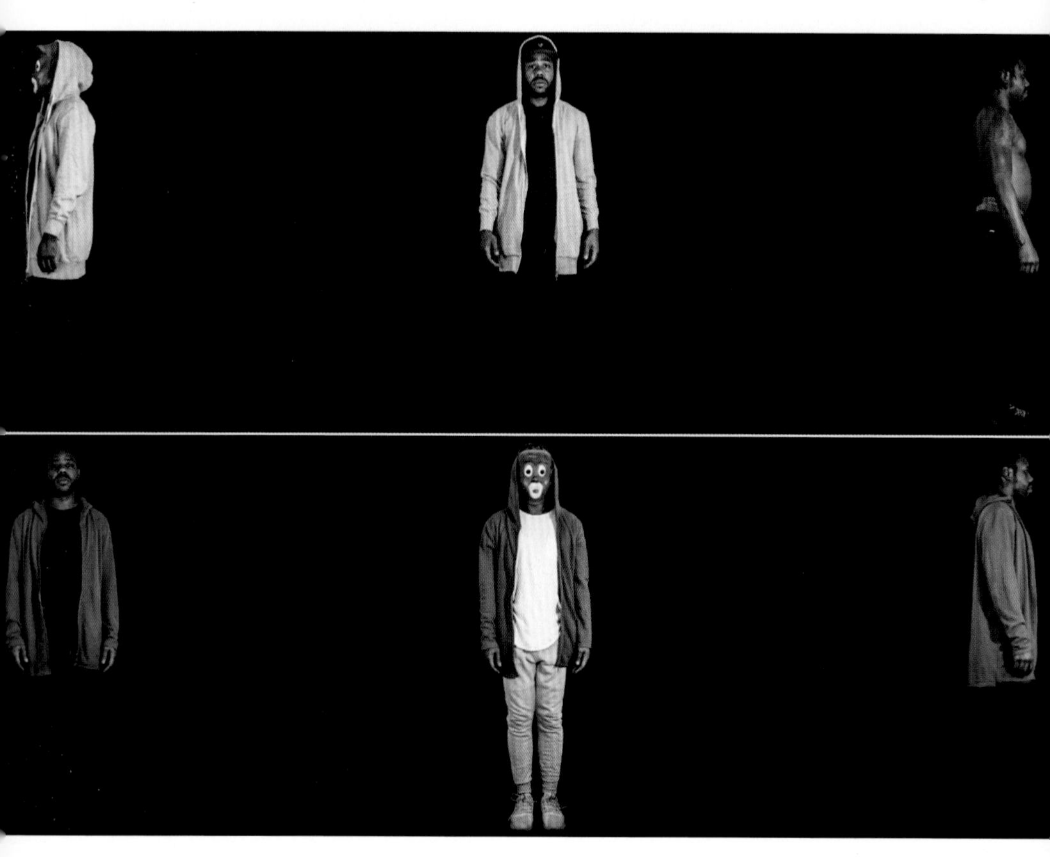

FIGURE. 4.9.
Marton Robinson, *Slot Machine*, 2020, video (stills). Courtesy of the artist.

scrutinized for perpetuating racist stereotypes, inciting national debates over racism in Costa Rica.[41]

For Robinson, as an Afro–Costa Rican who was forced to read the book as a child and who remembers the visceral experience of discomfort when he read it, the book exposes the anti-Blackness of Costa Rica that has always been present in the nation and the violence done to Afro–Costa Rican children. Thus, while the figure of the artist in the reels connects the racialized history of photography and criminality to the present technologies of surveillance, policing, and criminalization of Black bodies, it is important to emphasize that Robinson extends this violence beyond a US context by contextualizing it with the anti-Blackness of Costa Rica, and Central America and Latin America more broadly. With *Slot Machine*, the artist reminds us that anti-Blackness and an early inculcation of racial subordination in Black children with colonial narratives of inferiority and criminalization are tied to the policing and surveillance of Black bodies across borders. With an Afro-diasporic perspective, Robinson debunks any arbitrariness or "chance" in the criminalization of Black people by confronting the historical entanglements between colonial anti-Black narratives and visual technologies of criminalization from the nineteenth to twenty-first centuries.

In other works, Danny Zavaleta highlights how the Central America Free Trade Agreement (CAFTA-DR) outlaws those who work in unregulated, informal economies: that is, street vendors, bootleggers, and merchants of counterfeit clothes or pirated music and movies. For his Se busca series (2006–7), Zavaleta created vintage Western-style "wanted" posters featuring the street vendors of San Salvador (see figure 4.10). Each shows the portrait of a vendor with a pirate patch over his eye, in reference to their common label, *pirata* (pirate). Above the portrait the artist included the words "SE BUSCA, LOS PIRATAS DEL CENTRO" (Wanted, downtown pirates), and below are physical descriptions, including skin color, such as "piel morena" (dark skin); the "crime" the depicted person is wanted for, such as being a "vendor of CDs" or "vendor of toys"; and location. Zavaleta also spent time interviewing downtown vendors and learning of their work and challenges following the Salvadoran government's campaign to remove all "illegal" vendors from the city's downtown area without offering alternative economic opportunities, which would leave thirty-six thousand families unemployed. This campaign stems from a CAFTA-DR policy that requires participating nations to protect US intellectual property rights, which means policing and criminalizing vendors whose livelihood depends on this informal economy of piracy.[42] Such policies criminalize vendors, subjecting them to fines and imprisonment.

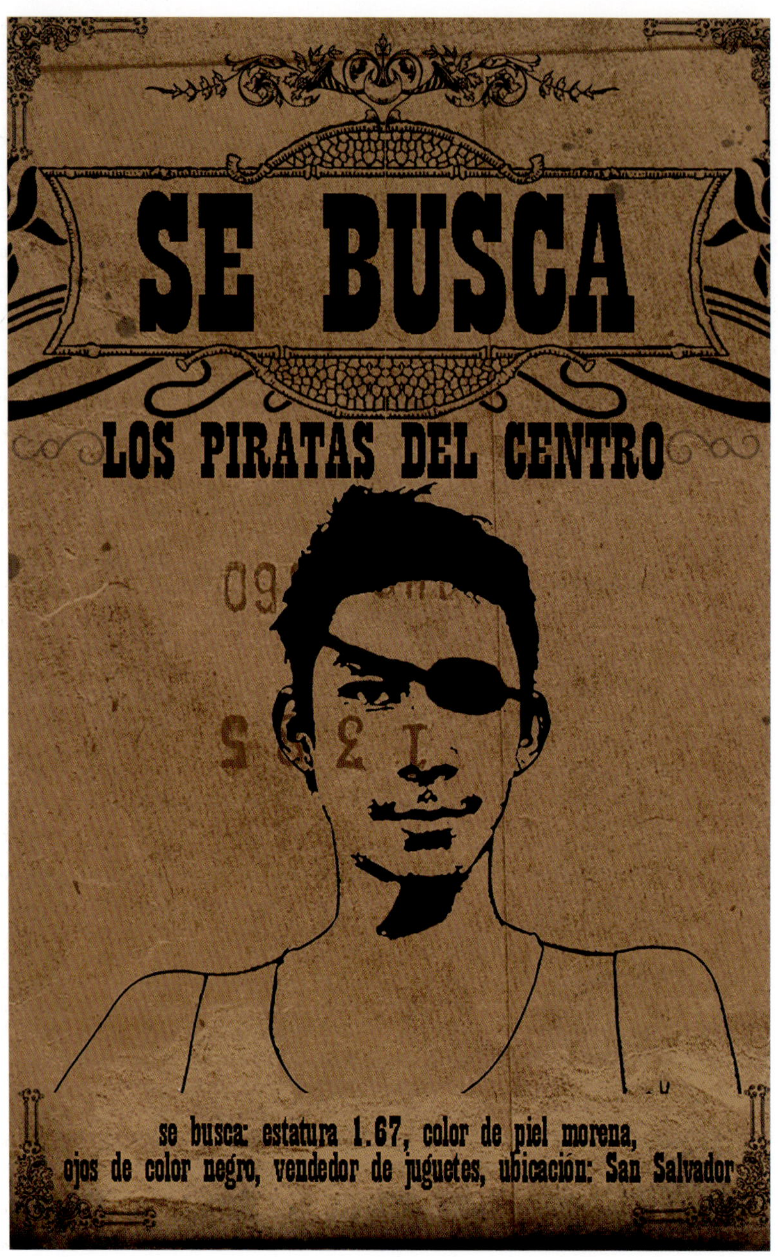

FIGURE 4.10.
Danny Zavaleta, Se busca series (vendor of toys), 2006–7, inkjet print. Courtesy of the artist.

Challenging the policing of vendors—who work in fear of authorities and are constantly on the move and in hiding—the artist re-created the vendors' portraits from the Se busca series onto the walls of the country's Museo de Arte de El Salvador (Museo MARTE, Museum of Art of El Salvador), exhibiting them as large-scale murals. Zavaleta collides an art space that celebrates creativity with the illegality of creative subsistence, forcing museumgoers to face the country's most vulnerable working sector, which is nonetheless a dynamic pillar of the Salvadoran economy. The artist also intervened in the city of San José, Costa Rica, plastering the wanted posters all over the city, often amid already existing graffiti, and thus blending them into aesthetics of unlawful practices. As people walked by and inquired about the wanted person, Zavaleta explained the context and critique behind his work, allowing him to engage with citizens on the injustice of such criminalizing practices, thus countering the dominant carceral logic that hinges on the criminalization of poor and racialized Salvadorans.

Siu, Zavaleta, and Robinson contest multiple forms of visual thingification and convey the relevancy of Roque Dalton's famous phrase "los siempre sospechosos de todo." They condemn the criminalization of everyday people perpetrated by both the US and Central American governments, which ascribe illegality through racialization, forced displacement, policing, and the criminalization of impoverished workers. They reveal how race and class are used as signifiers for criminality and that this practice is a historical continuum, as evidenced by the rhetoric of the threat of Indigenous communists in the 1930s, to the guerrillero in the civil wars, to the deported, campesinos, and informal workers, to the policing of Black bodies across borders. For the state, criminality is unrecognizable without the racialized, Indigenous, Black, poor, or migrant body precisely because the contemporary criminalization of poor and racialized Central Americans is a continuation of the so-called civilization project of colonialism and Western modernity.

DEFYING THE DEATH OF HUMANITY IN PRISON CAPTIVITY

In Central America, the state and its authorities use criminality as evidence for the ineligibility of personhood.[43] Under empire, personhood—the state of being a person with value, rights, and protection—depends on legal concepts of citizenship and legality defined by the state. Being ineligible to personhood thus refers to "the state of being legally recognized as rightless, located in the spaces of social death."[44] Central American prisons become the institutional spaces to both uphold that ineligibility and punish those deemed lacking personhood, not just by depriving them of liberty but by further attempting to break their humanity through captivity.

Regional studies conclude that the design of the penitentiary system in Central America violates the human rights of prisoners.[45] According to Mark Ungar, these violations include prison overcrowding, which leads to minimal sleeping space and increases sexual abuse and rape; poor infrastructure for food maintenance and preparation, which results in digestive illness and infections among inmates; and deficient medical staff and supplies due to a general lack of resources and poor administration.[46] Basic necessities, such as mattresses, are unaffordable, and inmates are often crammed into airless spaces or forced to sleep on stairs and in hallways. Most prisons lack potable water and are infested with rats and cockroaches. Moreover, slow processing of all prisoners violates pretrial detention limits and the right to a speedy trial. This means the majority of inmates are not tried and their captivity is prolonged indefinitely. Paul Hathazy and Markus-Michael Müller argue that the crisis of prison detention in Latin America is due both to human rights violations and the political denial of prison conditions by governments.[47] Scholars and activists have thus described the penitentiary system in Central America as a "subworld," and those who have been in it testify to the description, such as Panamanian artist Jhafis Quintero.[48]

In 1994, at the age of nineteen, Quintero was sentenced to ten years in prison, which he served in Costa Rica. Within that period, he simply describes: "Bad things happened. . . . I have seventeen stab wounds. . . . I was fortunate."[49] He refers to the penitentiary as a "subsociety with its own practices" where the biggest enemies are the prison guards who "act like gods."[50] In this world, he explains, "one only learns how to survive by force, that is, when the body is subjected to the [violent] circumstance."[51] Thus, in an attempt to bring to light all the "men and women who struggle in the shadows," Quintero documented a series of objects created by inmates from a Costa Rican prison in his artistic project titled In Dubia Tempora (2004), which he translates as "Critical Moments."

For the series, the artist claims he "rescued" objects made by inmates. He then exhibited them as art objects with an accompanying catalog that displays the individual objects against a white backdrop, removing any reference to their contextual origins or use.[52] The objects range from tattoo machines to marijuana smoking utensils, exercise devices, sexual stimulant books, and deadly weapons, which comprise the "natural order" of prison culture and are yet all prohibited by the prison system.[53] Their illegality speaks to the necessity of survival. Quintero displays each one with a label and text that describe its function as well as the required materials for its creation. With the belief that each object reflects the identity of its creator (the prisoner), the artist parodies the classification of "Otherness" in the name of scientific inquiry—as was the norm in fields of nineteenth-century anthropology, phrenology, and other discourses of scientific racism in the history of visual coloniality. Quintero labels and classifies each object in a guide for viewers, reminding them that the images in the catalog are criminalized and made into scientific objects to be observed: objects stripped of subjectivity that are simultaneously markers of identity.

The first image in the catalog presents a tattoo machine made of a child's race car toy with pink yarn wrapped around it; the yarn secures a needle on the side of the toy, while a piece of electric wire dangles from underneath (see figure 4.11). The title the artist gives to the object appears below in Latin: *Verba Volant, Scripta Manent*, which in English translates to "Words disappear, writing remains."[54] Quintero's use of Latin references the language of ancient Rome, the tool of an imperial dominating culture, and the verbalization of law and authority.[55] Viewers read the common name of the object (tattooing device), its materials (toy car, wool string, needle, and electric wire), and its use (permanently marking the skin). The appropriation of discarded consumer items and their transformation into illegal tools of the barest necessities points to capital and commodity as a system that links the "free" world with the captive world, the object with the viewer, the observer with the observed, and the object with the subject. This scientific lens, through its classification, convicts the object of illegality—in this case the unnatural use of a child's toy to mark the criminal body, or the forbidden union of innocence and guilt. The threat is contamination.

Quintero's work evokes the creative use of penal space, time, and matter, and what scholar and curator Nicole Fleetwood theorizes as a "carceral aesthetics."[56] For Fleetwood, penal space refers to the physical space of the prison and the disrupted relations it produces due to the prison's constrictions on mobility. She describes penal time as the various temporalities experienced, including time as punishment, the altered sense of time due to captivity, and the afterlife of time when freedom entails ongoing surveillance and monitoring. Finally, penal matter refers to the restriction of imprisonment, including limited access to materials, restrictions on what items the imprisoned can possess, and how they themselves become property of the state.[57] Through these creative uses of penal space-time and matter, Quintero not only creates art under conditions of unfreedom; his ultimate goal was to give the prisoners—the creators of these objects—the status of artist.

As handmade works of art, each object carries imprints of the creator's hand, survival, and thus existence. Although the use of the objects in the catalog serves the basic needs of prison culture (exercise, sexual stimulants, self-defense,

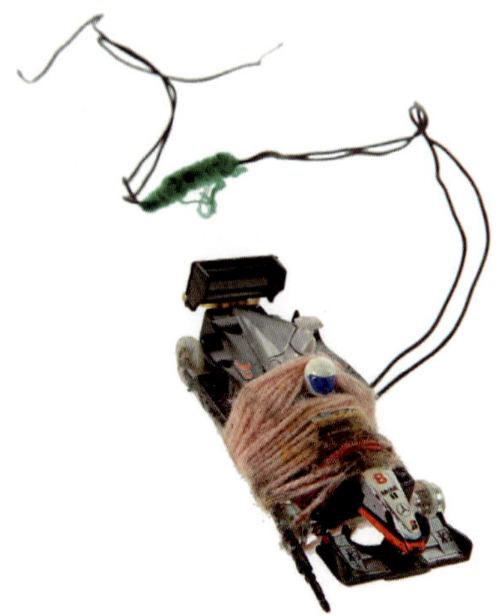

Verba Volant, Scripta Manent (Las palabras vuelan, los escritos perduran)
Nombre vulgar: Máquina de tatuar.
Materiales: Carrito de juguete, hilo de lana, aguja y alambre eléctrico.
Uso: Ornamental y decorativo. Estampar la piel de forma permanente, mediante procedimientos cuasi infantiles.

FIGURE 4.11.
Jhafis Quintero, In Dubia Tempora series, 2004, catalog. Courtesy of the artist.

entertainment, etc.), they are prohibited in prisons and are thus radical, criminal, and clandestine, like their creators (see figure 4.12). Every object was created, used, and concealed at risk, and thus the function of each object speaks to the most personal priorities of the inmate. Each object fulfills the most effective strategy of survival during incarceration. The objects' existence, therefore, speaks of survival not only in its resuscitation from the death of commodity but also as testament to desire, will, and creativity. Despite their objectification through the lens of consumerism, law, and science, the objects are encoded with the presence/aura of their makers.

Although the penitentiary system claims rehabilitation of prisoners, its function actually creates the perfect environment for repeated trauma through captivity.[58] Unable to escape, unable to flee, and under the control of a perpetrator, prisoners are susceptible to psychological domination.[59] In fact, one might say this is the goal. In captivity, a perpetrator destroys the victim's independence by inducing fear through scrutiny and a total control of the victim's body and bodily functions, thus destroying the victim's sense of autonomy.[60] In addition to demoralization, victims of captivity are coerced into believing, through their isolation, that no one cares for them and that even their family and allies have forgotten them. Thus, the ultimate goal of psychological control is achieved with the victim's total surrender, that is, when the victim conforms to a dependency on the perpetrator and becomes a submissive and compliant prisoner.[61] Prisoners are "broken" when they become willing victims who surrender for the sake of survival. Victims believe they have been reduced to "a nonhuman life form."[62] Likewise, Quintero's objects are not emotional organic objects but mechanical, functional objects, and more importantly, they reflect the dehumanization of the penitentiary system and thus the psychological and spiritual violence of prison captivity.

The catalog notes to the viewer: "If the logic of capitalism transformed subjects into objects, then the logic of the penitentiary corrupted objects into subjects."[63] Linking racial capitalism to the carceral logic, Quintero exposes the dehumanization practices of prison captivity. He points to the contradictory logic of the carceral state, in which the penitentiary, in contrast to its supposed rehabilitation, is actually a dehumanizing machine aimed to break and stigmatize those deprived of liberty with perpetual criminal and unhuman status, sabotaging and impeding reintegration into society. The objects from In Dubia Tempora are testimonials to the relation between visual thingification of racialized subjects and the dehumanization of carceral logic, a death of humanity Quintero defies by applying the title of artist, creative, and inventor to the makers.

FIGURE 4.12.
Jhafis Quintero, In Dubia Tempora series, 2004, intervened objects. Courtesy of the artist.

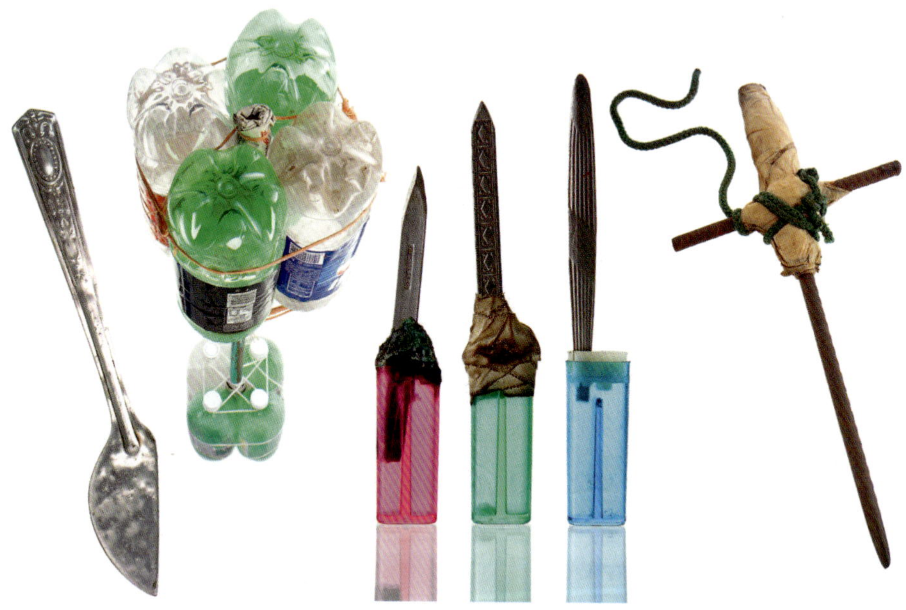

Whereas In Dubia Tempora reflected violence as it occurs on an individual and subjective level, in other works Quintero defies the prison system by creating informative and pedagogical tools for death and survival in prison confinement. In his performance *Máximas de seguridad* (Safety maxims) (2007), the artist smuggled survival manuals into the prison. In an illustrated pocket-size handbook, Quintero presented various scenarios of danger and offered instructional, practical solutions for the incarcerated reader (see figure 4.13). The manual coaches that if poisoned by another inmate or guard, one should drink milk, and a simple and didactic illustration accompanies the instruction. The manual further demonstrates where on the body one can conceal weapons (such as between the buttocks), it locates key body points that can cause severe injury to another, identifies where one can hide personal possessions within a prison, and how to maintain emotional connections with the outside world. By offering instructions on survival, the manual defies carceral violence and the logic of captivity.

For the performance component of the work, the artist distributed the manuals at a Costa Rican prison during visiting hours, when people wait hours in long lines to visit their loved ones. He approached those waiting, offered them a manual, and asked that they smuggle it inside for their loved ones and other inmates. According to Quintero, reactions ranged from curiosity and interest to acceptance of the mission and in some cases emotional responses, as some of the people he approached were also formerly incarcerated (see figure 4.14). The accuracy and precision of the manual's instructions and illustrations triggered a painful past for some but also an appreciation and support for Quintero's visual disobedience.

Quintero built on his pedagogical model of teaching survival skills for those in captivity with a video piece titled *Hágalo usted mismo* (Do it yourself) (2008), in which he parodies a Do-It-Yourself infomercial convincing viewers that captivity is a not-so-distant space. The protagonist, a Black man in a suit and tie, resembles an anchorman as he reads a script and speaks directly to viewers, explaining that they will inevitably encounter captivity and, once immersed in it, will experience its violence (see figure 4.15). Yet he also offers hope by stressing that viewers can take measures for their protection and survival. The video then transitions to a scene of the same individual, but this time nude, exposing his upper body full of scars and mutilation as we learn that the man was formerly deprived of liberty.

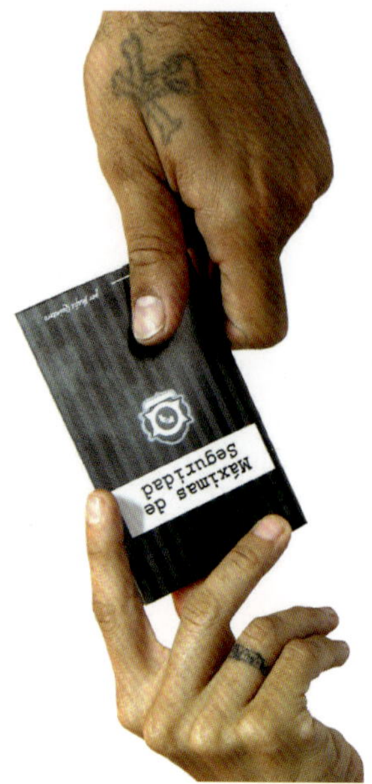

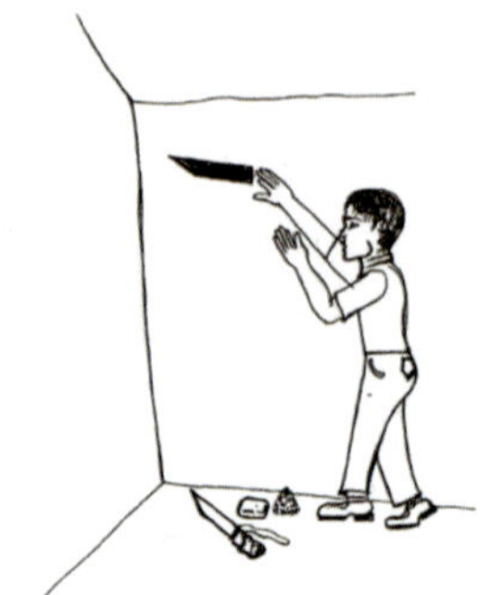

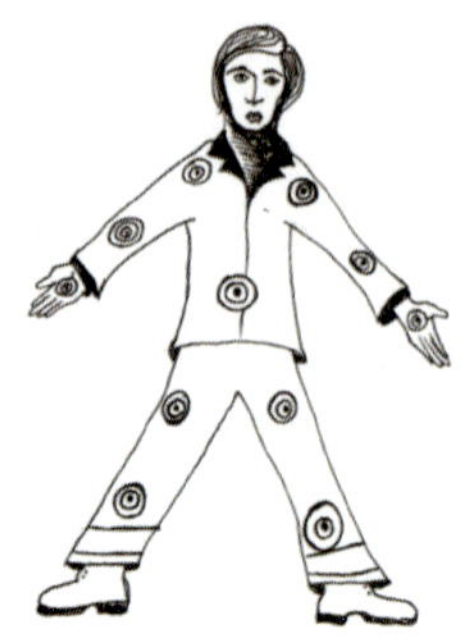

FIGURE 4.13.
Jhafis Quintero, *Máximas de seguridad*, 2007, book. Courtesy of the artist.

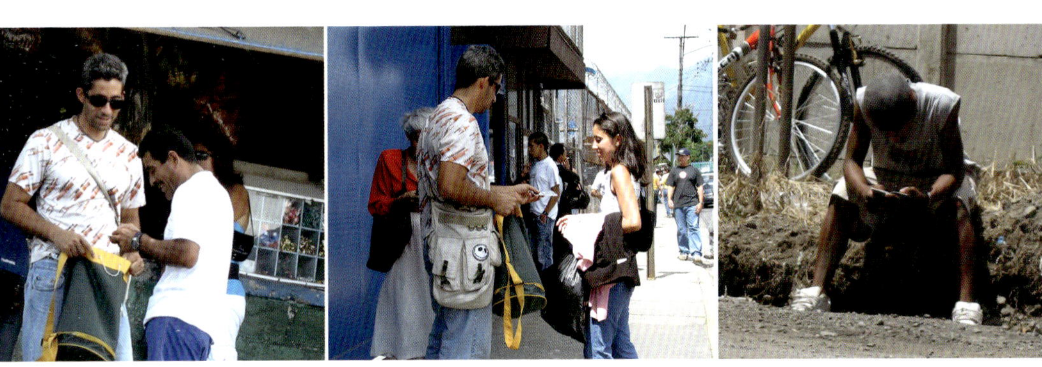

FIGURE 4.14.
Jhafis Quintero, *Máximas de seguridad*, 2007, performance. Courtesy of the artist.

As if in a cooking show, he begins his lesson on how to evade violent attacks from other inmates by describing how one can create weapons using materials already in a cell, such as a bed frame, and how to conceal said weapons. The commercial parody, as was also seen in Pricilla Monge's *Lección no. 1: Lección de maquillaje*, illustrates the popularity of infomercials as a means of social control in Central America (see figure 2.7). Evoking the genre's persuasive effect on citizens, Quintero alludes to the selling and consumption of fear as a mechanism of state control. Scholars have noted that across Latin America, political regimes turn to sensualist media coverage to capitalize on growing public concerns as they seek approval for their punitive "solutions" to the crime problem.[64] The man's switch in attire further challenges categories of criminal and perpetrator, as the man's monologue emphasizes the blurry line and easy slippage between the two. Once again, we see Quintero question boundaries between criminal and artist, showing that survival skills require a level of creativity and inventiveness no different than that of an artist. Art, like a weapon, is a means for survival.

As Quintero's artistic work testifies, each day in captivity is simultaneously an encounter with death and a feat of endurance. Physically and conceptually, those deprived of liberty in Central American prisons are immersed in a fear of death that is also tied to survival. Quintero reminds us that in reality inmates must kill or be killed.[65] Trauma studies have shown that the constant threat of death, and having survived that threat, constitutes a "death imprint," which includes death anxiety and its equivalents, such as disintegration of the self.[66] Out of necessity for survival, those deprived of liberty must be on constant alert, trustful of no one, and willing to defend themselves by injuring or killing another inmate who poses a threat. Inmates are forced to become perpetual victims *and* perpetrators of violence. It is in reference to such a hypervigilant lifestyle and consequent death anxiety that much of Quintero's art emerges.

The violence and trauma from captivity are unique not only in that they consist of a *prolonged* traumatic event—in Quintero's case ten years of incarceration—but also as they pertain to Central America, where issues of human rights violations and corruption in prisons are relegated as Third World concerns. Quintero demands that viewers question the Western system of justice, especially the penitentiary and its claim to rehabilitate. As Central American governments enforce extreme policies for mass incarceration of criminalized youth and the impoverished, Quintero's visual disobedience exposes how the penitentiary system creates the perfect environment for repeated violence and trauma in which those deprived of liberty are susceptible to both physical and psychological domination.

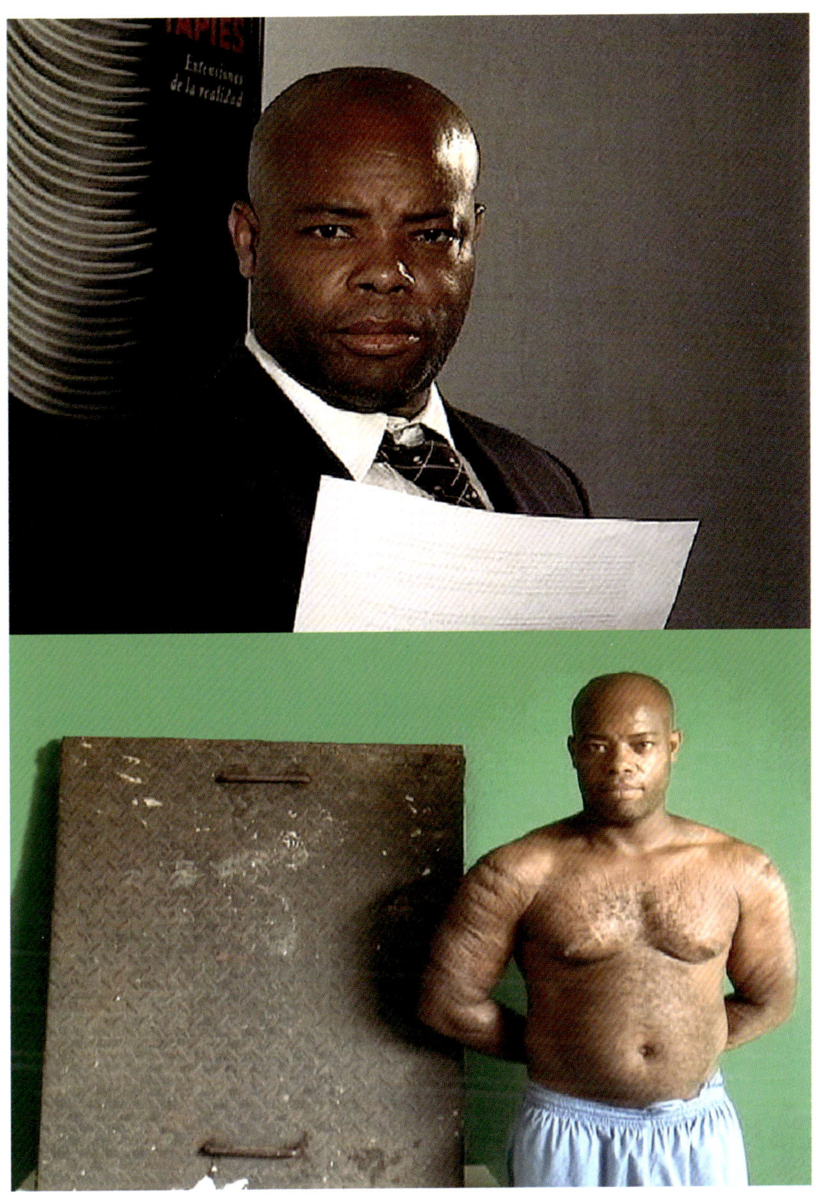

FIGURE 4.15.
Jhafis Quintero, *Hágalo usted mismo*, 2008, video (stills). Courtesy of the artist.

EXPOSING SITES OF SOCIAL CLEANSING

Social cleansing has been difficult to categorize by scholars, but its purpose remains clear: to force removal of a collective with "undesirable characteristics" that is viewed as a threat. The motives may differ, producing various forms of cleansing, such as racial, ethnic, ideological, political, or paradigmatic, which targets a range of undesirable characteristics, to which can be included class, religion, gender, and sexual orientation. Population removal ranges in extremes, from genocide to forced migration. Rather than rigid definitions of a collective, a group may encompass an intersectionality of targeted identities and characteristics.[67] Moreover, the ineligibility of personhood as a result of criminalization is a form of social death that "not only defines who does not matter, it also makes mattering meaningful."[68] By making these distinctions between those who matter (and deserve the state's protection) and those who don't (and deserve the state's discipline), Central American governments have initiated what I view as a new form of social cleansing in the region—the annihilation of the criminalized. While this has increased in the postwar period, artists such as Honduran Jorge Oquelí remind us that Central America has a long history of criminalization tied to social cleansing of the poor, radical, and Indigenous people on its lands.

In his performance *Exhumación (rito funerario)* (Exhumation, funeral rite) (2011), Oquelí enacted a funerary ritual at the National Penitentiary in Tegucigalpa, Honduras. The penitentiary was founded at a time of heavy repression and several massacres, such as the March 1937 massacre of Garifuna peoples in San Juan de Tela and the July 6, 1944, massacre of peaceful protestors in San Pedro Sula during the Tiburcio Carías Andino dictatorship (1932–49). Many political crimes were committed against those who resisted the dictatorship, and many others were criminalized and imprisoned, tortured, and assassinated for their protest, including the artist's father, who survived the imprisonment and shared stories of his peers' torture and disappearances within the prison walls. Many others were buried on its grounds. For the performance, Oquelí excavated a hole in the dirt and exhumed a human skull (see figure 4.16). His hands were painted blue, a color on the Honduran flag, as a reference to the nation-state's role in burying bodies and memory. With prayer and ritual, he used his corporal presence to intervene in a system of violence, historical erasure, and institutional compliance in the killing of Indigenous peoples, where the human skull he exhumed symbolized the recovery of forgotten crimes against humanity.

Amid a longer history of incarceration, artists note that the postwar period has seen a more extreme form of the prison as a site of social cleansing. In *100% Catracho* (2004), the Honduran artist Gabriel Galeano created small zipper

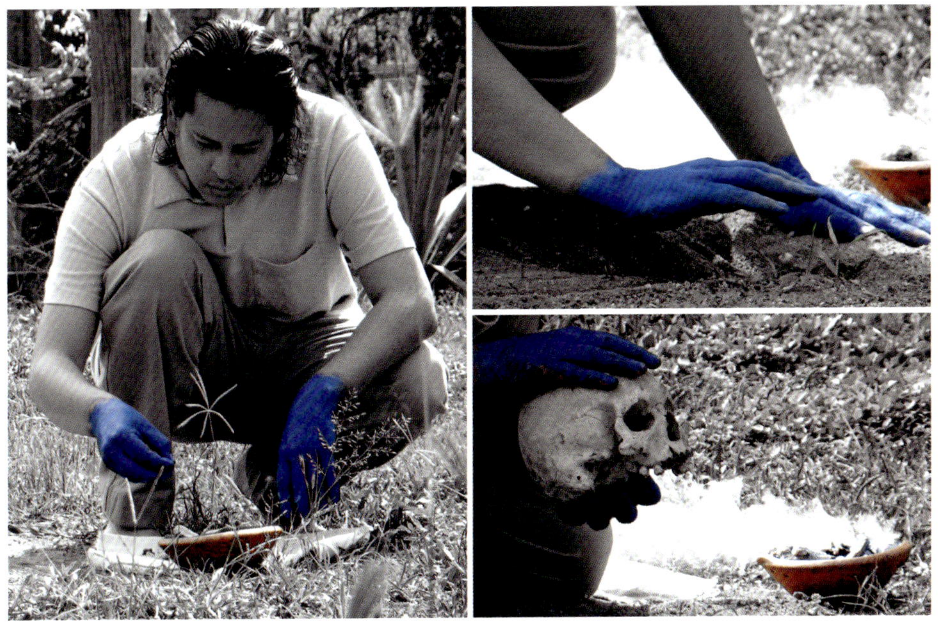

FIGURE 4.16.
Jorge Oquelí, *Exhumación* (*rito funerario*), 2011, performance. Courtesy of the artist.

bags filled with a gray ash substance and labels that read "product made in Honduras—100% Catracho," referring to the nickname given to Hondurans (see figure 4.17). He then distributed the small zipper bags to passersby in public spaces (see figure 4.18). The piece references the mysterious prison fires that have historically eliminated criminalized peoples in captivity. In Honduras, 61 people died while incarcerated in a prison fire in La Ceiba in 2003, and 107 people died while incarcerated in San Pedro Sula the following year. In 2010, a Salvadoran youth jail was engulfed in flames and left 16 imprisoned youths dead and 22 injured.[69] And in the biggest prison fire in Honduran history, 356 inmates died in Comayagua in 2012.[70] These mysterious fires are incinerating inmates alive, with little protest or concern from citizens, as the inmates are already deemed to be lacking social worth; their deaths are seen as beneficial for the safety of the meaningful. The lack of investigation or empathy for the victims or their families is driven by the shared consensus among authorities and large segments of the population that the deaths of inmates, seen as criminals and subhuman, are justified.

Refuting claims that prison fires are accidental, *100% Catracho* presents bystanders with the ashes of a Honduran citizen in the form of a product manufactured by the state. With contacts at the local morgue, Galeano retrieved the ashes of deceased inmates who died in prison fires. The distribution of the zipper bags in his performance physically brought the remains of the outcasts—men purged from society, who died under the responsibility of the state, unquestioned, and even celebrated—into the hands of citizens. His performance was a physical intervention that required citizens to open their eyes to ongoing social cleansing and to *feel* it in the palms of their hands, just as they would a product manufactured for consumption. Works like *100% Catracho* confront Hondurans with the reality that the only remedy the state pursues—criminalization and imprisonment—is amplifying rather than reducing Central America's violence.

This increased violence was also seen in Guatemala on March 8, 2017, when a fire broke out at the Virgen de la Asunción girls' shelter. Girls were detained there for various reasons that did not implicate criminal activity, yet popular consensus was that these were rebellious troublemakers or gang members. Some of the girls were orphans who became wards of the state; others were runaways who escaped bullying, familial physical and sexual abuse, and/or gang violence in their neighborhoods. Others were surrendered by their families to the state because they could not financially afford medical or specialized care. The shelter already had a long history of abuse. It was designed to hold a maximum of 350 youths but held around 700 children. In 2013, two teachers were arrested for sexually abusing girls, and a staff member was arrested for raping a thirteen-year-old girl with a cognitive disability. The girls often complained of mistreatment and sexual abuse within the youth shelter, but authorities and parents systematically ignored the allegations. A year before the fire, a court ordered the shelter to be shut down after an investigation documented forty-five complaints of children's rights violations and a possible sex trafficking network inside the shelter. However, it remained open, and forty-one girls died in the fire that day.

Outrage over the fire led many Guatemalans to protest the abuse and negligence, specifically the way the girls died, since their deaths could have been prevented. They were all in a room where the fire started, and they screamed and pleaded for nine minutes to be let out, but the guards refused. Twenty-five minutes later, the firefighters arrived and their scorched bodies were removed, while others died shortly after from smoke inhalation, and fifteen survived with severe injuries. In memory of the girls, the artist Regina José Galindo created a sound performance, *Las escucharon gritar y no abrieron las puertas* (They heard them cry and did not open the doors) (2017). Fifty-one women, including some of the mothers of the victims who volunteered to participate, joined Galindo in the performance (see figure 4.19). As both an act of catharsis and a protest, the women enclosed themselves in a room where they shouted for nine minutes, the amount of time the girls pleaded for help and were ignored. Microphones documented their yells and cries resulting in the audio piece, while photographs visually documented the women, whose distress and exhaustion become evident on their faces. The performance produces a memory archive that when heard counters the silence brought on by the guards' refusal and denial of the girls' supplications.

Artists like Oquelí, Galeano, and Galindo expose the penitentiary system as a site of social cleansing where, in addition to other human rights violations, the criminalized are increasingly abolished from existence through prison fires. Due to the popular acceptance that those criminalized are unworthy of personhood, their killings are little protested and rarely reported. The state has convinced people that their elimination is beneficial to society. Artists instead condemn the normalization of contemporary social cleansing of the racialized, impoverished, gendered, and criminalized and expose it as a project of coloniality facilitated by a carceral logic.

AGAINST CHILD MIGRANT DETENTION

When Central American migrants arrive at the US-Mexico border seeking asylum, it is this context of racialization, criminalization, and elimination that they often flee. Central Americans are often victims of institutional violence

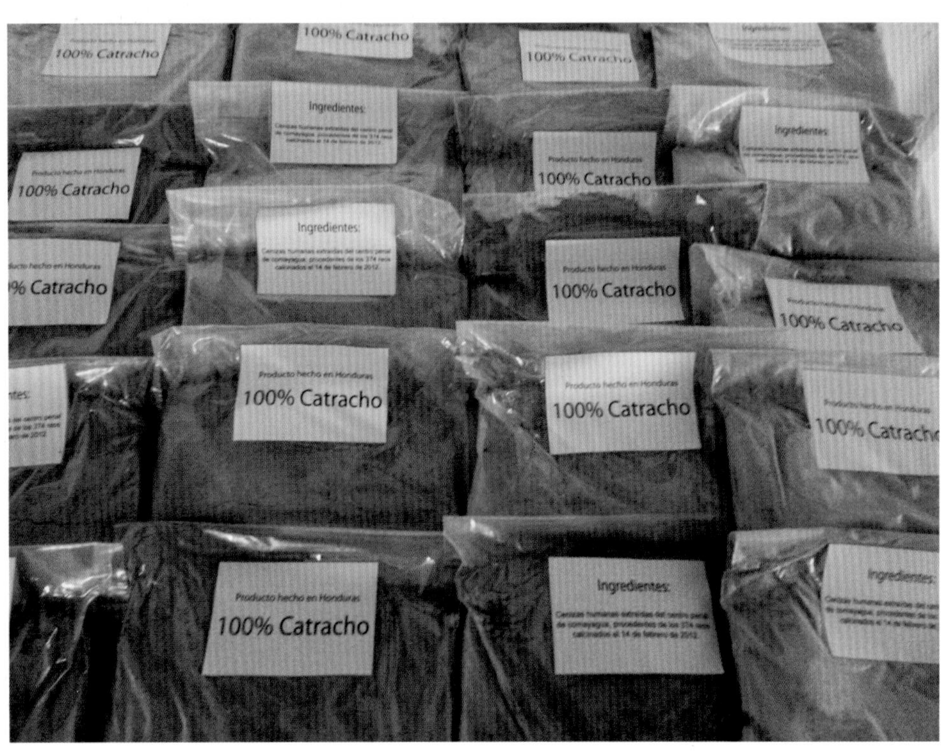

FIGURE 4.17.
Gabriel Galeano, *100% Catracho*, 2004, plastic zipper bags and mixed media. Courtesy of the artist.

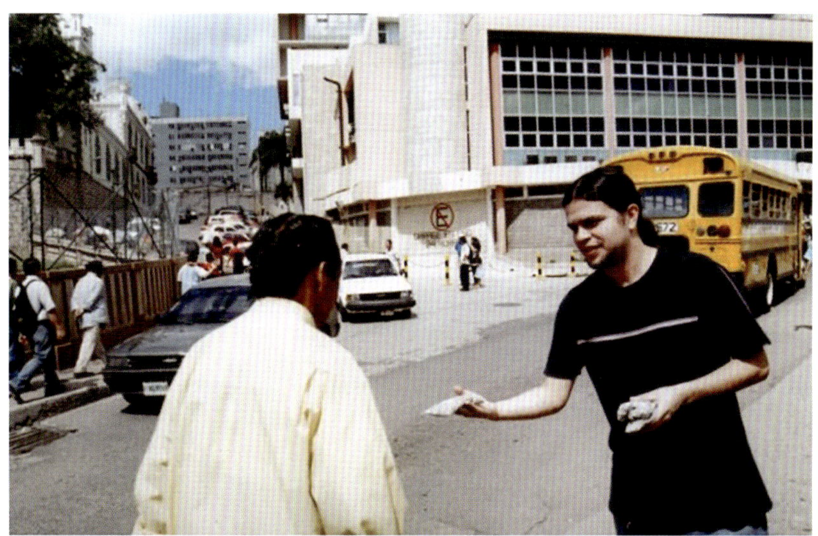

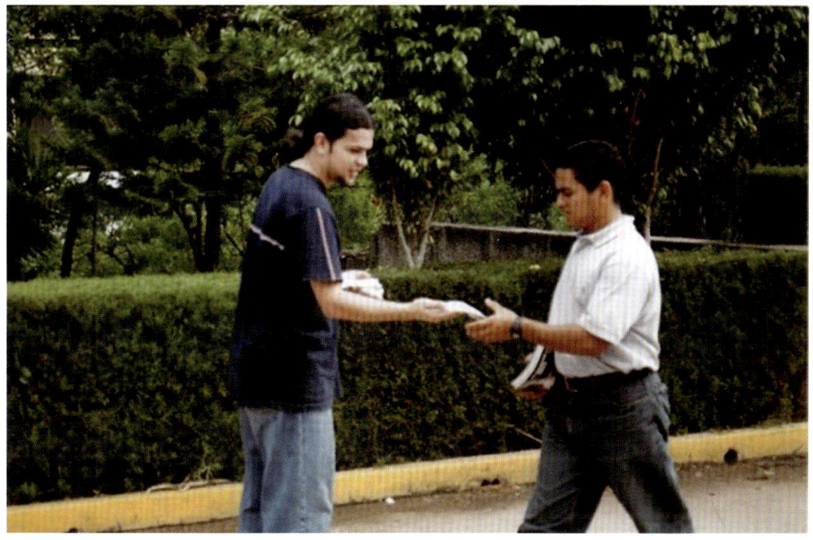

FIGURE 4.18.
Gabriel Galeano, *100% Catracho*, 2004, performance. Courtesy of the artist.

FIGURE 4.19.
Regina José Galindo, *Las escucharon gritar y no abrieron las puertas*, 2017, action. Courtesy of the artist.

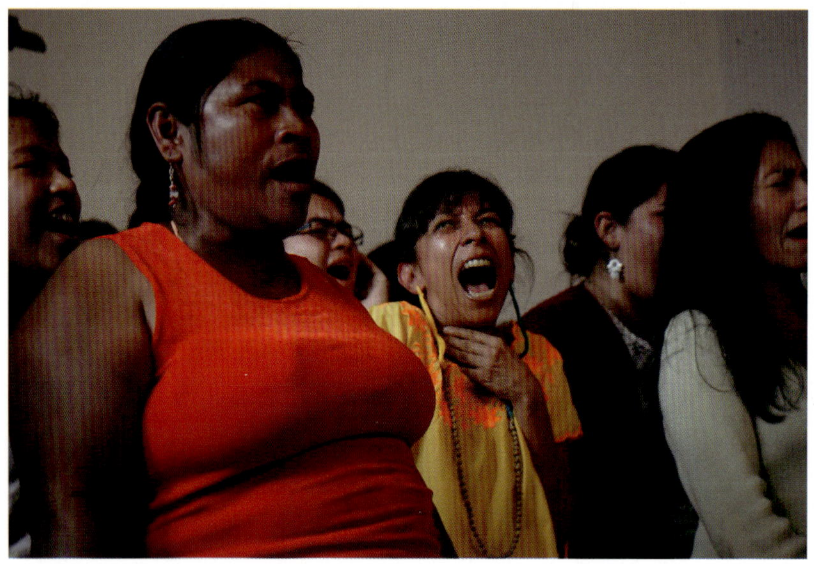

and then further criminalized through factors like poverty, gender, sexual orientation, and age to deem them criminal and ineligible for personhood. Refugees often arrive at the border looking for the opportunity to live, because to be poor and Central American is to be in persistent survival mode, constantly proving one's personhood in order to reach the status of the living and meaningful. Yet these safe-haven destinations become spaces of criminalization and dehumanization, especially when migrants encounter immigration detention centers—the United States' fastest-growing form of mass incarceration.[71] There, even migrant children are viewed as already lacking personhood and rights.

This logic of illegality led Galindo to create her performance *American Family Prison* (2008), in which she addressed child migrant imprisonment. For the performance, she placed herself and her family in captivity in a cell modeled after those in the T. Don Hutto Family Residential Center, which was once a medium-security prison and later run by Corrections Corporation of America (CCA). In 2016, CCA rebranded itself as CoreCivic following protest against the private prison industry. Galindo's small, fabricated cell included beds, a toilet, and a crib. She inhabited the cell along with her husband and two-year-old daughter for one and a half days (see figure 4.20). Museumgoers could see the family inside through a narrow window, and a video recorder documented the family's thirty-six-hour confinement. After the performance, the cell was left in the gallery as an installation, with remains such as drawings and a baby bottle, showing that the couple and their baby once inhabited the space.

While Galindo's detainment was voluntary and temporary, her performance superimposed a space of criminalization and illegality—one hidden from society—onto a space of art and culture, designed to exalt the creativity of human experience. Within this space of collision, she transformed her own body from artist to criminalized wife and mother, and that of her child into a metonym for the criminalization of innocence. In the performance space, located less than an hour-and-a-half drive from three out of the eleven major detention facilities in Texas, she made witnesses out of art viewers by facing them with what is easily purged from social consciousness on a daily basis, highlighting the irony of a culture that celebrates one Central American woman artist while simultaneously violating the human rights of thousands of other Central Americans detained only miles away.

The work also points to the threat of Central American motherhood to the United States and thus the racialized and gendered process of detention. As Martha D. Escobar has noted in her study, this process poses immigrant

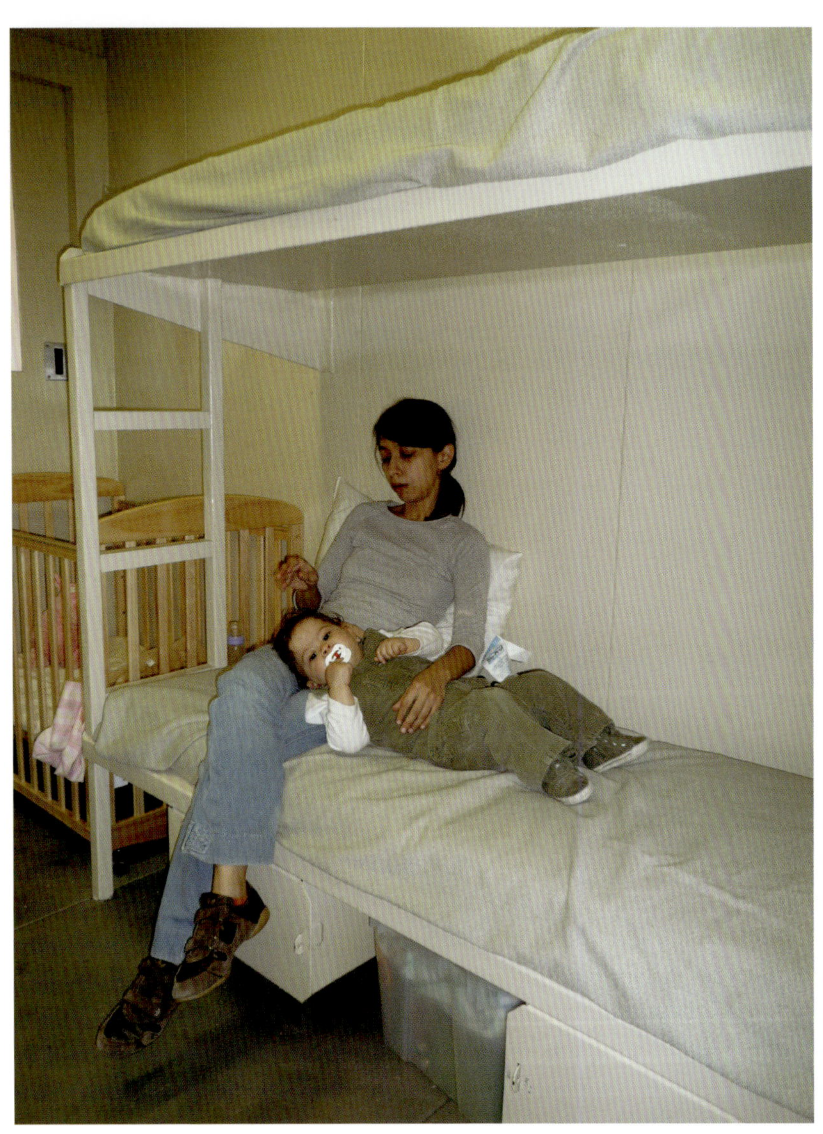

FIGURE 4.20.
Regina José Galindo, *American Family Prison*, 2008, multimedia installation and performance. Courtesy of the artist.

women as dependent and as reproducers of criminality.[72] Within a neoliberal state, their ability to have children presents permanent settlement and reduces their value as flexible laborers. Criminalization is thus a strategy to "separate their productive labor from their reproductive capabilities."[73] Galindo's performance confronts viewers with a US construction of Central American sexuality and motherhood as racialized national threats.

Along with mother migrants, the US government criminalizes asylum-seeking children. Under international law, Central American migrant children are considered refugees and asylum seekers since they are separated from their parents, without legal guardians, and unable to return to their countries of origin due to fear of violence, persecution, or lack of protection.[74] Between 2016 and 2017 alone, 41,435 children were detained at the southwestern US border.[75] In the 2018 fiscal year, 92 percent of unaccompanied children were of Central American origin.[76] In 2021, US Customs and Border Protection (CBP) reported that more than 65,000 unaccompanied children were apprehended while attempting to cross the US-Mexico border in the first five months of the year.[77] In October 2023, the Office of Refugee Resettlement reported that the youths in their care were approximately 47 percent Guatemalan, 29 percent Honduran, and 13 percent Salvadoran.[78]

The Obama administration's practice of detaining families together, beginning in 2014, and the Trump administration's family separation policy both continue to fuel the criminalization and detainment of children. President Joseph Biden continues to use Trump-era policies, such as the expulsion program known as Title 42, to deport children. In Guatemala, during her first overseas trip since taking office, Vice President Kamala Harris reflected the continuous anti-immigrant sentiments when she publicly warned Central American migrants: "Do not come. Do not come. The United States will continue to enforce our laws and secure our borders." She added: "If you come to our border, you will be turned back."[79]

The artist Guadalupe Maravilla draws from his own migration experience as an unaccompanied minor to condemn the absurdity of the criminalization of children. In *The OG of Undocumented Children* (2018), Maravilla merged singers, DJs, dancers, instruments, and a host of characters to create a spectacle of sound against the detention of unaccompanied minors. The performance began with the artist in front of a microphone on a small platform as he shared his personal migration story as an unaccompanied child migrant fleeing civil war. He described how he was sent with a coyote to unite with his parents in New York. The platform and artist were enclosed in metal fencing—referencing the rise of unaccompanied refugee minors held captive in detention centers, which protesting voices often describe as the United States placing "children in cages."

As the performance unfolded, Maravilla encountered an eight-year-old child, dressed in a mask and cape—the same age as the artist when he was an undocumented minor (see figure 4.21). The child belonged to a family of vampires, pointing to the absurdity of the government's fearmongering that immigrants are blood-sucking creatures draining resources and jobs from the country. Maravilla offered to invalidate the claim by asking audience members to come onstage, where he would bite and suck on their flesh. There could be only two outcomes: either the administration is proven right, and volunteers would immediately turn into vampires; or the government is proven wrong, and they could walk away with nothing more than a hickey. The absurdity of this exercise matches the absurdity of policies that oppress and marginalize children too young to understand they have been criminalized. Beyond the spectacle of sounds, performance, dance, a Mexican cumbia band, and the dance party that concluded the performance, all emblematic of immigrant resilience, Maravilla positions the undocumented child in a profound way. The performance forces viewers to ask: How are child migrants being harmed at this moment?

Amid the images of Central American children in detention centers, and the discourse of politicians, activists, and intellectuals, little space is given to the children's point of view. Salvadoran artist Ernesto Bautista counters the dominant perception of imprisoned children as helpless and uninformed by centering their philosophies on migration, detention, existence, and possible futurities. Bautista worked with children and their families in Tegucigalpa, Honduras, where through workshops and research they discussed the push-pull factors of migration and the implications of criminalization and detention of children. These conversations then informed a script performed by child actors in Bautista's art film *Teatro de desencuentro* (Theatre of missed encounters) (2021), first exhibited at Los Angeles Contemporary Exhibitions (LACE).

Through the lens of a moving surveillance camera inside the cage's ceiling, viewers see a group of children of various ages unable to escape their captivity. Nothing is visible beyond the darkness inside the cage and its red floor, on which the children sleep, sit, and lie, sometimes piled on top of each other, or where they move in frustration by their restricted mobility (see figure 4.22). Through voice-over, conversations between detained children range from philosophical dialogues to frustrations and annoyance with each other when they cannot agree to one child's question: "Are we dead or alive?"

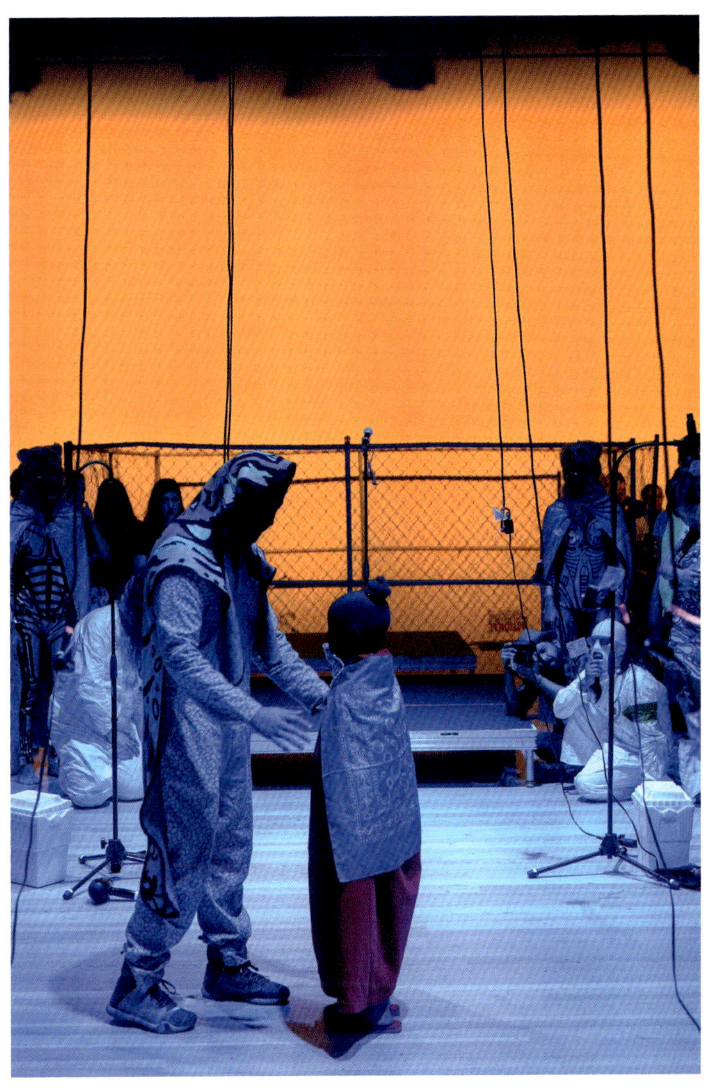

FIGURE 4.21.
Guadalupe Maravilla, *The OG of Undocumented Children*, 2018, performance. Photograph by Filip Wolak for the OG of Undocumented Children. Courtesy of the artist Guadalupe Maravilla.

In one conversation, the camera frames a teenage girl caring for a younger girl around five years old. The teenager tries to keep the restless and curious girl entertained and engaged. But unable to endure the length of her detention, the five-year-old expresses her desire to leave and proposes they escape. She is disappointed when the teenager reminds her that there is no certainty in escape, for they do not know what is outside the cage. What is out there could actually be worse for them. Unable to conceive a different escape plan, the younger girl replies: "I have an idea, what if we go to sleep and find someone in our dreams to tell us what to do?" To which the teenager responds: "You like to dream a lot?" The younger girl answers: "Yes. So, let's try." She lies on the floor and closes her eyes. With her concluding line, the five-year-old refuses defeat and maintains a commitment to freedom, despite the older girl's very real concerns of the unknown fate of those released. Likewise, she is not limited by a fear-based rationale, and she trusts that the answers can be found beyond the parameters of the earthly and scientific. No one inside the cage can help, but her dreams remain a site of encounters, perhaps with spirits and/or ancestors.

In another scene, we hear the voice of another child, Ariel, during his reflective monologue. He conveys how limits to freedom give way to imagination and creativity. "We are humans and we are trapped in a planet, that planet is trapped in a solar system, and that solar system is trapped in a galaxy, and that galaxy in a universe. We will always be trapped in a way, so why not create something inside instead of trying to get out of what you can't." Ariel's reflection speaks to the refusal of defeat, of ceasing to exist, even within the belly of the beast. This statement further reflects the containment of the cage as a metaphor for the barriers and walls placed on Central American existence through negation of humanity, anti-Indigenous and anti-Black violence, patriarchy, borders, US empire, and nation-state control, as I've shown so far in this book. For those who are never able to escape, or for those who escape one carceral violence only to land in another, there is no choice *but to create* from the space of one's geopolitical embodiment and location, whatever it may be. This is no everyday creation, for it's a defiance of death; it is a will to exist and assert one's humanity. That creation is a visual disobedience to the logic of colonialism, of heteropatriarchy, of carcerality, of empire—existence through creation. Ariel's philosophy is a reconfiguration of borders and walls. If it is not just the detained children but all humanity that is confined within boundaries, then focusing on creation rather than escape will give way to new communal solidarities and possibilities of liberation for all.

FIGURE 4.22.
Ernesto Bautista, *Teatro de desencuentro*, 2021, video (still). Courtesy of the artist.

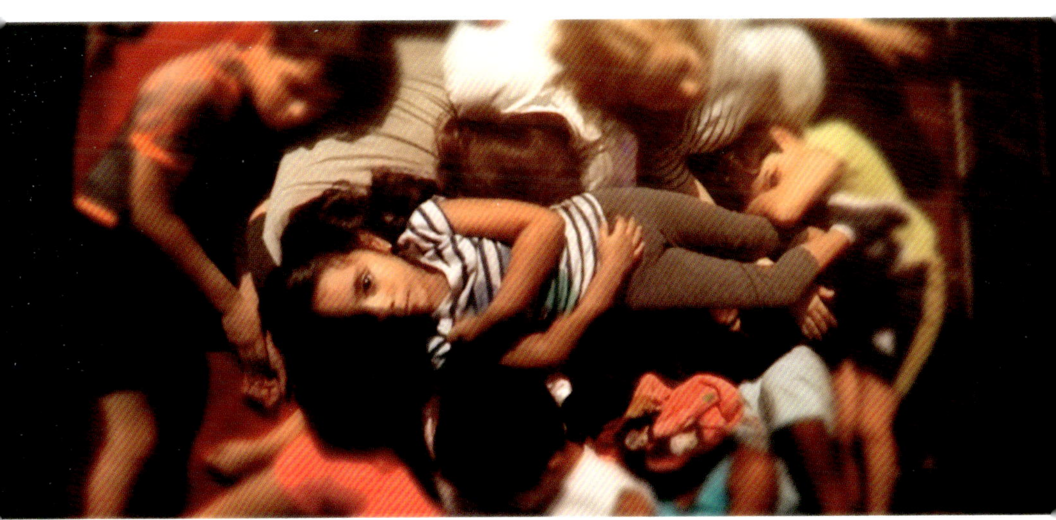

AGAINST DESERVINGNESS, TOWARD ABOLITION

Deservingness of rights, citizenship, and personhood is interlinked with the criminalization and imprisonment of poor racialized people. For many Central Americans, this criminalization happens before they reach the United States and before they leave the region, where criminalization relegates many of them to a nonhuman zone, which is yet another push factor for their migration, as was the case of Daniel Alemán (see figure 4.23). In 2022, both leaders of the collective Los Siempre Sospechosos de Todo were forced to flee El Salvador to the United States due to President Bukele's heightened criminalization and mass imprisonment of activists and poor youth. Alemán emigrated as a refugee, and Victor "Crack" Rodriguez is currently seeking political exile.

The detention and captivity of Central American men, women, children, and babies on US soil that we see today is possible because it builds on the already assumed illegality of Central Americans, who are viewed as already devoid of personhood and thus already outside the realm of human rights or protection. Thus, we fall into a trap when our only justification to vindicate the rights of Central American women and child migrants is contingent on their juxtaposition to violent transnational gangs as the *real* criminals—those who are supposedly truly undeserving of rights. The "bad/good immigrant dichotomies," as Escobar observes, such as felons/families, criminals/children, gang members/hardworking mothers, "assume that these categories are mutually exclusive; that 'felons' are not part of families, that 'criminals' are not children, that 'gang members' are not hard-working parents."[80]

Central American artists have opposed this reductive logic by exposing how the United States is complicit in the making of gangs and how governments perpetuate a carceral logic and fuel a system of criminalization that penetrates public and private spaces. They further condemn how the criminalization of Central Americans is sold to Central American people in order to ensure their approval and complicity in the elimination and social cleansing of the criminalized. While gang violence and criminal organization are indeed causes of desperation for many Central Americans, these artists disobey media, governments, popular consensus, and visual coloniality by refuting the colonialist binaries of guilty/innocent, good/evil, savage/civilized that have long been used against the colonized and question such boundaries. In doing so, I suggest their visual disobedience pushes not for immigration reform, not for selective citizenship, but rather for an abolition of the carceral logic, the carceral state, and the carceral state's mechanisms of violence. As "the always suspected

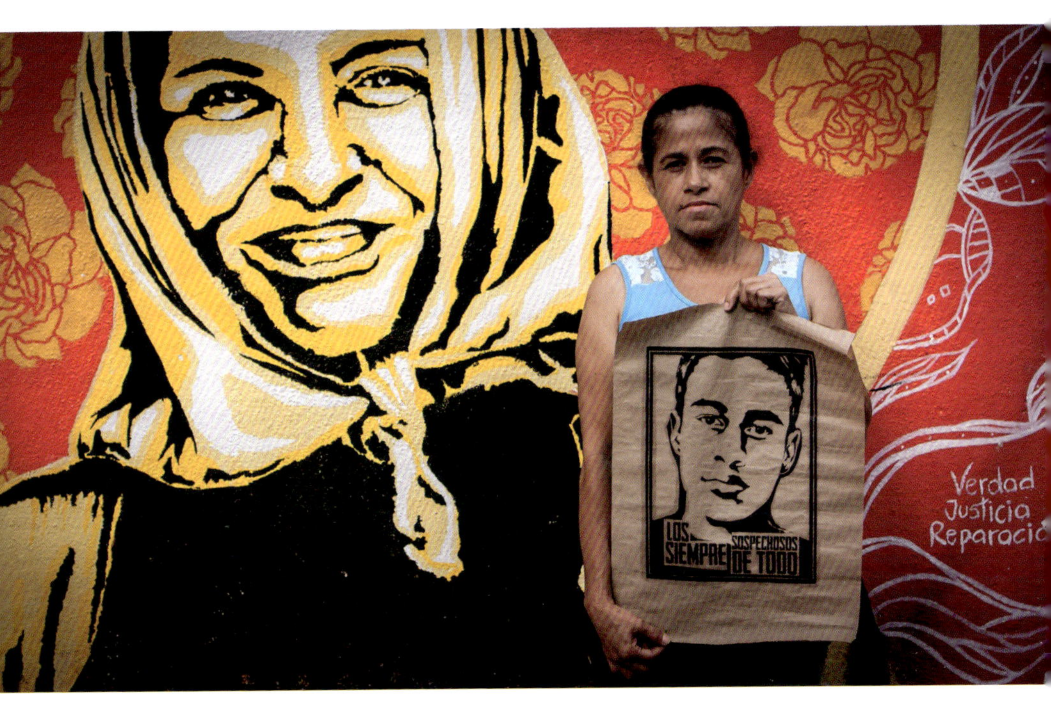

FIGURE 4.23.
Salvador Meléndez, *Meira Alemán, mother of Daniel Alemán, with a Los Siempre Sospechosos de Todo flyer depicting him*, 2017. Photograph published in *Revista Factum*.

ones" and "the eternally undocumented," as Dalton's poem once observed, the Central American artists in this chapter and their interventions should be considered in dialogue with other global projects of liberation that seek to dismantle borders, abolish carceral violence and its institutions, and counter colonial projects of extermination through creation and existence.

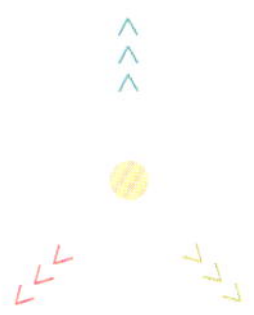

CONCLUSION

Visual Disobedience and Art Histories Otherwise

In a small village in Guatemala, an Indigenous child stands defiantly with an open chest, hands at his waist, as he gazes, against the sun's glare, straight ahead (see figure C.1). An Indigenous woman stands in a similar pose with an even more piercing stare (see figure C.2). The sun kisses their skin while behind them blue skies and water flank the volcanic landscape of Lake Atitlán, known as one of the most beautiful and deepest lakes in Central America. Nothing seems out of the ordinary in the image of this hopeful, young child and mature woman, except perhaps for the Superman shirts they wear, with the iconic *S*-emblazoned shield over their chests. The costume immediately connotes the characteristics and powers that made the original superhero character a worldwide sensation:

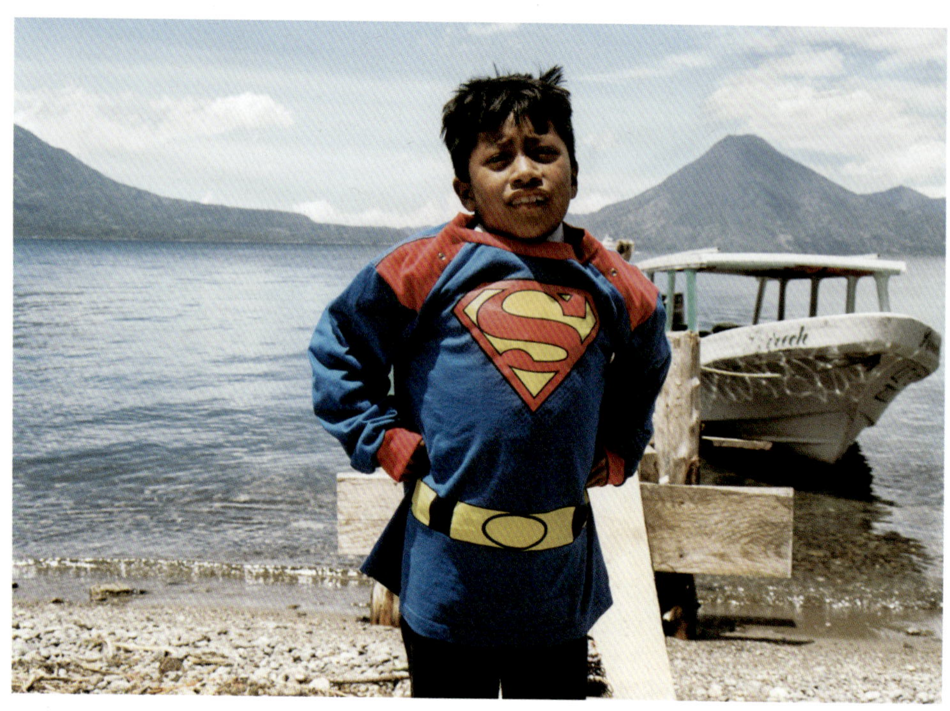

FIGURE C.1.
Walterio Iraheta, *Súper niño en Atitlán*, from Kriptonita series, 2007, photograph. Courtesy of the artist.

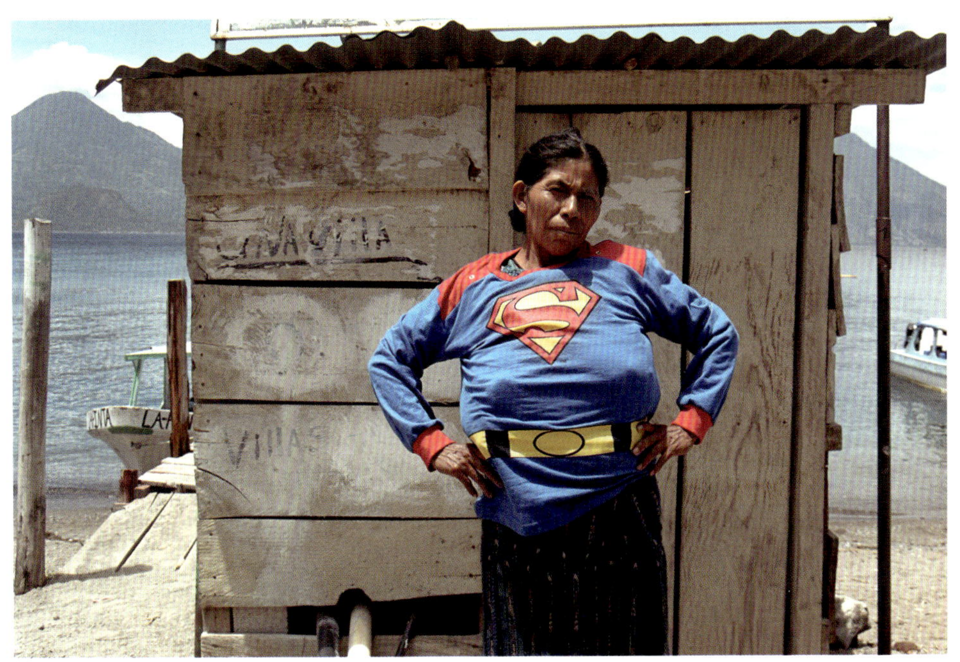

FIGURE C.2.
Walterio Iraheta, *Súper chica en Atitlán*, from Kriptonita series, 2007, photograph. Courtesy of the artist.

superhuman strength, the ability to fly, X-ray vision, breath with hurricane force, and a nonetheless noble, kind, and selfless personality.

The implication of a Guatemalan Mayan child and woman as an American superhero visually defies the hegemonic representations of Central American mothers and their children in detention centers that dominate media and US imaginaries today. Instead, with *Súper niño en Atitlán* and *Súper chica en Atitlán* (Super boy in Atitlán; Super girl in Atitlán; from the Kriptonita series) (2007), artist Walterio Iraheta reminds viewers that the iconic superhero and the child and woman have much more in common. Superman was the only survivor of his distant planet Krypton; he was sent by his parents to Earth when they realized that their planet, their home, would be destroyed. His common abilities on Krypton were "superpowers" on the new planet, and he used them to defend justice, coming to represent the "American" way and values.

Superman was a refugee. However, he was a white refugee, over six feet tall with blue eyes—a contrast to the Indigenous child and woman in the portraits. As we continue to see Central American, Indigenous, and Black refugees violently expulsed from the US-Mexico border, all the while we see the border opened for white, blond, blue-eyed refugees from Ukraine whose struggles are recognized as valid and whose lives are welcomed into safety and protection, images like Iraheta's expose more than racism or hypocrisy. They offer more than a social critique of "Americanness." They offer an acute perspective from below, an analysis of Empire, but more importantly a reminder that while the boy and woman may not have superhuman strength or the ability to fly, their mere existence evidences more than five hundred years of resistance and survival and a promise of hope for the future. Decolonial living *is* their superpower.

Collectively, the artistic interventions, embodiments, images, and practices in this book respond to the question: what happens when we create our own visual narratives, when we tell our (art) histories as we have lived them, and when we use our own modes of knowledge and communication? I have shown the answer can only be defiance. Creation and existence in the face of death and colonial violence will always be an act of insubordination—to the nation-state, to hegemonic narratives, to the violence of erasure, to empire, and to the art world and its institutions. Defiance occurs in many forms, from the physical confrontation in protests and demonstrations; to the subtle acts of looking back, speaking back, and writing back; to the production of ruptures and shifts in hegemonic thoughts, histories, and ways of seeing that make way for erased or repressed narratives.

This book has centered on those narratives that emerge through visual disobedience—narratives from Central American creative perspectives that reveal both a complex sociopolitical context ignored in the dominant media and histories and a creative ability and agency historically denied to us. I have shown that Mayan artists depart from Indigenous embodiments and cosmologies to reinsert, reinscribe, reconnect, and revalidate an Indigenous visual episteme. These Indigenous-led narratives provide a different notion of Mayan agency often denied to the Indigenous migrants currently arriving at the border, where new identities and labels are forced on them as conditions for existence in an imperial country. But moreover, as defiance to visual coloniality, these artists contest the colonial practice of relegating Indigenous peoples as subjects of study, objects for display, who are to be *seen* but who do not see.

These visual narratives also reveal how a turn to the body radicalized feminisms in Central America. Using one's own body as a site and weapon of intervention, especially in a postwar context, facilitated a critical theorization of race, gender, sexuality, and desire. In the postwar region, where gender-based violence became normalized and a fueling fact of migration, artists began to expand a class-based position with an intersection of positionalities leading to more radical enunciations on anti-Indigenous and anti-Black racism in the region and a condemnation of the policing and killing of gender nonconforming and nonheteronormative people. Their visual disobedience produced new forms of decolonial feminisms in the isthmus.

I have shown how through visual disobedience artists produce counternarratives of mass migration. In doing so, they alter our temporal, geographical, and embodied perceptions of war, migration, mobility, mapping, families, architecture, and economies as we understand them in the region. Central American governments are also held accountable for their participation in border regimes, including in the violence done to poor, Indigenous, and Black immigrants when Central American nation-states take on the role of border policing and enforcement. By shifting the border, these artists uncover the multiple border cultures Central American migrants navigate before ever reaching the US-Mexico border, demanding that we move beyond the US-Mexico dichotomy and question the war on mobility that is at the core of border imperialism.

Then, by shifting the border, the entanglements between criminalization of Central American asylum seekers and the larger history of mass incarceration in the United States become clear, further evidencing how US empire continues to violate Central American lives. Ultimately, these creative narratives push not for immigration reforms but for a rethinking of concepts of citizenship, value, and deservingness that are used to further the colonial projects of inhumanity. Their visual disobedience detours from selective citizenship and leads us toward an abolitionist movement. These narratives emerge from geopolitical embodiments, from creative ways of storytelling, witnessing, and testifying. They evidence the intellectual and creative abilities of racialized and gendered peoples when they are no longer relegated to images of suffering in the backdrop of magazines, anthropological subjects of study, or images of suffering but rather when recognized as thinkers, creatives, and storytellers of their own realities.

I have theorized the artworks in this book in terms of visual disobedience because beyond exposing the colonial practices by Central American governments and US empire that continue to subordinate Central American peoples, the artists in this book also defy visual coloniality. Their creative narratives offer anticolonial acts against what I have called visual erasure, visual thingification, and visual extractivism that have long been tactics of visual coloniality and the broader colonial project. They do not merely depict suffering or oppression but instead interrupt it; violence is not merely a subject matter but a testimony to it. Their visual disobedience is not representation but praxis. This praxis is one that stems from embodied knowledge through performance, actions, objects, and images that defy the uses of spaces that previously served as official spaces of state violence. The fusion of corporal, spatial, and visual praxis affirms an all-sensing and questioning existence that challenges Western and colonial notions of knowing and being.

This visual disobedience in Central America, which is constitutive of the wider Indigenous resistance and decolonial feminisms of the region, has unearthed new forms of witnessing sorrow, testifying to injustice, and insisting on accountability from systems of power. The perspectives and narratives that emerge from visual disobedience in this book reject the flattening and simplification of discourses that assign unlivable conditions in the region as "natural" to their people; instead, they make visible and tangible systems of power and domination of the nation-states, policing institutions, and patriarchal laws and policies that create unlivable conditions in Central America. They teach us that visual narratives matter. It matters who creates them, who receives them, and how they disrupt colonial logics to subtly or loudly demand a just world. Visual disobedience makes ways for narratives and art histories otherwise.

Some may see this book as a contribution to the discourse on migration and de/coloniality, while others may have come to this book seeking to learn about a people historically excluded from dominant art narratives. I hope to have shown in *Visual Disobedience* that these are not mutually exclusive. The omission of Central American art in art historical narratives, when the region itself has long been of geopolitical interest to US empire, cannot be rationalized as simple coincidence. For as I have argued, the denial and negation of a people's artistic capabilities form part of the broader colonial project of refusing people their humanity. Through the colonial theft of cultural objects, the erasure of the other systems of knowing, and the thingification of racialized people, visual coloniality has always already fueled the omission and elimination of peoples and their world making.

Therefore, there is no neutral erasure of history by art professionals, only a commitment to uphold imperial violence by relegating some to the past and others to the future. Neither does gifting back art and culture through so-called solidarity, curation, or discovery, to a people considered to have none, absolve one of complicity. In both the academic and the art world, colonial opportunism and the perpetuation of colonial narratives and displays reinforce a visual coloniality and impede cultural sovereignty. It is no coincidence, as Ariella Aïsha Azoulay reminds us, that the refugees of today (whether Syrian, Palestinian, Haitian, or Central American) are the descendants of civilizations plundered by colonialism. What we know today as the art world is historically indebted to that past (and in some cases ongoing) colonial pillage.

Exposing omission is thus not the ultimate goal. Neither will centering Central American artists and their visual disobedience in this book magically cease oppression and erasure in the region, for visual coloniality, plunder, and imperialism, are ongoing. Thus, my hope is in the reader. How will the reader recognize colonial ways of seeing and how will the reader disrupt processes that are often the most entrenched and normalized in our practices of seeing? Where can the reader recognize the mechanics of visual coloniality when considering other geopolitical spaces: Turtle Island? Palestine? Haiti? As a student, a scholar, or an art professional, how will the reader disobey visual coloniality?

A decolonial aesthetics cannot be a mere decorative backdrop to activist, political, or anticolonial work; rather, it is an essential component at the center of decolonial acts and in the struggle for self-determination and cultural sovereignty. In this manner, I also consider this book part of my own visual disobedience, which was to investigate and write from my own geopolitical space and embodiment, from the Central American diaspora, and from within and against the institutions that perpetuate such erasure. I cannot pretend it has been an easy task, as the themes I address in this book have touched my family and me in very real and tangible ways at various phases of my life and during multiple phases of the research and writing. After years of conversations and encounters, many of the artists I write about are allies and friends, and I thus cannot divorce myself from the emotional experiences that come with being witness to their testimonies and experiences. When a book project is not a popular new trend in scholarship, or another subject for study to publish or exhibit before moving on to the next, writing becomes a corporal and sensorial journey of pain, hope, rage, love, healing, and reasserted commitment. And it is no exaggeration to carry the feeling that one's life is at stake.

Yet this has been only an attempt to address some of the contemporary artists in the region who are currently receiving worldwide attention and to place their art, achievements, and concerns in a historical and anticolonial context, while focusing on one of many urgent issues: migration. There will have to be many more books. Subjects and artworks that I intended to include seemed impossible to condense into a book this size, and I quickly realized they merit their own books and future projects, some of which I have already begun. It is clear to me that the sociopolitical realities of the region are increasingly exposed and contested by artists, and thus Central American art will continue to intervene, disrupt, and teach us histories otherwise.

I hope to have conveyed that this book is not a call for inclusion and diversity of a field but a reminder that erasure of a peoples' creative abilities and narratives is directly tied to the devaluation of a peoples' worth, their dehumanization, and their elimination. Thus, in the face of such colonial violence, asserting artistic creation is directly connected to asserting one's existence and humanity. It is thus fitting to conclude with *Súper niño en Atitlán* and *Súper chica en Atitlán*, which reveal an alternative perspective of Central American children amid a time of detention, criminalization, and mass human rights abuses. It is a direct contrast to the fatally reductive depictions of Central American migrants that erase our histories and perpetuate further violence. Knowing that the violence enacted upon our communities today is part of a longer history of colonial violence reminds Central Americans that we have also long resisted, long survived, and long existed as a defiance to the colonial, patriarchal, and capitalist structures that negate our humanity. *Súper niño en Atitlán* and *Súper chica en Atitlán* are not only images that defy dominant narratives of destitution but ones that offer a different point of geopolitical departure and embodiment and thus a different knowledge and history—that of existence, resistance, and decolonial living.

NOTES

INTRODUCTION. AGAINST VISUAL COLONIALITY

1. For discussions on the tensions and conflation between Latin American and Latinx art and artists amid the emergence of multiculturalism or demands for difference in the artworld, see Dávila, *Latinx Art*, and Ramírez, "Brokering Identities."

2. Pérez-Ratton, *Un lugar inacabado*, 101.

3. In his review, Cameron stated: "Having offered such a promising curatorial thesis, it is disappointing that Mosquera, Ponce de León, and Weiss were not able to extend their research into any one of America's three most predominantly indigenous regions: the Andes (Peru, Bolivia and Ecuador), Central America (primarily El Salvador, Guatemala, Honduras and Nicaragua), and northern Canada (mainly Quebec, Saskatchewan and Northwest Territories) . . ." See Cameron, "Ante América," 96.

4. Some were in collaboration with curator Gerardo Mosquera, who since *Ante América* became a strong and constant supporter of art in the region. For documentation on these initiatives, see Pérez-Ratton and Castellano, *Mesótica II*; Mosquera and Samos, *Ciudad Múltiple City*; Olmo and Pérez-Ratton, *Todo incluído*; and Duran, *LANDINGS Ten (the Black Box)*. During his tenure as director of TEOR/éTica, Miguel López initiated a significant editorial series that recounts many of these events. Books in the series, Escrituras locales: Posiciones críticas desde América Central, el Caribe y sus diásporas, compile multiple essays by a single author into a standalone volume. They include Cazali, *Certezas vulnerables*; Díaz Bringas, *Crítica próxima*; Pérez-Ratton, *Un lugar inacabado*; Quintanilla, *Zona de turbulencia*; and Samos, *Divorcio a la panameña*.

5. In her seminal article, Juliet Hooker further points to the denial of culture in the erasure of Afro–Central Americans. Though both experience oppression, nation-states still attribute tradition, ancestral culture, and languages to Indigenous peoples, while Afro–Central Americans are seen as devoid of culture. The supposed lacking of culture, and of cultural identity, is one of several factors listed by Hooker that explains why Indigenous communities have been more successful at attaining collective rights over Afro–Central Americans. See Hooker, "Indigenous Inclusion/Black Exclusion." Regarding the US-based Garifuna, Paul Joseph López Oro has argued against US racial categories that continue to

view Blackness, Indigeneity, and Latinidad as mutually exclusive. See López Oro, "Garifunizando Ambas Américas."

6. Scholars wrestle with how these multiple deletions complicate the making of US Central Americans into ethnoracial subjects within the United States. Arturo Arias writes about "Central American-Americans" as an intentional reiteration of excess that points to how Central Americans are paradoxically positioned outside both Latino and Latin American signifiers. For Claudia Milian, Central Americans "disorient" US Latinidades, which are further problematized by the "Blackness" and "Dark-Brownness" of Central Americans (i.e., Garifuna and Maya migrants in the United States). As Milian explains, "Central Americans are introduced and kept at a safe distance so as not to disorient a U.S. Latino and Latina brownness" (*Latining America*, 128). See also Arias, "Central American–Americans"; and Maya Chinchilla's poem from which Arias develops the term: Chinchilla, "Central American–American," in *The Cha Cha Files*, 21–22.

7. Cárdenas, *Constituting Central American–Americans*.

8. Echavez See, *The Decolonized Eye*.

9. Early art historical analysis of revolutionary Nicaragua can be found in Kunzle, *The Murals of Revolutionary Nicaragua, 1979–1992*; and Craven, "The Nicaraguan Revolution (1979–1990)." The revolutionary group turned political party has since undergone drastic changes. Throughout the writing of this book, for instance, the former revolutionary leader of the Sandinistas, and since longtime president, Daniel Ortega, is protested by Nicaraguan citizens for human rights violations, and hundreds have been imprisoned or died in the span of a year at the hands of police repression, prompting artists, like Elyla and others, to respond and some to flee into exile.

10. This book draws from two bodies of work on Central American art from decades prior and the emerging discourse on US Central Americans. The first emerges from US scholars who traveled to El Salvador and Nicaragua in the 1980s and 1990s as part of the Central American solidarity movement. Notable are publications by curator Marilyn Zeitlin and art historians David Craven and David Kunzle, whose research highlighted war violence, testimony, and the revolutionary ideals of a liberated society, mostly in El Salvador and Nicaragua. The second body of literature comes from Central American curators, writers, and cultural workers who in the 1990s began to question the region's invisibility in the international art world and thus the need to produce critical reflection from the isthmus. From their dialogues and events, they produced a new body of literature from Central America led by curators and writers like Juanita Bermúdez, Rosina Cazali, Pablo Hernández-Hernández, Monica Kupfer, Rodolfo Molina, Virginia Pérez-Ratton, Raúl Quintanilla, Pablo José Ramirez, Adrienne Samos, and Sergio Villena, among others. The third comes from the Central American diaspora, from which I write this book. As either immigrants or the children of Central American immigrants, they began to analyze the sociopolitical conditions that made them a diasporic community and the challenges they endured as migrants, refugees, and Central Americans within a broader US Latinx population and beyond. Their intellectual work set the foundation for Central American studies, carving interventions into Latinx, Latin American, Indigenous, and African Diaspora studies. This includes work by Leisy Ábrego, Arturo Arias, Giovanni Batz, Floridalma Boj Lopez, Maritza Cárdenas, Gloria Chacon, Jorge E. Cuéllar, Juliet Hooker, Paul Joseph López Oro, Cecilia Menjívar, Claudia Milian, Yajaira M. Padilla, Andoni Castillo Perez,

Suyapa G. Portillo Villeda, Ana Patricia Rodriguez, and Arely Zimmerman, among others. Though strong in sociological, historical, political, and literary analyses, the role of art and visuality within the history of Central America and its diaspora, however, is only recently materializing, as in the work of Mauricio Ramirez, Tatiana Reinoza, Carlos A. Rivas, and Melanie White, and in the curatorial work of Armando Perla and Alma Ruiz.

11. Afro-descendants in Central America trace their history to both the forceful abduction and trafficking of enslaved Africans to the isthmus and labor migration from the Caribbean islands and the United States. The various peoples that make up the Afro–Central American population, such as the Garinagu, Miskito, Bay Island Creole, and West Indian migrants, have unique histories, challenges, and forms of resistance. In addition to the previously mentioned, see Cosgrove, et al., *Surviving the Americas*; Cunin and Hoffman, *Blackness and Mestizaje in Mexico and Central America*; Corinealdi, *Panama in Black* ; England, *Afro Central Americans in New York City*; Gómez Menjívar, *Black in Print*; Harpelle, *The West Indians of Costa Rica*.

12. Sylvia Wynter draws on Pierre Bourdieu to discuss these as "taste of reflection" (pure taste) versus "taste of the senses" (impure taste). See Wynter, "Rethinking 'Aesthetics.'"

13. The philosopher Immanuel Kant, a canonical figure in Western aesthetics, created an "Other" based on their assumed abilities to perceive aesthetics, which he claimed was determined by their racial category. Kant posited that these are aesthetic categories that serve as guides of conduct and are linked to moral experience, implying that art is not just a way of *seeing* things but a way of *being*. See Kant, *Observation on the Feeling of the Beautiful and the Sublime*.

14. Wynter, "Rethinking 'Aesthetics,'" 259.

15. Cusicanqui, "Experiencias de montaje creativo"; Cusicanqui, *Sociología de la imagen*.

16. Rickard, "Diversifying Sovereignty and the Reception of Indigenous Art."

17. Among members of the modernity/coloniality/decoloniality collective are Dalila Maria Benfield, Arturo Escobar, Raul Moarquech Ferrera-Balanquet, Pedro Pablo Gómez, Ramón Grosfoguel, Maria Lugones, Nelson Maldonado-Torres, Walter Mignolo, Miguel Rojas-Sotelo, Rolando Vazquez, and Catherine Walsh.

18. They attempt to expose how aesthetics is embedded within the colonial matrix of power, intervening in creative practices such as biennials and curatorial projects to decolonize the senses. See Barriendos, "La colonialidad del ver"; Maldonado-Torres, "On Metaphysical Catastrophe, Post-continental Thought, and the Decolonial Turn"; and Mignolo and Vázquez, "Decolonial AestheSis."Additionally, see Mirzoeff, *The Right to Look*.

19. Quijano, "Coloniality and Modernity/Rationality."

20. They include M. Jacqui Alexander, Aura Cumes, Maria Lugones, Xhercis Méndez, Mágara Millán Moncayo, Silvia Rivera Cusicanqui, Hortense J. Spillers, and Gladys Tzul Tzul, among others. The hemispheric emerging proposals for decolonizing feminism are thus led by Indigenous, Afro-descendant, poor, nonheteronormative, and gender nonconforming feminists. They include communal perspectives, Indigenous cosmovisions, relations to land and nature, diasporic histories, legacies of ancestral resistance, and other modes of knowing rooted in the embodied experience of those marked by the coloniality of gender, which is typically excluded from institutional feminism. See Alexander and Mohanty, *Feminist Genealogies, Colonial Legacies, Democratic Futures*; Cumes, "La 'India' como 'sirvienta,'"; Cusicanqui, "The Notion of 'Rights' and the Paradoxes of

Post-colonial Modernity"; Lugones, "Coloniality of Gender"; Mendez, "Notes Toward a Decolonial Feminist Methodology"; Moncayo, "Feminismos, Postcolonialidad, Descolonización"; and Spillers "Mama's Baby, Papa's Maybe."

21. Mignolo, "Epistemic Disobedience, Independent Thought, and Decolonial Freedom."

22. Gómez-Barris, *The Extractive Zone, 13*. See also Gómez-Barris, Lane, and Godoy-Anativia, "Decolonial Gesture."

23. In *The Archive and the Repertoire*, Diana Taylor identifies a parallel existence between two systems of historical memory and knowledge: the *archive*, the material and archival memory that is resistant to change (as in text, maps, and documents); and the *repertoire*, an ephemeral embodied practice that transmits memory and knowledge (as in dance, song, and gesture). Though they coexist, the repertoire, important to Indigenous epistemes, is often dismissed as outside the domain of legitimate Western knowledge. Meanwhile, the archive, valued for its permanance, is often preferred and preserved to serve the interest of the state and its colonial projects. These distinctions are fluid, as Amelia Jones has shown in her interrogation of the dichotomous relationship between archive and repertoire. Yet they are significant in decentering the Western privilege over the visual and material, and for reasserting the importance of the embodied, ephemeral, and performative, and thereby recentering the body and decolonizing the senses and knowledge. Such distinctions allow me to situate Mayan performances, beyond the Western definition of performance art that emerges from the United States and Europe, as rooted in a much longer history of Indigenous systems of sensing-knowing that predate art historical categories. See Jones, "Archive, Repertoire, and Embodied Histories," and Taylor, *The Archive and the Repertoire*.

24. Maldonado-Torres, "On Metaphysical Catastrophe, Post-continental Thought, and the Decolonial Turn."

25. Maldonado-Torres, "On Metaphysical Catastrophe, Post-continental Thought, and the Decolonial Turn," 256.

26. See Flores and Stephens, *Relational Undercurrents: Contemporary Art of the Caribbean Archipelago*, exhibited at the Museum of Latin American Art (MOLAA) in Long Beach, California, as part of the Getty Foundation–sponsored Pacific Standard LA/LA series.

27. Neruda, "The United Fruit Company," in *Canto general*, 179.

28. Gómez-Barris, *The Extractive Zone, 11–12*.

29. Castro-Gómez, *La hybris del punto cero*.

30. Tuck and Yang, "Decolonization Is Not a Metaphor."

31. Azoulay, *Potential History*, 63.

32. Scholars note that Maya scribes, known as *ah k'u huns*, meaning "he of the writing," were recruited and trained in special academies in calligraphy and the visual, and were depicted in unique dress in a myriad of reliefs, murals, and cultural objects. Their visual production included individual signatures and names, thus indicating a prestige and importance attributed to them by the Mayan court. Along with warriors, high-ranking scribes were even common targets for enemies seeking captives during combat. For an in-depth art historical account and analysis of the ancient Maya scribe, see Coe and Kerr, *The Art of the Maya Scribe*.

33. Mignolo, *The Darker Side of the Renaissance*.

34. For a discussion on the long effects of Vasari's writing in establishing a heteropatriarchal and exclusionary art canon, see Salomon, "The Art Historical Canon."

35. See Damisch, *The Origin of Perspective*; Edgerton, *The Renaissance Rediscovery of Linear Perspective*; and Elkins and Williams, *Renaissance Theory*.

36. Césaire, *Discourse on Colonialism*.

37. Césaire, *Discourse on Colonialism*, 41.

38. Césaire, *Discourse on Colonialism*, 83.

39. For further studies on the intersections of visual culture, landscape, travel, and tourism in relation to the colonial gaze, see Fusco and Wallis, *Only Skin Deep*; Mitchell, *Landscape and Power* ; Pratt, *Imperial Eyes*; and Thompson, *An Eye for the Tropics*.

40. For a history of human zoos, see Blanchard, *Human Zoos*; Cariou, "The Exhibited Body"; Corbey, "Ethnographic Showcases, 1870–1930"; and Egan, "Exhibiting Indigenous Peoples."

41. For more on display practices, see Kirshenblatt-Gimblett, *Destination Culture*.

42. Boëtsch, "From the Cabinets of Curiosity to the Passion for the Savage."

43. Aguirre, "Exhibiting Degeneracy."

44. Velasquez, Stephens, and Barnum's American Museum, *Illustrated Memoir of an Eventful Expedition into Central America*.

45. Aguirre, "Exhibiting Degeneracy," 50.

46. Aguirre, "Exhibiting Degeneracy," 49.

47. Yancy, "Colonial Gazing."

48. Yancy, "Colonial Gazing," 8.

49. Yancy, "Colonial Gazing," 8.

50. Veltmeyer and Petras, *The New Extractivism*.

51. Veltmeyer and Petras, *The New Extractivism*, 1.

52. Gómez-Barris, *The Extractive Zone*, 5.

53. For more on the colonial history of museums and exhibitions of Indigenous culture, see Azoulay, *Potential History* , and Sleeper-Smith, *Contesting Knowledge*.

54. From an interview included in Martínez Salazar, *Global Coloniality of Power in Guatemala*.

55. Boj Lopez, "Weavings That Rupture."

56. For instance, in El Salvador following the 1932 military-ordered execution of thirty thousand Indigenous men and boys, now known as La Matanza, terrorized Indigenous Salvadorans concealed their native clothing and ceased speaking native languages, resulting in a largely assimilated country today. See Tilley, *Seeing Indians*.

57. Martínez Salazar, *Global Coloniality of Power in Guatemala*, 67 (my emphasis).

58. For more on Indigenous textiles, intellectual property law, and the Indigenous challenge to Western concepts of authorship, see Chacón, "Material Culture, Indigeneity, and Temporality."

59. For further reading on the intersection of art, visual politics, and extractive policies and climate change, see Demos, *Decolonizing Nature*.

60. Maldonado-Torres, "Outline of Ten Theses on Coloniality and Decoloniality."

61. Fanon, *The Wretched of the Earth*; Sandoval, *Methodology of the Oppressed*; Guevara, "Socialism and Man in Cuba."

62. Walia, *Undoing Border Imperialism*.

I first published a shorter version of this chapter in 2013. Since then, the visibility and participation in the artistic sphere has increased. I am grateful to the artists discussed in this book for our decade-long conversations and friendships. See Cornejo, "Indigeneity and Decolonial Seeing in Contemporary Art of Guatemala."

1. For more on indigenismo, see Cornejo Polar, *Literatura y sociedad en el Perú*; Coronado, *The Andes Imagined*; and Mariátegui, *Seven Interpretive Essays on Peruvian Reality*. On the sentimental appeal of indigenismo to mestizo formation and contradictory goals, see Tarica, *The Inner Life of Mestizo Nationalism*.

2. For an art historical analysis of indigenismo related to gender and modernity and national identity in Mexico, see Zavala, *Becoming Modern, Becoming Tradition*. For indigenismo's reach from Mexico to a Pan-American context, see Cohen-Aponte, "Forging a Popular Art History"; Greet, *Beyond National Identity*; and Coronado, *The Andes Imagined*. For a focus on the state and the institutional museum's relation to indigenismo and paternalism, see Coffey, "From Nation to Community."

3. Rothenberg, *Memory of Silence*.

4. See Martínez Salazar, *Global Coloniality of Power in Guatemala*, 101–103.

5. Martínez Salazar, *Global Coloniality of Power in Guatemala*, 102.

6. Martínez Salazar, *Global Coloniality of Power in Guatemala*, 103.

7. Quoted in Martínez Salazar, *Global Coloniality of Power in Guatemala*, 103.

8. Esquit traces the concepts of *conciencia* and *superación* not to twentieth-century Catholicism or Paulo's Freire's *concientización* but to decades earlier, when Indigenous leaders used such concepts for unity and political Indigenous identity amid nation-state building. Therefore, the idea of a critically conscious Indigenous person is not one that derives from mestizo-led guerrillas but one rooted in Maya concepts and their relations to identity, the communal Indigenous experience, and autonomy. For instance, even the concept of *qawinaq* (*nuestra gente*) refers specifically to the Indigenous experience and is thus limited to the inclusion of Indigenous people. See Esquit, "Nociones Kaqchikel." See also Esquit, *La superación del indígena*.

9. Quoted in Martínez Salazar, *Global Coloniality of Power in Guatemala*, 103.

10. For the DIA document, see "Suspected Presence of Clandestine Cemeteries on a Military Installation," April 11, 1994, available via the National Security Archive, George Washington University, https://nsarchive2.gwu.edu/NSAEBB/NSAEBB11/docs/doc29.pdf.

11. Virgill Artiaga, "The Garifuna Voices of Guatemala's Armed Conflict."

12. Though beyond the spatial scope of this book, for my next book project I have been researching Afro–Central American cultural production across the isthmus and its US-based diaspora in conjunction with a larger project of contributing to Afro–Latin American art histories. Though I debated including a chapter in this book, I determined the topic deserves greater in-depth consideration and a book-length project is more appropriate. For more on Black Indigeneity, anti-Blackness, and Black experience in the isthmus and its diaspora, see Anderson, *Black and Indigenous*; Corinealdi, *Panama in Black*; Cosgrove et al., *Surviving the Americas*; Hooker, "'Beloved Enemies'"; and López Oro, "Garifunizando Ambas Américas."

13. Garrard-Burnett, "Living with Ghosts."

14. Tzul Tzul, " Rebuilding Communal Life," 404.

15. "Impact," FAFG, accessed March 2, 2021, https://fafg.org/our-impact/.

16. Ángel Poyón, Skype interview by the author, December 12, 2013.

17. For more on the Indigenous communities surrounding Lake Atitlán, see Macleod, *Santiago Atitlán, ombligo del universo tz'utujil*.

18. See Véliz, "Seguir hacia delante, volver la mirada hacia atrás."

19. Cabrera Padilla, "Artistas Guatemaltecos Kaqchikeles y Tz'utujiles."

20. Chavajay, quoted in "A los chunches no los transformo, los transfiguro, no hay nada que hacerles," interview by Beatriz Colmenares, May 12, 2013, http://www.elperiodico.com.gt/es/20130512/domingo/228140/.

21. In an interview, Chavajay uses the term *emplasticacion* to describe the arrival of modernity in San Pedro la Laguna. Benvenuto Chavajay, interview by the author, San Salvador, El Salvador, May 29, 2011.

22. See Düssel, *Invention of the Americas*, and *The Underside of Modernity*. See also Quijano, "Coloniality of Power, Eurocentrism, and Latin America."

23. Benvenuto Chavajay, interview by the author, San Salvador, El Salvador, May 29, 2011.

24. Benvenuto Chavajay, interview by the author, San Salvador, El Salvador, May 29, 2011.

25. Conversation with María Curruchiche, San Juan Comalapa, Guatemala, April 2011. See also "Diálogos formativos azul profundo," *Movimiento, Arte, Cultura* (blog), CREA, April 4, 2011, http://creaguatemala.blogspot.com/2011/04/dialogos-formativos-azul-profundo.html.

26. Cazali, *Migraciones*, 30.

27. Tuhiwai Smith, *Decolonizing Methodologies*, 52–53.

28. For example, the Virgin of Guadalupe was secretly worshipped as the pre-Columbian goddess Tonantzin. This imagery has been especially central to Chicana/o artists in the United States who root their spirituality through the incorporation of pre-Columbian imagery in their artwork. For a study on this relation between spirituality and Indigeneity in Chicano art, see Pérez, *Chicana Art*; and Latorre, *Walls of Empowerment*.

29. "El B'aktun pone de moda a los mayas aunque sus descendientes siguen olvidados," December 20, 2012, http://www.elcomercio.com/mundo/Guatemala-mayasfin_del_mundo_0_832116919.html.

30. Antonio Pichillá, Skype interview by the author, November 29, 2012.

31. Antonio Pichillá, Skype interview by the author, November 29, 2012.

32. Antonio Pichillá, Skype interview by the author, November 29, 2012.

33. Sandra Monterroso, interview by the author, Guatemala City, Guatemala, June 1, 2011.

34. Sandra Monterroso, interview by the author, Guatemala City, Guatemala, June 1, 2011.

35. Martínez Salazar, *Global Coloniality of Power in Guatemala*, 70.

36. Cumes, "La 'India' como 'sirvienta,'" 140.

37. Martínez Salazar, *Global Coloniality of Power in Guatemala*, 69.

38. For more on Maya dress in a diaspora context, see Boj Lopez, "Weavings That Rupture."

39. Belli was motivated to address the lack of critical pedagogical training for young artists with a series of projects that morphed into a regional center for artistic training now known as EspIRA/ESPORA. Its students continue to form the next generation of artists with the vocabulary, understanding, and techniques that enable them to participate in a contemporary art world, while addressing issues from their own context. EspIRA/ESPORA is now a recognized art school *from* Central America *for* Central American artists. For more on Belli's account, see López, "Don't Teach, Learn."

40. For a directory of Indigenous groups in Central America by country, see Minority Rights Group International, accessed December 1, 2018, https://minorityrights.org.

CHAPTER 2. A CREATIVE TURN TO THE BODY

1. See Craven, *Art and Revolution in Latin America, 1910–1990*; Davidson, *Latin American Posters*; and Kunzle, *Murals of Revolutionary Nicaragua, 1979–1992*.

2. Giunta, *Feminismo y arte latinoamericano*, 72–75.

3. Giunta, *Feminismo y arte latinoamericano*, 78 (my translation).

4. Lorde, "The Master's Tools Will Never Dismantle the Master's House," 26.

5. See Alexander and Mohanty, *Feminist Genealogies, Colonial legacies, Democratic Futures*; Mohanty, *Feminism without Borders*; and Spivak, "Can the Subaltern Speak?"

6. See Lugones, "Coloniality of Gender"; and Spillers, "Mama's Baby, Papa's Maybe."

7. Ana Marcela Montanaro Mena notes that in the 1990s, as Latin American countries moved toward a period of democratization, activists called for an autonomous feminism outside the Western and hegemonic feminism of institutions and nongovernmental organizations (NGOs) that from its position of privilege and discourse reinforced coloniality. For instance, they critiqued a Latin American feminism led by white, middle-class women who inherited feminist discourse from the Global North and replicated it in the Global South, thus causing more harm to those excluded: Indigenous peoples, Afro-descendants, campesinos, and the poor. See Montanaro Mena, *Una mirada al feminismo decolonial en América Latina*.

8. For country-focused studies on the rise of body, performance, and action art amid state repression, see Calirman, *Brazilian Art under Dictatorship*; Richard, *Márgenes e instituciones*; and Fusco, *Corpus Delecti*.

9. Fusco, *Corpus Delecti*, 9.

10. See Stiles, "Uncorrupted Joy."

11. Even before the 1990s, performance art was active in the region, though rarely documented. Guatemalan Margarita Azurdia (also known as Margot Fanjul), Panamanian Manuel Montilla, and Otto Opuy are among other pioneering artists who experimented with body art but are less known due to little or no documentation and now only exist in the memory of those who were present to witness the art actions. At the time, performances and actions were rarely considered "art" and became isolated cases, and some were dismissed as "acts of madness," which may be emblematic of how many others were received. For more, see Pérez-Ratton, "Performance and Action Work in Central America, 1960–2000."

12. Taylor, *¡Presente!*

13. See Cazali, *Pasos a desnivel*; Pérez-Ratton and Castellano, *Mesótica II*; Mosquera and Samos, *Ciudad Múltiple City*; Olmo and Pérez-Ratton, *Todo incluído*; Duran, LANDINGS *Ten (the Black Box)*; Díaz Bringas, *Crítica próxima*; Samos, *Divorcio a la panameña*; Cazali, *Certezas vulnerables*; Quintanilla, *Zona de turbulencia*; and Pérez-Ratton, *Un lugar inacabado*.

14. Some of these collectives included Imaginaria Group, Casa Bizarra, Arte Urbano Collective, and La Curandería (Healing Arts), among others. Most collectives in Guatemala, with the exception of Imaginaria gallery in Antigua, emerged in the city capital. Aside from the opportunity to dialogue, debate, and critically theorize with peers, many of Guatemala's collectives opened alternative spaces that would allow them to convene and to put their theorizations and experimentations into practice while engaging with broader audiences. See Cazali, *Pasos a desnivel*; and Cazali, "Ser contemporáneos."

15. The festival launched recognized performance artists such as Regina José Galindo, Aníbal López, Jorge de León, Benvenuto Chavajay, Sandra Monterroso, Ángel Poyón, Fernando Poyón, Jessica Lagunas, María Adela Díaz, and others.

16. For more on Jorge Oquelí's performance, see Vallecillo, *La otra tradición*; and Galeano, "La desestatización de la imagen de la violencia."

17. Hunt and Lessard, *Women and the Colonial Gaze*.

18. Mandel Katz, "La deconstrucción del 'deber ser' patriarcal."

19. Alvarado, *Abject Performances*.

20. Fregoso and Bejarano, *Terrorizing Women*, 4–5. I use both *femicide* and *feminicidio* interchangeably throughout this chapter.

21. Alvarez et al., *Translocalities/Translocalidades*.

22. Cházaro and Casey, "Getting Away with Murder."

23. Fregoso and Bejarano, *Terrorizing Women*, 10.

24. Cházaro and Casey, "Getting Away with Murder," 99.

25. Cházaro and Casey, "Getting Away with Murder," 97.

26. Geneva Declaration Secretariat, "When the Victim Is a Woman," 119; Prieto-Carrón, Thompson, and Macdonald, "No More Killings!," 31.

27. "The Northern Triangle in Data," WOLA: Advocacy for Human Rights in the Americas, 2021, https://www.wola.org/vcam/#violence.

28. Menjívar and Walsh, "Subverting Justice."

29. Peñas Defago, "El aborto en El Salvador."

30. Celina Escher, *Fly So Far* (Sweden, 2021) Pråmfilm Production.

31. Mengesha, "Defecting Witness," 146.

32. See also Barbosa, "Regina José Galindo's Body Talk"; Goldman, "Regina José Galindo"; Castro Flórez, "The Atrocious Incarnations of Regina José Galindo"; and Newman, "Regina José Galindo."

33. Quoted in Prieto-Carrón, Thompson, and Macdonald, "No More Killings!," 30.

34. Fregoso and Bejarano, *Terrorizing Women*, 13.

35. Amnesty International, "Justice and Impunity: Guatemala's Historical Clarification Commission 10 Years On," February 25, 2009, AMR 34/001/2009, http://www.refworld.org/docid/49a651682.html.

36. See Martínez Salazar, *Global Coloniality of Power in Guatemala.*

37. Hernández-Avila, quoted in A. Smith, *Conquest*, 79.

38. See Maldonado-Torres, "On the Coloniality of Being."

39. Maldonado-Torres, "On the Coloniality of Being," 255.

40. See Lakhani, *Who Killed Berta Cáceres?*

41. Batz, "The Fourth Invasion," 2.

42. See García-Peña, *Translating Blackness.*

43. García-Peña, *Translating Blackness*, 12. Though García-Peña refers to the US context of Black Latinidad, I still find her insightful theorization useful in the context of Afro–Latin American migrants within a Latin American context.

44. García-Peña, *Translating Blackness*, 12.

45. Ressini and Fabiola, "Estándares de belleza y cultura en la manifestación de anorexia en jóvenes del corregimiento de Bellavista en Ciudad de Panamá."

46. Ressini and Fabiola, "Estándares de belleza y cultura en la manifestación de anorexia en jóvenes del corregimiento de Bellavista en Ciudad de Panamá," 52.

47. Maria Raquel Cochez, "Artist Statement," accessed January 22, 2019, http://mariaraquelcochez.com/wp-content/uploads/2013/04/Artist-Statement-032013.pdf.

48. Alexander, "Erotic Autonomy as Politics of Decolonization."

49. See Muñoz, *Disidentifications*, 4.

50. Muñoz, *Disidentifications*, 11–12.

51. Méndez and Figueroa, "Not Your Papa's Wynter," 67.

52. Méndez and Figueroa, "Not Your Papa's Wynter," 67.

53. Human Rights Watch (HRW), "'Every Day I Live in Fear': Violence and Discrimination against LGBT People in El Salvador, Guatemala, and Honduras, and Obstacles to Asylum in the United States," October 2020, https://www.hrw.org/sites/default/files/media_2020/10/centralamerica_lgbt1020_web.pdf.

54. Human Rights Watch, "'Every Day I Live in Fear,'" 102.

55. Portillo Villeda, "'Outing' Honduras."

56. Human Rights Watch, "'Every Day I Live in Fear,'" 67.

57. See Human Rights Watch, "'Every Day I Live in Fear.'"

58. Human Rights Watch, "'Every Day I Live in Fear,'" 123.

59. Kampwirth, "Organizing the *Hombre Nuevo Gay.*"

60. See Kampwirth, "Organizing the *Hombre Nuevo Gay*," 320.

61. Kampwirth, "Organizing the *Hombre Nuevo Gay* , 323. See also, Howe, *Intimate Activism.*

62. McGee and Kampwirth, "The Co-optation of LGBT Movements in Mexico and Nicaragua."

63. See Gómez-Barris, *Beyond the Pink Tide.*

64. Elyla (Fredman Barahona), Zoom interview by the author, April 17, 2021.

65. Pierce, "I Monster," 316.

66. Gómez-Barris, *Beyond the Pink Tide*, 55–56.

67. Muñoz, *Cruising Utopia*, 1.

CHAPTER 3. SHIFTING THE BORDER

1. Anzaldúa, *Borderlands*, 3.

2. Hernández, *Coloniality of the U-S///Mexico Border*, 31.

3. Walia, *Undoing Border Imperialism*.

4. Hernández, *Coloniality of the U-S///Mexico Border*, 31.

5. For a discussion of the war on mobility and its management of movement into the European Union, see Casas-Cortés and Cobarrubias, "A War on Mobility."

6. The forgetting of US crimes against Central American people led Aviva Chomsky to begin her book on Central American history with some words on "invisibility and forgetting." See Chomsky, *Central America's Forgotten History*.

7. The US interventions that established a foundation and path toward the US-fueled wars in the 1980s included the secession of Panama from Colombia in 1903, which secured the Panama Canal Zone under US sovereignty; a series of military invasions in Honduras from the 1900s to the 1920s to protect the United Fruit Company (UFC) and Standard Fruit Company's economic interests, leading to the term *Banana Republic*; occupations in Nicaragua from 1912 to 1933 against a proposed Nicaragua Canal that would compete with the US-controlled Panama Canal; the 1954 coup in Guatemala, when president Jacobo Arbenz intended to repatriate land from UFC to land workers; and others.

8. García, *Seeking Refuge*.

9. For more on *El Sumpul* in the context of museums and memory and postwar El Salvador, see DeLugan, "Museums, Memory, and the Just Nation in Post–Civil War El Salvador."

10. García, *Seeking Refuge*, 39.

11. García, *Seeking Refuge*, 35.

12. García, *Seeking Refuge*, 35.

13. For a detailed analysis of *arpilleras* within the greater context of textile art and politics, see Bryan-Wilson, *Fray*.

14. See Walia, *Undoing Border Imperialism*.

15. Habacuc Guillermo Vargas, "El caso Natividad Canda," September 14, 2008, http://natividadcanda.blogspot.com/.

16. Habacuc Guillermo Vargas, "El caso Natividad Canda."

17. For a history of the border disputes between Nicaragua and Costa Rica and their connection to immigration issues, see Cordero, "Migraciones y medio ambiente." Also, for an understanding of how an otherwise lenient Costa Rican government began to change its immigration policies to restrict employment opportunities and benefits to Nicaraguan refugees, see Larson, "Costa Rican Government Policy on Refugee Employment and Integration, 1980–1990."

18. Sergio Villena Fiengo has written a comprehensive account of the varied positions and debates swirling around *Exposition #1* in Central America in his book *El perro está más vivo que nunca*.

19. Carlos Salinas Maldonado, "Nicaragua cierra el paso a los africanos que sueñan con EE UU," *El Pais*, October 11, 2016, https://elpais.com/internacional/2016/10/11/america/1476222901_255600.html.

20. Thomas Simonetti and Michael Robinson Chavez, "These Photos Show Why Migrants Desperately Want Out of Costa Rica," *Washington Post*, December 14, 2016.

21. José Adán Silva, "Migrants Are up against Nicaragua's 'Containment Wall,'" InterPress Service News Agency, February 15, 2018, http://www.ipsnews.net/2018/02/migrants-hit-hard-nicaraguas-closed-border-strategy/.

22. For more on the iconic Sandino figure in art and visual culture, see Craven, *Art and Revolution in Latin America, 1910–1990*; and Kunzle, *Murals of Revolutionary Nicaragua, 1979–1992*.

23. I have written in depth elsewhere about Habacuc's *Exposition #1*. See Cornejo, "No Text without Context."

24. For a discussion of anti-Blackness and its entanglements in the US border formation, see Walia, *Border and Rule*, 28–31.

25. Huerta, "La 'securitización' de la gubernamentalidad migratoria mediante la 'externalización' de las fronteras estadounidenses a Mesoamérica."

26. In 2002, Alianza para la Frontera México-Estados emerged. Plan Sur was then substituted in 2003 for Fortalecimiento de las Delegaciones Regionales de la Frontera Sur, from which emerged Grupo Beta, which increased the deportation of Central American migrants, and in 2005 Alianza para la Seguridad y la Prosperidad de América del Norte (ASPAN) was signed.

27. Huerta, "La 'securitización' de la gubernamentalidad migratoria."

28. Huerta, "La 'securitización' de la gubernamentalidad migratoria"; Torre-Cantalapiedra and Yee-Quintero, "México ¿una frontera vertical?," 90.

29. The southern region of Mexico includes Oaxaca, Veracruz, and Yucatán. The central region of Mexico includes Aguas Calientes, Colima, Mexico City, Guanajuato, Guerrero, Hidalgo, Jalisco, Mexico, Michoacán, Morelos, Nayarit, Puebla, Querétaro, San Luis de Potosí, Tlaxcala, and Zacatecas. The northern region of Mexico includes Baja California, Baja California del Sur, Chihuahua, Coahuila, Durango, Nuevo Léon, Sinaloa, Sonora, and Tamaulipas.

30. Torre-Cantalapiedra and Yee-Quintero, "México ¿una frontera vertical?," 93.

31. More recent numbers are higher. Not only do migrants endure violence; they are often also held captive and forced to work as slaves for organized crime groups and in some cases forced to perpetuate violence on others through vigilance work, robberies, or killings. Captors record such acts of violence to later use against them and prolong their captivity. See Palacios and Pedro, "Violencia postestructural."

32. Marta Sánchez Soler, "Recent Issues on Migration: US-Mexico-Central America," Movimiento Migrante Mesoamericano, Distrito Federal, Mexico, July 2019, https://www.academia.edu/14135885/Recent_issues_on_migration_US-Mexico-Central_America.

33. "Central American Migration: Root Causes and U.S. Policy," Congressional Research Service, March 31, 2022, https://crsreports.congress.gov/product/details?prodcode=IF11151.

34. This imbalance highlights Mexico's subordinate immigration relation to its northern neighbor, which it replicates and perpetuates onto its southern neighbor—an effort the United States has supported over the past few years through the allocation

of $3.5 billion in weapons to Mexico for the detainment and deportation of Central American migrants. Under the Trump administration, the Mexican government made an agreement with the US government to take unprecedented measures to halt Central Americans from reaching the United States by further militarizing the Guatemala-Mexico border with Mexican troops; the consequences of this agreement are still unfolding.

35. Broader externalization occurs in the United States, Europe, and Australia. For an analysis with case studies of each, see Frelick, Kysel, and Podku, "Impact of Externalization of Migration Controls on the Rights of Asylum Seekers and Other Migrants."

36. "MEXICO Human Cargo," *Advertiser* (Adelaide, South Australia), June 14, 2011, p. 26, Infotrac Newsstand, http://link.galegroup.com/apps/doc/A258727516/STND?u=albu78484&sid=STND&xid=049b9038.

37. Jasmine Aguilera and Simmone Shah, "San Antonio Migrant Smuggling Suspects Could Face Death Penalty: The Latest," *Time*, June 28, 2022, https://time.com/6191845/san-antonio-migrants-death/.

38. Parrini Roses and Flores Pérez, "El mapa son los otros."

39. For instance, in moments of waiting, resting, or seeking shelter, migrants congregate and share advice, experience, and warnings. This information, based on embodied experience and shared orally, reconfigures migrants' paths and is considered an inheritance of cultural knowledge. They are reconfigurable, shared knowledges that must change and adapt according to new obstacles, and are a disobedience to maps, to paths, and even to the singularity of knowledge. For more, see Parrini Roses and Flores Pérez, "El mapa son los otros."

40. Abrego, *Sacrificing Families*, 45.

41. Abrego, *Sacrificing Families*, 22.

42. Abrego, *Sacrificing Families*, 22.

43. Abrego, "Economic Well-Being in Salvadoran Transnational Families," 1078.

44. Abrego, *Sacrificing Families*, 151.

45. Abrego, "Economic Well-Being in Salvadoran Transnational Families," 1072.

46. See Held, "A Study of Remittances to Mexico and Central America," 75.

47. Olmo, *Utrópicos*, 123.

48. See Rocha, "Remittances in Central America."

49. Rocha, "Remittances in Central America," 468.

50. For an analysis of the rise of malls in Latin America, particularly in Colombia, see Dávila, *El Mall*.

51. Rocha, "Remittances in Central America," 471.

52. Rocha, "Remittances in Central America," 472.

53. Rocha, "Remittances in Central America," 472.

54. Rocha, "Remittances in Central America," 472.

55. Rocha, "Remittances in Central America," 474.

56. Garni and Weyher, "Dollars, 'Free Trade,' and Migration," 63.

57. Segovia, *Transformación estructural y reforma económica en El Salvador*.

58. See Gammage, "Exporting People and Recruiting Remittances"; and Garni and Weyher, "Dollars, 'Free Trade,' and Migration."

1. "The ones who widened the Panama Canal / the ones who repaired the Pacific fleet / at the military bases in California / the ones who rotted in jail in Guatemala / Mexico, Honduras, Nicaragua / for being thieves, smugglers, scammers / for being hungry / *the ever-suspected ones* / the ones who filled the bars and brothels / of all the ports and capitals in the region / the ones who grew corn in foreign jungles / the kings of the crime section / the ones who no one ever knows where they're from / the best craftsmen in the world / the ones who were mowed down with bullets / while crossing the border / the ones who died from malaria / or scorpion or snake bites / in banana plantation hell / the ones who cried drunk for the national anthem / under cyclones in the Pacific or snow in the north / the freeloaders, the beggars, the potheads / the Salvadorian sons of bitches / the ones who barely made it back / the ones who were a bit luckier / *the eternally undocumented* / the make-it-all, sell-it-all, eat-it-all / the first to pull out a knife / the saddest sad people in the world / my countrymen / my brothers." "Poema de amor," in Dalton, *Las historias prohibidas del Pulgarcito*, 199–200 (my translation).

2. See Fanon, *The Wretched of the Earth*.

3. The state charged the artist with electoral fraud and threatened him with six years of imprisonment, but he was eventually acquitted.

4. "CULPABLE por ser miembro de una familia pobre," "CULPABLE por vivir en zona de conflicto por pandillas," "CULPABLE porque perdimos identidad en el 1932," "CULPABLE por el incumplimiento de los acuerdos de paz." My translation.

5. Wolf, *Mano Dura*.

6. Cuellar, "No One Is Safe in Bukele's Gang War."

7. The prison consists of eight buildings made of reinforced concrete; each has thirty cells (100 square meters each) aimed to hold more than one hundred inmates while only offering eighty metal bunks, two sinks and two toilets, and no mattresses. Meanwhile, the recreational areas, such as dining halls and exercise rooms, are limited to prison guard use only. Human rights advocates warn of the risk of violence and human rights violations.

8. Cuellar, "No One Is Safe in Bukele's Gang War" (my emphasis).

9. Roy Walmsely, "World Prison Population List," 12th ed., Institute for Criminal Policy Research, Birkbeck, University of London, 2018, p. 19, https://www.prisonstudies.org/sites/default/files/resources/downloads/wppl_12.pdf.

10. Walmsley, "World Prison Population List," 5.

11. Walmsley, "World Prison Population List," 2.

12. Helen Fair and Roy Walmsley, "World Prison Population List," 13th ed., Institute for Criminal Policy Research, Birkbeck, University of London, 2020, pp. 2, 17, https://www.prisonstudies.org/sites/default/files/resources/downloads/world_prison_population_list_13th_edition.pdf.

13. Macías-Rojas, *From Deportation to Prison*.

14. Cacho, *Social Death*.

15. See Brandzel, *Against Citizenship*; and Escobar, *Captivity beyond Prisons*.

16. D. Rodríguez, "Abolition as Praxis of Human Being," 1575–1612.

17. Arana, "How the Street Gangs Took Central America," 100.

18. The most notorious gang is Mara Salvatrucha 13. The name derives from *mara*, a local street-Spanish term for "gang"; *salva*, which is short for "Salvadoran"; and *trucha*, slang for "watch out." Both MS-13 and the 18th Street gang originated in Los Angeles.

19. Narváez Gutiérrez, *Ruta transnacional*, 23.

20. The film *Voces inocentes* is based on the true story of Óscar Torres, who personally experienced the military practice of kidnapping and forcing boys to join the military at the age of twelve. Luis Mandoki, dir., *Voces inocentes*, Altavista Films (Hong Kong: Lucky Gems Group; Asia Video Publishing Co., 2005), DVD.

21. For more on Central American arrival in the Los Angeles area, see Lopez, Popkin, and Thales, "Central Americans at the Bottom"; and A. Rodríguez, "Departamento 15."

22. An estimated twenty thousand criminalized Central American youth were deported between 2000 and 2004 from Los Angeles to Central America. See Arana, "How the Street Gangs Took Central America," 101.

23. Zilberg, "Fools Banished from the Kingdom"; and "Gangster in Guerilla Face."

24. "Treasury Sanctions Latin American Criminal Organization," U.S. Department of the Treasury, Press Center, Washington, DC, October 11, 2012, https://home.treasury.gov/news/press-releases/tg1733.

25. Zilberg, "Gangster in Guerilla Face."

26. Hollywood films include *Sin nombre* (2009) and documentaries such as *National Geographic: World's Most Dangerous Gang*, which documents the Mara Salvatrucha. For a documentary by and from the perspective of MS-13 members, see *Fruits of War* (2008).

27. See Gilmore, *Golden Gulag*; and Foucault, *Discipline and Punish*, 298. For a brief overview of carceral geography as a field, see Moran, Turner, and Schliehe, "Conceptualizing the Carceral in Carceral Geography."

28. See Moran, Turner, and Schliehe, "Conceptualizing the Carceral in Carceral Geography."

29. Certeau, *The Practice of Everyday Life*, 97–98.

30. Taylor, *The Archive and the Repertoire*.

31. Foucault, *Discipline and Punish*, 216.

32. Though Vega is most known for his recent large-scale installations of spaceships and intergalactic vessels, in the same stitched-together style evoking First World and Third World confrontations, *Shanty Mall* and *Vigilantes invertidos* can be understood as precursors to his most recent work. His critiques of colonizing outer space began with critiques of criminalized space. For an analysis of Vega's installations in relation to science fiction, see Cornejo, "Decolonial Futurisms."

33. For more on the series Celda, see Reinoza, "The Other Side of Fear."

34. D. Rodríguez, "Abolition as Praxis of Human Being," 1583.

35. For the US context, see Berger, "Social Movements and Mass Incarceration." For Latin American art cases, see Calirman, *Brazilian Art under Dictatorship*; and Richard, *Márgenes e instituciones*.

36. These numbers have also been contested; it has been argued that the more accurate number was around ten thousand people. See Tilley, *Seeing Indians*.

37. Tilley, *Seeing Indians*, 144.

38. Tilley, *Seeing Indians*, 140.

39. Tilley, *Seeing Indians*, 165.

40. See Wallis, "Black Bodies, White Science"; C. Smith, "Upsetting the Archive"; and Barbash, Rogers, and Willis, *To Make Their Own Way in the World*.

41. For an account of these debates, see Muñoz-Muñoz, "Nacionalismo blanco."

42. Cacho, *Social Death*, 123.

43. Cacho, *Social Death*, 64.

44. Cacho, *Social Death*, 7.

45. For more on this investigation, see Molina, *¿Sistema penitenciario en Centroamérica o bodegas humanas?* For a history of the penitentiary system in Latin America, see Salvatorre and Aguirre, *The Birth of the Penitentiary in Latin America*. For a history of the penitentiary in Europe, its relation to modernity and capitalism, and a discussion on the role of prisons on the body and society, see Foucault, *Discipline and Punish*.

46. Ungar, "Prison Politics in Contemporary Latin America," 909–10.

47. Hathazy and Müller, "The Crisis of Detention."

48. Molina, *¿Sistema penitenciario en Centroamérica o bodegas humanas?*, 13.

49. Jhafis Quintero, communication with the author via telephone, October 12, 2008.

50. Jhafis Quintero, communication with the author via telephone, October 12, 2008.

51. Jhafis Quintero, communication with the author via telephone, October 12, 2008.

52. Quintero's original idea and investigation for the work was made possible with the collaboration of José Díaz (photographs), María Montero (texts), and José Alberto Hernández (graphic design).

53. Quintero, Díaz, and Montero, *In dubia tempora*, 7.

54. The correct translation from Spanish to English would be "words fly, the writings last," but here, and from now on, I refer to the English translation as it is offered in the catalog unless otherwise indicated.

55. Quintero, Díaz, and Montero, *In dubia tempora*, 9.

56. Fleetwood, *Marking Time*, 25.

57. For Fleetwood's discussion of penal space, time, and matter, see *Marking Time*, 37–47.

58. Molina, *¿Sistema penitenciario en Centroamérica o bodegas humanas?*, 5.

59. Herman, *Trauma and Recovery*, 33–95.

60. This assault on bodily autonomy occurs with the denial/command/supervision of organic functions like sleeping, releasing bodily waste, eating, exercising, and the deprivation of light and human contact. Herman, *Trauma and Recovery*, 77.

61. Herman, *Trauma and Recovery*, 83.

62. Herman, *Trauma and Recovery*, 84.

63. Quintero, Díaz, and Montero, *In dubia tempora*, 8.

64. See Hathazy and Müller, "The Crisis of Detention," 898.

65. According to Robert Jay Lifton, both victims and victimizers experience death immersion. See Lifton, "From Hiroshima to the Nazi Doctors," 12.

66. Lifton, "From Hiroshima to the Nazi Doctors," 17.

67. See Bell-Fialkoff, *Ethnic Cleansing* ; and Pegorier, *Ethnic Cleansing*.

68. Cacho, *Social Death*, 6.

69. Benjamin Witte-Lebhar, "Deadly Blaze Underscores Crisis in El Salvador's Prison System," NotiCen: Latin American Digital Beat,2010, https://core.ac.uk/download/pdf/287144819.pdf.

70. Javier C. Hernandez and Randal C. Archibold, "Blaze at Prison Underscores Broad Security Problems in Honduras," *New York Times*, February 15, 2012; Mario Cerna, "El 40% de los reos muertos en incendios están en Honduras," *El Heraldo*, February 16, 2012, https://www.elheraldo.hn/alfrente/564749-209/el-40-de-los-reos-muertos-en-incendios-est%C3%A1n-en-honduras.

71. Higuita et al., "U.S. Bound Journey of Migrant Peoples," 3. See also U.S. Immigration and Customs Enforcement, "Detention Management," accessed October 31, 2022, https://www.ice.gov/detain/detention-management.

72. Escobar, *Captivity beyond Prisons*.

73. Escobar, *Captivity beyond Prisons*, 10.

74. See Judith Kumin and Frances Nicholson, "Refugee Protection: A Guide to International Refugee Protection and Building State Asylum Systems," Inter-Parliamentary Union and the United Nations High Commissioner for Refugees, 2017, https://www.unhcr.org/us/media/refugee-protection-guide-international-refugee-law-handbook-parliamentarians.

75. Franco, "Trauma without Borders."

76. Office of Refugee Resettlement/ACF, Unaccompanied Alien Children Program Fact Sheet, May 2019, https://www.hhs.gov/sites/default/files/Unaccompanied-Alien-Children-Program-Fact-Sheet.pdf.

77. US Customs and Border Protection, "CBP Releases July 2021 Operational Update," August 12, 2021, https://www.cbp.gov/newsroom/national-media-release/cbp-releases-july-2021-operational-update.

78. Office of Refugee Resettlement (ORR), "Fact Sheet Unaccompanied Children (UC) Program," accessed October 21, 2023, https://www.hhs.gov/sites/default/files/uac-program-fact-sheet.pdf.

79. "'Do Not Come': VP Harris Sends Anti-migrant Message in Guatemala, Visits Mexico amid Deadly Election," Democracy Now!, June 8, 2021, https://www.democracynow.org/2021/6/8/kamala_harris_immigration_mexico_election_killings.

80. Escobar, *Captivity beyond Prisons*, 3.

BIBLIOGRAPHY

Abrego, Leisy J. "Economic Well-Being in Salvadoran Transnational Families: How Gender Affects Remittance Practices." *Journal of Marriage and Family* 71, no. 4 (2009): 1070–85.

Abrego, Leisy J. *Sacrificing Families: Navigating Laws, Labor, and Love across Borders*. Stanford, CA: Stanford University Press, 2014.

Aguirre, Robert D. "Exhibiting Degeneracy: The Aztec Children and the Ruins of Race." *Victorian Review* 29, no. 2 (2003): 40–63.

Alexander, M. Jacqui. "Erotic Autonomy as Politics of Decolonization: An Anatomy of Feminist and State Practice in the Bahamas Tourist Economy." In *Feminist Genealogies, Colonial Legacies, Democratic Futures: Thinking Gender*, edited by M. Jacqui Alexander and Chandra Talpade Mohanty, 63–100. New York: Routledge, 1997.

Alexander, M. Jacqui, and Chandra Talpade Mohanty, eds. *Feminist Genealogies, Colonial Legacies, Democratic Futures: Thinking Gender*. New York: Routledge, 1997.

Alvarado, Leticia. *Abject Performances: Aesthetic Strategies in Latino Cultural Production*. Durham, NC: Duke University Press, 2018.

Alvarez, Sonia E., Claudia de Lima Costa, Veronica Feliu, Rebecca Hester, Norma Klahn, and Millie Thayer, eds. *Translocalities/Translocalidades: Feminist Politics of Translation in the Latin/a Américas*. Durham, NC: Duke University Press, 2014.

Anderson, Mark. *Black and Indigenous: Garifuna Activism and Consumer Culture in Honduras*. Minneapolis: University of Minnesota Press, 2009.

Anzaldúa, Gloria. *Borderlands: The New Mestiza = La Frontera*. 4th ed., 25th anniversary. San Francisco: Aunt Lute Books, 2012.

Arana, Ana. "How the Street Gangs Took Central America." *Foreign Affairs* 84, no. 3 (2005): 98–110.

Arias, Arturo. "Central American–Americans: Invisibility, Power, and Representation in the US Latino World." *Latino Studies* 1, no. 1 (2003): 168–87.

Azoulay, Ariella Aïsha. *Potential History: Unlearning Imperialism*. New York: Verso, 2019.

Barbash, Ilisa, Molly Rogers, and Deborah Willis, eds. *To Make Their Own Way in the World: The Enduring Legacy of the Zealy Daguerreotypes*. Cambridge, MA: Peabody Museum Press; New York: Aperture, 2020.

Barbosa, Emilia. "Regina José Galindo's Body Talk: Performing Femicide and Violence against Women in 279 Golpes." *Latin American Perspectives* 41, no. 1 (2014): 59–71.

Barriendos, Joaquín. "La colonialidad del ver: Hacia un nuevo diálogo visual interepistémico." *Nómadas*, no. 35 (2011): 13–29.

Batz, Giovanni. "The Fourth Invasion: Development, Ixil-Maya Resistance, and the Struggle against Megaprojects in Guatemala." PhD diss., University of Texas at Austin, 2017.

Bell-Fialkoff, Andrew. *Ethnic Cleansing*. New York: St. Martin's, 1996.

Berger, Dan. "Social Movements and Mass Incarceration: What Is to Be Done?" *Souls* 15, nos. 1–2 (2013): 3–18.

Blanchard, Pascal. *Human Zoos: Science and Spectacle in the Age of Colonial Empires*. Liverpool: Liverpool University Press, 2008.

Boëtsch, Gilles. "From the Cabinets of Curiosity to the Passion for the Savage." In *Human Zoos: The Invention of the Savage*, edited by Pascal Blanchard, Gilles Boëtsch, and Nanette Jacomijn Snoep, 78–97. Arles: Actes Sud in association with Musée du Quai Branly, 2011.

Boj Lopez, Floridalma. "Weavings That Rupture: The Possibility of Contesting Settler Colonialism through Cultural Retention among the Maya Diaspora." In *U.S. Central Americans: Reconstructing Memories, Struggles, and Communities of Resistance*, edited by Karina D. Alvarado, Alicia Ivonne Estrada, and Ester E. Hernández, 189–203. Tucson: University of Arizona Press, 2017.

Brandzel, Amy L. *Against Citizenship: The Violence of the Normative*. Dissident Feminisms. Urbana: University of Illinois Press, 2016.

Bryan-Wilson, Julia. *Fray: Art + Textile Politics*. Chicago: University of Chicago Press, 2017.

Cabrera Padilla, Roberto. "Artistas Guatemaltecos Kaqchikeles y Tz'utujiles: Una nueva visión." In *Otra mirada: Atitlán + Comalapa*, exhibition pamphlet. Guatemala City: Embajada de México, 2007.

Cacho, Lisa Marie. *Social Death: Racialized Rightlessness and the Criminalization of the Unprotected*. Nation of Newcomers: Immigrant History as American History. New York: New York University Press, 2012.

Calirman, Claudia. *Brazilian Art under Dictatorship: Antonio Manuel, Artur Barrio, and Cildo Mereiles*. Durham, NC: Duke University Press, 2012.

Cameron, Dan. "Ante América." *Third Text* 8, no. 26 (1994): 94–96.

Cárdenas, Maritza E. *Constituting Central American–Americans: Transnational Identities and the Politics of Dislocation*. Latinidad: Transnational Cultures in the United States. New Brunswick, NJ: Rutgers University Press, 2018.

Cariou, Warren. "The Exhibited Body: The Nineteenth-Century Human Zoo." *Victorian Review* 42, no. 1 (Spring 2016): 25–29.

Casas-Cortés, Maribel, and Sebastian Cobarrubias. "A War on Mobility: The Border Empire Strikes Back?" In *Ways of Knowing Cities*, edited by Laura Kurgan and Dare Brawley, 177–91. New York: Columbia University Press, 2019.

Castro Flórez, Fernando. "The Atrocious Incarnations of Regina José Galindo." In *Regina José Galindo*, 113–21. Milan: Silvana Editoriale: 2011.

Castro-Gómez, Santiago. *La hybris del punto cero: Ciencia, raza e ilustración en la Nueva Granada (1750–1816)*. Colecciòn Pensar. Bogotá: Editorial Pointificia Universidad Javeriana, 2005.

Cazali, Rosina *Migraciones: Mirando al Sur*. Exhibition catalog. Edited by Ministerio de Asuntos Exteriores y de Cooperación. Mexico City: AECID, 2009.
Cazali, Rosina. *Pasos a desnivel: Mapa urbano de la cultura contemporánea en Guatemala*. Guatemala City: Artgrafic de Guatemala, 2003.
Cazali, Rosina. "Ser contemporáneos: Desde aquí." In *Certezas vulnerables: Crónicas de los debates artísticos desde Guatemala*, 114–34. San José: TEOR/éTica, 2017.
Certeau, Michel de. *The Practice of Everyday Life*. Translated by Steven Rendall. Berkeley: University of California Press, 1984.
Césaire, Aimé. *Discourse on Colonialism*. Translated by Joan Pinkham. 1972. New York: Monthly Review Press, 2000.
Chacón, Gloria Elizabeth. "Material Culture, Indigeneity, and Temporality." *Textual Cultures* 13, no. 2 (2020): 49–69.
Cházaro, Angelica, and Jennifer Casey. "Getting Away with Murder: Guatemala's Failure to Protect Women and Rodi Alvarado's Quest for Safety." *Hastings Women's Law Journal* 17, no. 2 (Summer 2006): 141–85.
Chinchilla, Maya. *The Cha Cha Files: A Chapina Poética*. San Francisco: Kórima, 2014.
Chomsky, Aviva. *Central America's Forgotten History: Revolution, Violence, and the Roots of Migration*. Boston: Beacon, 2021.
Coe, Michael D., and Justin Kerr. *The Art of the Maya Scribe*. London: Thames and Hudson, 1998.
Coffey, Mary K. "From Nation to Community: Museums and the Reconfiguration of Society under Neoliberalism." In *Foucault, Cultural Studies, and Governmentality*, edited by Jack Z. Bratich, Jeremy Packer, and Cameron McCarthy, 207–41. Albany: State University of New York Press, 2003.
Cohen-Aponte, Ananda. "Forging a Popular Art History: Indigenismo and the Art of Colonial Peru." *RES: Anthropology and Aesthetics*, no. 67/68 (2016): 273–89.
Corbey, Raymond. "Ethnographic Showcases, 1870–1930." *Cultural Anthropology* 8, no. 3 (August 1993): 338–69.
Cordero, Allen. "Migraciones y medio ambiente: ¿Una relación posible? El caso de la cuenca del río San Juan." *Revista Centroamericana de Ciencias Sociales* 3, no. 1 (July 2006): 123–49.
Corinealdi, Kaysha. *Panama in Black: Afro-Caribbean World Making in the Twentieth Century*. Durham, NC: Duke University Press, 2022.
Cornejo, Kency. "Artistas en Resistencia." In *Collective Situations: Readings in Contemporary Latin American Art 1995–2010*, edited by Bill Kelley Jr. and Grant Kester, 79–97. Durham, NC: Duke University Press, 2017.
Cornejo, Kency. "Decolonial Futurisms: Ancestral Border Crossers, Time Machines, and Space Travel in Salvadoran Art." In *Mundos alternos: Art and Science Fiction in the Americas*, edited by Robb Hernández and Tyler Stallings, 20–31. Riverside, CA: UCR ARTSblock, 2017.
Cornejo, Kency. "Indigeneity and Decolonial Seeing in Contemporary Art of Guatemala." *FUSE Magazine* 36, no. 4 (2013): 24–31.
Cornejo, Kency. "No Text without Context: Habacuc Guillermo Vargas' *Exposition #1*." *Art and Documentation/Sztuka i Dokumentacja*, no. 10 (2014): 53–59.
Cornejo Polar, Antonio. *Literatura y sociedad en el Perú: La novela indigenista*. Lima: Lasontay, 1980.

Coronado, Jorge. *The Andes Imagined: Indigenismo, Society, and Modernity*. Pittsburgh, PA: University of Pittsburgh Press, 2009.

Cosgrove, Serena, José Idiáquez, Leonard Joseph Bent, and Andrew Gorvetzian. *Surviving the Americas: Garifuna Persistence from Nicaragua to New York City*. Cincinnati, OH: University of Cincinnati Press, 2020.

Craven, David A. *Art and Revolution in Latin America, 1910–1990*. New Haven, CT: Yale University Press, 2002.

Craven, David A. "The Nicaraguan Revolution (1979–1990)." In *Art and Revolution in Latin America, 1910–1990*, 117–68. New Haven, CT: Yale University Press, 2002.

Cuellar, Jorge E. "No One Is Safe in Bukele's Gang War." *North American Congress on Latin America (NACLA) Report*, June 23, 2022. https://nacla.org/bukele-gang-war.

Cumes Simón, Aura Estela. "La 'India' como 'sirvienta': Servindumre doméstica, colonialism y patriarcado en Guatemala." PhD diss., Centro de Investigaciones y Estudios Superiores en Antropología Social, Mexico City, 2014.

Cunin, Elizabeth, and Odile Hoffman. *Blackness and Mestizaje in Mexico and Central America*. The Harriet Tubman Series on the African Diaspora. Trenton, NJ: African World, 2014.

Cusicanqui, Silvia Rivera. "Experiencias de montaje creativo: De la historia oral a la imagen en movimiento ¿Quien escribe la historia oral?" *Chasqui*, no. 120 (December 2012): 14–18.

Cusicanqui, Silvia Rivera. "The Notion of 'Rights' and the Paradoxes of Postcolonial Modernity: Indigenous Peoples and Women in Bolivia." *Qui Parle* 18, no. 2 (Spring/Summer 2010): 29–54.

Cusicanqui, Silvia Rivera. *Sociología de la imagen: Miradas Ch'ixi desde la historia andina*. Buenos Aires: Tinta Limón, 2015.

Dalton, Roque. *Las historias prohibidas del Pulgarcito*. Colección Gavidia 29. San Salvador: UCA Editores, 1991.

Damisch, Humbert. *The Origin of Perspective*. Cambridge, MA: MIT Press, 1994.

Davidson, Russ, ed. *Latin American Posters: Public Aesthetics and Mass Politics*. Santa Fe: Museum of New Mexico Press, in association with University of New Mexico Center for Regional Studies, UNM University Libraries, and National Hispanic Cultural Center, 2006.

Dávila, Arlene. *El Mall: The Spatial and Class Politics of Shopping Malls in Latin America*. Oakland: University of California Press, 2016.

Dávila, Arlene. *Latinx Art: Artists, Markets, Politics*. Durham, NC: Duke University Press, 2020.

DeLugan, Robin. "Museums, Memory, and the Just Nation in Post–Civil War El Salvador." *Museum and Society* 13, no. 3 (July 2015): 266–79.

Demos, T. J. *Decolonizing Nature: Contemporary Art and the Politics of Ecology*. Berlin: Sternberg, 2016.

Díaz Bringas, Tamara. *Crítica próxima*. San José: TEOR/éTica, 2016.

Duran, Joan, ed. *LANDINGS Ten (the Black Box)*. Belize City: five-o-one art projects, 2009.

Düssel, Enrique. *The Invention of the Americas: Eclipse of the Other and the Myth of Modernity*. New York: Continuum, 1995.

Düssel, Enrique. *The Underside of Modernity: Apel, Ricoeur, Rorty, Taylor, and the Philosophy of Liberation*. Translated by Eduardo Mendieta. Atlantic Highlands, NJ: Humanities, 1996.

Echavez See, Sarita. *The Decolonized Eye: Filipino American Art and Performance*. Minneapolis: University of Minnesota Press, 2009.

Edgerton, Samuel Y., Jr. *The Renaissance Rediscovery of Linear Perspective*. New York: Basic Books, 1975.

Egan, Nancy. "Exhibiting Indigenous Peoples: Bolivians and the Chicago Fair of 1893." *Studies in Latin American Popular Culture*, no. 28 (2010): 6–24.

Elkins, James, and Robert Williams, eds. *Renaissance Theory*. New York: Routledge, 2008.

England, Sarah. *Afro Central Americans in New York City: Garifuna Tales of Transnational Movement in Racialized Space*. Gainesville: University Press of Florida, 2006.

Escobar, Martha D. *Captivity beyond Prisons: Criminalization Experiences of Latina (Im)migrants*. Austin: University of Texas Press, 2016.

Esquit, Edgar. *La superación del indígena: La política de la modernización entre las élites indígenas de Comalapa, siglo XX*. Guatemala City: Instituto de Estudios Interétnicos, Universidad de San Carlos de Guatemala, 2010.

Esquit, Edgar. "Nociones Kaqchikel sobre la opresión y la lucha política en Guatemala, siglo XX." *REP: Revista Espacio Pedagógico* 17, no. 2 (2010): 252–66.

Fanon, Frantz. *The Wretched of the Earth*. Translated by Constance Farrington. New York: Grove, 1965.

Fleetwood, Nicole. *Marking Time: Art in the Age of Mass Incarceration*. Cambridge, MA: Harvard University Press, 2020.

Flores, Tatiana, and Michelle A. Stephens, eds. *Relational Undercurrents: Contemporary Art of the Caribbean Archipelago*. Los Angeles: Museum of Latin American Art, 2017.

Foucault, Michel. *Discipline and Punish: The Birth of the Prison*. 1977. New York: Vintage, 1995.

Franco, Diana. "Trauma without Borders: The Necessity for School-Based Interventions in Treating Unaccompanied Refugee Minors." *Child and Adolescent Social Work Journal* 35, no. 6 (2018): 551–65.

Fregoso, Rosa Linda, and Cynthia L. Bejarano, eds. *Terrorizing Women: Feminicide in the Américas*. Durham, NC: Duke University Press, 2010.

Frelick, Bill, Ian M. Kysel, and Jennifer Podkul. "The Impact of Externalization of Migration Controls on the Rights of Asylum Seekers and Other Migrants." *Journal of Migration and Human Security* 4, no. 4 (2016): 190–220.

Fusco, Coco, ed. *Corpus delecti: Performance Art of the Americas*. New York: Routledge, 2000.

Fusco, Coco, and Brian Wallis. *Only Skin Deep: Changing Visions of the American Self*. New York: International Center of Photography in association with Harry N. Abrams, 2003.

Galeano, Rodnie Gabriel. "La desestatización de la imagen de la violencia: Análisis desde el arte contextual en Guatemala, El Salvador, Honduras." PhD diss., Universidad de Granada, 2020.

Gammage, Sarah. "Exporting People and Recruiting Remittances: A Development Strategy for El Salvador?" *Latin American Perspectives* 33, no. 6 (2006): 75–100.

García, María Cristina. *Seeking Refuge: Central American Migration to Mexico, the United States, and Canada*. Berkeley: University of California Press, 2006.

García-Peña, Lorgia. *Translating Blackness: Latinx Colonialities in a Global Perspective*. Durham, NC: Duke University Press, 2022.

Garni, Alisa, and L. Frank Weyher. "Dollars, 'Free Trade,' and Migration: The Combined Forces of Alienation in Postwar El Salvador." *Latin American Perspectives* 40, no. 5 (September 2013): 62–77.

Garrard-Burnett, Virginia. "Living with Ghosts: Death, Exhumation, and Reburial among the Maya in Guatemala." *Latin American Perspectives* 42, no. 3 (2015): 180–92.

Geneva Declaration Secretariat. "When the Victim Is a Woman." In *Global Burden of Armed Violence 2011: Lethal Encounters*, 113–44. Cambridge: Cambridge University Press, 2011. https://www.smallarmssurvey.org/sites/default/files/resources/GBAV2011_WEB-full-report-REV.pdf.

Gilmore, Ruth Wilson. *Golden Gulag: Prisons, Surplus, Crisis, and Opposition in Globalizing California*. American Crossroads 21. Berkeley: University of California Press, 2007.

Giunta, Andrea. *Feminismo y arte latinoamericano: Historias de artistas que emanciparon el cuerpo*. Buenos Aires: Siglo Veintiuno Editores, 2018.

Goldman, Francisco. "Regina José Galindo." *BOMB* no. 94 (December 2005): 38–44.

Gómez-Barris, Macarena. *Beyond the Pink Tide: Art and Political Undercurrents*. Oakland: University of California Press, 2018.

Gómez-Barris, Macarena. *The Extractive Zone: Social Ecologies and Decolonial Perspectives*. Dissident Acts. Durham, NC: Duke University Press, 2017.

Gómez-Barris, Macarena, Jill Lane, and Marcial Godoy-Anativia, eds. "Decolonial Gesture." Special issue, *E-misférica*, May 2014. https://hemisphericinstitute.org/en/emisferica-11-1-decolonial-gesture.html.

Gómez Menjívar, Jennifer Carolina. *Black in Print: Plotting the Coordinates of Blackness in Central America*. Albany: State University of New York Press, 2023.

Greet, Michele. *Beyond National Identity: Pictorial Indigenism as a Modernist Strategy in Andean Art, 1920–1960*. University Park: Pennsylvania State University Press, 2009.

Guevara, Che. "Socialism and Man in Cuba." Marxists Internet Archive. From *Che Guevara Reader: Writings on Politics and Revolution*, Melbourne: Ocean, 2005. https://www.marxists.org/archive/guevara/1965/03/man-socialism.htm.

Harpelle, Ronald N. *The West Indians of Costa Rica: Race, Class, and the Integration of an Ethnic Minority*. Montreal: McGill-Queen's University Press, 2001.

Hathazy, Paul, and Markus-Michael Müller. "The Crisis of Detention and the Politics of Denial in Latin America." *International Review of the Red Cross* 98, no. 3 (2016): 889–916.

Held, Mary L. "A Study of Remittances to Mexico and Central America: Characteristics and Perspectives of Immigrants." *International Journal of Social Welfare* 26, no. 1 (2017): 75–85.

Herman, Judith. *Trauma and Recovery: The Aftermath of Violence—From Domestic Abuse to Political Terror*. New York: Basic Books, 1992.

Hernández, Robert D. *Coloniality of the U-S///Mexico Border: Power, Violence, and the Decolonial Imperative*. Tucson: University of Arizona Press, 2018.

Higuita, Nelson Agudelo, Jose Antonio Suarez, Eugenia Millender, Elizabeth Garcia Creighton, Michaele Francesco, et al. "U.S. Bound Journey of Migrant Peoples in Transit across Dante's Inferno and Purgatory in the Americas." *Travel Medicine and Infectious Disease* 47 (February 2022): 1–5.

Hooker, Juliet. "'Beloved Enemies': Race and Official Mestizo Nationalism in Nicaragua." *Latin American Research Review* 40, no. 3 (October 2005): 14–67.

Hooker, Juliet. "Indigenous Inclusion/Black Exclusion: Race, Ethnicity and Multicultural Citizenship in Latin America." *Journal of Latin American Studies* 37, no. 2 (2005): 285–310.

Howe, Cymene. *Intimate Activism: The Struggle for Sexual Rights in Postrevolutionary Nicaragua*. Durham, NC: Duke University Press, 2013.

Huerta, Amarela Varela. "La 'securitización' de la gubernamentalidad migratoria mediante la 'externalización' de las fronteras estadounidenses a Mesoamérica." *Contemporánea*, no. 4 (July–December 2015). https://revistas.inah.gob.mx/index.php/contemporanea/article/view/6270.

Hunt, Tamara L., and Micheline R. Lessard, eds. *Women and the Colonial Gaze*. New York: New York University Press, 2002.

Jones, Amelia. "Archive, Repertoire, and Embodied Histories in Nao Bustamante's Performance Practice." In *Artists in the Archive: Creative and Curatorial Engagements with Documents of Art and Performance*, edited by Paul Clarke, Simon Jones, Nick Kaye, and Johanna Linsley, 151–76. New York: Routledge, 2018.

Kampwirth, Karen. "Organizing the *Hombre Nuevo Gay*: LGBT Politics and the Second Sandinista Revolution." *Bulletin of Latin American Research* 33, no. 3 (2014): 319–33.

Kant, Immanuel. *Observation on the Feeling of the Beautiful and the Sublime.* Berkeley: University of California Press, 1960.

Kirshenblatt-Gimblett, Barbara. *Destination Culture: Tourism, Museums, and Heritage.* Berkeley: University of California Press, 1998.

Kunzle, David. *The Murals of Revolutionary Nicaragua, 1979–1992*. Berkeley: University of California Press, 1995.

Lakhani, Nina. *Who Killed Berta Cáceres? Dams, Death Squads, and an Indigenous Defender's Battle for the Planet*. New York: Verso, 2020.

Larson, Elizabeth M. "Costa Rican Government Policy on Refugee Employment and Integration, 1980–1990." *International Journal of Refugee Law* 3, no. 4 (1992): 326–42.

Latorre, Guisela. *Walls of Empowerment: Chicana/o Indigenist Murals of California.* Austin: University of Texas Press, 2008.

Lifton, Robert Jay. "From Hiroshima to the Nazi Doctors: The Evolution of Psychoformative Approaches to Understanding Traumatic Stress Syndromes." In *International Handbook of Traumatic Stress Syndromes*, edited by John P. Wilson and Beverley Raphael, 11–23. New York: Plenum, 1993.

Lopez, David E., Eric Popkin, and Edward Thales. "Central Americans at the Bottom: Struggling to Get Ahead." In *Ethnic Los Angeles*, edited by Roger David Waldinger and Mehdi Bozorgmehr, 279–304. New York: Russell Sage Foundation, 1996.

López, Miguel A. "Don't Teach, Learn: The Educational Experiments in EspIRA. Interview with Patricia Belli." In *Patricia Belli: Equilibrio y colapso*, edited by Miguel A. López, 196–203. San José: TEOR/éTica, 2018.
López Oro, Paul Joseph. "Garifunizando Ambas Américas: Hemispheric Entanglements of Blackness/Indigeneity/AfroLatinidad." *Postmodern Culture* 31, no. 1 (2020): unpaginated.
Lorde, Audre. "The Master's Tools Will Never Dismantle the Master's House." In *Feminist Postcolonial Theory: A Reader*, edited by Reina Lewis and Sara Mills, 25–28. New York: Routledge, 2003.
Lugones, Maria. "Coloniality of Gender." *Worlds and Knowledges Otherwise* 2, no. 2 (Spring 2008): 1–17. https://globalstudies.trinity.duke.edu/sites/globalstudies.trinity.duke.edu/files/documents/v2d2_Lugones.pdf.
Macías-Rojas, Patrisia. *From Deportation to Prison: The Politics of Immigration Enforcement in Post–Civil Rights America*. The Latina/o Sociology Series. New York: New York University Press, 2016.
Macleod, Morna. *Santiago Atitlán, ombligo del universo tz'utujil: Cosmovisión y ciudadanía*. Guatemala City: Cholsamaj, 2000.
Maldonado-Torres, Nelson. "On Metaphysical Catastrophe, Post-continental Thought, and the Decolonial Turn." In *Relational Undercurrents: Contemporary Art of the Caribbean Archipelago*, edited by Tatiana Flores and Michelle Ann Stephens, 247–59. Long Beach, CA: Museum of Latin American Art; Albuquerque, NM: SF Design/Fresco Books, 2017.
Maldonado-Torres, Nelson. "On the Coloniality of Being: Contributions to the Development of a Concept." *Cultural Studies* 21, nos. 2–3 (2007): 240–70.
Maldonado-Torres, Nelson. "Outline of Ten Theses on Coloniality and Decoloniality." Frantz Fanon Foundation, October 23, 2016. https://fondation-frantzfanon.com/wp-content/uploads/2018/10/maldonado-torres_outline_of_ten_theses-10.23.16.pdf.
Mandel Katz, Claudia. "La deconstrucción del 'deber ser' patriarchal." *Cuadernos de Antropología*, nos. 17–18 (January 2007): 151–62.
Mariátegui, José Carlos. *Seven Interpretive Essays on Peruvian Reality*. Translated by Marjory Urquidi. Austin: University of Texas Press, 1971.
Martínez Salazar, Egla. *Global Coloniality of Power in Guatemala: Racism, Genocide, and Citizenship*. Lanham, MD: Lexington Books, 2012.
McGee, Marcus J., and Karen Kampwirth. "The Co-optation of LGBT Movements in Mexico and Nicaragua: Modernizing Clientelism?" *Latin American Politics and Society* 57, no. 4 (Winter 2015): 51–73.
Méndez, Xhercis. "Notes toward a Decolonial Feminist Methodology: Revisiting the Race/Gender Matrix." *Trans-scripts* 5 (2015): 41–56.
Méndez, Xhercis, and Yomaira C. Figueroa. "Not Your Papa's Wynter: Women of Color Contributions toward Decolonial Futures." In *Beyond the Doctrine of Man: Decolonial Visions of the Human*, edited by Joseph Drexler-Dreis, 66–68. New York: Fordham University Press, 2019.
Mengesha, Lilian. "Defecting Witness: The Difficulty in Watching Regina José Galindo's PERRA." *TDR: The Drama Review* 61, no. 2 (2017): 140–57.

Menjívar, Cecilia, and Shannon Drysdale Walsh. "Subverting Justice: Socio-legal Determinants of Impunity for Violence against Women in Guatemala." *Laws* 5, no. 3 (2016). https://doi.org/10.3390/laws5030031.

Mignolo, Walter. *The Darker Side of the Renaissance: Literacy, Territoriality, and Colonization*. 1995. Ann Arbor: University of Michigan Press, 2003.

Mignolo, Walter. "Epistemic Disobedience, Independent Thought, and Decolonial Freedom." *Theory, Culture and Society* 26, nos. 7–8 (2009): 159–81.

Mignolo, Walter, and Rolando Vázquez. "Decolonial AestheSis: Colonial Wounds/Decolonial Healing." *Social Text Online*, July 15, 2013. https://socialtextjournal.org/periscope_article/decolonial-aesthesis-colonial-woundsdecolonial-healings/.

Milian, Claudia. *Latining America: Black-Brown Passages and the Coloring of Latino/a Studies*. The New Southern Studies. Athens: University of Georgia Press, 2013.

Mirzoeff, Nicholas. *The Right to Look: A Counterhistory of Visuality*. Durham, NC: Duke University Press, 2011.

Mitchell, W. J. T. *Landscape and Power*. 2nd ed. Chicago: University of Chicago Press, 2002.

Mohanty, Chandra Talpade. *Feminism without Borders: Decolonizing Theory, Practicing Solidarity*. Durham, NC: Duke University Press, 2003.

Molina, Alma Benítez. *¿Sistema penitenciario en Centroamérica o bodegas humanas?* San José: CODEHUCA, 1999.

Moncayo, Márgara Millán. "Feminismos, Postcolonialidad, Descolonización: ¿Del centro a los márgenes?" *Andamios* 8, no. 17 (2011): 11–36.

Montanaro Mena, Ana Marcela. *Una mirada al feminismo decolonial en América Latina*. Colección Religión y Derechos Humanos. Madrid: Dykinson, 2017.

Moran, Dominique, Jennifer Turner, and Anna K. Schliehe. "Conceptualizing the Carceral in Carceral Geography." *Progress in Human Geography* 42, no. 5 (2018): 666–86.

Mosquera, Gerardo, and Adrienne Samos, eds. *Ciudad Multiple City: Arte > Panamá 2003; arte urbano y ciudades globales, una experiencia en contexto/Urban Art and Global Cities, an Experiment in Context*. Amsterdam: KIT, 2003.

Muñoz, José Esteban. *Cruising Utopia: The Then and There of Queer Futurity*. 10th Anniversary edition. New York: New York University Press, 2019.

Muñoz, José Esteban. *Disidentifications: Queers of Color and the Performance of Politics* Minneapolis: University of Minnesota Press, 1999.

Muñoz-Muñoz, Marianela. "Nacionalismo blanco, prensa e enversión de las víctimas durante la 'Polémica Cocorí.'" *Revista de Filología y Lingüística de la Universidad de Costa Rica* 45, no. 2 (September 1, 2019): 73–98.

Narváez Gutiérrez, Juan Carlos. *Ruta transnacional: A San Salvador por Los Angeles, espacios de interacción juvenil en un contexto migratorio*. Mexico City: Universidad Autónoma de Zacatecas, 2007.

Neruda, Pablo. *Canto general*. Translated by Jack Schmitt. Berkeley: University of California Press, 2000.

Newman, Lia. "Regina José Galindo: Bearing Witness/Dar Testimonio." In *Regina José Galindo: Bearing Witness/Dar Testimonio*. Davidson, NC: Van Every/Smith Galleries, 2015.

Olmo, Santiago, ed. *Utrópicos: Centroamérica y Caribe*. Exhibition catalog, Museo de Pontevedra. Pontevedra: Gráficas Anduriña, 2010.

Olmo, Santiago, and Virginia Pérez-Ratton, eds. *Todo incluído: Imágenes urbanas de Centroamérica*. Exhibition catalog. Madrid: Centro Cultural del Conde Duque, 2004.

Palacios, Izcara, and Simón Pedro. "Violencia postestructural: Migrantes centroamericanos y cárteles de la droga en México." *Revista de Estudios Sociales*, no. 56 (April 2016): 12–25.

Parrini Roses, Rodrigo, and Edith Flores Pérez. "El mapa son los otros: Narrativas del viaje de migrantes centroamerianos en la frontera sur de México." *Íconos: Revista de Ciencias Sociales*, no. 61 (May 2018): 71–90.

Pegorier, Clotilde. *Ethnic Cleansing: A Legal Qualification*. London: Taylor and Francis, 2013.

Peñas Defago, María Angélica. "El aborto en El Salvador: Tres décadas de disputas sobre la autonomía reproductiva de las mujeres/Abortion in El Salvador: Three Decades of Disputes over Women's Reproductive Autonomy." *Península* 13, no. 2 (2018): 213–34.

Pérez, Laura E. *Chicana Art: The Politics of Spiritual and Aesthetic Alterities*. Durham, NC: Duke University Press, 2007.

Pérez-Ratton, Virginia. "Performance and Action Work in Central America, 1960–2000: A Political and Aesthetic Choice." In *Arte ≠ Vida: Actions by Artists of the Americas, 1960–2000*, edited by Deborah Cullen, 204–13. New York: El Museo del Barrio, 2008.

Pérez-Ratton, Virginia. *Un lugar inacabado: Construyendo infraestructura artística en Centroamérica*. San José: TEOR/éTica, 2021.

Pérez-Ratton, Virginia, and Rolando Castellon, eds. *Mesótica II: Centroamérica, re-generación*. San José: Museo de Arte y Diseño Contemporáneo, 1996.

Pierce, Joseph M. "I Monster: Embodying Trans and Travesti Resistance in Latin America." *Latin American Research Review* 55, no. 2 (2020): 305–21.

Portillo Villeda, Suyapa G. "'Outing' Honduras: A Human Rights Catastrophe in the Making." *NACLA Report on the Americas* 45, no. 3 (Fall 2012): 6–7.

Pratt, Mary Louise. *Imperial Eyes: Travel Writing and Transculturation*. New York: Routledge, 2008.

Prieto-Carrón, Marina, Marilyn Thompson, and Mandy Macdonald. "No More Killings! Women Respond to Femicides in Central America." *Gender and Development* 15, no. 1 (2007): 25–40.

Quijano, Aníbal. "Coloniality and Modernity/Rationality." *Cultural Studies* 21, nos. 2–3 (2007): 168–78.

Quijano, Aníbal. "Coloniality of Power, Eurocentrism, and Latin America." *Nepantla: Views from the South* 1, no. 3 (2000): 533–80.

Quintanilla, Raúl. *Zona de turbulencia: Arte en Nicaragua, de la Revolución al neoliberalismo.* San José: TEOR/éTica, 2018.

Quintero, Jhafis, José Díaz, and María Montero. *In dubia tempora (momentos críticos)*. San José: Estrecho Dudoso, 2006.

Ramírez, Mari Carmen. "Brokering Identities: Art Curators and the Politics of Cultural Representation." In *Thinking about Exhibitions*, edited by Reesa Greenberg, Bruce W. Ferguson, and Sandy Nairne, 15–27. New York: Routledge, 1996.

Reinoza, Tatiana. "The Other Side of Fear: Alma Leiva's Prison Cells." In *Counter-archives to the Narco-City/Contra-archivos de la ciudad del narco*, edited by Tatiana Reinoza and Luis Vargas-Santiago, 54–73. South Bend, IN: Snite Museum of Art, 2015.

Ressini, Salinas, and Daniela Fabiola. "Estándares de belleza y cultura en la manifestación de anorexia en jóvenes del corregimiento de Bellavista en Ciudad de Panamá." *Punto Cero* 31, no. 35 (2015): 35–54.

Richard, Nelly. *Márgenes e instituciones: Arte en Chile desde 1973*. 2nd ed. Santiago: Ediciones/Metales Pesados, 2007.

Rickard, Jolene. "Diversifying Sovereignty and the Reception of Indigenous Art." *Art Journal* 76, no. 2 (Summer 2017): 81–84.

Rocha, José Luis. "Remittances in Central America: Whose Money Is It Anyway?" *Journal of World-Systems Research* 17, no. 2 (2011): 463–81.

Rodríguez, Ana Patricia. "'Departamento 15': Cultural Narratives of Salvadoran Transnational Migration." *Latino Studies* 3, no. 1 (April 2005): 19–41.

Rodríguez, Dylan. "Abolition as Praxis of Human Being: A Foreword." *Harvard Law Review* 132, no. 6 (April 2019): 1587–88.

Rothenberg, Daniel, ed. *Memory of Silence: The Guatemalan Truth Commission Report*. New York: Palgrave Macmillan, 2012.

Salomon, Nanette. "The Art Historical Canon: Sins of Omission." In *(En)Gendering Knowledge*, edited by Joan E. Hartman and Ellen Messer-Davidow, 222–36. Knoxville: University of Tennessee Press, 1991.

Salvatorre, Ricardo D., and Carlos Aguirre, eds. *The Birth of the Penitentiary in Latin America*. Austin: University of Texas Press, 1996.

Samos, Adrienne. *Divorcio a la panameña: Saltos y rupturas en el arte de Panamá, 1990–2015*. San José: TEOR/éTica, 2016.

Sandoval, Chela. *Methodology of the Oppressed*. Minneapolis: University of Minnesota Press, 2000.

Segovia, Alexander. *Transformación estructural y reforma económica en El Salvador: El funcionamiento económico de los noventa y sus efectos sobre el crecimiento, la pobreza, y la distribución del ingreso*. Guatemala City: F y G Editores, 2002.

Sleeper-Smith, Susan. *Contesting Knowledge: Museums and Indigenous Perspectives*. Lincoln: University of Nebraska Press, 2009.

Smith, Andrea. *Conquest: Sexual Violence and American Indian Genocide*. Cambridge, MA: South End, 2005.

Smith, Cherise. "Upsetting the Archive: Lessons from Brian Wallis's 'Black Bodies, White Science.'" *American Art* 31, no. 2 (January 2017): 17–18.

Spillers, Hortense J. "Mama's Baby, Papa's Maybe: An American Grammar Book." *Diacritics* 17, no. 2 (Summer 1987): 64–81.

Spivak, Gayatri Chakravorty. "Can the Subaltern Speak?" In *Marxism and the Interpretation of Culture*, edited by C. Nelson and L. Grossberg, 271–313. Urbana: University of Illinois Press, 1988.

Stiles, Kristine. "Uncorrupted Joy: International Art Actions." In *Out of Actions: Between Performance and the Object, 1949–1979*, edited by Paul Schimmel, 227–329. Los Angeles: Museum of Contemporary Art, 1998.

Tarica, Estelle. *The Inner Life of Mestizo Nationalism*. Minneapolis: University of Minnesota Press, 2008.

Taylor, Diana. *The Archive and the Repertoire: Performing Cultural Memory in the Americas*. A John Hope Franklin Center Book. Durham, NC: Duke University Press, 2003.

Taylor, Diana. *¡Presente! The Politics of Presence*. Durham, NC: Duke University Press, 2020.

Thompson, Krista A. *An Eye for the Tropics: Tourism, Photography, and Framing the Caribbean Picturesque*. Durham, NC: Duke University Press, 2006.

Tilley, Virginia. *Seeing Indians: A Study of Race, Nation, and Power in El Salvador*. Albuquerque: University of New Mexico Press, 2005.

Torre-Cantalapiedra, Eduardo, and José Carlos Yee-Quintero. "México ¿una frontera vertical? Políticas de control del tránsito migratorio irregular y sus resultados, 2007–2016." *Revista LiminaR: Estudios Sociales y Humanísticos* 16, no. 2 (2018): 87–104.

Tuck, Eve, and K. Wayne Yang. "Decolonization Is Not a Metaphor." *Decolonization, Indigeneity, Education, and Society* 1, no. 1 (2012): 1–40.

Tuhiwai Smith, Linda. *Decolonizing Methodologies: Research and Indigenous Peoples*. London: Zed, 1999.

Tzul Tzul, Gladys. "Rebuilding Communal Life: Ixil Women and the Desire for Life in Guatemala." *NACLA Report on the Americas* 50, no. 4 (2018): 404–7.

Ungar, Mark. "Prison Politics in Contemporary Latin America." *Human Rights Quarterly* 25, no. 4 (November 2003): 909–34.

Vallecillo, Adan, ed. *La otra tradición: Un encuentro con el arte contemporáneo en Honduras, 2000–2010*. San Salvador: Talleres Albacrome, 2011.

Vasari, Giorgio. *The Lives of Artists*. Translated by Julia Conaway Bondanella and Peter Bondanella. Oxford: Oxford University Press, 1998.

Velasquez, Pedro, John Lloyd Stephens, and Barnum's American Museum. *Illustrated Memoir of an Eventful Expedition into Central America, Resulting in the Discovery of the Idolatrous City of Iximaya, in an Unexplored Region; and the Possession of Two Remarkable Aztec Children, Maximo (the Boy) and Bartola (the Girl), Descendants and Specimens of the Sacerdotal Caste (Now Nearly Extinct), of the Ancient Aztec Founders of the Ruined Temples of That Country*. New York: Wynkoop, Hallenbeck and Thomas, printers, 1860.

Véliz, Maria Victoria. "Seguir hacia delante, volver la mirada hacia atrás." In *Suave chapina: Benvenuto Chavajay*. Exhibition pamphlet. Guatemala City: Centro Cultural Metropolitano, 2007.

Veltmeyer, Henry, and James Petras. *The New Extractivism: A Post-neoliberal Development Model or Imperialism of the Twenty-First Century?* London: Zed, 2014.

Villena Fiengo, Sergio. *El perro está más vivo que nunca: Arte, infamia y contracultura en la aldea global*. San José: Editorial Arlekín, 2011.

Virgill Artiaga, Scherly. "The Garifuna Voices of Guatemala's Armed Conflict." *NACLA Report on the Americas* 52, no. 2 (2020): 422–29.

Walia, Harsha. *Border and Rule: Global Migration, Capitalism, and the Rise of Racist Nationalism*. Chicago: Haymarket Books, 2021.

Walia, Harsha. *Undoing Border Imperialism*. Oakland, CA: AK Press, 2013.

Wallis, Brian. "Black Bodies, White Science: Louis Agassiz's Slave Daguerreotypes." *American Art* 9, no. 2 (1995): 39–61.

Wolf, Sonja. *Mano Dura: The Politics of Gang Control in El Salvador*. Austin: University of Texas Press, 2017.

Wynter, Sylvia. "Rethinking 'Aesthetics': Notes towards a Deciphering Practice." In *EX-ILES: Essays on Caribbean Cinema*, edited by Mbye Cham, 248–51. Trenton, NJ: Africa World Press, 1992.

Yancy, George. "Colonial Gazing: The Production of the Body as 'Other.'" *Western Journal of Black Studies* 32, no. 1 (2008): 1–15.

Zavala, Adriana. *Becoming Modern, Becoming Tradition: Women, Gender, and Representation in Mexican Art*. University Park: Pennsylvania State University Press, 2010.

Zilberg, Elana. "Fools Banished from the Kingdom: Remapping Geographies of Gang Violence between the Americas (Los Angeles and San Salvador)." *American Quarterly* 56, no. 3 (2004): 759–79.

Zilberg, Elana. "Gangster in Guerilla Face." *Anthropological Theory* 7, no. 1 (2007): 37–57.

INDEX

Page numbers ending with *f* refer to figures.